PUTNAM'S HISTORY OF AIRCRAFT

Aircraft of the
Second World War

PUTNAM'S HISTORY OF AIRCRAFT

Aircraft of the Second World War

The Development of the Warplane 1939–45

Series Editor: Philip Jarrett

PUTNAM

Title page photograph: USAAF P-51 Mustangs on line (US Air Force / M J H Taylor)

Aircraft of the Second World War
The Development of the Warplane 1939–45

Series Editor: Philip Jarrett
Philip Jarrett is a freelance author, editor, sub-editor and consultant specialising in aviation. He began writing on aviation history in 1967, and in 1971 became assistant editor of *Aerospace*, the Royal Aeronautical Society's newspaper. He was assistant editor of *Aeroplane Monthly* from 1973 to 1980, and production editor of *Flight International* from 1980 to 1989.

M J F Bowyer
Michael Bowyer's interest in aviation was awoken when the huge R.101 airship passed low overhead. By the mid-1930s he was recording and soon photographing aircraft, and throughout the hostilities he compiled copious records of the events from a ringside seat. After serving in the RAF he became a leading aviation historian, journalist and author, combining these activities with an academic career.

Captain Eric Brown
Captain Eric Brown, the Fleet Air Arm's most decorated pilot, had a thirty-one-year career in the Royal Navy. He served as test pilot from 1942, eventually being appointed Chief Naval Test Pilot at RAE Farnborough and commanding the Enemy Aircraft Flight, the High Speed Flight and the Aerodynamics Flight. He continued test flying after the war, amassing a world record total of 487 basic aircraft types before retirement.

R Wallace Clarke
R Wallace Clarke has written widely on aircraft armament for specialist journals, and his two authoritative volumes on *British Aircraft Armament*, published in 1993 and 1994, were widely acclaimed. He is also the UK representative of the 492nd Group Association, and has produced an account of the group's secret Second World War operations.

Les Coombes
After service in the RAF from 1939–46 Les Coombes became a researcher and writer on avionics and ergonomics. He specialises in the history of air force technology and in the design and history of the aircraft cockpit. He is the author of *The Aircraft Cockpit* and *The Fighting Cockpit 1914–2010*.

Norman Friedman
Norman Friedman works as a naval analyst at the Hudson Institute in New York and lectures around the world. Described as 'America's leading naval writer', he is the author of over 20 books and numerous articles including *British Carrier Aviation*, *Warship Design and Development* and *Naval Radar*. His updated edition of the highly acclaimed *Naval Institute Guide to World Naval Weapons Systems* has recently been published.

John Golley
John Golley trained in Canada on Tiger Moths and Harvards, then completed an AFU course on Masters in the UK before converting to Hurricanes and Typhoons. During 1943–45 he flew with 245 Squadron, and then became a flying instructor. His books include *Aircrew Unlimited*, the story of the Commonwealth Air Training Plan.

Patrick Hassell
Patrick Hassell, an aerodynamicist, worked for Handley Page, BAC, Douglas and Saab. After twenty-five years in industry he left Dowty Propellers in 1994 to concentrate on researching aviation history, particularly in the areas of aeronautical technology, air transport, and the political control of aviation development.

Peter Hearn
Group Captain Peter Hearn, AFC, served 30 years as an RAF Parachute Jumping Instructor, training and serving with Airborne Forces and the SAS. He is the author of seven books on aviation topics including *The Sky People*, his internationally acclaimed history of parachuting. He is also a novelist, a published poet and a teacher of creative writing.

E R Hooton
E R Hooton, a defence writer, has written numerous articles for international publication. He produces naval reference publications for Jane's Information Group, and has written books on the Chinese Civil War, the Tanker War and the Luftwaffe from 1918 to 1940. He is currently completing another book on the Luftwaffe for Arms & Armour Press, taking the story to 1944.

Andrew Nahum
Andrew Nahum has been fascinated by engines ever since his mother bought him a noisy Italian model aircraft motor as a young boy. He has written widely on automotive history and his books include *The Rotary Aero Engine*, *Alec Issigonis*, and, as co-author, *The Rolls-Royce Crecy*. He is Curator of Aeronautics at the Science Museum, London.

Dr Alfred Price
Dr Alfred Price served as an aircrew officer in the RAF, specialising in electronic warfare and air fighting tactics. Upon leaving the Service in 1974 he became a full-time aviation writer, and is the author or co-author of 41 books, including *Instruments of Darkness*, *Battle of Britain: the Hardest Day*, and *The Spitfire Story*. He holds a History PhD from Loughborough University and is a Fellow of the Royal Historical Society.

Elfan ap Rees
Elfan ap Rees has been involved with helicopters for more than thirty years, owning and publishing the news journals *Helicopter International* and *Helidata News* and, from 1969, building up a unique collection of historic rotorcraft which formed the nucleus of today's International Helicopter Museum. He also represents the helicopter industry on several national and international bodies, and at weekends flies his own vintage helicopter to relax and maintain currency.

Derek Wood
Derek Wood was founder editor/publisher of *Jane's Defence Weekly*. He has been an aviation and defence writer for over 45 years, and was the London editor of Interavia group of publications from 1953 to 1986 and air correspondent for various newspapers from 1961 to 1986. His books include *The Narrow Margin*, *Project Cancelled*, *Target England* and *Attack Warning Red*.

© Putnam Aeronautical Books 1997

First published in Great Britain in 1997 by Putnam Aeronautical Books, an imprint of Brassey's (UK) Ltd
33 John Street
London WC1N 2AT
Telephone: 0171 753 7777
Fax: 0171 753 7794
E-mail: brasseys@dial.pipex.com

North American orders: Brassey's, Inc., PO Box 960, Herndon, VA 22070, USA.

A CIP catalogue record for this book is available from the British Library.
Library of Congress Cataloging-in-Publication Data: A catalog record for this book is available on request.

ISBN 0 85177 875 5

Typeset in Monotype Plantin by Strathmore Publishing Services, London N7
Printed and bound in Italy by LEGO SpA

Contents

[Bibliographies are included at the end of each chapter]

Introduction

Philip Jarrett

The years 1939–45 saw rapid and unprecedented development in all spheres of aviation, as the warring nations vied to gain a technological edge over their opponents and win mastery of the skies, and thereby secure ultimate victory. Designers, engineers and scientists in industry and in research institutions laboured to improve the aeroplane and enhance its capabilities and equipment.

By the end of the Second World War enormous strides had been made, not only in weaponry and destructive power, but in all of the essential technologies that would revolutionise air transport in the years ahead. For all its grim horror, the war accelerated the aeroplane's development as nothing else could have done. While it is undeniably true that much wartime research and development work concentrated on what might be termed the destructive arts, equal or greater effort was devoted to the saving of lives and improving the performance, reliability and ergonomics of the complex machine that the aeroplane was becoming.

Supercharging enhanced the altitude performance of the piston engine, radar helped the pilot find his way at night and locate other aircraft, new systems made flying safer and more comfortable for aircrew, and the advent of the jet engine heralded a new era in the conquest of the skies, offering hitherto undreamed-of speeds just as the piston engined, propeller-driven aeroplane was reaching the limits of its development.

In these pages leading aviation writers present an authoritative account of this dramatic era in the history of aviation technology. To set the scene, E. R. Hooton surveys the air arms of the Axis forces at the outbreak of hostilities in 1939, examining their equipment and the political, military, economical and technological factors or philosophies that had shaped them and either furthered or frustrated their development. It was not numerical strength that made Germany's air force the most powerful, as in this sense it was dwarfed by the Soviet Air Force. The secret of its strength lay in the modern design of the vast majority of its aircraft. Italy's Regia Aeronautica, although regarded as second only to the German air force, suffered as a result of an under-capitalised aircraft industry, an apparent reluctance to abandon biplane fighters, a lack of suitably powerful aero engines and the absence of a doctrine of air power. Both arms, however, had used the Spanish Civil War as a testing ground for their new front-line aircraft, allowing both pilots and ground crew to become familiar with them under combat conditions, and enabling initial mechanical or operational shortcomings to be pinpointed and resolved.

Japan's proving ground was the conflict with Russia in 1939, where the inadequacies of its aircraft became disastrously evident. The problems in this case were that technologically modern aircraft were being built to outmoded requirements, and the conservatism of military traditionalists inhibited the development of modern tactical philosophies.

Derek Wood's survey of the development of Allied aircraft in the early war years spotlights the manner in which Germany's neighbours left the modernisation of their air arms too late, some adhering to the naive belief that their neutrality would be respected, and others trusting in static defences or outmoded tactical concepts. The failure of the European aviation industry to meet the sudden and overwhelming demand for modern combat aircraft resulted in the USA's manufacturers receiving orders for a variety of types. This had the fortuitous effects of bringing about an expansion of the American companies' production facilities and of enabling them to assess their products' performance in operational service and introduce improvements before the USA actually entered the war. In some instances, however, this had unfortunate results for the customer nations. Those who ordered the Bell Airacobra, Brewster Buffalo and Curtiss Hawk 75A, for example, found to their dismay that their investments had been wasted, and that their brand new fighters were no match for the Luftwaffe's Bf 109s. Tragically, the need was so desperate that some of these aircraft were then put to work in India and the Far East, where they proved equally vulnerable to their Japanese counterparts.

However, there were great success stories. Outstanding examples were the North American Mustang and Mitchell, Lockheed Hudson, Douglas Boston, Boeing B-17 and Consolidated Liberator, all of which saw widespread use after initial teething troubles were resolved.

Britain's industry, too, had its share of failures and successes. The Fairey Battle and Westland Whirlwind did not come up to expectations, but others, such as the Avro Manchester and Hawker Typhoon, were transformed from problem children into mature and potent warriors. Development potential is the hallmark of great design, and the aircraft lacking in this attribute, such as the Hurricane and Stirling, flew briefly into the spotlight and then receded. Those having it in abundance were the Spitfire and Mosquito, the latter also being endowed with extraordinary versatility; a great asset in war. One thing many of the successful machines had in common was the Rolls-Royce Merlin engine, another product which had great development potential.

Russia's great strength at the war's outset lay in its ability to take the aggressor's first mighty and unexpected blow and then, after a massive logistics exercise in which its threatened factories were withdrawn to the depths of this vast country, to rally, recoup its losses and hit back with a vengeance. It was fortunate for both Britain and the USSR that Germany had failed to develop a successful long-range bomber. Had Hitler been able to cripple the centres of manufacture of either nation, the outcome would have been very different.

The story of fighter development from 1941 onwards is taken up by Dr Alfred Price, who begins by surveying the continuing and parallel development of Britain's Spitfire and Germany's Bf 109, and the disadvantages of such prolonged continuation of a line. He then turns his attention on new fighter types introduced into service during the war by Britain, Germany, the USA, Japan and the USSR, underlining the essential requirements of engine and armament and how these were affected by the specific role or operational situation. Comparative performance data highlight the relative merits and demerits of the principal types.

Nightfighting placed the emphasis on quite different fighter attributes, and the section dealing with this aspect opens with an outline of Britain's night air defence system, at the time the only really effective system of its type in the world, and the way in which the fighters operated within it. The Luftwaffe system evolved on similar lines but took longer to develop, and the incessant 'battle of the boffins' to devise increasingly better radars and, in response, more effective radar countermeasures, is a central theme.

The use of the fighter-bomber was pioneered by the Luftwaffe, but once its advantages were perceived by their opponents the type became an important component of all of the combatant forces. Unlike a bomber, the fighter-bomber could revert to its pure fighter role and defend itself once it had released its bombs. Moreover, it was cheaper, required fewer crew, and had far better speed and altitude performance. Disadvantages were the small bomb load and limited radius of action. Such aircraft demanded new operational techniques and specially developed weapons, particularly for use against difficult targets such as tanks. Dr Price exposes the fallacy of the much-vaunted air-launched unguided rocket projectile, which lacked accuracy and was quite ineffective against armoured vehicles.

He concludes with a survey of the development and use of rocket- and jet-propelled fighters. Interestingly, both Luftwaffe and RAF senior officers initially

regarded their respective types, the Me 262 and Meteor, with almost casual interest, seeing them as outside of their requirements. However, once the Me 262 had proved its worth against US heavy bombers and the British got word of German developments, both sides pursued the subject with vigour. Dr Price dismisses the postwar myths that the Me 262 was not put into large-scale production early enough, and that Hitler's edict that the aircraft should initially be used as a fighter-bomber caused any appreciable delay in its operational introduction as a fighter. The great weaknesses of the Me 262 were its unreliable engines and poor serviceability, and a comparison of victories claimed against losses reveals poor results.

The spectacular nature of the diminutive Me 163 rocket-propelled interceptor belied its disappointing and dangerous Service use, and again we are presented with figures which show it to have been far from successful in combat.

Speculation can be a pointless pursuit, but the revelation of the outstanding superiority of the Vampire I when compared with the Spitfire XIV, in all aspects of combat performance, makes one wonder how the jet fighter might have affected air combat had the war continued. In truth, however, the jet fighters had a negligible influence on the war.

In his chapter 'The Bomber Revolution', Mike Bowyer stresses the differing tactical philosophies that determined the approaches taken by the various warring nations. While Germany had concentrated on the smaller, short-range twin engined medium bombers and single engined Stukas, believing dive-bombing to be an essential capability if accuracy was to be achieved, Britain's bomber force was initially formed with the aim of waging a strategic campaign to destroy the enemy's industries and navy, and therefore comprised long-range twin engine bombers, with a new generation of four engine heavy bombers under development. In both cases the resulting machines initially proved inadequate and vulnerable in the face of determined opposition, and both sides learned their respective lessons the hard way, suffering little success and heavy losses.

While Britain upgraded only the Wellington, preferring to introduce completely new types, Germany followed a path of continual updating of the original designs. A significant contribution to the Allied cause came from the USA, where several excellent bombers of various classes were developed, as mentioned earlier. In Russia the emphasis was again on twin-engined medium bombers, though one four engined strategic heavy bomber, the Pe-8, was developed. Germany's only true bomber in this class, the He 177, was dogged throughout its operational life by interminable powerplant problems, and never realised its potential.

Japan put range before defence in bomber design,

and its twin engine bombers were suited to both army and navy use. Again vulnerability was a major problem. An alternative solution was the high-speed unarmed bomber. This concept was embodied with great success in the Mosquito, originally dismissed by Bomber Command's Commander-in-Chief as being of no use, but soon to prove its worth - and with a significantly lower loss rate compared with its Bomber Command contemporaries, as the author shows.

Japan was the only nation to resort to the desperate measure of mass suicide or Kamikaze attacks, mostly using ageing aircraft adapted for the purpose, but also with the purpose-designed Ohka, essentially nothing more than a rocket-propelled piloted bomb. Although there can be no doubting the success of many of these operations, the cost in pilots' lives was horrendous.

The aeroplane which brought the war with Japan to its climactic end was the B-29 Superfortress, the evolution of which had begun in 1938, before the war had even started. It was the most technologically advanced piston engined heavy bomber of the war, but Germany progressed a stage further, developing the world's first operational jet bomber, the Arado Ar 234B. As the author points out in his conclusion, the principal elements of the Cold War were ready at the war's end; the jet bomber, the cruise missile (embodied in the V1) and the atomic bomb.

Airmobility, or the transport of troops and equipment by aircraft, came into its own in the Second World War. Peter Hearn describes how the German assault on the Low Countries, using paratroops and glider-borne infantry, took the defenders completely by surprise. Although both the Russians and Italians, as well as the Germans, had developed the concept of airborne operations in the interwar years, Britain was conspicuously slow in recognising both the threat and the potential of such assaults, and lacked not only the aircraft but also the knowledge to follow suit. Thus disadvantaged, Britain's armed services had an uphill struggle to catch up with the technology, but were able to begin operations in 1941. In the USA as well the military were slow to adopt the concept, but at least they had the C-47, a purpose-built transport which was to become the Allies' principal air-support aircraft, and ample production facilities well beyond the enemy's reach. The successful use of airborne divisions in the invasion of Europe and to support the Rhine crossing demonstrated that the lesson had been learnt, but the disaster at Arnhem underlined the cost of bad planning.

As Norman Friedman shows, the part of the aeroplane in the war at sea was significant. Neither Germany nor Italy had any aircraft carriers, but large forces of these vessels were operated by Britain, Japan and the USA. In addition, land-based aircraft and seaplanes were used in maritime roles by all of the major powers.

Although reconnaissance and fleet protection were the roles initially performed by naval aircraft, the carriers also served as floating bases from which strikes could be launched, using torpedo and dive bombers. Naval aircraft also proved an effective deterrent to submarines, and convoy protection by land- and carrier-based aircraft, using progressively improved radar systems, became a vital and effective duty.

Both Britain and the USA suffered from the inability of the different Services to agree on their respective responsibilities. Thus the RAF regarded its flying boats as an alternative to the fleet, and the Royal Navy was not permitted to have land-attack aircraft. In the USA it was some time before the US Navy assumed responsibility for all maritime patrol aircraft, having hitherto been restricted to carrier aircraft and water-based machines. On the other hand, the Japanese navy's freedom to use whatever aircraft it wanted resulted in much duplicated effort and imposed a strain on the nation's industries.

New technology and techniques had to be developed for attacking capital ships, both with bombs and torpedoes, and for operating aircraft from carriers which, in turn, imposed limits on aircraft size and weight. Furthermore, the limited number of aircraft that could be carried meant that one aircraft type might be required to perform several different roles, which effectively compromised its design. The great variety of aircraft developed to meet the wide range of requirements is apparent in the author's country-by-country survey.

It might be thought that rotary-winged aircraft played an insignificant part in the Second World War, but Elfan ap Rees' chapter shows that the leading combatant nations evinced a continued interest in their possibilities, and that rotorcraft were more active than is generally realised. Britain, France, Germany, Japan and Russia all employed autogyros of various types in a variety of roles, and helicopter developments by Focke-Achgelis and Flettner in Germany and Sikorsky in the USA resulted in practical machines which saw Service use in the latter years of the war. In Britain, development of the Weir helicopter having been abandoned early in the war, the Sikorsky helicopter was adopted, but was not used operationally before the war's end.

R Wallace Clarke's study of the development of aircraft armament is divided of necessity into sections dealing with guns, gunsighting, powered gun turrets and rocket weapons, each section then being subdivided into the respective nations. As in all other aspects of the aeroplane's evolution, the 'baptism of fire' quickly revealed the shortcomings of the various weapons and weapon installations. Some lessons were surprising. Few pilots could hit anything at ranges greater than two or three hundred yards, density and rate of fire was more important than the calibre of the shells, and solid steel shells were more destructive than high-explosive projectiles.

While Britain and the USA concentrated on output, reliability and commonality of ammunition, Germany upgraded its weapons constantly and produced a wide range of new types of gun. Nor was commonality a priority of the Japanese, the navy using different weapons to the army, and both Services mixing types and calibres.

The sights used with the guns, and the turrets in which the guns were mounted, were as rich in their variety as the guns themselves, and both were subject to constant development and improvement. Unguided rockets were fairly basic devices, but Germany pioneered the guided missile with its wire-guided X4 and radio-guided Hs 293.

Every aeroplane embodies a number of systems and an assortment of equipment, some vital to the machine itself or its crew, and some to enable the aircraft to perform its appointed task. In Chapter 9 Les Coombs vividly illustrates the great advances made in the war years, and the rapidly increasing complexity of the machine that was the aeroplane. 'Well-equipped' is, of course, a relative term that changes in accordance with the standards of each particular period. Although the aircraft of the early war period might have been regarded as representing the latest in technological accomplishment, they were not total 'weapons systems' as we now understand the term. Indeed, compared with the machines of the late war period they seem relatively simple in some respects. The incessant battle to increase safety and save valuable pilots' lives, improve the performance and capabilities of the machine and counter or outsmart the opponent meant that significant progress was made in the five years of war.

Andrew Nahum's short chapter on aero engines establishes the state of engine development at the war's outbreak and looks at the problems engine designers faced as they sought to improve efficiency and reliability. The allied and inseparable subjects of high-octane fuels and supercharging are also covered, as are problematic engines. Finally, the hurdles confronting the designers of the first jet engines are outlined.

Chapter 11 comprises contributions from two authors. Capt Eric Brown, an accomplished test pilot, describes the role of flight testing in wartime and highlights some specific aspects and aircraft. His assessment of the Me 163 as a 'landmark in aviation technology' might seem to be at variance with the opinion expressed by Dr Price, but while one author is considering the aircraft from the point of view of the technology it embodied, the other is concerned with its effectiveness as a combat aircraft. This serves to remind us that there are at least two sides to every question, and that conclusions depend to a large degree on the approaches on which they are based.

The second part of this chapter, contributed by Patrick Hassell, looks at the extraordinary business of aircraft ferrying, both within the British Isles from factory to Service unit, and across vast oceans and continents. It is no use having new aeroplanes pouring from the production lines if you cannot get them to the places where they are desperately needed, and the accomplishments of the Air Transport Auxiliary, the Atlantic Ferry Organisation and the Return Ferry Service were impressive, to say the least. The impact of the experience gained in intercontinental operations on the postwar development of commercial air transport was surely profound.

This volume concludes with John Golley's account of the training systems adopted by Germany and the Allies. The title 'Vital Command', chosen by him, stresses the importance of training to all air arms, and the essential and basic need for a system that ensures a continual flow of well-trained aircrew. Closely allied to this, of course, was the provision of suitable aircraft on which to train them. The author shows that the Luftwaffe had ample facilities and recruits, but that its training system was inadequate and began to fragment owing to the urgent need to replace combat losses, whereas the Empire Flying Training Scheme tapped resources around the world. Moreover, the significant contribution of the USA ensured that there was an ample supply of well-trained aircrew to operate the machines.

Last, but by no means least, mention must be made of artist Frank Munger's splendid cutaway drawing of the Hawker Typhoon, undoubtedly the first such drawing of this aircraft ever produced. The aim in this series is to feature a cutaway in each volume, the aircraft selected being typical of the period covered rather than exceptional. The Typhoon suits this criterion admirably, being very much a product of the Second World War era with regard to its design, structure and powerplant.

Philip Jarrett

1

Axis Aircraft at the Outbreak of War

E R Hooton

Germany

At the outbreak of war in September 1939 Germany's Reichsluftwaffe was the world's most powerful air force. This status was achieved not merely numerically, for its first-line strength of 4,093 aircraft was nearly half that of the Soviet Air Force (which had 7,321 on New Year's Day 1939), but on the fact that the vast majority of its aircraft (92 per cent) were of modern design and construction.

Germany's success in completing aerial re-equipment before its enemies gave the Luftwaffe an edge which it used to devastating effect over the next three years. The edge was made keener by the structure and philosophy of the Luftwaffe, which was far more than the purely tactical force which most post-war aviation historians claim. Indeed, had it been a tactical force it would never have spearheaded Nazi Germany's success, but to understand its philosophy requires a slight diversion into German military thought.

In the aftermath of the Napoleonic wars the German General Staff recognised that the appearance of mass armies meant that the old division of military operations into Tactics and Strategy was inadequate. They therefore confined Tactics to operations by army corps and their component units (although these could be extended to armies in certain circumstances), and the activities of armies and army groups now came under the new concept of the Operational (*Operativer*) Art, with Strategy confined to activity above army group level. This philosophy subsequently helped define military aircraft requirements.

Tactical operations were largely the responsibility of the Nahaufklärungsstaffeln on land and the Seenahaufklärungsstaffeln as well as the Bordfliegerstaffeln at sea. The former were attached to Armee Korps and Panzer Divisionen and were essentially what the Royal Flying Corps in the First World War had called Corps Aeroplanes, single-engined two-seaters with the roles of tactical reconnaissance (visual and photographic), artillery observation and direction, ground attack and resupply. Their floatplane equivalents in the Royal Naval Air Service had similar tactical reconnaissance and artillery support duties, but responsibility for coastal anti-submarine operations replaced ground-attack/resupply duties.

In most of Europe's air forces, Corps Aeroplanes comprised 20 to 40 per cent of the total first-line strength, but in the Luftwaffe they were only 7.5 per cent. The majority of the Nahaufklärungsstaffeln were equipped with the Henschel Hs 126, a stressed-skin monocoque, braced-wing monoplane with a radial engine and fixed undercarriage. It was typical of the last generation of such aircraft, being designed for operation from small, roughly prepared fields to a requirement which emphasised visibility from the semi-enclosed

The Henschel Hs 126 Corps aircraft had largely replaced the Heinkel He 45 and He 46 in the Nahaufklärungsstaffeln by the outbreak of war.

The Focke-Wulf Fw 189 V3 was the third prototype of the twin-engined Corps aircraft designed to replace the Hs 126. The type began to enter service from the autumn of 1940.

cockpit. The radio and the topographic camera in the rear bay (supplemented by a hand-operated camera on the port side) were the most important items of equipment, while the armament, typically, was derisory, comprising a single fixed 7.9mm (0.30in) MG 17 machine-gun for the pilot and a similar-calibre MG 15 on a movable mounting for the observer. The maximum bomb load was only 100kg (220lb). Against the latest generation of high-performance fighters, such aircraft were dead meat with only their manoeuvrability to protect them.

Many of the Nahaufklärungsstaffeln retained some of the older Heinkel He 45 biplanes and He 46 braced monoplanes with wooden wings and fuselages of welded steel tube covered by doped fabric and metal panels. This form of construction had appeared in the First World War and was extensively employed until the early 1930s, when it was supplanted by all-metal, stressed-skin monocoque construction techniques which produced lighter but stronger airframes. Yet the Corps Aeroplane itself was becoming an anachronism, able neither to fight nor flee, and the Luftwaffe had begun developing a more modern concept from 1937 based upon tactical reconnaissance and higher performance. By 1939 prototypes of the new aircraft, the Focke-Wulf Fw 189, were flying. Following a trend common in the late 1930s, it was a twin-boom design, like the Fokker G.I and Lockheed P-38. Like the contemporary Potez 637 army co-operation aircraft, the Fw 189 (which entered service late in 1940) had twin engines, a retractable undercarriage and a fully enclosed cockpit, which made it seem a world away from the Hs 126, although their performance and combat capability were similar.

One prototype Fw 189 was modified to meet the close-support or 'Schlacht' requirement. This mission was developed by the German Army during the First World War, when Schlacht aircraft were essentially flying storm troops designed to assist an advance on the ground by attacking enemy troops with automatic weapons and small bombs. Its wartime success meant that in 1934 an updated requirement was issued as the Light Divebomber, for which the Henschel Hs 123 was selected. This was a curious mixture of old and new, with sesquiplane configuration, fixed undercarriage and open cockpit but all-metal monocoque construction and mixed-construction wings. The 'Ein-Zwei-Drei', as it was popularly called, formed the basis of the Stuka (Sturzkampfflugzeug) Gruppen, and despite the support of the Luftwaffe's head of development, Oberst Wolfram von Richthofen, it was gradually withdrawn from service.

In 1937, however, Richthofen (a cousin of the famous 'Red Baron' and minor 'ace' in his own right) became chief of staff to the Condor Legion, the German expeditionary force fighting in Spain for Franco's Nationalists. The Legion had copied the Spanish and used its obsolete Heinkel He 51 fighters for the Schlacht role with great success, and had recommended the development of dedicated ground-attack aircraft with armoured protection for the Tactical role. It is interesting to note that the Russians came to a similar conclusion, leading to the development of the Ilyushin Il-2 'Ilyusha'.

At the outbreak of war only one Schlachtgruppe existed, and this was equipped with the ageing Hs 123, which was essentially a flying machine-gun nest, with two MG 17s which could be supplemented by up to 200kg (440lb) of bombs or two 20mm (0.78in) MG FF cannon. Its potential replacements, the Fw 189 V1b and the Hs 129, both twin-engined aircraft, were flying in prototype form by the outbreak of war. The former was a two-seat armoured version of the Fw 189 (the Schlacht model of which was to be designated Fw 189C), with four MG 17s and two MG FF forward and two 7.9mm MG 81s aft, while the latter was a dedicated single-seat design with armour plate 6–12mm thick, 75mm thick armoured glass and an armament of two MG 17s and two MG FF. The Hs 129's protection was its only advantage, for the aircraft proved severely underpowered as

Entering service from July 1939, the Arado Ar 196 replaced the Heinkel He 60. Designed as a spotter aircraft, it was used for a variety of duties including escort fighter, and could sometimes match the Beaufighter. Two of these aircraft helped to capture the British submarine HMS Seal.

Inadequate defensive armament led to redesign of the Dornier Do 17's forward fuselage, and this version entered service in the summer of 1938 as the Do 17Z, seen here. Although the aircraft had only a small bomb bay, it was frequently used for low-level surprise attacks because its shoulder mounted wings made it easier for pilots to judge their altitude.

well as cramped, but it was cheaper to build and in 1941 was selected for production.

The naval equivalent of the Hs 126 was the Arado Ar 196 floatplane, an elegant all-metal twin-float design of modern construction which was to prove surprisingly agile. At the outbreak of war the Arado was being introduced into the Bordfliegerstaffeln, but these still had many He 60 biplanes which also equipped the Seenahaufklärungsstaffeln and may be regarded as the floatplane equivalent of the He 45.

Curiously, the Luftwaffe's first *de facto* chief of staff, Oberst (later Generalleutnant) Walther Wever, brought with him when he transferred from the army the latter's belief in the supremacy of Tactical air power, but extensive reading led him to change his mind. Within a year Wever had not only accepted that the Luftwaffe should have an *operativer* role with the emphasis upon bombers interdicting the enemy rear at army/army group or fleet level and destroying enemy air power, but he had also 'sold' the concept to the Army's high command. The concept was also acceptable to his political masters because the bombers could also be used to cow Germany's neighbours in peacetime by threatening to annihilate their cities and factories.

Luftwaffe bombers were therefore designed to strike at Germany's immediate neighbours, and four designs emerged during the mid 1930s. The Luftwaffe requirements had assigned priority to bomb load, followed by speed, defensive armament and range, but the general requirement was for an aircraft with a 1,000km (600-mile) range, a maximum speed of 350km/h (215mph) and a 1 tonne (2,200lb) bomb load. The requirement was met by three designs which were essentially complementary, the Dornier Do 17, Heinkel He 111 and Junkers Ju 86, the emphasis in each design being on speed, bomb load and range respectively. By 1939 the Ju 86 had been withdrawn from service because its Junkers

Jumo 205C diesels proved extremely unreliable, although they provided exceptional operating economy. However, radial engined versions proved popular abroad and they served with five air forces.

The other two were designed to follow another typical 1930s fashion, the concept of a bomber fast enough to outpace enemy fighters. The concept reflected the technological revolution created by combining lightweight monocoque, stressed-skin airframes with powerful engines at a time when fighter design emphasised manoeuvrability at the expense of speed and firepower. Against biplane or braced-wing monoplane fighters the fashion proved sound, as the He 111 and Do 17 were to demonstrate during the next two years. Both were elegant, streamlined designs, but experience in the Spanish Civil War, and natural caution, dictated a strengthening of defensive armament to supplement self-sealing tanks. The He 111P-1 had only three MG 15

The Heinkel He 111V3 (formerly He 111b) of 1935 was the second bomber prototype and the pattern for the underpowered He 111A series with BMW VI 6.0Z engines. Only when the Daimler-Benz 600 and Junkers Jumo were introduced did the He 111 become the formidable aircraft which was the 'third leg' of the Kampfgruppen.

13

A design which was in the right place at the right time. Like several passenger aircraft of the time, the Junkers Ju 52 could be adapted to a bomber, and several despatched to Spain in 1936 performed both roles. Large numbers were built as bombers owing to the failure of the Dornier Do 11/13/23 family, and virtually all had been transferred to transport units by September 1939. At that time it was also used for training and electronic intelligence, while during the war it was fitted with a large magnetic coil for magnetic minesweeping.

machine-guns in nose, dorsal and ventral positions, but later versions such as the P-4 had armour protection for the pilot, a second MG 15 in the nose and two firing from the side with a fifth crew member to operate them. Similar improvements were made in the He 111H-2, while the Do 17Z expanded its defensive armament from three to four MG 15s but ventral cover was improved through a redesigned nose. The Do 17 was exported to Yugoslavia and an improved export version with DB 601A in-line engines was under development at the outbreak of war as the Do 215, and was destined to join the specialised Aufklärungsstaffeln of the Luftwaffe High Command (ObdL). By the beginning of the war the Luftwaffe had 1,171 medium bombers or 28.5 per cent of its first-line strength, but their individual bomb load was limited. The horizontal bomb bays of the Do 17 could not accommodate anything larger than 250kg (550lb) bombs, and with a full bomb load the tactical radius was reduced to about 320km (200 miles). The He 111 had three times this range, but the vertical cells of its bomb bay could accommodate nothing larger than 500kg (1,120lb) bombs, heavier loads, including a 1,000kg bomb, having to be carried externally, with the resulting drag limiting range.

One feature of Luftwaffe bombers not generally noted was their ability to operate in all weathers. This requirement came from Milch, whose direction had ensured that Lufthansa possessed such a capability before the Nazis came to power. This was emulated by the Luftwaffe, which established a network of radio beacons throughout the Reich, and every multi-engined aircraft

received the appropriate direction-finding (DF) loop aerial. The RAF by contrast was slow not only creating a beacon network and equipping its aircraft but also providing sufficient navigators. The Lufthansa practice of all-weather operation extended into the night, and this, too, was copied by the Luftwaffe, all of whose major bases had Lorenz instrument-landing systems and all of whose bombers had the appropriate receivers. The system was modified into an instrument bombing system, 'X-Verfahren', one of three in service or at advanced stages of development at the outbreak of war.

The Junkers Ju 87 V3 prototype first flew in 1935, and a year later a pre-production aircraft served briefly in Spain under the supervision of Oberst Wolfram von Richthofen. It returned to Germany in 1937, but later in the year a number of production dive-bombers were sent to Spain and began the type's famous career. By the outbreak of war eight Stukagruppen were in service, three under Richthofen as Fliegerführer zbV (later Fliegerkorps VIII).

The performance of the Junkers Ju 88 V3, the first prototype to have Junkers Jumo 211s, clinched the award of the 'Schnellbomber' contract to the manufacturer. Production of the Ju 88 was under way in September 1939, and the type became one of the Luftwaffe's most useful aircraft.

A major weakness of the first generation of German bombers (Do 11/13/23 and Ju 52) had been poor bomb sights, which led to intense interest in dive-bombing for greater accuracy. From its earliest days the Luftwaffe had Sturzkampfflugzeug units, and the Light Dive-bomber requirement which led to the Hs 123 was accompanied by a Heavy Dive-bomber requirement drafted around the Ju 87, the emphasis of this latter requirement being on bomb load. Despite the acquisition of the Lotfe 7D tachometric bomb sight by September 1939, the Luftwaffe was the only land-based air arm with a large dive-bomber force, which comprised 24 per cent of all German bombers. The Ju 87 could carry a 500kg (1,102lb) bomb some 600km (370 miles), and could be used for either tactical or *operativer* missions, but defensive armament (two fixed MG 17s forward and one movable MG 15 aft) was limited and it required conditions of aerial superiority to operate effectively. A longer-ranged version was completing development for anti-shipping operations as the Ju 87R, and a study was also under way of a carrier-borne version of the Ju 87B, the Ju 87C.

Dive-bombing fascinated the Luftwaffe development organisation not only under Generalleutnant Ernst Udet,

who assumed the position of Generalluftzeugmeister in 1938, but also under his predecessor, Richthofen, who initially went to Spain to test new types including prototype Ju 87s. Another enthusiast was Oberst Hans Jeschonnek, the Luftwaffe chief of staff in 1939, whose earlier staff appointment gave him considerable influence in aircraft development. The combination of influences was to have a pernicious effect upon Luftwaffe bomber development, as was becoming clear at the outbreak of war.

A demand for a dive-bombing capability was included in the requirement for the Luftwaffe's next-generation medium and heavy bombers, the Ju 88, Do 217 and He 177. The first, envisaged as a high-speed three-seat aircraft with a speed of 500km/h (310 mph), a range of 3,000km (1,850 miles) and a maximum bomb load of 2 tonnes (4,410lb), had added to it a requirement to conduct 30°-angle dive-bombing attacks, and Spanish experience indicating the need for better defensive armament led to a fourth crew member being added. As a result of numerous design changes, the weight of the Ju 88 doubled and performance dropped, so that the initial production aircraft, which was entering service at the outbreak of war, had a maximum speed of 460km/h

Unlike the RAF, the Luftwaffe developed a long-range escort fighter/interceptor in the Messerschmitt Bf 110. Production was slow during the summer of 1939, and only a few Zerstörergruppen had received the type when Poland was invaded. The situation gradually improved, and within a year the Bf 110 was being used for other roles including reconnaissance, for which this Bf 110C-5 was developed.

(286mph) and a range of 1,770km (1,100 miles). The maximum internal bomb load was 1,800kg (3,960lb) or 2,000kg externally, the internal bomb load being confined to 50kg bombs.

The dive-bombing requirement was also extended to Germany's four-engined bomber, the He 177, which was scheduled to be in widespread service by 1942. Unfortunately for the Luftwaffe this extremely sophisticated aircraft, designed to the Bomber A requirement, was to be plagued by development problems. The prototype's four Daimler-Benz DB 601 engines were paired in two nacelles as the DB 606, and were prone to overheating. This exacerbated the aircraft's weight problem caused by the need for strengthening to meet a 60° dive-angle requirement. It had been anticipated that the loaded weight of the operational He 177 would be approximately 27 tonnes (59,500lb), but successive prototypes increased in weight until the first production version (He 177A-1) had a loaded weight of 30 tonnes (66,100lb).

The idea of a four-engined bomber diving at 60° has been much derided by aviation historians, but it should be noted that RAF Specification P.13/36, which led directly to the Halifax and indirectly to the Lancaster, included an unspecified dive angle requirement, 70° at one time being seriously considered. In the event Göring personally authorised removal of the dive-bomber requirement early in the He 177's development, but Udet's compartmentalised organisation with its blinkered engineers was unable to resolve the bomber's problems until 1943. The absence of the He 177, which was to have been the backbone of the long-range anti-shipping force, created a major problem for the Luftwaffe at the

outbreak of war. Fortunately Focke-Wulf had been designing a long-range maritime reconnaissance version of the Fw 200B four-engined airliner for the Japanese Navy as the Fw 200C, and in September the Luftwaffe placed an order for a small number.

Interestingly Dipl Ing Heinrich Hertel, who had conducted initial design work on the He 177, joined the Junkers organisation in the summer of 1939 and took charge of the Bomber B design. This was a Ju 88 replacement, the requirement for which was issued in July 1939 and the development of which proved as accident prone as that of Bomber A. In this programme also the Luftwaffe was to prove too ambitious and Udet's organisation inadequate.

The dive-bombing requirement also plagued the Do 217, a genuinely twin-engined heavy bomber which may be regarded as the equivalent of the Avro Manchester. The maiden flight was in August 1938 and development was under way in 1939, but the umbrella-like dive brake in the tail proved a major headache and eventually, in 1939, Udet authorised the temporary suspension of the dive-bomber requirement. As the handling characteristics of the aircraft proved unsatisfactory, a major redesign was authorised, leading to the Do 217E the following year.

The Luftwaffe's bombers (and those of Italy's Regia Aeronautica) were also its 'eyes', both in their normal configuration and in dedicated long-range reconnaissance versions. The latter were assigned to separate Army and Luftwaffe Fernaufklärungsstaffeln, although the Kampfgeschwader themselves conducted a great deal of reconnaissance for their own missions and German bombers were noted for their extensive

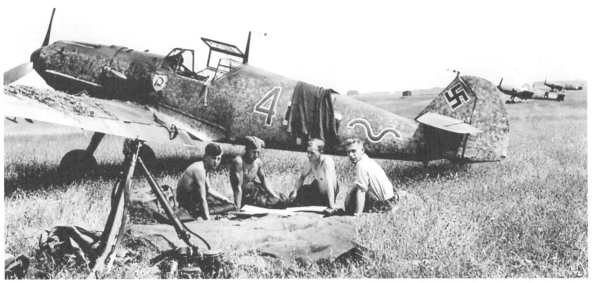

In September 1939 the Messerschmitt Bf 109E-1, represented here by an aircraft of JG 2 'Richthofen', was becoming the prime workhorse of the Jagdgruppen. It remained so for a year before being largely replaced by the Bf 109E-4.

fenestration. The majority of reconnaissance aircraft were Do 17F/P versions of the Do 17E/M bombers, with cameras in the bomb bay, supplemented by small numbers of Ju 88As and He 111Hs. The philosophy of using bombers for long-range reconnaissance was part of the First World War philosophical baggage, when dual use was the norm, such aircraft being capable either of outpacing or outfighting the few fighters which might intercept them. As the Luftwaffe quickly discovered, this philosophy depended upon the enemy having old-fashioned fighters, and the introduction of high-performance interceptors placed aircraft such as the Do 17 in the invidious position where they could neither out-fight nor out-run their opponents, especially when the latter had radar to provide early warning of their victim's approach.

The solution was based upon adapting fighter designs for reconnaissance using their high speed at lower altitudes or, even more effectively, flying at very high altitudes which even forewarned interceptors had difficulty in reaching. To meet the former requirement the Messerschmitt Bf 110C-5 was already being developed at the outbreak of war, while for the latter requirement, for which the British swiftly used modified Spitfires, the Luftwaffe again used bombers. A proposal was received from Junkers to convert Ju 86 airframes with pressurised cabins and improved engines as the Ju 86H (later Ju 86P), and this appeared in the summer of 1940 together with the Bf 110C-5.

The only Luftwaffe reconnaissance units with dedicated reconnaissance aircraft were the Seefernaufklärungsstaffeln and the Küstenmehrzweckstaffeln, the former with the Do 18 flying boat and the latter with the

He 59 twin-engined multi-role floatplane which was used also for anti-ship operations and minelaying. Experience quickly confirmed that both were at the end of their operational lives, but the replacement for the Do 18, the three-engined Blohm und Voss Bv 138 with Jumo 205 diesel engines, required considerable redesign and was not available until the following summer. Fortunately there were no such problems with the He 115 multi-role floatplane which was to replace the He 59. The new aircraft was the antithesis of its predecessor, an all-metal monoplane with enclosed crew positions and a bomb bay which could hold mines or torpedoes. The floatplane configuration was to impose increasingly severe performance restrictions, but the He 115 was to prove a robust and reliable design.

Unlike its rivals, the Luftwaffe had only one modern single-engine fighter design at the outbreak of war, and virtually all the Jagdgruppen had the Bf 109, with a strength of 1,151 aircraft. The selection of the Bf 109 was a political and operational triumph for its designer, Professor Willi Messerschmitt, who had had to overcome personal prejudice (from the Luftwaffe's second-in-command, Generaloberst Eberhard Milch) and conservatism which might have been epitomised in Udet (whose 62 victories were won in traditional fighters). Far from being a stick-in-the-mud, however, Udet quickly recognised the value of the Bf 109 and his demonstrations undoubtedly helped to extinguish any opposition from traditionalists. The Bf 109E was the prime first-line aircraft, with a maximum speed of 550km/h (342mph) and a formidable armament of two 20mm MG FF cannon and two MG 17 machine-guns, but a substantial number of the older Bf 109Ds were in service with the

To supplement the Bf 109, development had begun of the Focke-Wulf Fw 190, the V1 prototype depicted here flying for the first time in June 1939. As with the Hawker Typhoon, the design was plagued by engine problems, although in the case of the German aircraft they were exacerbated by bureaucracy in the RLM

Zerstörergruppen pending the delivery of adequate numbers of Bf 110s, and also in the Nachtjagdgruppen. Development of the replacement Bf 109F with higher performance, including a maximum speed of 600km/h (373mph) but weaker armament, was already under way, and mention should also be made of a carrier-borne version with improved range, the Bf 109T, under development at the outbreak of war.

The success of the Bf 109 made the higher echelons in the Luftwaffe reluctant to consider another fighter, but the value of heavier armament and a more robust undercarriage led Udet's organisation reluctantly to consider just such a requirement. By the outbreak of war, therefore, work was well advanced on the Fw 190 with a radial, air-cooled engine, and in June 1939 the prototype made its maiden flight. The lack of integration within Udet's organisation meant that two years were to elapse before the new fighter entered service, and it required a Jagdgeschwader technical officer to provide the direction which was to make the Fw 190 one of the great fighters of the Second World War.

Udet's influence, and that of the Nazi Party in the shape of Messerschmitt's good friend Rudolf Hess, also helped ensure the Luftwaffe had a long-range fighter (*Zerstörer* or Destroyer in German terminology) in the Bf 110, of which 102 were available. The Bf 110 was typical of attempts by many air forces during the 1930s to develop an aircraft which could either accompany bomber formations throughout their missions or intercept enemy bombers far from their targets (an important requirement in the days before radar was widely available). Curiously, although the Luftwaffe had developed drop-tanks by the outbreak of war, the idea of extending single-engine fighter range by these means does not appear even to have been considered, although a similar criticism might also be applied to the US Eighth Air Force in 1942.

Twin-engined aircraft with two- or three-man crews, such as the Bf 110, were greatly influenced by experience in the First World War, notably with the Bristol Fighter and the Caudron C.11. In the face of the high-performance fighters such as the Bf 109 which emerged in the late 1930s, all of the long-range fighters were to prove a disappointment, lacking the speed or manoeuvrability to dogfight with the single-engined aircraft. Most were to be reduced in status to ground-attack duties in daytime, although some, like the Bf 110, were to earn a new lease of life as nightfighters.

Certainly the outbreak of the war saw the Luftwaffe actively considering two designs as successors to the Bf 110 in the Zerstörergruppen. The Messerschmitt Me 210, of which the prototype flew on 5 September 1939, was the favourite, given Messerschmitt's experience, prestige and influence, while the Arado Ar 240, which first flew in May 1940, was the back-up programme. Both were extremely sophisticated designs with defensive armament including remotely controlled barbettes. Unfortunately both designs displayed appalling handling characteristics, especially with regard to stability. The Me 210 programme in particular proved prolonged and so disastrously unsuccessful that it provided Milch with an opportunity for revenge upon the designer, whom he humiliated in 1942.

In one respect at least the Luftwaffe was streets ahead of its rivals. That was in the provision of air transport, although this was by accident rather than design. In its early days the Luftwaffe intended supplementing its Do 11 bombers with a small number of Ju 52/3m transports which would be operated by Lufthansa and be capable of conversion into bombers with the appropriate kit. Although it was an all-metal monoplane with a cantilever wing, the 'Tante Ju' (Auntie Junkers), as the aircraft was nicknamed, was technically an older-generation design with a structure of corrugated aluminium over a tubular steel framework, a strong fixed undercarriage and three BMW 132 radial engines.

The failure of the Do 11 series, despite radical redesign, led to the decision to use the Ju 52/3m as a stop-gap pending the arrival of the second-generation bombers (Do 17, He 111, Ju 86). The air bridge which allowed General Franco to move thousands of troops from Morocco to Spain in the early days of the Spanish Civil War, mostly relying upon converted Ju 52/3m bombers, alerted the Luftwaffe to the advantages of air transport. At the outbreak of war some 550 were in service, and apart from a dozen aircraft in an X-Verfahren bombing unit, all were transports. Half of them were assigned to general transport duties (including those requisitioned from Lufthansa), ready to fly in replacements and supplies to forward units, while the remainder were assigned to Fliegerdivision 7 with crews trained either to drop troops by parachute or to fly them into airfields behind enemy lines. Not even the Soviet Air Force, which had pioneered airborne operations, had such a force.

Italy

Second only to the Luftwaffe in prestige at the outbreak of the Second World War was Italy's Regia Aeronautica. Europe's second autonomous air force, it had some 2,800 first-line aircraft in September 1939. The prestige had been gained through the inheritance of the mantle of the great prophet of air power, Gen Guilio Douhet, through its operational experience in Ethiopia and Spain as well as numerous record-breaking flights. Consequently many air forces ordered Italian aircraft before the Second World War, and as late as the summer of 1940 even the RAF was seeking Caproni light bombers.

The reality was that the Regia Aeronautica was a turkey rather than an eagle, due largely to Italy's weak industrial base, with both aircraft companies and component manufacturers under-capitalised, leading to low rates of production. Nevertheless, industry was seeking to meet the Regia Aeronautica's expansion plan, Programme R, and all the modern bombers such as the CRDA Cant Z.1007bis Alcione (Kingfisher), Fiat BR 20 Cicogna (Stork) and Savoia-Marchetti S.79-I Sparviero (Sparrow Hawk), were low-wing cantilever monoplanes with retractable undercarriages, while the other component of the Gruppi Bombardamento Terreste, the S.81 Pipestrello (Bat) bomber-transport had a fixed undercarriage. However, as with most of the Regia Aeronautica's combat aircraft, their fuselages were all of

Like the Ju 52, the Savoia-Marchetti S.81 Pipistrello (Bat) was a bomber transport which saw extensive service in Spain, where it proved obsolescent, yet even in 1939 it formed the backbone of the Gruppi BT, although increasingly it was restricted to night bombing.

traditional construction, with steel tube or wooden airframes covered with wood or doped fabric, and most of the bombers had similar coverings on their wings. Compared with the all-metal monocoque, these weaker structures took a higher proportion of the take-off weight, imposing penalties upon both range and payload, while the materials were more vulnerable to environmental conditions which reduced aircraft life.

The problem was compounded by the inability of Italian aero-engine manufacturers to provide high-power, water-cooled, in-line motors, which forced them to rely upon radials often developed from foreign

Italy's elegant Cantieri Riuniti dell'Adriatico (Cant) Z.1007bis Alcione (Kingfisher) entered service in 1939 and helped form the backbone of the wartime Gruppi Bombardamente Terreste, yet it also summarised the weaknesses of the Italian aircraft industry, being of all-wooden construction because there was insufficient investment for all-metal aircraft, and having three engines because the industry was incapable of producing high-powered engines.

The prototype Società Anonima Piaggio P.108 four-engined bomber flew in 1939, and was the only Axis dedicated heavy bomber design with separate engines to see operational service. Although the Focke-Wulf Fw 200 flew bomber missions over Britain, it was designed as an airliner, while the engines of the contemporary Heinkel He 177 were paired in two nacelles.

designs. The Piaggio P.XI RC 40 in the Z.1007bis developed 1,000hp at take-off, and the Alfa Romeo 126 RC 34 in the S.79-I developed only 780hp at a time when the latest version of the contemporary Junkers Jumo 211 in the Ju 88 developed 1,200hp. To compensate for increased structural weight the designers of both the Alcione and Sparviero adopted a three-engine solution which increased drag, even with long-chord engine cowlings. The Cicogna had two Fiat A.80 RC 41 18-cylinder engines rated at 1,000hp but proved decidedly underpowered, partly because the heavy structure also included a nose gun turret. In this respect the Cicogna was unique in the Regia Aeronautica, whose leadership piously (and somewhat optimistically) hoped their bombers would outrun most interceptors. The defensive armament of all Italian bombers was based upon single, rifle-calibre (7.7mm) machine-guns, although these were often supplemented by one or two heavy-calibre (12.7mm) weapons, the Z.1007bis having two.

Curiously for an air force allegedly shaped in Douhet's image, the Regia Aeronautica had no war-winning airpower doctrine like the RAF and, increasingly, the US Army Air Corps. When created in 1925 the Regia Aeronautica was based upon a strike force (Aerial Army) of bomber and fighter squadrons, of which a fixed number were assigned to co-operate with the army and navy, supplementing their dedicated reconnaissance squadrons. In 1931 the then Air Minister, Marshal Italo Balbo (who was killed by his own AA gunners in 1940), introduced a more flexible arrangement. As a result the Gruppi Bombardamento were assigned *ad hoc* missions dependent upon the situation, and might be called upon to attack targets on land or at sea. However, there was no practical co-ordination between the three services and the

Regia Aeronautica therefore shaped air missions to its own whim.

Nevertheless, during 1939 experiments were well advanced with torpedo bombing by Gruppi Bombardamento, and during that year the S.79-II began to enter service. This had the same engines as the Z.1007bis but could carry two torpedoes externally, and the squadrons which received these aircraft put Italy in the forefront of anti-shipping operations. Indeed, the Germans paid the Italians the compliment later in the war of emulating their tactics and acquiring their torpedoes. At the outbreak of the Second World War a successor to the S.79 was being developed, originally as the S.79bis and later as the S.84 (a designation shared with an unsuccessful DC-3 lookalike). The new bomber featured an improved aerodynamic shape with twin fins and rudders, but while it had a heavier armament (six 12.7mm machine-guns) than the S.79, its performance proved inferior, although it was to see operational service from 1941 onwards.

The Regia Aeronautica was also not blind to the advantages of modern four-engined bombers. The Piaggio company had been working on various experimental designs since the mid-1930s, beginning with the P.23 (sometimes referred to as the P.123) and the P.50, and the expertise gained led to the all-metal, monocoque construction P.108, which first flew in 1939. It featured a strong defensive armament including two remotely-controlled wing turrets and six 12.7mm machine-guns, but while this flying fortress was quickly ordered into production, it did not enter service until 1942. Like the Germans, the Italians were also interested in the concept of dive-bombing, although it was never embraced with such fervour in Rome. The Savoia S.85, with two 500hp Piaggio P.VII RC 35 radials, was issued to Squadriglie in

20

An important lesson of the Spanish Civil War was the requirement for a dedicated dive-bomber, and an Italian response was the Savoia-Marchetti S.85, which was in service with 96o Gruppo in 1939. The design proved a failure and the S.85s were replaced by Ju 87s at the earliest opportunity.

1939 but had a totally inadequate performance and never saw active service, being replaced by the Ju 87B late in 1940.

A major problem for the Regia Aeronautica (and the Armée de l'Air) was the fragmentation of the development and procurement organisation under Balbo's influence. Aircraft selection and orders were primarily (but not exclusively) the responsibility of the Direzione Generale Costruzioni e Approvigionamenti (DGCA), from which technicians were excluded, while technical development and evaluation were the responsibility of the Direzione Superiore Studi Esperienze (DSSE), the specifications being drawn up by the Air Staff. This arrangement compartmentalised development, with little exchange of ideas, and its most pernicious effects were seen in fighter development.

By the mid-1930s it was clear that the traditional fighter, designed largely to destroy enemy Corps Aeroplanes, with its light armament and emphasis upon manoeuvrability and pilot visibility, could not meet the new generation of high-speed bombers. High performance and heavy armament were required for this task, and reluctantly air staffs ordered fighters with these characteristics – except in the Regia Aeronautica.

In September 1939 more than 70 per cent of the Italian fighter force consisted of biplanes built in the traditional manner, and the Regia Aeronautica was still re-equipping Gruppi Caccia Terreste with biplanes! The backbone of these Gruppi were equipped with the Fiat CR.32, powered by a Fiat A.30 RA liquid-cooled vee engine, the aircraft being a development of the CR.30 with the same powerplant. The only concession to technical advance was the provision of two 12.7mm machine-guns rather than the traditional rifle-calibre weapons, while

the later CR.32bis had two such weapons added in the lower wings. By the end of 1939 this was being replaced by the CR.42 Falco (Falcon) with the Fiat A.74 RC 38 radial and one heavy and one rifle-calibre machine-gun in the cowling. Relatively fast at 430km/h (267mph), the Falco was an anachronism, although it was purchased by several air forces, including that of Hungary.

While the Regia Aeronautica appeared reluctantly to accept the low-wing monoplane fighter, a specification not being issued until 1936, in practice it sought to mould the new generation of aircraft in the shape of the traditional virtues. The successful designs, the Fiat G.50

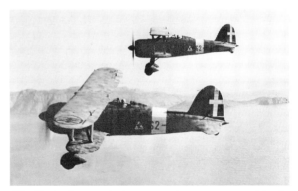

The Regia Aeronautica's conservatism was expressed in the selection of the fixed-undercarriage Società Anonima Aeronautica d'Italia (Fiat) CR.42 sesquiplane as its standard fighter in 1939, when the world's major air forces were selecting all-metal cantilever monoplanes for this role. Nevertheless, this aircraft not only maintained the First World War fighter tradition, but also proved an export success, being selected, like its Fiat predecessors, by several air forces, including those of Belgium, Hungary and Sweden.

21

A step in the right direction for the Gruppi Caccia Terreste was the Fiat G.50 Freccia (Arrow), which entered service from 1938. Yet the design still owed more to tradition than to technology, being slow and lacking firepower.

First flown in 1939, the Fiat CR.25 was also an attempt to produce a long-range escort fighter like the Bf 110, and one production machine was used as a 'hack' by the Italian Air Attache in Berlin. Its inadequacies as a fighter were quickly realised and it was produced only for the strategic reconnaissance role, although it was also used to escort transport aircraft.

Freccia (Arrow) and the Macchi MC.200 Saetta (Thunderbolt) both embodied modern construction techniques, but the emphasis was upon manoeuvrability and they had only two 12.7mm machine-guns, while transparent canopies in each design were replaced by open cockpits at pilots' request to provide better visibility. Both aircraft were handicapped by having to use the 840hp Fiat A.74 RC 38 at a time when the Bf 109E-1 had a 1,050hp liquid-cooled, inverted vee, Daimler-Benz DB 601A which gave it a top speed of 550km/h (342mph) compared with the Saetta's 505km/h (314mph) and the Freccia's 470km/h (293mph), the latter being only 42km/h (26mph) faster than the Falco bi-plane. The same radial engine was also used in the Caproni Vizzola F.5, which competed against the Freccia and Saetta and resembled the former, though featuring traditional construction techniques. Although it was not selected for mass production, a small number of pre-production aircraft entered service in a home defence unit.

The Fiat A.74 RC 38 was also selected for the only Italian attempt at a long-range fighter, the Fiat CR.25, which first flew in 1939. Only a handful of this twin-engined aircraft, with a pair of heavy machine-guns in the nose and one in the dorsal turret, saw service from 1942, largely in the air transport escort role.

To support the army the Regia Aeronautica had its Gruppi and Squadriglie Osservazione equipped largely with the Meridionali Ro 37, a fixed-undercarriage sesquiplane of traditional construction which was a typical contemporary Corps Aeroplane. The original production version had the Fiat A.30 RA liquid-cooled twelve-cylinder vee engine, but this aircraft was supplemented later by the radial-engined Ro 37bis with either the Piaggio P.IX RC 40 or Piaggio P.XR.

The Italians had been quicker than most to perceive

the requirement for ground-attack aircraft, largely through the efforts of Col Amedeo Mecozzi in the late 1920s. By 1939 Italian divisions could call upon the Squadriglie Assalto, which had three purpose-built designs. The Breda Ba 64 was an all-metal, cantilever monoplane design with open cockpit and retractable undercarriage, while the Caproni Bergamaschi AP.1 was similar but of traditional construction and with fixed undercarriage. The Breda design had four rifle-calibre machine-guns in the wings, while the AP.1 had three machine-guns, one each in the wheel fairings and one in the fuselage, but there was a considerable degree of commonality, both aircraft carrying a total bomb load of 400kg (880lb) and being available in single-seat fighter/attack and two-seat reconnaissance versions, and both being at the end of their service lives.

The Ba 65, which formed the backbone of the Squadriglie Assalto, was powered by a Gnôme-Rhône 14 radial built under licence as the Isotta-Fraschini K.14, and was also produced in single-seat attack (Ba 65) and two-seat reconnaissance-bomber (Ba 65bis) versions. It featured substantial improvements in armament, with two rifle-calibre and two heavy machine-guns and up to 1 tonne (2,200lb) of bombs, but its obsolescence was demonstrated during the Spanish Civil War, by which time a potential replacement was under development by Breda. This was a twin-engined attack bomber of ultra-modern construction with three heavy machine-guns in the nose and a single 7.7mm weapon in the open rear cockpit. Production began in 1939 as the Ba 88 Lince (Lynx). The Lince could carry up to 500kg (1,010lb) of bombs, but it was underpowered and the massive nacelles for the Piaggio P.XI RC 40 radials created tremendous drag in an otherwise clean airframe.

An unusual feature of Regia Aeronautica policy was a series of requirements for aircraft dedicated to the

The SA Industrie Mecchaniche e Aeronautiche Meridionali Ro (Romeo) 37 entered service in the mid 1930s as a fighter-reconnaissance aircraft. No attempt was made to enforce the former requirement, and it was the basic Corps aircraft of the Regia Aeronautica. A radial engined version, the Ro 37bis, supplemented the Ro 37 in the Squadriglie Osservazione Aerea.

One of Europe's leading aircraft exporters was the Società Italiana Caproni, which produced a succession of conservative designs. Indeed, as late as 1940 Britain's Air Ministry was in the late stages of ordering some Ca 310s. The Ca 133, of which an air ambulance version is seen here, was a typical bomber-transport design, and formed the backbone of the colonial air force in Africa by 1939.

colonial policing role. The original design was Caproni's Ca 133 bomber-transport, a high-braced-wing monoplane with three radial engines capable of carrying 500kg (1,100lb) of bombs externally or eighteen soldiers internally. A new generation of multi-role aircraft was in production by 1939 from Caproni Bergamaschi, based upon the Borea (North Wind) light airliner. All were twin-engined, cantilever-wing monoplanes of traditional construction. The Ca 309 Ghibli (Desert Wind) having a fixed undercarriage, but the Ca 310 Liberccio (Southwest Wind) and the Ca 311 had retractable undercarriages. Although lightly armed (three 7.7mm machine-guns) and carrying a bomb load of only 400kg (880lb) these aircraft and evolutionary developments were to be used extensively during the Second World War and many were exported. The Ca 309 was manufactured under licence in Bulgaria with 240hp Argus As 10C engines as the Papagal (Parrot).

Given Mussolini's determination to ensure that the Mediterranean was *Mare Nostrum* (Our Sea) the Italian fleet was well served with seaplanes which could patrol the waters around the navy's extensive network of bases. The twin-hulled Savoia S.55, used for many record-breaking flights, was being withdrawn and had been largely replaced by the single-engined Cant Z.501 Gabbiano (Seagull) flying boat. In the offensive role the elegant trimotor Cant Z.506 Airone (Heron) floatplane had entered service with the Gruppi Bombardamento Marittimo in 1938, and could carry a torpedo or a 800kg (1,764lb) bomb internally. To direct the navy's guns the battleships and cruisers carried the Meridionali Ro 43 floatplane, although its performance both in the air and in waters other than flat calm were poor. To provide air protection for the fleet at sea, a fighter version of the Ro 43 was produced as the Ro 44.

Italian aircraft were extensively exported to Europe,

the Middle East and Latin America. In addition to aircraft selected for the Regia Aeronautica, a number of designs were built specifically for export or built under licence. One of the most successful was a twin-engined version of the S.79, the S.79B, which was fitted with a variety of engines depending upon the customer's choice. Romania's first batch had 1,000hp Gnôme-Rhône K.14 II C32s, while the second batch, JRS.79B, had the 1,220hp Junkers Jumo 211 Da liquid-cooled vee engine and was manufactured under licence from 1940 with a redesigned tail.

The Caproni Bergamaschi Ca 135 had been an unsuccessful competitor with the Cant Z.1007 and S.79, but it had some export success, customers including Hungary, which selected the version with Piaggio P.XI RC 40 radials (Ca 135bis), this version featuring a manually operated dorsal turret. Hungary also selected the

The Officine Meccaniche 'Reggiane' SA (Caproni), commonly called Reggiane, produced the Re 2000 Intercettore (Interceptor) to meet a Regia Aeronautica requirement for a monoplane fighter. Although it was not selected for domestic use, from 1939 it was exported to and also manufactured in Hungary under licence by MAVAG as the Héja I (Hawk I), pictured here.

The Industria Aeronautica Romana (IAR), backbone of Rumania's aircraft industry, produced the sesquiplane IAR 37 Corps aircraft. It proved unsatisfactory owing to its IAR 14K engine, a derivative of the Gnome-Rhône 14K, and alternative power was sought. With the BMW 132A the aircraft became the IAR 38, which first flew in January 1939, and the following year, powered by the IAR 14K II C32, it was designated IAR 39, seen here, and became the prime front-line version.

Reggiane Re 2000 Serie I fighter which had competed unsuccessfully against the G.50 and MC 200. An all-metal fighter powered by a Piaggio P.XI RC 40, it later proved more manoeuvrable than the Bf 109E, but its unprotected wing fuel tanks were a weakness. The fighter was sold to Hungary, where it was dubbed Héja (Hawk), and produced under licence from 1942 with Gnôme-Rhône 14K as the Héja II.

A design which flew only in prototype form was the Caproni Bergamaschi Ca 335 Maestrale (Mistral). This was a two-seat fighter reconnaissance design with Hispano-Suiza 12 Ycrs liquid-cooled vee engine, and a licence was acquired by Belgium's SABCA, which was producing the aircraft as the S.47 at the time of the German invasion in 1940.

The Balkan allies of Germany and Italy had small aircraft industries whose limited facilities were largely employed to produce aircraft of traditional construction, usually of obsolete German, Italian, Czechoslovak, French and Polish design. By 1939 only Hungary and Romania had produced indigenous combat aircraft, the former's Corps Aeroplane squadrons including the Manfred Weiss WM 16 Budapest. A derivative of the Fokker VD biplane with a Gnôme-Rhône radial engine, this was produced in two versions, with the 9K Mistral (Budapest I) and the 14K Mistral-Major (Budapest II).

Romania produced a similar aircraft with the same powerplant as the Budapest II, the IAR 37 sesquiplane with enclosed cockpit. The unreliability of early licence-built Mistral-Majors led to the stop-gap installation of the BMW 132A as the IAR 38, but by 1939 improvements in Mistral-Major reliablity led to renewed installations in the IAR 39. The same engine was also selected for the country's first modern fighter, the IAR 80, which made its maiden flight in April 1939. This all-metal monocoque fighter capitalised upon existing production

to the extent that it used the tail of the PZL P.24E fighter. It was scheduled to receive four rifle-calibre (7.92mm) machine-guns, but the difficulties of acquiring these and other components in a Europe now at war, as well as the lack of machine tools, prevented the fighter entering service until early 1941.

Japan

Italian aircraft sold to Japan participated without distinction in a conflict which ended immediately before the outbreak of the Second World War. In May 1939 a dispute on the Manchurian-Mongolian border between the Khalkin Gol river and the village of Nomonhan flared into a full-scale war in which the Fiat Type I (BR.20) was used. The battle ended in ignominious defeat for the Japanese, who lost 158 aircraft destroyed or damaged beyond repair. This conflict actually saw the third clash between Russian and Japanese pilots, who had met on the Korean border in 1938 and in China from 1937. On paper Japan had more than 2,000 first-line aircraft, but Janus-like organisation fragmented its strength into the Army Air Force (JAAF) and Navy Air Force (JNAF), and it was the former Service's air arm which was humiliated.

The role of the Japanese Army was to secure national interests on the east Asian mainland, the prime threat being perceived from the Soviet Union, while in the absence of any Japanese enthusiasts of Douhet, its air arm existed to support that role. Its early leaders had been officers 'ticket punching' before transferring to other commands, one of the most distinguished being Lt Gen Tojo Hideki, who was Inspector General of the JAAF between December 1938 and July 1940, then became War Minister, and in 1941 the Prime Minister. In 1939 a new plan to expand the JAAF by a third to 142 squadrons (Chutai) was accepted. By this time the JAAF was developing its own career structure, yet the definition of aircraft requirements still tended towards the conservative while benefiting from a substantial capital investment into the aviation industry made during the early 1930s. This investment meant that by 1939 most Japanese combat aircraft were cantilever monoplanes with monocoque airframes, although the failure to develop modern liquid-cooled in-line motors meant that most aircraft had radial engines. Most JAAF aircraft represented First World War requirements in the shape of late 1930s technology, although there were signs of philosophical development.

This conservatism is especially striking in the bomber force, which continued to follow the First World War division into single-engined, two-seat light bombers and multi-engined heavy bombers. The majority of bombers were in the former category, and both they and the multi-engined aircraft suffered from notably small bomb loads. The May 1936 requirement for a new generation

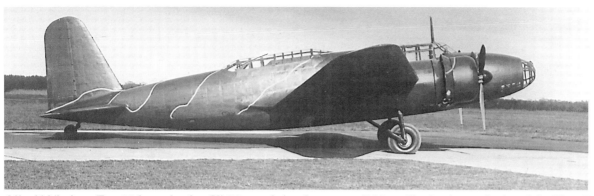

Mitsubishi's Army Type 97 heavy bomber (Ki-21) was designed to meet a 1936 specification, but production of the Ki-21-I depicted here was slow, and some heavy-bomber Chutais had the misfortune to receive the Fiat BR.20. In the Second World War the Ki-21 was codenamed 'Sally' by the Allies.

of light bombers specified a maximum speed of 400km/h and a normal bomb load of 300kg (661lb) to replace the Army Type 93 (Kawasaki Ki-3). This requirement led to two low-wing aircraft with enclosed cockpits and fixed undercarriages. The Mitsubishi Army Type 97 Single-engined Light Bomber (Ki-30) differed from the Kawasaki Army Type 98, also a Single-engined Light Bomber (Ki-32), in that the latter, uniquely for Japanese combat aircraft of this period, had a liquid-cooled vee engine (Kawasaki Ha-9). The bombs, up to a maximum of 450kg (993lb), were carried internally, and their defensive armament consisted of a single rifle-calibre (7.7mm) machine-gun facing forward and one in the rear cockpit. At the suggestion of a Capt Fujita Yuzo, a ground-attack aircraft specification based upon the Ki-30 was issued in December 1939, and prototypes made their appearance in the summer of 1939. Although lightly armed (two fixed and one movable rifle-calibre machine-guns) and with a small, externally carried bomb load of 180kg (400lb), the aircraft was armoured. It entered service from 1940 as the Mitsubishi Army Type 99 Assault Aeroplane (Ki-51).

The traditional light bomber concept was challenged when the Japanese encountered the Tupolev SB-2-M100 in China in November 1937. This led almost immediately to a requirement for a twin-engined light bomber with a maximum speed of 480km/h (298mph), a 400kg (882lb) internal bomb load and a defensive armament of up to four rifle-calibre machine-guns. The Kawasaki Army Type 99 Twin-engined Light Bomber (Ki-48) was a four-man aircraft and development was well advanced in 1939, the aircraft entering service the following year.

By 1939 the heavy bomber Chutais had received the Mitsubishi Army Type 97 Heavy Bomber (Ki-21), which was designed to meet a 1936 specification to replace the Mitsubishi Army Type 92 (Ki-20) and Mitsubishi Army Type 93 (Ki-1). The specification included a five-hour endurance, a maximum speed of

400km/h (248mph) and a normal bomb load of 750kg (1,653lb) which might be extended for short-range missions to 1 tonne (2,205lb). Initial production models of the Ki-21 had a long, enclosed, dorsal machine-gun position. Later production models had improved protection including a fifth machine-gun in a remotely-operated tail position and laminated rubber sheets added to the fuel tanks. Delays in production of this aircraft led to the purchase of the Fiat BR.20 as a stop-gap, but this was an experiment the Japanese did not repeat.

The limitations of the Ki-21 were evidently acknowledged by the Army, which issued in 1938 a replacement heavy bomber specification. This called for a maximum speed of 500km/h (311mph), a 3,000km (1,864-mile) range, a 1 tonne bomb load and improved active/passive protection including self-sealing tanks. The prototype of what became the Nakajima Army Type 100 Heavy Bomber (Ki-49) made its maiden flight in August 1939 and entered service two years later, but the type never supplanted its predecessor.

In fighter design, too, the Japanese Army proved as conservative as the Regia Aeronautica. The last biplane fighter, the Kawasaki Army Type 95 (Ki-10), had almost disappeared by 1939 and had been replaced by the Nakajima Army Type 97 (Ki-27), combining modern construction techniques with a fixed undercarriage, open cockpit and a pair of rifle-calibre machine-guns. The Ki-27, which evolved from a private-venture design, the Type PE, was clearly designed to traditional fighter concepts, although later production versions had enclosed cockpits and could carry either four 25kg (55lb) bombs for ground-attack missions or two 130 litre (28.6 Imp gal) drop tanks to extend range. The replacement, the Nakajima Army Type I (Ki-43), was already flying in prototype form in September 1939, and while

it featured a retractable undercarriage and higher speed (the specification of 1937 called for 500km/h

The prototype Nakajima Army Type 1 (Ki-43) Hayabusa (Peregrine Falcon) flew as the war began and was a replacement for the Ki-27, although built according to the same philosophy. Widely encountered during the war, it was codenamed 'Oscar'.

In 1939 most of the Japanese Army Air Force's Corps squadrons had the Tachikawa Army Type 98 direct co-operation aeroplane (Ki-36), which, like Ki-27 and Ki-43, was a traditional design exploiting new technology. It was extremely popular with its crews, one reason why a trainer version appeared in 1939 as the Army Type 99 advanced trainer (Ki-55), codenamed 'Ida'.

(311mph)), it was still a traditional design. Indeed, the specification demanded manoeuvrability at least equal to that of the Ki-27. The new fighter, dubbed Hayabusa (Peregrine Falcon), entered service in 1941.

Like its contemporaries in Europe, the Japanese Army was interested in the twin-engined, long-range fighter concept, although the specification issued in March 1937 was essentially a blank sheet of paper. The responses from Kawasaki, Mitsubishi and Nakajima

then led to a more detailed specification nine months later which included a maximum speed of 540km/h (335mph) and a five-hour endurance with an armament of two forward-firing and one movable rear-facing machine-gun. Only Kawasaki responded, with the Army Experimental Ki-45, which first flew in January 1939. Engine problems delayed its introduction into service, however, and these were not overcome for two years.

Inevitably the majority of JAAF aircraft were Corps

Virtually all of the Japanese Army fighter Chutais in 1939 were equipped with the Nakajima Army Type 97 (Ki-27), which was mutton dressed as lamb, the traditional fighter concept embodied in new technology. It was still the backbone of these Chutais in 1941, receiving the codename 'Nate'.

Aeroplanes. Small numbers of the Nakajima Army Type 94 Reconnaissance Aeroplane (Ki-4) sesquiplane remained in first-line service, but they had largely been supplanted by the Tachikawa Army Type 98 Direct Co-operation Aeroplane (Ki-36). This had a modern airframe with an enclosed cockpit, yet essentially reproduced the earlier aircraft with such features as its fixed undercarriage, light armament (two 7.7mm machine-guns and 150kg (330lb) bomb load), but despite (or because of) them it proved very popular.

Captain Fujita Yuzo, who influenced the Ki-51 attack bomber specification, also drafted one in July 1935 for a high-speed reconnaissance aircraft to support armies and army groups. The specification for what became the Mitsubishi Type 97 Command Reconnaissance Aeroplane (Ki-15) included a requirement for a maximum speed of 450km/h (280mph) and a combat radius of 400km (250 miles). With its fixed undercarriage and long, enclosed cockpit it resembled contemporary mailplanes, but it proved successful, and in September 1939 production of an up-engined version with a Mitsubishi Ha-26-I entered service as the Army Type 97 Command Reconnaissance Aeroplane Model 2 (Ki-15-II) with a top speed of 510km/h (317mph). Unusually, this latter aircraft so impressed the Japanese Navy that they ordered similar aircraft as the Mitsubishi Navy Type 98 Reconnaissance Aeroplane (C5M).

It was Fujita, now a Major, who drafted the specification for a successor in December 1937. This called for an aircraft with six hours' endurance at 400km/h (249mph) and a maximum speed of 600km/h (373mph). The elegant, twin-engined prototype first flew in November 1939 and, despite failing to meet the official specification, it was faster than the Ki-43 fighter. This facilitated its entry into service the following year as the Mitsubishi Army Type 100 Command Reconnaissance Aeroplane (Ki-46).

In contrast to the JAAF, the Japanese Navy laid great emphasis upon range for both land- and ship-based aircraft. The Navy's role was to protect both the maritime approaches to the homeland and the Empire's island possessions, which extended into the central Pacific, primarily against the USA. The ability to detect and to engage enemy forces as early as possible, and if possible beyond the range of enemy aircraft, was a key factor in Japanese naval aircraft specifications and operations. Indeed, it was exploited by Japanese carrier task forces as late as the summer of 1944. The ability of land-based aircraft to reach distant targets was demonstrated in China from 1937 onwards, and the Japanese Navy anticipated striking the enemy fleet with both land- and carrier-based air power. Yet in 1939 it was universally believed that the role of naval air power was to support the battle fleet, detecting and tracking the enemy and then eroding his strength through bomb and

Captain (later Major) Fujita Yuzo was one of the few visionaries in the Japanese Army Air Force, and his demand for a high-performance reconnaissance aircraft led to the appearance in November 1939 of the prototype Mitsubishi Army Type 100 command reconnaissance aeroplane (Ki-46). The second version, pictured here, was the Ki-46-II with Mitsubishi Ha 102 engines, which was faster than the Ki-43 and entered service in 1940.

torpedo attacks until the battleships could fight the decisive action, their guns being directed by observation aircraft.

The Japanese Navy was no exception, and even until the end of the Second World War it was dominated by traditionalists who believed in the supremacy of the battleship. This orthodoxy was challenged by two men, the most notable of whom was Admiral Yamamoto Isoroku, newly appointed commander-in-chief (officially commander of the Combined Fleet) in September 1939, and the charismatic Commodore (Rear Admiral in November) Onishi Takajiro. A brilliant staff officer who had exploited every opportunity to broaden his horizons, Yamamoto had lectured on the importance of air power, and especially torpedo bombers, as an instructor in the Naval Academy in the 1920s. He had headed the JNAF in the mid-1930s, and as a Navy Minister encouraged the construction of aircraft carriers to take the battle to the enemy. He was complemented by Onishi, a founder of the Nakajima Aircraft Company and by 1941 chief of staff of the land-based 11th Air Fleet, who sought also to exploit the numerous islands on the eastern edge of Japan's Pacific empire for land-based air power.

The majority of the aircraft in service in 1939 came from programmes initiated between the 8th and 11th years of the Showa reign (8-Shi to 11-Shi), i.e. 1933 to 1937. The long-range, land-based strike force largely had the Mitsubishi Navy Type 96 Attack Bomber (G3M), developed at the instigation of Yamamoto when he headed the Naval Bureau of Aeronautics' Technical Division. The specification he issued in 1933 went only to Mitsubishi and produced a twin-engined torpedo bomber whose operational debut in August 1937 involved a 2,000km (1,250-mile) transoceanic bombing

Development of the Mitsubishi Navy Type 96 attack bomber (G3M) was begun at the instigation of Capt (later Admiral) Yamamoto Isoroku, and gave the Japanese Navy an unrivalled long-range strike arm in 1939. Two years later, when these bombers received the codename 'Nell', some helped to sink the British capital ships HMS Prince of Wales *and* Repulse.

mission against Chinese targets in bad weather. The biggest drawbacks to this family were that their 800kg (1,746lb) bomb load had to be carried externally, and their three rifle-calibre machine-gun defensive armament (in three retractable turrets, two dorsal and one ventral) was inadequate.

In September 1939 a prototype replacement aircraft developed to a 12-Shi requirement made its first flight, and was to provide the Japanese Navy with an aircraft capable of carrying an 800kg torpedo internally 3,700km (2,000nm). The cigar-like Mitsubishi Navy Type 1 Attack Bomber (G4M) was to have a heavier armament, with a 20mm cannon in a tail position and four 7.7mm machine-guns, but there was no provision for armour or self-sealing fuel tanks. The previous year saw work begin on an even more ambitious project for an attack bomber with a range of up to 6,500km (3,500nm). Based upon the Douglas DC-4E four-engined airliner, the first prototype of the Nakajima Experimental 13-Shi Attack Bomber Shinzan (Mountain Recess) flew at the end of the year and had the

By 1939 the Japanese Naval Air Force had largely re-equipped its carrier groups with modern strike aircraft such as this Nakajima Navy Type 97 carrier attack bomber (B5N1). During the war these aircraft, codenamed 'Kate', were used for both level and torpedo bombing as well as reconnaissance.

simplified designation G5N, but it proved unsuccessful.

Like the JAAF, the JNAF strike force consisted mainly of single-engined aircraft, although in this case because they were designed primarily to operate from aircraft carriers. By 1939 a wholesale change in the dive-bomber and torpedo-bomber squadrons was well advanced, with traditional-construction biplanes of the 8-Shi and 9-Shi programmes being replaced by monocoque-construction, cantilever monoplanes.

Re-equipment of the torpedo bomber units had been given priority, for the Yokosuka Navy Type 96 Carrier Attack Bomber (B4Y) was never more than a stop-gap design following the failure of the Yokosuka Type 92 (B3Y). The 10-Shi (1935) specification laid great emphasis upon endurance, which was to be up to seven hours, and an external payload of 800kg (1,760lb). The winner of the competition was the Nakajima Navy Type 97 Carrier Attack Bomber (B5N), which entered service in 1938 and was the first Japanese carrier-borne aircraft with a retractable undercarriage. The aircraft possessed a formidable range of between 1,110km (normal) and 2,260km (maximum) (590nm and 1,220nm), which was unmatched by American torpedo bombers even in 1944. So radical was the design that a conservative fall-back design with a fixed undercarriage was produced by Mitsubishi as the B5M, but saw little active service. In 1939 a 14-Shi specification for a replacement aircraft was issued, calling for a range of between 1,850km (with 800kg load) to 3,300km (without bombs) (1,000 to 1,800nm), which led in 1941 to the Nakajima Navy Carrier Attack Bomber Tenzan (Heavenly Mountain), or B6N.

In re-equipping dive-bomber units the Navy proved more conservative, and during 1939 the Aichi Navy Type 96 Carrier Bomber (D1A1), strongly influenced by the Heinkel He 66, was due for replacement by the Aichi Navy Type 99 Carrier Bomber (D3A), which retained a fixed undercarriage but was strongly influenced by the Heinkel He 70. Production was delayed by the need to redesign the cowling and improve the tail, but when the aircraft entered service in 1940 these design changes gave it great manoeuvrability as compensation for the inadequate defensive armament of three 7.7mm machine-guns. The offensive load was no more than 370kg (815lb), although the bomber had a range of 1,470km (795nm).

Its replacement was already on the drawing board, and also reflected German influence. To meet an 13-Shi (1938) requirement for an aircraft with a range of 1,480km (with bombs) and 2,200km (without bombs) (800-1,200nm), Yokosuka designed an aircraft influenced by the Heinkel He 118 but with many radical features including internal bomb load, retractable under-carriage and a liquid-cooled vee engine (the prototypes had imported Daimler-Benz DB 600Gs). Although the

Yokosuka Navy Carrier Bomber Susei (Comet), or D4Y, first flew at the end of 1940, nearly three years elapsed before it joined dive-bombing units, owing to development problems.

The Navy's fighter in 1939 was typical of its contemporaries, being produced to a 9-Shi (1934) requirement. The Mitsubishi Navy Type 96 Carrier Fighter (A5M) was an all-metal gull-wing design with an open cockpit and fixed undercarriage. The usual pair of rifle-calibre machine-guns were fitted, although later models augmented this with a 20mm cannon. Development of a replacement was well advanced, having begun in 1937 in the light of combat experience over China, and while manoeuvrability was stressed, the speed and armament requirements (500km/h or 311mph and two 20mm cannon with two 7.7mm machine-guns) clearly demonstrated that the JNAF was seeking a radical design. The Mitsubishi Navy Type 0 Carrier Fighter (A6M) entered service in 1940 and was to prove one of the great fighters of the Second World War, with a phenomenal range (for the period) of 1,870km (1,010nm).

The limited range of its predecessor forced the JNAF to send attack bombers unescorted deep into Chinese territory, where many fell victim to enemy fighters. Recognising the problem, and influenced by the French Potez 631, a long-range, twin-engine fighter specification was issued in 1938. This called for an aircraft with a maximum speed of 520 km/h (322mph), good manoeuvrability to meet single-seat fighters and a normal range of 2,400km which could be extended to

The other element of the carrier strike force was to be the Aichi Navy Type 99 carrier bomber (D3A1), which entered service in 1940. Codenamed 'Val', this dive bomber was greatly influenced by the Heinkel He 70, Heinkel and Aichi having had a strong business relationship since the late 1920s.

3,700km (1,300 to 2,000 nm). The prototype of the Nakajima Navy Experimental 13-Shi three-seat escort fighter did not fly until 1941, and proved a failure, but redesigned it became the Navy Type 2 Reconnaissance Aeroplane (J1N).

The Navy's desire for a bomber destroyer was underlined in a 14-Shi requirement issued in September 1939, which had actually been drafted the previous year. This called for a land-based aircraft with 600km/h (373mph) maximum speed and the ability to reach 6,000m (19,700ft) in 5.5 minutes. Three years were to elapse before the prototype Mitsubishi Navy Interceptor Fighter Raiden (Thunderbolt), or J2M, first flew, and

Mitsubishi's Navy Type 96 carrier fighter (A5M), later codenamed 'Claude', formed the third element of the carrier triumvirate and was a conservative design exploiting modern technology. A replacement for this fighter was about to enter service in the form of the Mitsubishi Navy Type 0 carrier fighter (A6M2), the famed Zero or 'Zeke'.

For long-range reconnaissance the Japanese Navy relied in 1939 upon the four engined Kawanishi Navy Type 97 flying boat (H6K), with a normal range of more than 2,200nm (4,000km). It was frequently encountered during the war, when it was co-denamed 'Mavis'.

engine problems were to have a detrimental effect upon development.

The single-engined attack bombers all had a secondary reconnaissance role. Indeed, the Yokosuka D4Y actually entered service in 1942 with a reconnaissance unit, but the eyes of the fleet were its seaplanes. Long-range reconnaissance requirements were met by two 9-Shi designs with braced wings, the four-engined Kawanishi Navy Type 97 Flying Boat (H6K) and the twin-engined Yokosuka Navy Type 99 Flying Boat (H5Y). The latter was supposed to complement the former but proved underpowered, but the H6K proved a great success, having a normal range of more than 4,000km (2,200nm). By 1939 a replacement Large Flying Boat was under development to meet a 13-Shi

Every Japanese major warship from cruiser size upwards carried a floatplane, and in 1939 most were the Nakajima Navy Type 95 reconnaissance seaplane (E8N1).With a large island empire to defend, the Japanese made extensive use of this seaplane, later codenamed 'Dave', from shore bases as well as from seaplane tenders and carriers.

requirement for an aircraft with a range of 8,300km (4,500nm). The prototype of what became the Kawanishi Navy Type 2 Flying Boat (H8K) did not appear until the following year, and when it entered service it was to prove a valuable tool, with armour protection and a defensive armament of five 20mm cannon and three 7.7mm machine-guns.

Seaplanes were embarked in many Japanese ships to provide tactical reconnaissance and fire control, but seaplane carriers as well as seaplane tenders were also available to strengthen reconnaissance and anti-submarine forces. One of the most widely used floatplanes in 1939 was the Nakajima Navy Type 95 Reconnaissance Seaplane (E8N), a single-float open-cockpit biplane of traditional construction, and its successor adopted a similar design philosophy, entering service as the Mitsubishi Navy Type 0 Observation Seaplane (F1M).

For longer-range reconnaissance in cruisers and seaplane carriers the Navy used the Kawanishi Navy Type 94 Reconnaissance Seaplane (E7K), a twin-float design otherwise similar to the E8N. Development of a replacement had been under way since 1937, and was to be won in 1940 by the Aichi Navy Type 0 Reconnaissance Seaplane (E13A), a twin-float, all-metal monoplane with an enclosed cockpit. A potential replacement for which a 14-Shi (1939) requirement was issued called for a high-speed reconnaissance seaplane which could evade fighters. Two years were to elapse before the first flight of what became the Kawanishi Navy Type 2 High-speed Reconnaissance Seaplane Shiun'(Violet Cloud), or E15K, and the aircraft was not a success.

The Japanese Navy placed much emphasis upon night operations in which the enemy would be struck first by very long-range torpedoes and then by gunfire, and in this field the Japanese were to win several victories, even against enemy forces who had the advantage of radar. To support this role small numbers of the single-engined Aichi Navy Type 96 Night Reconnaissance Seaplane (E10A1) biplane flying boat were in service, embarked in the light cruisers which led the destroyer flotillas, but from 1938 these were being replaced by the similar Aichi Type 98 Night Reconnaissance Seaplane (E11A1), designed to an 11-Shi requirement.

The submarine arm, whose tasks were to provide advanced warning of enemy fleet movements to the Combined Fleet and to erode enemy fleet strength, naturally had a seaplane requirement. In 1939 this was met by Watanabe Navy Type 96 Small Reconnaissance Seaplanes (E9W1), which were kept dismantled in small hangars and re-assembled when required. A 12-Shi requirement for a replacement saw the appearance in 1939 of the prototype of what became the twin-float Yokosuka Navy Type 0 Small Reconnaissance Seaplane (E14Y1). This little-known aircraft entered service in 1941 and had the unique distinction of bombing the American mainland the following year.

Bibliography

There is a wealth of literature on German aircraft, of which the author has relied upon:

Green, W, *Warplanes of the Third Reich* (Galahead Books, New York, 1990);

Homze, E L, *Arming the Luftwaffe* (University of Nebraska Press, Lincoln, 1976);

Smith, J R & Kay, A, *German Aircraft of the Second World War* (Putnam, London, 1972).

For the Luftwaffe at this time see:

Hooton, E R, *Phoenix Triumphant* (Arms & Armour Press, London, 1994).

Little has been written in English about Italian aircraft or the Regia Aeronautica. The only comprehensive work on aircraft is:

Thompson, Jonathan W, *Italian Civil and Military Aircraft 1930–1945* (Aero Publishers, USA, 1963).

For the Regia Aeronautica see:

Ceva, L & Curami, A, 'Air Army and Aircraft Industry in Italy' in Boog, Horst (ed), *The Conduct of the Air War in the Second World War* (Berg Publishers, Oxford, 1992), and

Green, W & Fricker, J, *The Air Forces of the World* (MacDonald, London, 1958).

For an exhaustive study on Japanese aircraft see:

Francillon, R J, *Japanese Aircraft of the Pacific War* (Putnam, London, 1970).

There is little in English about the development of the Japanese air forces apart from:

Eiichiro Sekigawa, *Pictorial History of Japanese Military Aviation*, edited by Taylor, J W R and Monday, D (Ian Allan, Shepperton, 1975)

as well as

Green & Fricker (op cit).

For the JAAF, see a series of US Army post-war monographs published in microfilm form by the US Government Printing Office:

No 76, 'China Area air operations record July 1937 to August 1945';

No 77, 'Japanese preparations for operations in Manchuria 1931–1942';

Japanese Studies on Manchuria series No 4, 'Air operations 1931–1945', is also of interest. Also see *passim*:

Saburo Hayashi & Coox, A D, *Kogun* (The Marine Corps Association, Quantico, Virginia, 1959).

For the JNAF, there is:

Masatake Okumiya & Jiro Horikoshi with Caidin, M, *Zero* (Cassell & Company, London, 1957), and

Mitsuo Fuchida & Masatake Okumiya, *Midway: The battle that doomed Japan* (Hutchinson & Co, London, 1957).

Note: It should be noted that the family name comes first in Japan.

Polish PZL P.37 Los light bombers. A useful aircraft, the Los was overwhelmed in the sudden Luftwaffe attack in September 1939. Some escaped to Romania and were eventually used against Russia.

Belgian Air Force Gloster Gladiators. In surprise attacks they were virtually wiped out in 1940. The Gladiator was highly manoeuvrable, but, as a biplane, was outclassed by modern monoplane fighters. One unit operated with the RAF in the Battle of Britain, and the type was for a period the only defence of Malta. The Gladiator also saw action in Norway and in the Western Desert.

2

Allied Aircraft Development in the Early War Years

Derek Wood

The first real moves towards air rearmament among the European nations that would eventually face Germany in war came in 1935. In that year, Adolf Hitler renounced the terms of the Treaty of Versailles, introduced conscription and unveiled the new Luftwaffe. On Germany's borders were potential enemies – Poland, Belgium, France, Holland, Denmark and Switzerland. Beyond Poland lay the great enigma, Russia. In the distance was Great Britain, while across the Atlantic lay the United States of America. The attitude of these countries to a forthcoming conflict varied, as did their ability to produce modern aircraft and build them rapidly in quantity.

Poland had a well-developed aircraft industry with some basically sound designs, including a modern twin-engined light bomber, the PZL P.37 Los. A high-performance modern fighter was, however, lacking. A dozen squadrons equipped with Bristol Mercury-engined PZL P.11c fighters went to war, but proved no match for the Messerschmitt Bf 109. The P.11c was an all-metal, high gull-wing machine with a fixed undercarriage and a top speed of 242mph (390mph).

Belgium had expected that its neutrality would be respected; a forlorn hope. It had a small aircraft industry, the products of which included several foreign types built under licence. Arrangements had been made for the Hawker Hurricane to be assembled under licence in Belgium, but the invasion put a stop to that after just a few had been completed; a squadron of purchased Hurricanes was wiped out on the ground. Twenty-two Gloster Gladiator biplane fighters had been purchased before the war, but all this was to no avail. The Belgian Air Force also possessed Fiat CR.42 biplane fighters and sixteen Fairey Battle light bombers.

A modern monoplane fighter designed by Renard had been under test in 1939, but it crashed during trials. In its last variant it was the Renard 38 with a Merlin engine. It had a speed of over 300mph (480km/h) and a mixed cannon and machine-gun armament, but although it showed great potential it did not go into production.

In Holland the key aircraft manufacturer was Fokker, which supplied the Dutch armed services. The standard fighter was the Fokker D.XXI, first flown in 1936. Powered by an 830hp Bristol Mercury radial engine, the D.XXI had a fixed undercarriage and a maximum speed of 270mph (434km/h). It was highly manoeuvrable, but not fast or well-enough armed to match the Bf 109. The Fokker G.Ia was a twin-engined, twin-boom fighter ground-attack aircraft of high performance but was

The standard single-seat fighter in Holland in 1940, the Fokker D.XXI was outnumbered and outperformed by the Bf 109.

The Rolls-Royce-Merlin-powered Renard 38 prototype. A promising modern design, but development ceased after the invasion of Belgium in 1940.

available only in small numbers. Holland, like Belgium, was neutral and it did not consider that it would be directly threatened in any war.

Potentially, the two most powerful foes that Germany faced were France and Great Britain. France had had a succession of governments with various aircraft policies – most of them bad. The disorganisation was such that many different types were ordered in small quantities. The great disaster came in 1936, when the Popular Front took office. It proceeded to nationalise a greater part of the industry and split it into six companies which, in turn, acquired factories from the remaining private sector. The result was chaos.

Guy La Chambre became Air Minister in 1938 and tried to pick up the pieces with very little time to spare. He made great efforts, but the overall situation was hopeless. A new production programme was initiated in 1938 requiring the construction of 2,500 up-to-date military aircraft, but the bulk of the defence budget went to the army and funds were therefore inadequate, even if the industry could have coped with the expansion. There were at least two promising fighters under development and two or three bombers but, in the main, front-line equipment was obsolescent or obsolete.

Far and away the best fighter produced in France was the single-seat Dewoitine D520. Powered by a supercharged 910hp Hispano 12Y 45 in-line engine, it had a maximum speed of 326mph (524km/h) and a service ceiling of 36,000ft (11,000m), and its range was 615 miles (990km). Its 28ft 9in (8m) span and 33ft 6in (10m) length made for a fast and highly manoeuvrable combat aircraft. Armament consisted of one 20mm cannon firing through the airscrew hub and four 7.5mm machine-guns in the wings. Originally a private venture, the D520 flew in October 1938. The first order for 200 was placed in 1939, although this was later increased to 2,200, plus 120 for the Aeronavale. The first batch was

delivered in January 1940, but when the German offensive opened on 10 May only thirty-six were operational. Further units were re-equipped with the type before the armistice, and they all performed well. In total, 905 D520s were built, and a number subsequently operated with air forces of the Axis powers. Limited further development of this promising design took place during the war.

The Bloch 152 radial-engined fighter also had a reasonable performance, with a top speed of 316mph (274km/h) and a service ceiling of 38,000ft (11,600m). Several hundred were in use in 1940, but not enough to affect the outcome of the battle in the air. The most widely used French fighter was the Morane MS406, powered by the 860hp Hispano-Suiza 12Y 31 in-line engine. With a maximum speed of 303mph (488km/h), the MS 406 was sturdily built and manoeuvrable; it could not, however, match the performance of the Bf 109 and suffered accordingly.

Before the war the French bomber fleet was declared obsolete or obsolescent and replacement programmes were hastily initiated. The most promising of the new types was the Lioré et Olivier LeO 451 medium bomber, powered by two Gnôme-Rhône radials. Streamlined, and with a maximum speed of 285mph (485km/h), the LeO 451 had a service ceiling of 26,500ft (8,000m) and carried up to 2,800lb (1,270kg) of bombs. However, its defensive armament was poor, with single 7.5mm machine-guns in the nose and ventral positions and one 20mm cannon in a poorly engineered dorsal mounting.

Despite problems over the non-availability of certain vital items of equipment, and other delays, there were just over 470 LeO 45s in service by May 1940 and eight groups were fully equipped. After the armistice the aircraft were used operationally by the Vichy French and later by the Free French.

Another streamlined modern bomber was the Amiot

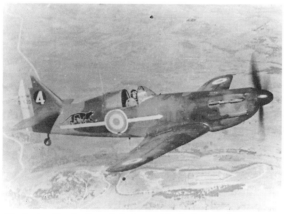

Undoubtedly the French fighter with the best performance in 1940 was the Dewoitine D.520; however, there were not enough of them.

The most numerous interceptor in the French Air Force in 1940 was the Morane MS.406, which had a 20mm cannon firing through the propeller shaft and two wing-mounted machine-guns. Despite a top speed of just over 300mph it was no match for the German Bf 109.

The Lioré et Oliver Leo 451, shown in the foreground in this picture, was the best medium bomber in the Armée de l'Air in 1940, but too few were available. It had high performance, but poor armament.

351/354, which was also used for reconnaissance. Powered by two Gnôme-Rhône radials, the 351/354 had a crew of four and could attain a top speed of 265mph (426km/h). Its range was 1,500 miles (2,400km) and its armament consisted of one 20mm cannon and two 7.5mm machine-guns. A bomb load of 2,500lb (1,130kg) could be carried. The 351 had twin fins, while the 354 had a single fin and rudder. The first production aircraft left the factory in late 1939 and about fifty had been delivered by the time of the invasion; the factory near Paris was subsequently overrun by the Germans.

Out of the motley assortment of machines that went to war with the French Services, one other stands out, the Bloch 174/175 twin-engined reconnaissance bomber (see photograph overleaf). With a span of 39ft 10in (11m) and powered by two Gnôme-Rhône 14N 49 radials, the twin-finned 174/175 had a range of 1,000 miles (1,600km). Its maximum speed was 325mph (522km/h), and it had the remarkable service ceiling of over 35,000ft (10,670m). These capabilities, plus good manoeuvrability, made the 174/175 difficult to intercept. Its armament comprised seven 7.5mm machine-guns and, as a bomber, the 175, it could carry 1,000lb (450kg) of bombs. Marcel Bloch (better known after the war as Marcel Dassault) was a good designer, yet his efforts were to have little practical effect, as only forty-nine 174/175s were used operationally and production was very slow.

Overall, France had too little time available and too chaotic an industry to re-equip the Armée de l'Air and the Aeronavale with sufficient numbers of the right aircraft. A shortage of parts, and even sabotage, contributed to the gloomy picture. After the armistice, development at French factories all but ceased, and this seriously affected the industry after the war. It had to catch up with five years of lost technology and design know-how, not to mention missing the beginning of the jet age.

The USA, although not in the conflict until December 1941, was indirectly a major participant in the air war from 1939 onwards. In the late 1930s France, Belgium, Norway, Greece and Britain ordered military aircraft from the USA to fill gaps in their inventories. This had two effects. First, it enabled US factories to expand at a time of acute contract shortage, and second, it gave firms invaluable operational experience with their products before the country entered the war.

A Bloch 175 bomber in German markings. The 175 and its reconnaissance counterpart, the 174, had high speed and altitude performance. There were, however, so few of them that they did not affect the outcome of the air war over France.

The main list of aircraft is as follows: Bell P-39 Airacobra, Boeing B-17 Fortress, Brewster F2A Buffalo, Consolidated PBY Catalina, Consolidated B-24 Liberator, Curtiss Hawk 75, Curtiss P-40 Warhawk/Tomahawk, Chance-Vought V-156F Chesapeake, Douglas DB-7A/B Havoc/Boston, Grumman F4F Wildcat/Martlet, Lockheed Hudson, Martin 167 Maryland, North American Harvard, North American P-51 Mustang and Vultee Vengeance.

Some of these types were very successful either in the short or long term, while others proved quite unsuited to operations in the European theatre when pitted against the Luftwaffe. A typical example of the latter was the Bell P-39 Airacobra. One of the first interceptors to have a tricycle undercarriage, the Airacobra was unique in having its 1,150hp Allison V-1710-E4 engine mounted behind the pilot, the propeller being driven via a long extension shaft. A 20mm cannon fired through the

A very modern-looking, streamlined fighter, the Bell P-39 Airacobra did not have a performance to match, particularly at altitude, and was therefore unsuited to the European air war. Many were supplied to the USAAF and to Russia, where they were used for ground attack. The P-39 was unique in having the engine behind the pilot, driving the propeller through an extension shaft.

Ordered for the US Navy as the Brewster F2A, this fighter was also the subject of a misguided RAF order in 1939, where it was known as the Buffalo. Unsuitable for European operations, RAF Buffaloes were sent to Malaya and Singapore, where they fell victim to high-performance Japanese fighters.

The first American fighter to see action in the Second World War, the Curtis Hawk 75A (P-36) saw service with the French Air Force and, later, the RAF. The latter sent them, as the Mohawk, to India and Burma. Several USAAC squadrons were equipped with the P-36.

airscrew boss, while there were two nose-mounted and four wing-mounted 0.30in machine-guns.

Airacobras were initially ordered by France, but after the armistice the contract was taken over by Britain. Following Air Fighting Development Unit trials, one squadron, No 601, was re-equipped with the type. It was found that performance at altitude was very poor and mechanical unreliability led to serious serviceability problems. The Airacobra was briefly used for ground strafing, but was withdrawn from operations after four months. The bulk of the 670 ordered were cancelled and, instead, went to the US Army Air Corps, while many were supplied to Russia, where they proved suitable for low-level attacks.

Two other interceptors were ordered which also proved unsuitable for the European conflict, namely the Brewster Buffalo and the Curtiss Hawk 75A. The Buffalo, an ugly barrel-shaped fighter, was first ordered by the US Navy as the F2A. In 1939 the British Purchasing Commission decided to order a land-based version, as did Belgium. After Belgium collapsed, its order for 28 was taken up to add to the 170 for the RAF, where they were named Buffalo. First deliveries were made in July 1940, but flight trials showed conclusively that the Buffalo would be no match for the Bf 109. Its speed of 292mph (470km/h) and general performance were low, and the armament of four 0.5in machine-guns was inadequate. The Buffaloes were, therefore, shipped to the Far East, where they later suffered severely at the hands of Japanese fighters.

Britain ordered another radial-engined fighter, the Curtiss Hawk 75A, which in RAF service was named Mohawk. Again, this was an aircraft ordered and operated in quantity by the French air force, the remaining orders being switched to Britain after the armistice. The

P-36A Hawk was a standard fighter with the USAAC.

The French Hawks were powered by the Pratt & Whitney Twin Wasp engine, and these were designated Mohawk III by the RAF. The majority of the 100-plus Mohawks delivered to the RAF in 1940 were, however, powered by the 1,200hp Wright Cyclone GR-1820 radial, and in this form were designated Mohawk IV. With a top speed of 302mph (485km/h), a service ceiling of 32,000ft (9,750m) and six 0.30in machine-guns, the Mohawk was a good deal better than the Buffalo, although it was still unsuitable for Europe. Later the Mohawks were operated in India and Burma against the Japanese air forces.

Two further fighters had useful careers with the RAF, neither in its original intended role. These were the P-40 Tomahawk and the P-51 Mustang. The Curtiss Tomahawk was virtually a liquid-cooled-engine development

A development of the Curtiss P-36 with an Allison liquid-cooled engine in place of a radial, the P-40 was built in large numbers for the USAAC and for export. With the RAF, as the Tomahawk, the aircraft was used for low-level tactical reconnaissance in the UK and fighter ground attack in the Middle East. As an interceptor its lack of altitude performance ruled it out in the European theatre.

Designed and built in 117 days to meet a British wartime specification, the North American Mustang had a laminar-flow wing which gave it very good low-altitude performance. It was used by the RAF for tactical reconnaissance, and later, when fitted with the Rolls-Royce Merlin in place of the Allison engine, it became the outstanding long-range, high-altitude fighter of the war.

of the Mohawk. France ordered 140 export P-40s, but these were not delivered; they were taken up by the RAF along with an additional 606 machines. Variants covered Tomahawks Mk I, IIA and IIB.

The Tomahawk served as a low-level tactical reconnaissance aircraft with army co-operation squadrons in Britain, as poor altitude performance did not allow fighter operations in the European theatre. Tomahawks

Named the Wildcat in the US Navy and Marines and Martlet in the British Fleet Air Arm, the Grumman F4F fighter was built in large numbers and saw service throughout the war on board ships and from land bases. The Martlet, in December 1940, was the first American aircraft in British service to force down an enemy machine in the Second World War. In this pre-delivery photograph the Martlet II bears an American civil registration together with British markings overpainted in white.

did, however, work as interceptors in the Western Desert in addition to performing effective ground-attack operations. With a 1,040hp Allison V-1710-33 engine, the aircraft had a top speed of 345mph (555km/h) at 15,000ft (4,570m) and carried six 0.303in machine-guns.

In 1940 the RAF took the unprecedented step of commissioning the design of a fighter in the USA to incorporate the lessons learned in the first eight months of the war. A prototype of the NA-37, destined to become the Mustang, was designed and built in the remarkable time of 117 days. It had a laminar-flow wing, a low-drag radiator and a very high standard of finish. As a result the Mustang had a maximum speed of 390mph (625km/h) at low altitude and a range of just over 1,000 miles (1,600km). The 1,100hp Allison engine, however, as on the Airacobra and the Tomahawk, did not give the required performance at altitude, thus making it better suited to low-level tactical reconnaissance. Some 800 Allison-engined Mustangs were acquired by the RAF.

With an armament of four 0.50in and four 0.30in guns and an oblique camera, the type was used from early 1942 onwards, replacing Tomahawks. The Mustang was to come into its own later as the war's most successful long-range interceptor when re-engined with the Rolls-Royce Merlin. This development is dealt with in another chapter.

The Royal Navy also took an interest in US fighter designs, and on the fall of France took over a French order for single-seat Grumman G-36A aircraft,

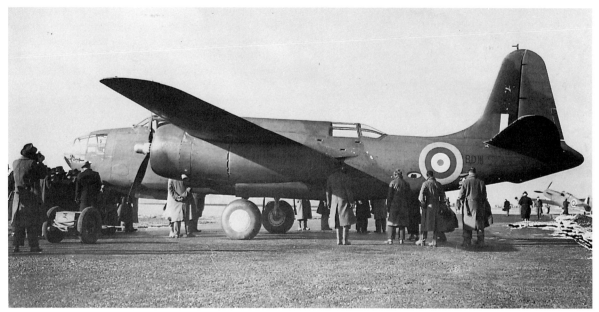

Designated A-20 by the USAAC and called Boston by the RAF, this Douglas design was a very effective bomber/attack aircraft and was also used as a fighter. The aircraft shown here is an RAF Boston I, BDIII. Boston Is were converted in Britain into Havocs as night fighter/intruders, and later BDIII was fitted with a Turbinlite airborne searchlight.

designating them Martlet I. This was followed by an order for 100 G-36Bs, 90 of them with folding wings. Initially the 1,200hp Wright Cyclone was fitted, but the second batch had the Pratt & Whitney Twin Wasp radial of the same power, these being known as Martlet Mk II. Deliveries were made in 1940, the second batch following in 1941–2. A Greek order was also taken over in 1941.

Tough, reliable and armed with four or six 0.5in machine-guns, the Martlet was a godsend to the Fleet Air Arm (FAA). It was used in every theatre of war, operating from fleet and escort carriers. Under Lend-Lease, enacted in the USA in 1941, the FAA received a steady stream of Martlets and Wildcats, the latter being the name for the type used by the US Navy and US Marines and then standardised on by Britain in 1944. The Martlet had a span of 38ft (11m), a maximum speed of 328mph (527km/h) at 21,000ft (6,400m), a service ceiling of 37,500ft (11,435m) and a normal range of 845 miles (1,300km). Its loaded weight was 7,002lb (3,175kg).

In the fields of light and medium bombing, reconnaissance and training, the USA was able to provide first-class aircraft, several of which were continuously developed through the war. One of the most successful from the outset was the tricycle-undercarriage Douglas DB-7 light bomber. Originally the subject of a large pre-war French order and one for the RAF, the DB-7 first flew in August 1939 and, after the German invasion, the outstanding French orders were taken over by the RAF.

Thereafter, the US Army Air Forces adopted the type as the A-20, the 'A' prefix standing for attack.

The RAF used its first DB-7s as trainers, the name Boston being adopted. A quantity of DB-7s and DB-7As were converted into night intruders and nightfighters in Britain and called Havocs. The Mk I had two 1,200hp Twin Wasp radials, while later deliveries were fitted with 1,600hp Wright Double-Row Cyclones. As a nightfighter the Havoc had a 'solid' nose housing eight 0.303 machine-guns and airborne radar, while the intruder version had a glazed nose with guns in the lower nose, a Vickers K gun in the dorsal position and 2,400lb (1,000kg) of bombs.

The Havoc II nightfighter had an unglazed nose accommodating no fewer than twelve 0.303in machine-guns. The light bomber version of the aircraft, the Boston III, was the most widely used variant with the RAF, deliveries beginning in spring 1941. It proved the ideal replacement for the obsolescent Blenheim, which had borne the brunt of the daylight bombing since the war began and had suffered heavy casualties. The Boston III was fast, with a maximum speed of over 300mph (482km/h), manoeuvrable and well liked by its crews. The Mark III had a span of 61ft 4in (18m) and a range of just over 1,000 miles (1,600km) when fully loaded. With a crew of four it had a maximum bomb load of 2,000lb (907kg). Gun armament consisted of four fixed 0.303in machine-guns in the nose, and twin 0.303s in the dorsal and ventral gun positions. An intruder version of the Boston III carried four 20mm cannon in an

Named the Maryland by the British, this Martin bomber was not ordered by the USAAC. Most of those supplied to the RAF were sent to the Middle East, where they were used for bombing and reconnaissance. The Maryland was also used by South African Air Force squadrons. From the Maryland was developed the larger Baltimore bomber for the RAF, which had better performance and less cramped crew accommodation.

underfuselage pack. The Marks IV and V which appeared later in the war had a power-operated twin-gun dorsal turret.

A light attack bomber which failed to gain a US contract but which was supplied to Europe was the Martin 167, named Maryland by the RAF. A three-seater, the Maryland was powered by two 1,200hp Twin Wasp radials initially, with single and later two-stage superchargers. It carried up to 2,000lb (907kg) of bombs and six machine-guns, four of which were in the wing. Some seventy-five Marylands were taken over from French orders, and altogether the RAF acquired 225, the majority being shipped to the Middle East for bombing and

The Martin Baltimore development of the Martin Maryland which was originally designed to French requirements and later used by the RAF. Classified as a light bomber, the Baltimore was larger and faster than its forebear and carried better defensive armament. The Baltimore served in the Middle East and Italy.

photographic reconnaissance work. It had very cramped crew positions separated by bulkheads, and was only moderately successful. A more capacious, higher powered development to British requirements was the Martin Baltimore, which first flew in June 1941 and entered RAF service early in 1942. Like the Maryland, the Baltimore was employed in the Mediterranean area. A total of 1,473 was produced for the RAF.

Two important and widely produced American medium bombers began flight tests in 1940, the North American B-25 Mitchell and the Martin B-26 Marauder. The original prototype for the B-25, the NA-40, was destroyed during initial flight tests in 1939, but the USAAC was so impressed that it called for major design changes to be incorporated and had enough faith to place an order for 184 of the new NA-62, the first of which flew in August 1940.

A mid-wing 67ft 7in (20m)-span aircraft with two 1,700hp R-2600 radials, the B-25, had a five-man crew, a five-gun armament and carried 3,000lb (1,360kg) of bombs. The range was 1,350 miles (2,100km), and it had a maximum speed of over 300mph (482km/h). To solve stability problems, dihedral on the outer wing panels was deleted. Over 9,700 Mitchells of all marks were built, of which 800-plus were delivered to the RAF. The changes in the Mitchell, particularly concerning armament (a prime consideration in the Second World War), are considered elsewhere in this work.

When the US Army Air Corps issued a requirement for a high-performance medium bomber in January 1939, the emphasis was laid on speed. The Glenn Martin company's submission was based on an aircraft with a very high wing loading (i.e. a small wing area) and a high degree of streamlining. Like the B-25, the resulting aircraft by Martin, the B-26 Marauder, had a tricycle undercarriage. The high wing loading inevitably led to high landing speeds and training problems. With a shoulder-wing, the B-26 had plenty of fuselage capacity, allowing a bomb load of 4,800lb (2,177kg). Armament consisted of nose and tail 0.30in machine-guns plus two 0.50s mounted in a dorsal turret. Powered by two 1,850hp R-2800 Double Wasp radials, the Marauder could achieve 315mph (500km/h) at 15,000ft (4,570m) and cruised at 265mph (426km/h). Range was 1,000 miles (1,600km) and service ceiling 25,000ft (7,600m).

The US Army Air Corps became the US Army Air Force in June 1942, and its first Marauders were delivered that year, while aircraft supplied to the RAF did not become operational until mid 1942. On subsequent variants the wingspan was increased from 65ft to 71ft (19m to 21m) and armament was steadily increased. Production continued through to April 1945.

Two American four-engined bombers were to have a major effect on the outcome of the Second World War, namely the Boeing B-17 Flying Fortress and the

A heavily armed high performance medium bomber, the Martin B-26 Marauder had a high wing loading, which meant long take-offs and landings. Well streamlined, it had a top speed of over 300 mph. A standard bomber in the newly-created USAAF, the Marauder also equipped squadrons of RAF and South African Air Force in the Mediterranean theatre of war. Depicted is an RAF Marauder I.

One of the most successful American front-line aircraft of the Second World War, the North American Mitchell was produced to a total of nearly 11,000 and served in every theatre of war. It was named after the aviation pioneer General 'Billy' Mitchell. A medium bomber with a crew of five, it had a top speed of over 280 mph and a range of 1,350 miles. The example shown is a Mitchell I (B-25B), the first delivered to the UK, wearing RAF prototype markings and the serial FK16I.

Consolidated B-24 Liberator. Both benefited from early service experience with the RAF.

The B-17 dated back to a far-sighted Army Air Corps design competition of 1934 for a bomber to carry 2,000lb of bombs for at least 1,020 miles at a speed of over 200mph. The prototype was flown in 1935, and steady development continued thereafter.

Because of lack of money and political opposition, the first fully operational version, the B-17B, was not ordered until 1938. Thereafter the B-17C was procured, of which thirty-eight were supplied to the USAAC and, in 1941, twenty to the RAF as the Fortress I. The B-17C had a 67ft 10in-long fuselage of circular cross-section, four Wright Cyclone R-1820 engines of 1,200hp each with turbosuperchargers, and a crew of ten. Wingspan was 103ft 9in (31m) and all-up weight 45,750lb (20,750kg).

The lessons learned by the RAF were incorporated

A Boeing B-17C Flying Fortress I of the RAF. Twenty of these aircraft were supplied to Bomber Command in 1941. Owing to mechanical and other problems, together with poor armament, they were not a success. The redesigned B-17E corrected these deficiencies, its improvements including a new fin and a tail turret. In this form it opened the offensive by the US 8th Air Force from Britain and, with later marks, became famous as one of the most important heavy bombers of the war.

A Liberator I of RAF Coastal Command. This type and its successors made a major contribution to the war against the U-boat by closing the Atlantic air gap, as the Liberator had a range of 2,400 miles. The early air-to-surface-vessel (ASV) radar aerials can be seen on the wings, nose and above the rear fuselage. The Liberator went on to become the stablemate of the B-17 in the US daylight bombing offensive in Europe, and served in all war theatres.

in the next major variant of the Fortress, the B-17E. Mechanical reliability was improved, the bomb sight modified and gun freezing dealt with. Most important, though, was an increase in the defensive armament. The rear fuselage was redesigned to incorporate a tail gun turret, and an enlarged tail unit was fitted. Armament was increased to twelve 0.5in guns and one 0.30in (including two power-operated twin-gun turrets) and the bomb load rose from 10,500lb to 17,600lb (4,760 to 7,980kg). The B-17E had a service ceiling of 36,600ft (11,155m), a maximum speed of 317mph (510km/h) and cruised at 210mph (337km/h). Its all-up weight was 53,000lb (24,000kg). The B-17E came into service in the Pacific and European war theatres in 1942.

The second heavy day bomber to achieve fame, the B-24, was a later and very different-looking aircraft. It also had the distinction of being produced in larger quantities than any other single Allied type during the Second World War (a total of over 18,000).

When, in 1939, the Army Air Corps formulated a specification for a heavy bomber, it demanded better range and capacity than the B-17, together with high speed. Consolidated Aircraft set out to meet these using the Davis patented long-span, narrow-chord wing. This high-aspect-ratio wing had a low angle of attack, and its design thus gave high lift and low drag, which meant increased range.

On the Consolidated Model 32 bomber, which became the B-24, the shoulder-mounted wing allowed for a large bomb bay with the bombs stowed vertically, and a catwalk between the front and rear sections of the fuselage. It also had roller-shutter bomb doors which reduced airflow disturbance associated with conventional bomb-bay doors. Finally, the Model 32 was the first heavy bomber with a nosewheel undercarriage, the main legs retracting outwards into the wings.

While the USAAC ordered a small number of early Liberators, the RAF ordered 285, of which 120 had originally been ordered by France. The first of these were used as transports. As a result of operational experience, the RAF Liberator Is were fitted with 0.5in machine-guns, one each in the nose and tail, one either side of the fuselage and one in a tunnel gun position underneath. In addition, self-sealing fuel tanks and internal armour were fitted.

The Liberator went into RAF squadron service with Coastal Command in June 1941. With its range of 2,200 miles (3,530km) it was known as a VLR (very long range) aircraft, and for the first time Britain could begin to close the gap in mid-Atlantic where German U-boats had been operating unhindered by land-based aircraft surveillance and attack. The B-24 Liberator was steadily developed and had a distinguished career in bomber, maritime and transport roles.

The early marks had four 1,200hp Pratt & Whitney R-1830-33 engines with mechanical superchargers. Span was 110ft (33m) and length 63ft 9in (19m). Gross weight was 53,600lb (24,300kg), maximum speed 292mph (460km/h), cruising speed 228mph (366km/h)

First flown in 1939, the Lockheed P-38 Lightning remained in production until the end of the war. Fast, and possessed of long range, the Lightning carried a heavy nose armament, and turbosuperchargers for the Allison engines were carried in the booms. One famous event in the Lightning's history was the shooting down of a bomber carrying the Japanese Admiral Yamamoto, 500 miles from the fighters' base.

and service ceiling 30,500ft (9,300m). Bomb load was 4,000lb (1,800kg).

Britain pioneered the use of air-surface-vessel (ASV) radar for airborne maritime surveillance. This became a major factor in the U-boat war. The equipment was steadily developed for longer range and clearer presentation for the operator. With its exceptional range the Liberator made full use of ASV in both British and American service, the former from June 1941 onwards.

The first Coastal Command aircraft to be fitted with ASV was also American, the ubiquitous Lockheed Hudson. This type was the first American aircraft to be used operationally by the RAF in the Second World War. The Hudson was a military conversion of the Lockheed 14 civil transport, and was purchased in quantity by the British in 1938. It was a classic example of a good basic airframe being adapted to undertake numerous tasks in a wide variety of climates. The Hudson was used for maritime reconnaissance/attack, general reconnaissance, bombing, training and as a transport.

Powered by two 1,100hp Wright Cyclone radial engines, the Hudson had a maximum speed of 246mph (395km/h), cruised at 170mph (273km/h), and had an endurance of 6hr. The weapon load (of bombs or depth charges) was 750lb (340kg), and armament consisted of two 0.303 machine-guns in the nose, two in a dorsal Boulton Paul turret and one in the belly. A crew of five was carried.

The successor to the Hudson was another adaptation of a Lockheed transport, this time the Model 18. Bearing a close resemblance to the Hudson, the type was known as the B-34/B-37 Lexington in the USAAF, the PV-1 with the US Navy, and the Ventura in the RAF. With two 2,000hp Pratt & Whitney Double Wasp engines, the Ventura had a maximum speed of 300mph (480km/h), cruised at 260mph (420km/h), had a range of 1,000 miles (1,600km) and a service ceiling of 25,000ft (7,260m). Armament was two 0.50 and six or eight 0.303in guns plus 2,500lb (1,135kg) of bombs. The Ventura saw limited service with Bomber Command in 1943 and then served with Coastal Command and the air forces of Australia, New Zealand, South Africa and Canada.

A radical American fighter design was ordered in quantity by Britain in 1940 but later cancelled, which caused arguments and recriminations. The aircraft, the Lockheed P-38 Lightning, was designed to meet a 1937 USAAC requirement for an interceptor to attain 360mph at 20,000ft (6,000m) and reach that height in six minutes – very ambitious for that prewar period. Lockheed chose a twin-boom, twin-engine layout with radiators and turbosuperchargers mounted in the booms behind the Allison in-line engines. The pilot sat in a central nacelle which also housed the single cannon plus four machine-gun armament.

The RAF had ordered 143 Lightnings in March 1940, and there was also a French contract. These were all to be powered by the same unsupercharged 1,040hp Allison V-1710-33 engine as the Curtiss Tomahawk, also ordered by both nations. The orders were placed before the long-drawn-out Battle of Britain had been fought and many lessons about air fighting had been learned, particularly the need for climb and altitude performance. Without superchargers the Lightning clearly did not meet European conditions, and the RAF cancelled the order following trials with three aircraft at A&AEE Boscombe Down in late December 1941 and early 1942.

Lockheed wanted the contract adhered to on the original terms, but this was not found possible. At the time there was also a shortage of superchargers in the USA. As a result, the USAAF took over the British order and placed a larger one following America's entry into the conflict. The USAAF subsequently used the Lightning in all war theatres as a long-range fighter, fighter-bomber and reconnaissance aircraft. Production continued until 1945. The final version, the P-38L, had a top speed of 414mph (666km/h), could climb to 20,000ft (6,000m) in seven minutes and had a service ceiling of 44,000ft (13,400m).

In addition to the aircraft detailed above, a variety of other types were purchased by Britain, usually in smaller quantities. One exception was the North American NA-16 Harvard two-seat advanced trainer, which remained in RAF service until the late 1950s. First ordered by the RAF in 1938, the Harvard was entering service by the end of that year. Contracted and paid for up to early 1941, Harvards for the RAF totalled 1,100. Under Lend-Lease a further 4,000 were delivered. The USA employed the type in large numbers as the T-6 Texan.

The Harvard was used under the air training scheme in Canada and Southern Rhodesia and the commonality with the Texan was a major asset after December 1941. The Harvard was of metal construction and powered by a single 550hp Pratt & Whitney Wasp radial. Maximum speed was 205mph (330km/h) and endurance 3.9hr.

The arrangements between the USA and Britain were quite remarkable. A non-combatant up to December 1941, America was supplying large quantities of war material, including hundreds of aircraft, to a friendly nation at war. By 1941 Britain was quite literally running out of dollars, and faced a situation where she would be unable to pay for the aircraft she so desperately needed. On 11 March 1941 President Roosevelt signed a Congressional 'Lend-Lease' Bill which completely altered the situation right through until the defeat of Japan in 1945.

Under 'Lend-Lease' the USA could sell, transfer, exchange, lease or lend any defence article, providing the receiving country's defence was deemed to be vital to the defence of the USA. Continued deliveries to Britain were thus assured.

It had not, however, been a one-way street. In the 1938–9 period British contracts with American firms were worth more than those placed by the USAAC. These served to 'prime the pump' of US industry at a time when American rearmament had hardly begun and, as mentioned earlier, allowed for much needed factory and workforce expansion. In addition, as noted

The North American AT-6, named Texan in the USA and Harvard by the RAF, was undoubtedly the key advanced trainer of the Second World War. Thousands of aircrew flew the type in the USA and throughout the British Commonwealth countries. It had a top speed of 205 mph. After the war it was also used for counterinsurgency work.

An early production Hurricane Mk I eight-gun fighter, L1621 of No 87 Squadron, with two-blade, fixed-pitch propeller. The Hurricane was very manoeuvrable and a stable gun platform, and bore the brunt of the air fighting in France and in the Battle of Britain.

previously, both industry and the USAAC/USAAF received a steady flow of combat information which indicated where improvements on aircraft needed to be made. These included the fitting of self-sealing fuel tanks, aircrew armour protection, heavier armament for both fighters and bombers and, for fighters, the necessity for higher altitude performance and better rates of climb. The requirement for greater range/endurance meant larger internal fuel capacity and reliable drop tanks. Operational experience also showed up mechanical defects and maintenance problems which could be remedied on types which would ultimately be flown on a war basis by both air forces.

A further British contribution in 1941 was to open the door on British technical secrets to the Americans. This included providing the cavity magnetron, a high-power valve developed at Birmingham University which made possible the production of centimetre wavelength radar. This was to revolutionise air-to-surface, air-to-air and ground-based radars.

Finally, the ferrying of American-built aircraft across the Atlantic had been organised. The ferry service was inaugurated on 10–11 November 1940 with seven Lockheed Hudsons led by Capt (later Air Vice-Marshal) D C T Bennett of British Overseas Airways Corporation. It took them ten and a half hours to fly from Gander, Newfoundland, to Northern Ireland. This trailblazer was to lead in later years to vast numbers of multi-engined aircraft traversing what was to be the longest oversea main air supply route in the world. To get ferry crews back to North America an east-west service was begun in September 1941 by BOAC, initially using six converted Liberator bombers. In August 1941 Pan American Airways began ferrying American aircraft to the RAF in the Middle East via West Africa.

Britain

The period September 1939 to April 1940, known as the 'Phoney War', hardly prepared Britain for the disasters to come. The air fighting over the Western Front was sporadic and, apart from giving RAF pilots some combat in Hurricanes, it did not give the overall experience necessary to counter later massive German air attacks. Certain lessons were learned, the most important of which was that the then-current generation of twin-engine bombers, such as the Blenheim and Wellington, could not survive in daylight without escort when confronted with modern enemy fighters. During the Battle of France the single-engine standard light bomber, the Fairey Battle, proved to be a disaster and suffered severe casualties.

After the evacuation from Dunkirk and the Franco-German armistice, Britain's situation as an island fortress off an enemy-held European land mass was perilous in the extreme. During May and June 1940, 959 aircraft were lost, of which 477 were fighters.

The aircraft raw material situation had radically altered. Delivery of aluminium-containing bauxite from France ceased with the armistice, and supplies had to be shipped all the way from British Guiana, in the face of a growing U-boat campaign. Canada was a key aluminium supplier. In the last quarter of 1939 some 12,000 tons (12,200 tonnes) of ingots of aluminium arrived in Britain; in 1940 this rose to 48,000 tons (48,770 tonnes). Canada also supplied quantities of high-purity magnesium and cryolite, essential for top-grade aluminium

Probably the most famous of all fighter aircraft, the Merlin-powered Vickers-Supermarine Spitfire. With its elegant lines, it proved capable of steady development throughout the war as more engine power became available. Shown here is a Spitfire Mk I.

production. Refining and crushing cryolite ore had been a Danish speciality, but this source was cut off with the German invasion. Specialised timber, textiles, paper and rare materials like platinum and radium had to be purchased and imported from all over the world.

Production of aircraft in Britain exceeded that of Germany in 1940, and continued to grow despite the bombing of factories up and down the country in 1940–41.

The basis for the aircraft industry and its transition to a rearmament state was established in the period 1935 to 1938 by a very far-sighted politician, Lord Swinton, who became Secretary of State for Air in mid-1935. First, he cut the existing lengthy time between fully tested prototype and in-service date by ordering 'off the drawing board' and incorporating modifications on the line. He also ordered common engine mountings which allowed for easy fitment of alternative powerplants.

Swinton's greatest achievement, however, was to provide for massive production expansion when the emergency came. He launched an Air Ministry scheme whereby state-owned factories would be set up by non-aviation companies such as car manufacturers. They would equip and manage the works and turn out aircraft and aero engines from a 'parent' company in the aircraft industry. This was known as the shadow factory scheme, and was announced by the Prime Minister in March 1936.

The parent company had to provide specifications for plant, jigs, tools, etc, full drawings and training for key people. In addition to the shadow scheme, the system of subcontracting parts and components was widely extended. By including small engineering works, garages, and even such companies as toy makers, a country-wide network of around 15,000 subcontractors was created.

The only major failure in the shadow scheme was at Castle Bromwich. Swinton had wanted it to be parented by Vickers, as it was for Spitfire manufacture. When Swinton was replaced by Sir Kingsley Wood in 1938, Castle Bromwich was placed in the hands of the Nuffield Organisation. As a result, instead of a massive output of Spitfires, by May 1940 nothing had come off the line. Lord Beaverbrook, the Minister of Aircraft Production, immediately placed the factory in the hands of Vickers, and by the end of September 1940 125 Spitfires had been produced there.

The key to fighter production was the supply of Rolls-Royce Merlin engines. Any disruption of Merlin production during the Battle of Britain would have left Hurricane and Spitfire airframes sitting useless at the end of the line. While Bristol chose to have a motor car company operate its shadow factory, Rolls-Royce decided to run a shadow itself at Crewe. The new factory finished its first Merlin in May 1939. During the summer of 1940 Rolls-Royce worked up to a rate of delivery of 400 engines per month.

A further Rolls-Royce factory, at Hillington near Glasgow, was completed in October 1940. In the USA Ford turned down a licence contract to build the Merlin, but it was taken up by the Packard Motor Company, which later built thousands of Merlins, including those

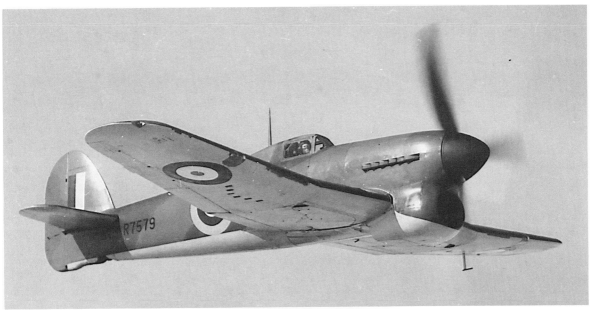

An early production Hawker Typhoon IA with an armament of twelve machine-guns. The Mark IB had four 20mm cannon, which became standard. The Sabre-engined Typhoon was designed as a low- to medium-altitude interceptor, but it suffered from early structural and engine problems. Ultimately it became one of the most successful ground-attack aircraft of the war, using rocket projectiles, bombs and cannon.

for the later marks of Mustang fighter. The Merlin-engined Mustang became one of the best interceptors of the Second World War.

Despite the many setbacks of war, the industry was able to provide the fighting machines to defend Britain and to strike back. The air battles over France and the subsequent Battle of Britain taught many lessons which affected then current production and future developments. Both the Hurricane and Spitfire had been improved with higher-rated Merlins and constant-speed propellers. To provide more firepower an improved 20mm cannon installation was to be available for both aircraft by 1941. There was, however, clearly an upper limit to Hurricane performance improvements.

In 1937 the Air Ministry issued specification F.18/37 for a high-speed fighter intended to utilise new 2,000hp engines. One example was to be fitted with the Napier Sabre, which had cylinders arranged in an 'H' configuration. The other was to have the Rolls-Royce Vulture engine with an 'X' cylinder arrangement, the Vulture also being scheduled as the powerplant for the Avro Manchester heavy bomber. Both engines had 24 cylinders. Hawker submitted a common airframe design for both the engines specified, the Vulture-engined machine becoming known as the Tornado and the Sabre-engined one as the Typhoon.

The Tornado flew first, but was later abandoned because of technical problems with the Vulture and

The Spitfire V was a major update of the Spitfire I and II, with more power and varied armament. It was the first variant to be used as a fighter-bomber. The Spitfire V, in early 1941, was in time to meet the improved German Bf 109F. This photograph shows Spitfire Vbs of No 340 Ile de France Squadron, with two cannon and four machine-guns.

A promising design, the Westland Whirlwind was the first twin-engined single-seat fighter to serve with the RAF. Unfortunately it required long runways for landing, and had problems with its Rolls-Royce Peregrine engines, which were not used on other types. It was fast at low altitude and was used for bomber escort. Later it was fitted with two 500 lb bombs, supplementing its four 20mm cannon, and was used for ground attack.

The twin-Hercules Bristol Beaufighter was the RAF's first effective nightfighter when equipped with airborne-interception (AI) radar. It replaced the slow Blenheim and, with four cannon and six machine-guns, had devastating firepower. Beaufighters were used in Europe and the Middle and Far East, being adapted to carry rocket projectiles, bombs and even torpedoes. The version shown here is a Beaufighter IC long-range fighter of RAF Coastal Command.

subsequent cancellation due to Rolls-Royce's concentration on the Merlin. The Typhoon was first airborne in February 1940, but unfortunately the specification was drawn up in the era when it was anticipated that most air fighting would be at low and medium altitudes. Consequently the Typhoon did not have the necessary climb and high altitude performance, and it suffered from rear-fuselage structural problems. The engine also continued to give trouble owing to its use of sleeve valves, which eventually had to be manufactured in a different material using imported American machine tools.

At one point the Typhoon programme was nearly cancelled. Fortunately this did not happen, and the machine evolved into one of the best fighter/ground-attack aircraft of the war, with four 20mm cannon and either eight 60lb-warhead rocket projectiles (27kg) or two 500lb (227kg) or 1,000lb (454kg) bombs. The Typhoon in its final in-service form had a maximum speed of 412mph (660km/h) at 19,000ft (5,790m). Other details on the Typhoon are covered in a later chapter.

The main development in RAF single-seat fighters devolved on the Spitfire, which proved itself capable of remarkable improvements in performance and, in many versions, remained in large-scale production through to the war's end. The Spitfire II, with a 1,175hp Rolls-Royce Merlin XII, went into service in August 1940 and was succeeded, in February 1941, by the Spitfire V with a Merlin 45 of 1,440hp. Carrying either eight machine-guns (Mk VA) or two 20mm cannon and four machine-guns (Mk VB), it had a maximum speed of 374mph (600km/h), could climb to 20,000ft (6,000m) in 7½min and had a normal range of 470 miles (760m). Its ceiling was 37,000ft (11,200m). The Spitfire VC had a 'universal' wing which could accommodate the armament of the VA or VB or four 20mm cannon. The Mk V became available as the Luftwaffe was putting the improved-performance Bf 109F into service.

In the meantime, camera-equipped unarmed Spitfires had been doing exceptional work as high-altitude photographic reconnaissance aircraft. The PR Spitfire was later put into production as the Mark IV, and 229 were built.

Another fighter for which there were high hopes but which suffered from lack of altitude performance was the Westland Whirlwind. Like the Lockheed Lightning it was a twin-engined, single-seater with heavy armament concentrated in the nose. Designed to meet specification F.37/35, the Whirlwind was powered by 885hp Rolls-Royce Peregrine I in-line engines, developed from the famous Kestrel. The aircraft went into squadron service in July 1940 but was not operational until December owing to lack of engines, Rolls-Royce being totally involved in Merlin production. The Whirlwind was fast and effective at low altitude, particularly as a bomber es-cort and later as a fighter-bomber, but it required long runways to cope with its high landing speed. With no Peregrine development in view, the Whirlwind's operational life and production were limited. Armed with four 20mm cannon in the nose, the Whirlwind had a maximum speed of 360mph (580km/h) at 15,000ft (4,570m) and a service ceiling of 30,000ft (9,100m). Climb was 5.8min to 15,000ft (4,570m), and range was 800 miles (1,280km).

One very successful twin-engined fighter emerged from the Munich Crisis of 1938. Cannon armament was being introduced in Germany, and France, and the RAF had no long-range fighter for use as a nightfighter and for escorting bombers.

Bristol evolved a design which would use the wings, rear fuselage, tail unit and undercarriage of the Beaufort torpedo bomber, already under development. These were married to a new front fuselage. Called the Beaufighter, and powered by Hercules radials, this air-craft first flew in July 1939. Four prototypes were ordered, followed by Specification F.17/39 covering the production of 300 aircraft. A number of modifications were introduced before the first Beaufighters were delivered to the RAF in August 1940, in the middle of the Battle of Britain. The RAF's Blenheim fighters were proving very disappointing against modern opposition as they were too slow and poorly armed; they could even be outpaced by the Junkers Ju 88 bomber!

With night defence becoming of paramount importance, the Beaufighter was the obvious answer. It could carry the new air interception (AI) radar previously installed in the Blenheim, and its armament of four nose-mounted 20mm cannon plus six machine-guns in the wings was the heaviest of any fighter of the period. During the night blitz against Britain in 1940/41 the number of Beaufighters in service rose and so did the tally of night 'kills'. The first Luftwaffe aircraft destroyed at night by a Beaufighter with AI radar was a Ju 88 on 19 November 1940.

The aircraft was also fitted with Rolls-Royce Merlins (the Mk II) as an alternative to the Hercules, but the majority of production machines had the Hercules engine. The Beaufighter proved itself to be extremely versatile. It became Coastal Command's standard long-range fighter and was equipped with bombs, rocket projectiles or a torpedo. It served in the Middle East and Far East theatres, in the latter being known by the Japanese as 'whispering death'. The Beaufighter I had a span of 57ft 10in (17m), a loaded weight of 21,000lb (9,500kg), a maximum speed of 330mph (530km/h) and a range of 1,500 miles (2,400km). Its Hercules III engines delivered 1,365hp each.

This was a classic example of the adaptation of a sound basic airframe to perform a variety of tasks. After the campaign in France it was realised that a

First flown in 1936, the Armstrong Whitworth Whitley night bomber was a standard RAF 'heavy' in the early war years. On the early variants, as shown here, the engines were Tiger radials, but from the Mark IV onwards the powerplant changed to Rolls-Royce Merlins. In addition to Bomber Command, the Whitley was used in Coastal Command and as a paratroop trainer and glider tug.

strike/ground-attack aircraft had to have the ability to deliver weapons directly and then fight if necessary with a reasonable chance of survival. The Fairey Battle light bomber concept was truly dead.

Versatility along these lines went further with another design which was to become one of the really great military aircraft of the Second World War, the de Havilland Mosquito. When, in 1938, the Hatfield-based company proposed a bomber design without armament but with faster speed than proposed fighters, the idea was greeted by the RAF with little enthusiasm; what they wanted was a bomber with heavy armament. Largely due to the efforts of Sir Wilfrid Freeman, the Air Member for Research, Development and Production, the project was kept alive. An order was placed for fifty aircraft in March 1940 to meet specification B.1/40. The prototype was completed in eleven months and flew in November 1940.

What emerged was a streamlined two-seat aircraft with two 1,250hp Merlin engines, a speed of over 380mph (600km/h) at 17,000ft (5,180m) which, as a bomber, carried a load of 2,000lb (900kg) for 1,370 miles (2,200km). Even more revolutionary was that it was of all-wooden construction. It was clear that the Mosquito was admirably suited to fulfil other roles. Accordingly, prototypes for photographic reconnaissance and interception followed.

The long-range PR Mosquito was urgently needed by the RAF and was the first into service, in September 1941. The fighter Mosquito with AI radar was not in service until January 1942, but thereafter it replaced the Beaufighter and the Havoc. Its armament was four

20mm cannon plus four machine-guns in the nose. The logical follow-up was the fighter-bomber Mosquito, with bombs in addition to guns. The Mosquito was steadily developed through the war, achieving faster speeds, greater range and higher altitude. For two-and-a-half years from its entry into service, the Mosquito was faster than any other type in service with the Allies or the Axis. In Bomber Command it was the fastest aircraft throughout the war.

When the war began, Britain's long-range medium bomber force relied on three types, the Whitley, (see photograph, page 52), Wellington and Hampden. Of these the best all-round operational aircraft was the Vickers Wellington. It was, however, clear to the Air Ministry that larger, heavier machines with increased defensive armament would ultimately be needed. In 1940/41 operations highlighted the usual crop of deficiencies: lack of self-sealing fuel tanks, low performance, defective armour plate and, above all, poor defensive armament. Lack of suitable navigational aids was an added factor, but hardly the fault of the airframe manufacturers. By the end of 1940 medium bombers were used only at night, as daylight raids were too costly.

Of the three aircraft, the Wellington (affectionately known as the Wimpy) proved to be the best and most reliable, and it therefore had the longest Service life, ultimately in a variety of roles. It used geodetic, lattice, construction which was very strong, and the aircraft could take a lot of punishment. Originally fitted with two Bristol Pegasus engines, the Wellington was also produced with Rolls-Royce Merlins and then Bristol Hercules. With 1,145hp Merlins, the Mk II carried a

Nicknamed the 'Wimpy', the Vickers Wellington bomber was a contemporary of the Whitley and Hampden in the RAF, but served in much larger numbers. Initially with Pegasus engines and also produced with Merlins (Mk II), the Wellington from the Mk III onwards was powered by Hercules. Geodetic lattice structure was extremely tough and could withstand a lot of damage. The Wellington played a major role with Coastal Command and also operated as a bomber in the Middle and Far East. These are Wellingtons Is of No 9 Squadron.

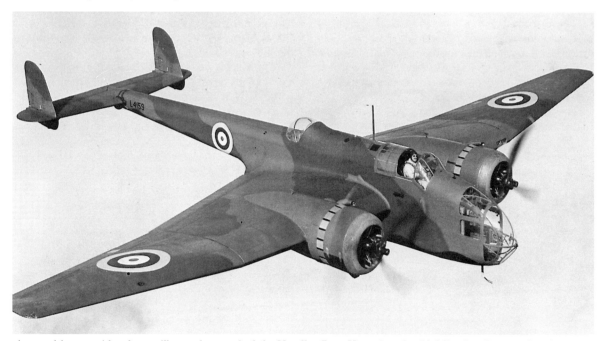

An usual layout with a long tailboom characterised the Handley Page Hampden, the third Bomber Command main type to enter the war. It suffered, however, from poor accommodation for the crew and ineffective defensive aramament. It was fast and had long range; modifications were made and it went on to perform well, later working as a Coastal Command torpedo-bomber. Basic power was two Pegasus radials, but 100 were built as Herefords with Napier Dagger engines.

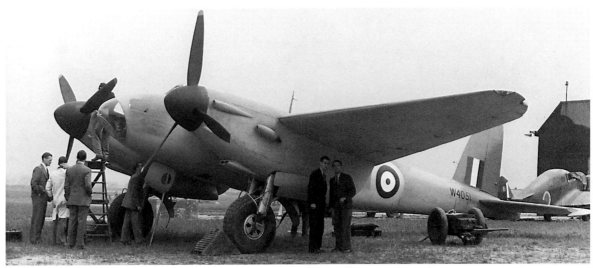

The most versatile high-performance warplane of the Second World War, the de Havilland Mosquito was a brilliant design. Of wooden construction, it was faster than any interceptor then in service when it first flew in November 1940. Used for for long-range precision bombing, pathfinding, day and night fighting, low-level attack, reconnaissance, maritime attack and special duties, it remained in RAF service until the advent of the Canberra jet bomber. Illustrated is the third (PR) prototype, W4051.

pilot and four crew. Bomb load was 4,000lb (1,180kg) and range 2,200 miles (3,540km) at 180mph (290km/h) at 15,000ft (4,570m). Armament comprised a twin-gun nose turret, a four-gun tail turret and two beam guns. Span was 86ft 2in (26m), and length 64ft 7in (19m). Wellington production totalled 11,461.

The medium bombers had emerged as a result of RAF specifications issued in 1932 and 1934. By 1936 the Air Staff, watching the growing power and size of the Luftwaffe, issued far-sighted specifications for new and larger bombers carrying increased bomb loads. Two were to be twin-engined and one four-engined.

Avro and Handley Page had the Rolls-Royce Vulture engine specified, while the Shorts design was to have four Bristol Hercules radials. The Vulture consisted of two Rolls-Royce Peregrines one above the other, driving a single crankshaft. This resulted in an X-configuration engine rated at 1,800hp, but with considerably higher power potential. The Avro bomber design, the Type 679, subsequently named the Manchester, retained the Vulture, while the Handley Page project, which became the Halifax, was switched to a four-Merlin layout in 1937.

The Manchester soldiered on with the Vulture. It flew in prototype form in July 1939 and first entered service with Bomber Command in November 1941. The airframe was excellent, but the Vulture was a constant source of trouble. It did not reach its designed power

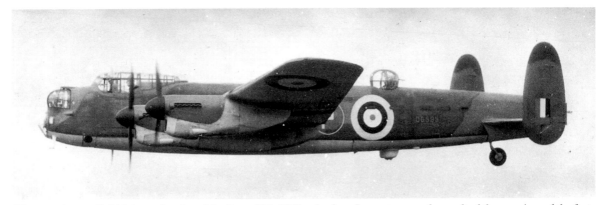

The most famous British heavy bomber of the Second World War, the Avro Lancaster, was the result of the marriage of the first-class Manchester airframe, which had two unreliable Vulture engines, with four Rolls-Royce Merlins. In the second half of the war the Lancaster formed the backbone of Bomber Command, along with the Halifax, and carried the largest bombs, including the giant 22,000lb 'Grand Slam'. Illustrated is the prototype Lancaster I, a converted Manchester.

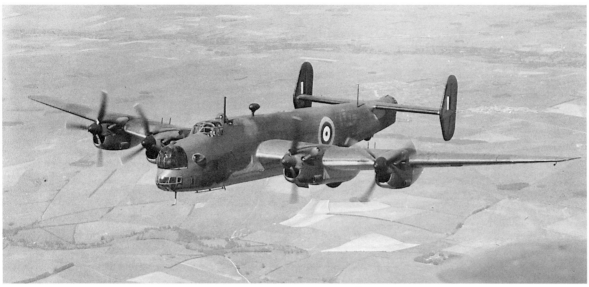

With the Lancaster, the Handley Page Halifax was the mainstay of the RAF's bomber offensive against Germany. Early marks had Merlin engines until, with the Mk III, the aircraft standardised on the Hercules radial. The Halifax was also widely used for maritime work with Coastal Command and as a glider tug.

output and engine failures were frequent. If Rolls-Royce had not had all its efforts concentrated on the Merlin, the company would certainly have developed the Vulture to an acceptable standard. As it was, time and effort were at a premium and the Vulture was an also-ran.

There then occurred one of the most remarkable aircraft transformations in wartime. Avro fitted a Manchester airframe with four Merlins and flew it in January 1941. The result, as the Lancaster, became the best-known and most successful RAF heavy bomber of the war; it was also the largest load-carrier of all Allied bombers, being capable of delivering the giant 22,000lb (9,980kg) 'Grand Slam' bomb.

Apart from a change to Hercules radials on 300 Lancaster IIs and modified bomb bays, the Lancaster airframe was to remain virtually the same throughout the war; a tribute to good design. The Lancaster I had four 1,280hp Merlin XX engines, carried a crew of seven and was armed with twin 0.303in machine-guns in nose and dorsal positions and a four-gun turret in the tail. Its span was 102ft (31m), length 69ft 4in (21m) and its all-up weight was 50,000lb (22,680kg). Maximum speed was 287mph (460km/h), cruising speed 200mph (320km/h) and range 1,660 miles (2,670km) with 14,000lb (6,350kg) bomb load; ceiling was 19,000ft (5,790m).

The four-Merlin Halifax flew on 25 October 1939, the first production aircraft following on 11 October 1940. By the following month the first squadron was being formed. Like the Lancaster, the Halifax had a crew of seven and a range of 1,860 miles (3,000km) with 5,800lb (2,630kg) of bombs; its maximum speed was 265mph (426km/h) at 17,500ft (5,330m) and service ceiling 22,800ft (6,950m). Its span was 98ft 10in (29m) and loaded weight 58,000lb (26,300kg). Armament was two 0.303in guns in a nose turret and four in the tail, while some aircraft had beam guns. The maximum bomb load was 13,000lb (5,900kg). Many detail modifications were carried out on sub-marks until the Hercules-engined Mark III became a definitive production variant.

The history of the Short Stirling was a somewhat different matter. Air Ministry policy changed with the increasing perceived threat and, as a result, apart from the Manchester and Halifax, which were initially classified as medium bombers to P.13/36, a further requirement, B.12/36, was issued for a fast four-engine, long-range heavy bomber. The word 'fast' has to be taken in terms of the aircraft in service in 1936. For example, the Fairey Hendon and the Handley Page Heyford bombers had top speeds of 155mph and 142mph respectively.

Short's submission for B.12/36 was for a large four-Hercules aircraft with a crew of seven or eight, using technology based on the company's proven flying boats. The Air Ministry, however, placed several restrictions on the specification including, ridiculous as it may seem, a limit on the wingspan to fit a standard RAF hangar. This meant that the wing was of low aspect ratio, thus limiting the operational ceiling – a definite draw-back when in service.

The Stirling had a wing span of 99ft 1in (30m) and a length of 87ft 3in (26m). As it had a shoulder-wing it possessed a very tall main undercarriage. Production of the Stirling was held up by Luftwaffe bombing raids, but it went into service with No 7 Squadron in August 1940,

The first four-engined bomber to be used operationally in the war, the Short Stirling with four Hercules radials initially went into squadron service in August 1940. Because of its low-aspect-ratio wing its service ceiling was limited. As a bomber the Stirling was last used in 1944, but it was widely employed as a glider tug and transport.

during the Battle of Britain. The Stirling thus achieved two 'firsts', the first four-engined monoplane bomber to go into service with the RAF and the first to go on operations in the Second World War.

The Hercules delivered 1,400hp, and with these the Stirling had a maximum speed of 260mph (420km/h) and a maximum cruising range of 2,330 miles (3,750km) with 3,500lb (1,590kg) of bombs, or 590 miles (950km) with 14,000lb (6,350kg) of bombs. Its all-up weight was 59,400lb (26,940kg). Its armament comprised a two-gun nose turret, a four-gun tail turret and, initially, a ventral two-gun 'dustbin'. Later the ventral turret was removed and a two-gun dorsal turret fitted. The turrets had hydraulic recuperators, but unfortunately the location of two of them coincided with the RAF roundel on the fuselage. By using the roundel as a target, enemy fighters were able to put the turrets out of action. As a result, the recuperators had to be moved.

Through 1940 and 1941 Britain was developing and gaining operational experience on the types of large long-range bomber which would form the backbone of Bomber Command's operations at night. At the same time, the USAAF was modifying and perfecting its own key four-engined day bombers, the B-17 Fortress and the B-24 Liberator, described earlier. In 1943–45 the two great air fleets would conduct a round-the-clock campaign, a form of air warfare never before seen.

Two events of May 1941 were ultimately to change military and civil aviation completely on the one hand, and bring untold destructive power from the air on the other. On 15 May 1941 a 29ft-span (8m) single-seat monoplane, the E.28/39, took off from Cranwell,

Lincolnshire, flown by P E Sayer. In one vital respect it differed from all other aircraft in Britain, for it had no propeller. It was in fact jet-propelled, and the only machine of its kind, apart from two in Germany, the Heinkel He 178 and He 280, which had also flown in prototype form.

Neither side was aware of the other's gas turbine work. Flight Lieutenant (later Air Commodore Sir) Frank Whittle had pioneered gas turbine design development, and his firm Power Jets Ltd was given a contract in 1939 to build a flight engine. Design and development of the airframe was entrusted to the Gloster Aircraft Company under the terms of specification E.28/39, the 'E' standing for experimental.

Outside Germany the first jet aircraft to fly was the Gloster E.28/39, which took to the air with a Whittle W.I turbojet engine on 15 May 1941. From this design grew the two great jet engine industries of the USA and Britain, and it led the way to the civil and military jet fleets of today.

The Boeing B-29 Superfortress represented a quantum leap in aircraft design. With its high speed of 350mph, pressurised cabin, remotely controlled gun turrets and range of over 3,000 miles, it was remarkable in that the original official requirement was issued in February 1940. The B-29 was the type which dropped the first two atomic bombs on Hiroshima and Nagasaki in 1945.

Powered by an 860lb-thrust Power Jets W.1 gas turbine, the E.28/39 had a maximum speed of 466mph (750km/h), well in excess of any piston-engined aircraft of the period. It could climb to 30,000ft (9,000km/h) in 22min, and had a service ceiling of 32,000ft (9,750m) and a loaded weight of 3,748lb (1,700kg).

A second prototype was built, but later crashed when the ailerons became jammed during a high-altitude flight. The first prototype continued flying at intervals through to 1944 with higher powered engines and other refinements. In 1946 it was put on permanent display in the Science Museum in London.

In November 1940 the RAF issued a specification for a twin-engined jet fighter based on designs submitted by Gloster Aircraft. In February 1941 an order was placed for twelve 'Gloster-Whittle' aircraft, a type which was to become the Gloster Meteor.

As related earlier, Britain shared its technical secrets with USA and this included Whittle's aero gas turbine work. It was to have far-reaching consequences as companies in both countries turned towards the gas turbine first for fighters, then for bombers and later transports. The technology gap became ever wider between the victorious Western Allies and those nations defeated or left to mark time during the Second World War. It can all be traced back to Whittle and the E.28/39.

The second key event of May 1941 was the issue of a letter by the USAAC to Boeing, stating that an order would be placed for 250 aircraft of a 'superbomber' type. Boeing had received an official requirement for such an aircraft in February 1940. It was to carry 2,000lb (900kg) of bombs at a speed of 400mph (640km/h) and have a range of 5,333 miles (8,580km). A tricycle undercarriage, pressurisation and heavy defensive armament were specified.

Boeing had been working on designs of such a bomber since 1938, and three prototypes had been ordered in 1940. The project was known as the model 345, the army designation was XB-29, and it later became famous as the B-29 Superfortress which was to lay waste the cities of Japan by dropping the first two atomic bombs on Hiroshima and Nagasaki. Even to consider such an incredibly advanced project in 1940–41, with little money available, represented one of the most far-sighted acts in the history of military aviation.

Russia

In the early hours of 22 June 1941 Hitler invaded the Soviet Union in Operation Barbarossa. Surprise was complete, and by noon on the same day 1,200 Russian aircraft had been destroyed on the ground and in the air.

Losses of bases and equipment continued as the German army advanced. In the early stages the main opposition came from Polikarpov I-152/I-153 biplane and

The Il-2 Shturmovik armoured ground-attack aircraft played a major part in the ultimate Soviet victory over the German invasion columns. Heavily armed, the Il-2 was produced at the rate of 1,200 per month, and production far outstripped most other Second World War types. Illustrated is an Il-2M3.

I-16 monoplane fighters, both of which had been combat-tested in Spain. Most of the bombers in Soviet operational service were also obsolescent and suffered accordingly at the hands of the Luftwaffe.

However, a number of modern designs were already well into the development/production phase. As the Germans approached Moscow a remarkable operation was undertaken. Threatened factories were moved by railway to east of the Ural mountains and to Siberia. It was a mammoth undertaking, but it was successfully concluded. The Luftwaffe had failed to develop a suitable long-range bomber and, therefore, the new factory sites were safe from attack.

In these factories Yak-1, MiG-1, MiG-3 and LaGG-3 fighters were steadily produced and developed, incorporating the lessons learned from combat experience. Designer Ilyushin built the Il-2 single-engine close support/anti-tank aircraft which became famous as the 'Shturmovik'. This was flown in October 1940 and put into large-scale production in March 1941. Its armament was two cannon and two machine-guns, and it had a top speed of 292mph (470km/h). Ultimately the Russians built 36,000 Il-2s.

Like the Luftwaffe, the Soviet Air Force concentrated on light and medium twin-engine short-range aircraft. A typical example was the Petlyakov Pe-2 with a three-man crew, two M-105R in-line engines of 1,100hp and carrying a bomb load of up to 2,200lb (1,000kg).

Armament consisted of four machine-guns. The Pe-2 had a span of just over 51ft (15m) and a maximum speed of 335mph (540km/h).

The very heavy aircraft losses incurred by the Soviet Air Force in 1941 led to urgent requests to Britain and America for warplanes. There then began a steady flow of fighters and bombers including Tomahawks, Kittyhawks, Hurricanes, Airacobras and Bostons. As the war progressed more advanced types were supplied. In total, the USA ultimately sent 14,833 aircraft to Russia, while Britain's direct contribution included no fewer than 2,952 Hurricanes.

Capable of over 330 mph, the Petlyakov Pe-2 was a first-class light bomber design, also used as a fighter and for reconnaissance. It was produced in large numbers.

Bibliography

Andrews, C F, *Vickers Aircraft since 1908* (Putnam, London 1969)

Angle, G D, (ed), *Aerosphere 1939* (Aircraft Publications, New York 1939)

Balchin, N, *The Aircraft Builders* (HMSO, London 1947)

Barnes, C H, *Shorts Aircraft since 1900* (Putnam, London 1967)

Barnes, C H, *Bristol Aircraft since 1910* (Putnam, London 1964)

Bowers, P M, *Boeing Aircraft since 1916* (Putnam, London 1966)

Bridgman, L (ed), *Jane's All the World's Aircraft 1941* (Sampson Low, London, 1941)

Brown, D, Shores, C & Macksey, K, *The Guiness History of Air Warfare* (Guiness Superlatives, Enfield 1976)

Francillon, R J, *Grumman Aircraft since 1929* (Putnam, London 1989)

Francillon, R J, *McDonnell Douglas Aircraft since 1920, Vol 1* (Putnam, London 1988)

Jackson, A J, *Avro Aircraft since 1908* (Putnam, London 1965)

Jackson, R, *Air War over France 1939–40* (Ian Allan, London 1974)

James, D N, *Gloster Aircraft since 1917* (Putnam, London 1971)

Lumsden, A, *British Piston Aero-Engines and their Aircraft* (Airlife, Shrewsbury 1994)

Mason, F K, *Hawker Aircraft since 1920* (Putnam, London 1961)

Nowarra, N J & Duval, G R, *Russian Civil and Military Aircraft, 1884–1969* (Fountain Press, London 1971)

Swanborough, G & Bowers, P M, *United States Military Aircraft since 1909* (Putnam, London 1989)

Swanborough, G & Bowers, P M, *United States Navy Aircraft since 1911* (Putnam, London 1968)

Tapper, O, *Armstrong Whitworth Aircraft since 1913* (Putnam, London 1973)

Taylor, M J H (ed), *Jane's Encyclopedia of Aviation* (Bracken Books, London 1989)

Thetford, O, *Aircraft of the Royal Air Force since 1918* (Putnam, London 1971)

The Spitfire XIV, powered by the 2,035hp Rolls-Royce Griffon 61 engine with a two-stage supercharger, was one of the most effective air superiority fighters in service at the end of the Second World War. (Vickers) (See pages 60–61.)

The Vought F4U Corsair was the fastest and most effective carrier-borne fighter/fighter-bomber type to see large-scale service during the Second World War. (See pages 64 and 74–5)

3
Fighter Development, Mid-1941 to Mid-1945
Dr Alfred Price

The air superiority fighter in mid-1941

In the middle of 1941, nearly two years into the Second World War, two aircraft stood out as representing the state of the art among the air superiority fighters then in service: the Supermarine Spitfire Mark VB and the Messerschmitt Bf 109F-2. Both fighters were developed versions of designs that made their initial flights more than half a decade earlier, and both were in large-scale production.

When, in the mid-1930s, they had designed the two fighters, both Reginald Mitchell and Willi Messerschmitt had the same goals in mind. Each sought to produce a short-range interceptor fighter with the highest possible speed and climbing performance, mating the smallest possible airframe to the most powerful engine then available. Given the similarity of the requirements, it is hardly surprising that the resultant aircraft should have several points in common. Both were low-wing monoplanes with all-metal stressed-skin construction, faired cockpits and retractable undercarriages.

When considering the relative merits of these fighters, however, one must bear in mind that aircraft design is largely a matter of compromise. If the designer concentrates on improving one aspect of performance or combat capability, almost inevitably this will be at the expense of something else.

Arguably, Willi Messerschmitt did slightly better than Reginald Mitchell in designing the smallest possible airframe to meet his requirement. The Bf 109 was a smaller machine all round, and its wing area of 16.17m² (174 sq ft) was one quarter less than the Spitfire's 242 sq ft (22.48m²).

The engine fitted to the Bf 109F-2 was the 1,200hp Daimler Benz DB 601N engine, while the Spitfire V had the 1,470hp Rolls-Royce Merlin 45. Both fighters had a maximum speed of just over 595km/h (370mph), however. At this time drop tanks were little used, and without them both fighters were limited to an effective combat radius of about 100 miles (160km).

The Bf 109 'Friedrich' was the lighter of the two fighters, its loaded weight of 2800kg (6,173lb) being about 160kg (350lb) less than that of the Spitfire VB. On the other hand, the larger wing of the Spitfire gave it a wing loading at 27lb/sq ft (1.13kg/m²), compared with 35.5lb/sq ft (1.49kg/m²) for the German fighter. That meant the Bf 109 was inferior to the British fighter in a turning fight.

The Spitfire VB was the more heavily armed, carrying two 20mm Hispano cannon and four 0.303in machine-guns spaced out across the wings. The 'Friedrich-2', in contrast, was armed principally for fighter-to-fighter combat and had a single 15mm cannon and two 7.9mm machine-guns grouped close together in the nose of the aircraft.

Throughout the remainder of the war the development of fighter aircraft in Great Britain and Germany

Two broadly comparable machines which ranked as the most effective air superiority fighters in service in mid-1941. Left: *A Supermarine Spitfire VB of No 92 Squadron.* Right: *A Messerschmitt Bf 109 'Friedrich' of Jagdgeschwader 2, outside its camouflaged hangar in northern France. (Spitfire: Vickers; Messerschmitt: via Schliephake)*

The Spitfire XII was optimised for operations at low altitude, and had its wings clipped to give an increased rate of roll.

followed one of two separate paths. On one of these paths, the well-proven Spitfire and Bf 109 designs were developed to squeeze the last drop of performance out of them. On the other path, new fighter types were built and introduced into service.

In the next two sections we shall observe the aircraft that emerged from each path of development, and see how they fared in service.

Pushing the Well-proven Designs

The Spitfire VB and the Bf 109F-2 were well into their respective development processes in mid-1941. These had followed, and would continue to follow, more or less common lines. Successive variants of these fighters employed more powerful (and therefore heavier) engines to boost their maximum speed and climbing performance. They carried more powerful (and therefore heavier) armaments. They carried larger (and therefore heavier) fuel loads to provide the increases in range that operational pilots demanded. And they carried more (and therefore heavier) armour and other items of operational equipment.

Each improvement in performance or combat capability brought with it a weight increase, which in turn led to other problems. The late-war Spitfire Mk XIV, for example, weighed more than a tonne more than the Mark I when it entered service before the war. When the fighter was on the ground or in normal flight the increased weight was not important, but in combat it was a quite different matter. In a 6g turn every part of the fighter and those items attached to it weighed six times as much. If the airframe was not strong enough to support the additional weight, multiplied by the 'g' factors, the structure was liable to suffer a catastrophic failure and break up. To cope with each major increase in weight, therefore, a fighter's airframe had to be strengthened to restore its safe loading factor. And, naturally, each such increase in strength brought with it a further twist to the weight spiral.

During the Second World War Supermarine pushed the process of incremental development of the Spitfire further than anybody else. After the Mark VB, the next major improvement to the performance came in the spring of 1942 with the introduction into service of the Spitfire Mark IX. This was powered by the new Merlin 61 engine fitted with two supercharger blowers in series, one feeding into the other. At sea level the new engine developed a maximum of 1,565hp, just under 100hp more than the Merlin 45. At high altitude the effect of the two-stage supercharger was more profound. At 30,000ft (9,150m) the Merlin 45, with the single-stage supercharger, developed about 720hp. At the same altitude the Merlin 61, the same basic engine but with the two-stage supercharger, developed about 1,020hp, or nearly one-third more. With its additional blower and casing, the Merlin 61 was 9in (23cm) longer and about 200lb (about 90kg) heavier than the Mark 45.

After the Mark IX, the next major improvement to the performance came early in 1944 with the introduction into service of the Spitfire Mark XIV. The new fighter was powered by the 2,035hp Griffon 61 engine, a 36.75-litre 'banger' with a cubic capacity one-third greater than the Merlin. By inspired juggling with the ancillary components Rolls-Royce designers kept the frontal area of the new engine to within six per cent, its length to within 3in (7.5cm) and its weight to within

A close-up of the Griffon engine fitted to a Spitfire XIV. Although it had a cubic capacity one-third greater than the Merlin, by inspired juggling with the ancillary components its designers kept the frontal area of the new engine to within 6 per cent, its length to within 3in (7.5cm) and its weight to within 600lb (272kg) of the equivalent figures for the Merlin. (Costain)

600lb (270kg) of the Merlin. It speaks equally highly for the design staff at Supermarine that they were able to re-design the Spitfire to take the new engine.

The box below summarises Spitfire development. It puts some figures to the improvement in performance that resulted from that extra power. It also shows the in-creases in weight and their progressive effect on the fighter's wing loading (for each mark for which figures are given, the fighter's wing area remained the same). It will be seen that the Spitfire Mk XIV had a wing loading more than 10lb/sq ft (0.4kg/m²) greater than the Mk I.

The 'bottom line' of these changes was that during its long development life the handling characteristics of the Spitfire deteriorated steadily. Test pilot Alex Henshaw described their effect:

> I loved the Spitfire, in all of her many versions. But I have to admit that the later Marks, although they were faster

Development of the Spitfire				*Figures for initial production version of each variant*
Mark	Entered service	Engine power	Maximum speed	Weight (normal loaded)	Wing loading
I	Sep 1938	1,030hp	362mph 583km/h	5,819lb 2,639kg	24lb/sq ft 1.01kg/m²
V	Feb 1941	1,470hp	371mph 597km/h	6,525lb 2,959kg	27lb/sq ft 1.13kg/m²
IX	June 1942	1,560hp	409mph 658km/h	7,400 lb 3,356 kg	30.6lb/sq ft 1.29 kg/m²
XIV	Jan 1944	2,035hp	446mph 718km/h	8,400lb 3,809kg	34.7lb/sq ft 1.46kg/m²

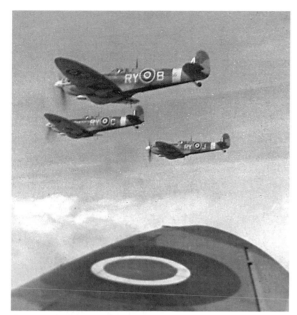

Spitfire IXs of No 313 Sqn. Each fighter carries a 90gal (408-litre) drop-tank under the fuselage.

than the earlier ones, were also much heavier and so did not handle so well. You did not have such positive control over them. One test of manoeuvrability was to throw the Spitfire into a flick roll and see how many times she rolled. With the Mark II ... one got two and a half flick rolls, but the Mark IX was heavier and you got only one and a half. With the later and still heavier versions one got even less. The essence of aircraft design is compromise, and an improvement at one end of the

performance envelope is rarely achieved without a deterioration somewhere else.

That deterioration in the Spitfire's handling characteristics came at the same time as major and sought-after improvements in performance. That alone made them acceptable in time of war.

Other fighter designs proved much less able to accommodate the development process, however. A prime example of fighter design that suffered problems from over-development was the Messerschmitt Bf 109. When the Bf 109 'Berta' entered service in February 1937 its wing loading was an acceptable 1.14kg/m² (27.2lb/sq ft), and it handled beautifully.

The Bf 109 'Friedrich' provided the best compromise in terms of performance, fighting ability and handling characteristics. From then on, however, each increase in performance or combat capability was bought at a high cost in terms of the aeroplane's handling characteristics.

Ideally, the Bf 109 should have been superseded in production by a new design in the spring of 1942. But the Me 209 and Me 309 fighters intended to replace it were not yet ready to go into production (they never would be). There was no alternative but to continue developing the older fighter. As has been said, Willi Messerschmitt did rather better than Reginald Mitchell when it came to designing the smallest possible airframe to meet the original requirement for an interceptor. But when the German fighter was subjected to the rigours of the development process, that advantage became a major handicap.

The next major production variant of the Bf 109, the 'Gustav-6', entered service in September 1942 and had

A late production Spitfire XIV fitted with a bubble canopy. The latter gave greatly improved visibility in the rear hemisphere, an important advantage in combat.

The Messerschmitt Bf 109 'Kurfurst', the final version of the fighter to go into large-scale production. (via Schliephake)

a wing loading of 1.68kg/m² (40lb/sq ft). That was bad enough, but sub-variants of the 'Gustav' optimised to engage Allied heavy bombers carried even heavier weapon loads which pushed their wing loading up to 1.81kg/m² (43lb/sq ft). Box 2 below summarises the development.

The combination of the small wing, overloaded airframe, narrow-track undercarriage and big 1,800hp engine driving a broad bladed propeller, produced some really vicious handling traits in the Bf 109G-6. If an inexperienced pilot opened the throttle too quickly during take-off, or if he tried to lift the fighter into the air before it had reached flying speed, the aircraft was liable to roll on its back and smash into the ground. Nobody did that twice.

The ultimate production variant of the Bf 109, the K-4, was even more of a handful than the 'Gustav'. Both sub-types of the Bf 109 remained in large scale production in Germany until the last days of the war, though as combat aircraft they were much inferior to the Spitfire Mk XIV.

The Spitfire and the Bf 109 equipped the bulk of the fighter units in the RAF and the Luftwaffe, respectively, throughout the whole of the period under review. These two fighters illustrated the extent to which the development process could be pushed in time of war, but they also highlighted its shortcomings. In the next section we shall examine some of the new-generation piston-engine fighter designs that entered service after the middle of 1941 and proved successful in combat.

Development of the Messerschmitt Bf 109				*Figures for initial production version of each variant*	
Variant	Entered service	Engine power	Maximum speed	Weight (normal loaded)	Wing loading
Berta	Feb 1937	680hp	465km/h 289mph	2,150kg 4,741lb	1.14kg/m² 27.2lb/sq ft
Emil	Feb 1939	1,100hp	550km/h 342mph	2,504kg 5,523lb	1.31kg/m² 31.3lb/sq ft
Friedrich	Mar 1941	1,200hp	600km/h 373mph	2,800kg 6,173lb	1.49kg/m² 35.5lb/sq ft
Gustav-6	Sep 1942	1,475hp	621km/h 386mph	3,147kg 6,940lb	1.68kg/m² 40lb/sq ft

A Messerschmitt Bf 109G taxies in after a sortie, past a bomb crater being filled in, in the summer of 1944. By this stage the German fighter was developed past its best and it had acquired some vicious handling traits.

How they Compared:

Spitfire Mark XIV *versus* Messerschmitt Bf 109G

Maximum speed The Spitfire XIV is 40mph (64km/h) faster at all heights except near 16,000ft (4,900m), where it is only 10mph (16km/h) faster.

Maximum climb The same result: at 16,000ft the two aircraft are identical, otherwise the Spitfire XIV out-climbs the Me 109G. The zoom climb is practically identical when the climb is made without opening the throttle. Climbing at full throttle, the Spitfire XIV draws away from the Me 109G quite easily.

Dive During the initial part of the dive, the Me 109G pulls away slightly, but when a speed of 380mph (612km/h) is reached, the Spitfire XIV begins to gain on the Me 109G.

Turning circle The Spitfire XIV easily out-turns the Me 109G in either direction.

Rate of roll The Spitfire XIV rolls much more quickly.

Conclusion The Spitfire XIV is superior to the Me 109G in every respect.

Note: This box and the following 'comparison boxes' in this chapter contain verbatim excerpts from official reports of combat trials carried out during the Second World War using captured aircraft.

The new generation of fighters

Between the middle of 1941 and the spring of 1944 each of the major air forces involved in the conflict fielded one or more new air superiority fighters. The Luftwaffe brought into action the Focke-Wulf Fw 190. The RAF introduced the Hawker Typhoon and later the Tempest, and the US Army Air Force brought in the P-47 Thunderbolt and the P-51A Mustang, followed later by Merlin-engined variants of the P-51. The US Navy

A Republic P-47 Thunderbolt of the 376th Fighter Squadron, 361st Fighter Group, during the spring of 1944. The Thunderbolt was the first really effective single-engined long-range escort fighter to go into service in quantity. This example carries a 90gal (408-litre) pressurised drop-tank under the fuselage. (USAF)

introduced the Grumman F6F Hellcat and later the Vought F4U Corsair. The Japanese Navy introduced the Mitsubishi A6M3 (Allied codename 'Hamp'), followed much later by the Mitsubishi J2M3 'Jack' and the Kawanishi N1K1-J 'George'. The Japanese Army began its war with the Nakajima Ki-43 'Oscar' and in the closing stages of the conflict its best fighter was the Nakajima Ki-84 'Frank'. The Soviet Air Force introduced a long

A close-up of the Pratt & Whitney R-2800-59 Double Wasp engine fitted to a Thunderbolt. Note the large duct under the engine, to carry carburettor air to the turbosupercharger fitted in the rear fuselage. (USAF)

The Hawker Typhoon and Tempest				*Figures for initial production version of each type*	
Type	Entered service	Engine power	Maximum speed	Weight (normal loaded)	Wing loading
Typhoon I	Sep 1941	2,180hp	405mph 652km/h	11,400lb 5,170kg	40.8lb/sq ft 1.72kg/m^2
Tempest V	Apr 1944	2,420hp	435mph 700km/h	11,400lb 5,170kg	37.7lb sq ft 1.58kg/m^2

line of Mikoyan and Gurevich, Yakovlev and Lavochkin fighter designs.

Each of these fighter types employed the same basic layout as a low-winged monoplane with single fin and rudder, fixed forward-firing armament, the engine mounted in the nose driving a tractor airscrew, and a tailwheel undercarriage.

It goes without saying that fighter performance depends on engine power. In this respect British and US designers were indeed fortunate in having support from highly effective engine manufacturers such as Rolls-Royce, Napier and Pratt & Whitney. During 1942 each of these companies began production of engines in the 2,000hp class suitable for use in fighters. In Germany the first such engines did not become available until 1944. The Soviet Union and Japan both failed to bring into service any single-engined fighter type powered by an engine in that class.

The armament carried by a fighter depended on the type of opponent it was intended to engage. The American Thunderbolts and Mustangs were intended to fight mainly against enemy fighters or fighter-bombers, and for that purpose their armament of eight and six 0.5in (12.7mm) machine-guns respectively was sufficient. For much the same reason, many Russian fighters carried one 20mm cannon and two 0.5in weapons. Japanese fighters at the beginning of the period carried two 20mm cannon and two rifle-calibre machine-guns. The RAF Spitfires and Typhoons were armed to engage enemy bombers and fighters, the former carrying a combination of rifle-calibre machine-guns, 0.5in weapons, and two 20mm cannon and the latter twelve 0.303in machine-guns which were soon replaced by four 20mm cannon.

The Luftwaffe also armed its fighters to engage enemy bombers and fighters, and the initial production version of the Fw 190 carried four 20mm cannon and two rifle-calibre machine-guns. In action against US heavy bombers even this armament proved insufficient, however. To provide additional firepower, some Fw 190s carried a launcher under each wing for a Wgr 21, a 210mm-calibre (8¼in) spin-stabilised air-to-air rocket.

Among the new generation of single-engined fighters the largest and the heaviest, by a wide margin, was the Thunderbolt. The initial production version, the P-47C,

Armourers prime the warhead of a Wgr 21 rocket before loading it into the launching tube. This spin-stabilised unguided rocket weighed 110kg (242lb) at launch, including the high-explosive warhead weighing 36kg (79lb).

Close-up of the Wgr 21 launcher fitted to an Fw 190.

weighed 13,500lb (6,125kg) in the normal loaded condition. That was more than double that of the Messerschmitt Bf 109G, and nearly twice that of the Spitfire Mk IX. The American fighter was powered by the Pratt & Whitney R-2800-59 Double Wasp turbo-supercharged radial, which developed 2,300hp at 31,000ft (9,500m). The weight and size of the turbo-supercharger unit dictated that it be fitted in the rear fuselage. Locating it so far from the engine gave rise to several problems. Air for the engine carburettor was collected by a large inlet at the base of the engine cowling, and from there it was ducted some 20ft (6m) rearwards to the turbosupercharger. After compression, the air was

At the end of the war the Kawanishi N1K2 'George' was one of the best Japanese Navy fighters in service, but too few were available for them to influence events.

US Army Air Force Fighters				*Figures for initial production version of each type*	
Type	Entered service	Engine power	Maximum speed	Weight (normal loaded)	Wing loading
P-51A Mustang	Apr 1942	1,200hp	390mph 628km/h	8,600lb 3,900kg	36.9lb sq ft 1.55kg/m^2
P-47C Thunderbolt	Apr 1943	2,300hp	433mph 697km/h	13,500lb 6,122kg	45lb sq ft 1.89kg/m^2
P-51B Mustang	Dec 1943	1,620hp	440mph 708km/h	9,200lb 4,172kg	39.5lb sq ft 1.66kg/m^2

Japanese Navy Fighters				*Figures for initial production version of each type*	
Type	Entered service	Engine power	Maximum speed	Weight (normal loaded)	Wing loading
Mitsubishi A6M3 'Hamp'	Apr 1942	1,130hp	554km/h 338mph	2,543kg 5,609lb	1.02kg/m^2 24.2lb/sq ft
Mitsubishi J2M3 'Jack'	Jan 1944	1,820hp	597km/h 371mph	3,434kg 7,573lb	1.47kg/m^2 35lb/sq ft
Kawanishi N1K2-J 'George'	Late 1944	1,990hp	596km/h 370mph	4,099kg 9,039lb	1.39kg/m^2 33lb/sq ft

Development of the Focke-Wulf Fw 190				*Figures for initial production version of each variant*	
Variant	Entered service	Engine power	Maximum speed	Weight (normal loaded)	Wing loading
Fw 190A-3	Apr 1942	1,700hp	673km/h 418mph	3,977kg 8,770lb	1.87kg/m^2 44.5lb/sq ft
Fw 190A-8	Apr 1944	1,700hp	657km/h 408mph	4,381kg 9,660lb	2.06kg/m^2 49lb/sq ft
Fw 190D-9	Sep 1944	2,240hp	686km/h 426mph	4,299kg 9,480lb	2.02kg/m^2 48.1lb/sq ft

Development of US Navy Fighters					*Figures for initial production version of each type*
Type	Entered service	Engine power	Maximum speed	Weight (normal loaded)	Wing loading
F6F-3 Hellcat	Jan 1943	2,000hp	376mph 605km/h	11,381lb 5,161kg	34lb/sq ft 1.43kg/m^2
F4U-1D Corsair	May 1944	2,250hp	425mph 684km/h	12,039lb 5,460kg	38.3lb/sq ft 1.61kg/m^2

ducted forwards some 20ft (6m) and into the inlet of a mechanically driven second-stage supercharger at the rear of the engine. The hot exhaust gases had to be ducted 20ft (6m) to the rear to drive the turbine before they emerged from the rear fuselage. This arrangement meant there was about 60ft (18m) of ducting running up and down the fuselage, under the cockpit. The duct carrying the compressed air had to be of the high-pressure type, while that carrying the hot exhaust gases rearwards had to have sliding joints to allow for the expansion of the metal. With all that ducting and a 256 Imp gal (1,162 litre) fuel tank inside the fuselage, the Double Wasp engine in the front and the turbosupercharger in the rear, it is hardly surprising that the Thunderbolt was so big. Once its pilots learned to exploit the fighter's high speed and its excellent diving performance, however, the P-47 proved successful as a long-range escort fighter even against smaller and more nimble opponents.

The 166 Imp gal (753-litre) ferry tank fitted initially to the P-47C was unpressurised, and so would not deliver fuel at altitudes above 20,000ft (6,100m). Thunderbolts flew to the enemy coast below that altitude, using the fuel from the ferry tank. When they reached the coast they dropped the tanks, often before they were empty, and commenced a climb to be in position to engage enemy fighters when they met them.

The next major advance to the Thunderbolt's escort range came with introduction of the 90 Imp gal (408-litre) pressurised drop tank. It became available in

September 1943 and, since it worked at any altitude, it permitted a more flexible mode of operation. Using the new tank the fighter had a radius of action of about 400 miles (645km). Later, small numbers of Thunderbolts were modified to carry two 90gal drop tanks, thus increasing their operational radius of action to 475 miles (765km).

The lightest fighter type of this period was the Japanese Mitsubishi A6M3 Model 32 'Hamp'. This carrier-borne fighter appeared in April 1942 and had a loaded weight of only 5,609lb (2,544kg). To achieve a performance comparable with that of contemporary fighters in other countries, using a less powerful engine, designer Jiro Horikoshi had to produce a very 'tight' design. But that meant the fighter had very little potential for development. During the first year of the war in the Pacific the 'Hamp' and its predecessor, the 'Zero', had struck fear in the hearts of its opponents. Yet the real reason for this success was not so much the fighter but the highly trained pilots who flew it. During the first eighteen months of the conflict, that band of prewar-trained Japanese Navy fighter pilots was wiped out almost to a man. Their hastily trained replacements were far less effective.

Another fighter type that became the bane of its opponents when it first appeared was the Focke-Wulf Fw 190. A more sturdy machine than the Bf 109, the Fw 190 was powered by the 1,600hp BMW 801 radial. The Fw 190 had a clear performance margin over the Spitfire

The Mitsubishi A6M5, Allied code-name 'Zeke 52', whose performance was outclassed by those of the US Navy's Hellcat and Corsair fighters.

The Fw 190D, which entered service in the autumn of 1944, had a performance comparable with that of the P-51B, the Spitfire XIV and the Tempest.

Focke-Wulf Fw 190s of Jagdgeschwader 51 operating under harsh winter conditions at a forward airfield in Russia. Note that the aircraft in the background is having its engine changed in the open. (Romm)

VB which soldiered on until the Spitfire IX entered service. From then on the performance of the Spitfire advanced the faster, and the Mk XIV had a clear margin of superiority even over the Fw 190D.

For the Japanese Navy the moment of truth came in the summer of 1943, when the US Navy introduced the Grumman F6F Hellcat. This was powered by a 2,000hp Pratt & Whitney R-2800-10W, an engine similar to that fitted to the Thunderbolt. The new American fighter had a maximum speed of 376mph (605km) at 22,800ft (6,900m), giving it a comfortable performance margin over the 'Hamp'. With the next generation of Japanese fighters still more than a year from service, the outclassed 'Hamp' had to continue to bear the brunt of the

The Nakajima Ki-84 'Frank' was one of the best fighters in service with the Japanese Army Air Force.

Japanese Army Air Force Fighters				*Figures for initial production version of each type*	
Type	Entered service	Engine power	Maximum speed	Weight (normal loaded)	Wing loading
Nakajima Ki 43-IIB 'Oscar'	Jul 1943	1,130hp	515km/h 320mph	2,412kg 5,320lb	0.96kg/m^2 22.9lb/sq ft
Nakajima Ki 84 'Frank'	Aug 1944	1,900hp	624km/h 388mph	3,612kg 7,965lb	1.26kg/m^2 29.9lb/sq ft

The Grumman F6F Hellcat carrier fighter had a considerable performance advantage over the Japanese A6M5 'Zeke 52', and played a major part in the US Naval victories in the Pacific theatre during 1943 and 1944

air fighting over the Pacific. Now the 'tightness' of its original design was a liability, because the airframe could not accept an engine developing more than 1,300hp. Mitsubishi did its best to squeeze more performance from the existing airframe, but with little success.

The cleanest airframe design of any fighter of this period was that of the North American P-51 Mustang. The P-51A, the initial production version, was powered by the Allison V-1710 engine and was quite an effective low-altitude fighter. When the fighter was re-engined with the Merlin 61 built under licence by the US Packard company as the V-1650-3, the Mustang really came into its own. The Spitfire IX used the Rolls-Royce-built version of the same engine. Yet, when the two fighters flew at similar throttle settings, the Mustang was between 20

and 30mph (32 and 48km/h) faster, depending on altitude.

With a maximum speed of 440mph (708km/h), the Mustang was faster than any piston-engined fighter opposing it. Moreover, carrying two 75 Imp gal (340 litre) tanks, its operational radius of action of 650 miles (1,045km) took it to Berlin and beyond.

The appearance of large numbers of Thunderbolts and Mustangs over Germany in the spring of 1944 caused a crisis in the Luftwaffe. Home defence units flying the Bf 109 and Fw 109 found themselves in a sort of '*Catch 22* situation'. If a fighter carried enough firepower to destroy the American heavy bombers, it was too heavy and unwieldy to engage with the American escorts. If the armament was reduced so that the fighter could dogfight with the American escorts, it could not engage the bombers with much chance of success.

As a makeshift solution, the Luftwaffe introduced separate Gruppen equipped with 'heavy' and 'light' fighters. The 'heavy' fighter type was the specially modified Focke-Wulf Fw 190A-8 'Sturmbock' ('battering ram') fitted with two 20mm and two 30mm MK 108 cannon. This version carried extra steel armour to protect the cockpit area and extra panels of toughened glass on either side of the canopy to enable it to engage in slugging matches against American heavy bombers from short range. The weight of the heavy cannon and the extra armour made the Sturmbock highly vulnerable if it was engaged by American fighters, however. Because of this, each Gruppe of Sturmbock fighters was escorted into action by two 'light' fighter Gruppen equipped with lightly armed Bf 109s fitted with uprated engines. The task of the latter was to protect the 'heavy' fighters from the US escorts. These tactics enjoyed some success during the early summer of 1944, until the numerically superior American fighter force devised countermeasures.

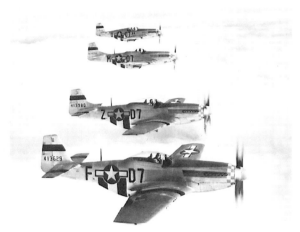

North American P-51 Mustangs of the 503rd Fighter Squadron, 339th Fighter Group, in the summer of 1944. The three aircraft nearest the camera are the 'D' version with the bubble canopy. The furthest aircraft is a 'C' version with the original faired canopy.

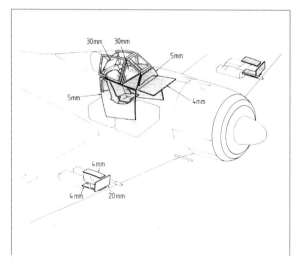

Additional armour fitted to the Fw 190A-8 Sturmbock.

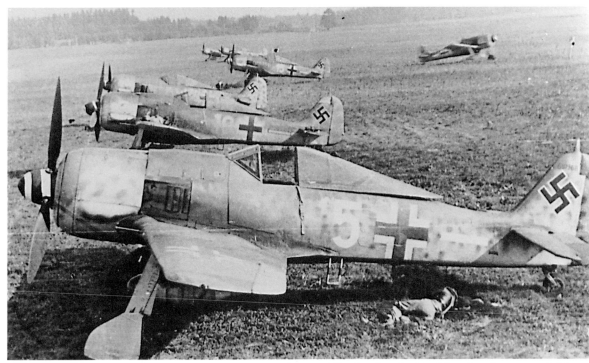

Focke Wulf Fw 190A-8 'Sturmbock' fighters of II. (Sturm) Gruppe of Jagdgeschwader 300. These heavily armoured fighters carried two wing-mounted 30mm cannon, and were modified to engage in short-range fire-fights with US heavy bomber formations. (Romm)

Left: *Yakovlev Yak-9 fighters of the Soviet Air Force. This aircraft entered service in August 1942 and was built in large numbers. It had a maximum speed of 584km/h (363mph) and weighed 3,199kg (7,055lb).*

Soviet Air Force Fighters				*Figures for initial production version of each type*	
Type	Entered service	Engine power	Max. speed	Weight (normal loaded)	Wing loading
Mikoyan-Gurevich MiG-3	Autumn 1941	1,350hp	655km/h 407mph	3,284kg 7,242lb	1.61kg/m² 38.3lb/sq ft
Yakovlev Yak-9	Aug 1942	1,260hp	584km/h 363 mph	3,199kg 7,055lb	1.60kg/m² 38.1lb/sq ft
Lavochkin LA-5FN	Spring 1943	1,640hp	647km/h 402mph	3,358kg 7,406lb	1.66kg/m² 39.4lb sq ft

How they Compared:

Spitfire Mark VB *versus* **Focke-Wulf Fw 190A-3**

General The Fw 190 was compared with a Spitfire VB from an operational squadron for speed and all-round manoeuvrability at heights up to 25,000ft. The Fw 190 is superior in speed at all heights, and the approximate differences are as follows:

At 2,000ft (600m) the Fw 190 is 25–30mph (40–48km/h) faster than the Spitfire VB
At 3,000ft (900m) the Fw 190 is 30–35mph (48–56km/h) faster than the Spitfire VB
At 5,000ft (1,500m) the Fw 190 is 25mph faster than the Spitfire VB
At 9,000ft (2,700m) the Fw 190 is 25–30mph faster than the Spitfire VB
At 15,000ft (4,600m) the Fw 190 is 20mph (32km/h) faster than the Spitfire VB
At 18,000ft (5,500m) the Fw 190 is 20mph faster than the Spitfire VB
At 21,000ft (6,400m) the Fw 190 is 20–25mph faster than the Spitfire VB

Climb The climb of the Fw 190 is superior to that of the Spitfire VB at all heights. The best speeds for climbing are approximately the same, but the angle of the Fw 190 is considerably steeper. Under maximum continuous climbing conditions the climb of the Fw 190 is about 450ft/min (2.28m/sec) better up to 25,000ft (7,600m).

Dive Comparative dives between the two aircraft have shown that the Fw 190 can leave the Spitfire with ease, particularly during the initial stages.

Manoeuvrability The manoeuvrability of the Fw 190 is better than that of the Spitfire VB except in turning circles, when the Spitfire can quite easily out-turn it. The Fw 190 has better acceleration under all conditions of flight and this must obviously be most useful during combat.

When the Fw 190 was in a turn and was attacked by the Spitfire, the superior rate of roll enabled it to flick into a diving turn in the opposition direction. The pilot of the Spitfire could experience great difficulty in following this manoeuvre, and even when prepared for it, was seldom able to allow the correct deflection. A dive from this manoeuvre enabled the Fw 190 to draw away from the Spitfire, which was then forced to break off the attack.

The above trials have shown that the Spitfire VB must cruise at high speed when in an area where enemy fighters can be expected. It will then, in addition to lessening the chances of being successfully 'bounced', have a better chance of catching the Fw 190, particularly if it has the advantage of surprise.

How they Compared:

Spitfire Mark XIV *versus* **Focke-Wulf Fw 190A-3**

Maximum speeds From 0–5,000ft (0–1,500m) and 15,000–20,000ft (4,600–6,100m) the Spitfire XIV is only 20mph (32km/h) faster; at all other heights it is up to 60mph (97km/h) faster than the Fw 190A.

Maximum climb The Spitfire XIV has a considerably greater rate of climb than the Fw 190A at all altitudes.

Dive After the initial part of the dive, during which the Fw 190 gains slightly, the Spitfire XIV has a slight advantage.

Turning circle The Spitfire XIV can easily turn inside the Fw 190, though in the case of a right-hand turn this difference is not quite so pronounced.

Rate of roll The Fw 190 is very much better.

Conclusions In defence, the Spitfire XIV should use its remarkable maximum climb and turning circle against any enemy aircraft. In the attack it can afford to 'mix it' but should beware of the quick roll and dive. If this manoeuvre is used by an Fw 190 and the Spitfire XIV follows, it will probably not be able to close the range until the Fw 190 has pulled out of its dive.

Hawker Typhoon Mk IB

(see page 64 ff)

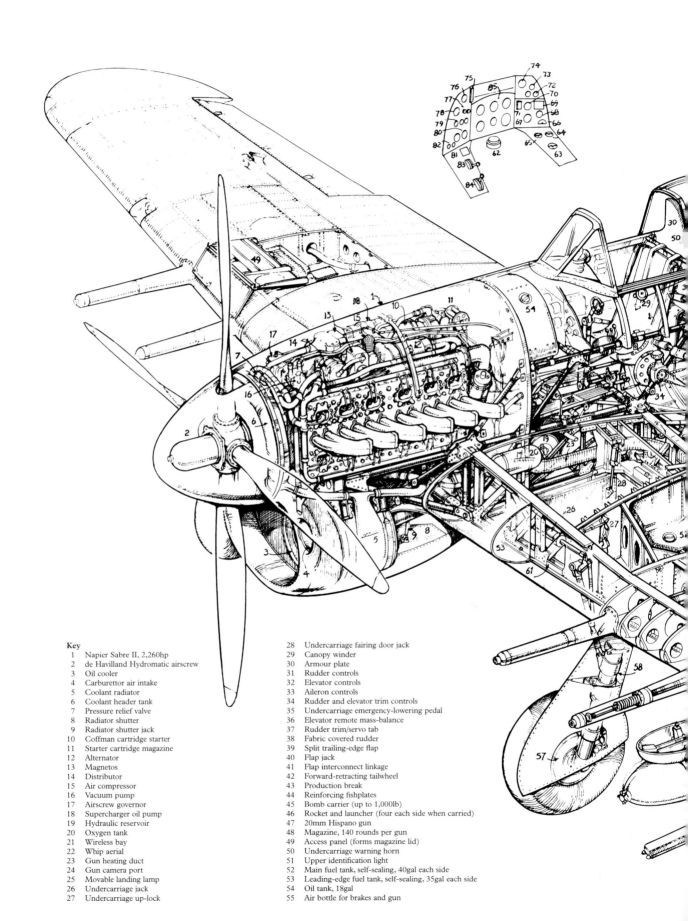

Key

1 Napier Sabre II, 2,260hp
2 de Havilland Hydromatic airscrew
3 Oil cooler
4 Carburettor air intake
5 Coolant radiator
6 Coolant header tank
7 Pressure relief valve
8 Radiator shutter
9 Radiator shutter jack
10 Coffman cartridge starter
11 Starter cartridge magazine
12 Alternator
13 Magnetos
14 Distributor
15 Air compressor
16 Vacuum pump
17 Airscrew governor
18 Supercharger oil pump
19 Hydraulic reservoir
20 Oxygen tank
21 Wireless bay
22 Whip aerial
23 Gun heating duct
24 Gun camera port
25 Movable landing lamp
26 Undercarriage jack
27 Undercarriage up-lock

28 Undercarriage fairing door jack
29 Canopy winder
30 Armour plate
31 Rudder controls
32 Elevator controls
33 Aileron controls
34 Rudder and elevator trim controls
35 Undercarriage emergency-lowering pedal
36 Elevator remote mass-balance
37 Rudder trim/servo tab
38 Fabric covered rudder
39 Split trailing-edge flap
40 Flap jack
41 Flap interconnect linkage
42 Forward-retracting tailwheel
43 Production break
44 Reinforcing fishplates
45 Bomb carrier (up to 1,000lb)
46 Rocket and launcher (four each side when carried)
47 20mm Hispano gun
48 Magazine, 140 rounds per gun
49 Access panel (forms magazine lid)
50 Undercarriage warning horn
51 Upper identification light
52 Main fuel tank, self-sealing, 40gal each side
53 Leading-edge fuel tank, self-sealing, 35gal each side
54 Oil tank, 18gal
55 Air bottle for brakes and gun

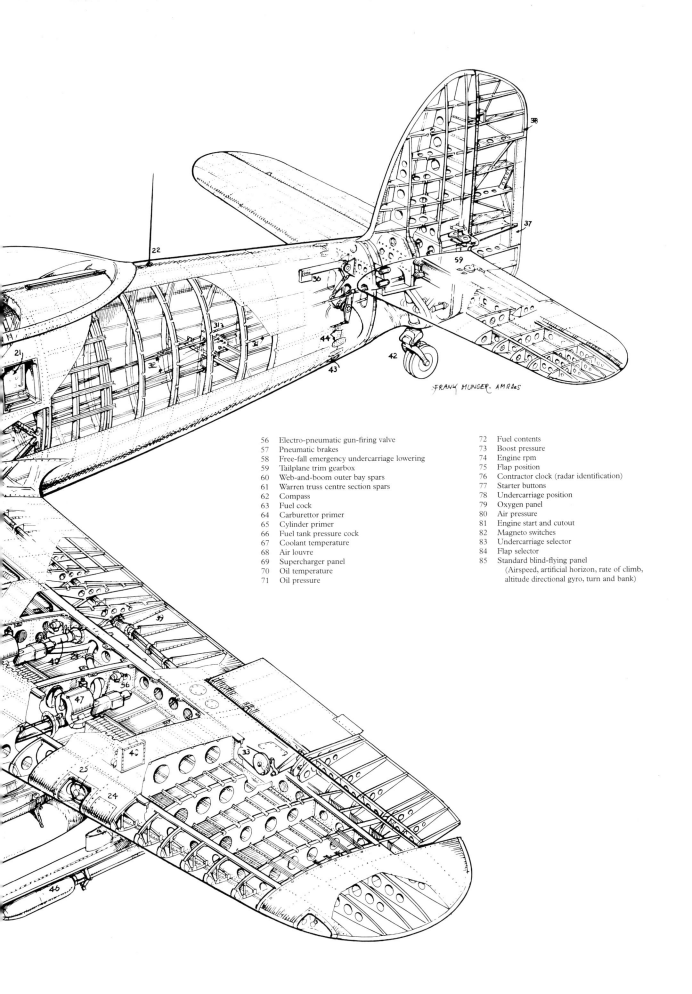

FRANK MUNGER. AMRAeS

56	Electro-pneumatic gun-firing valve	72	Fuel contents
57	Pneumatic brakes	73	Boost pressure
58	Free-fall emergency undercarriage lowering	74	Engine rpm
59	Tailplane trim gearbox	75	Flap position
60	Web-and-boom outer bay spars	76	Contractor clock (radar identification)
61	Warren truss centre section spars	77	Starter buttons
62	Compass	78	Undercarriage position
63	Fuel cock	79	Oxygen panel
64	Carburettor primer	80	Air pressure
65	Cylinder primer	81	Engine start and cutout
66	Fuel tank pressure cock	82	Magneto switches
67	Coolant temperature	83	Undercarriage selector
68	Air louvre	84	Flap selector
69	Supercharger panel	85	Standard blind-flying panel
70	Oil temperature		(Airspeed, artificial horizon, rate of climb, altitude directional gyro, turn and bank)
71	Oil pressure		

How they Compared:

North American P-51B Mustang *versus* **Focke-Wulf Fw 190A-3**

Maximum speed The Fw 190 is nearly 50mph (80km/h) slower at all heights, increasing to 70mph (112km/h) above 28,000ft (8,500m).
   Climb There appears to be little to choose in the maximum rate of climb. It is anticipated that the Mustang will have a better climb than the new Fw 190D. The Mustang is considerably faster at all heights in a zoom climb.
   Dive The Mustang can always out-dive the Fw 190.
   Turning circle Again, there is not much to choose. The Mustang is slightly better. When evading an enemy aircraft with a steep turn, a pilot will always out-turn the attacking aircraft initially because of the difference in speeds. It is therefore still a worthwhile manoeuvre with the Mustang when attacked.
   Rate of roll Not even a Mustang approaches the Fw 190.
   Conclusions In the attack, a high speed should be maintained or regained in order to regain the height initiative. A Fw 190 could not evade by diving alone. In defence a steep turn followed by a full throttle dive should increase the range before regaining height and course. Dog-fighting is not altogether recommended. Do not attempt to climb away without at least 250mph (400km/h) showing initially.

How they Compared:

North American P-51B Mustang *versus* **Messerschmitt Bf 109G**

Maximum speed The Mustang is faster at all heights. Its best heights, by comparison, are below 16,000ft (4,900m) where it is 30mph (50km/h) faster, approximately, and above 25,000ft (7,600m) where it is 30mph faster, increasing to 50mph at 30,000ft (80km/h at 9,100m).
   Maximum climb This is rather similar. The Mustang is very slightly better above 25,000ft but inclined to be worse below 20,000ft (6,100m).
   Zoom climb The Me 109G appears to have a very good high-speed climb, making the two aircraft similar in a zoom climb.
   Dive On the other hand, in defence the Mustang can still increase the range in a prolonged dive.
   Turning circle The Mustang is greatly superior.
   Rate of roll Not much to choose. In defence (in a tight spot) a rapid change of direction will throw the Me 109G's sight off. This is because the 109G's maximum rate of roll is embarrassing (the slots keep opening).
   Conclusions In attack, the Mustang can always catch the Me 109G, except in any sort of climb (unless there is a high overtaking speed). In defence, a steep turn should be the first manoeuvre, followed, if necessary, by a dive (below 20,000ft). A high-speed climb will unfortunately not increase the range. If above 25,000ft keep above by climbing or all-out level flight.

How they Compared:

Grumman F6F-5 Hellcat and Vought F4U-1D Corsair *versus* **Mitsubishi A6M5 'Zeke 52'**

F6F-5
The F6F ranged from 25mph (40km/h) faster at sea level to 75mph (120km/h) faster at 25,000ft (7,600m). In the climb the Model 52 was superior below 14,000ft (4,250m), at altitudes above that the F6F was superior. Below 230mph (370km/h) the rate of roll of the two fighters was similar, above that speed the F6F was much the better. Below 200mph (322km/h) the Model 52 was far more manoeuvrable than the F6F, while above 230mph (370km/h) the F6F was the more manoeuvrable.

continued

continued

Grumman F6F-5 Hellcat and Vought F4U-1D Corsair *versus* Mitsubishi A6M5 'Zeke 52'

F4U-1D Corsair
The F4U ranged from 48mph (77km/h) faster at sea level to 80mph (129km/h) faster at 25,000ft (7,600m). In the climb it was equal to the Model 52 below 10,000ft (3,000m), at all altitudes above that the F4U was superior, up to 750ft/min (3.81m/sec) better at 18,000ft (5,500m). Below 230mph (370km/h) the rate of roll of the two fighters was similar, above that speed the F4U was much the better. Below 200mph (322km/h) the Model 52 was far more manoeuvrable than the F4U, while above 230mph the F4U was the more manoeuvrable.

General
Do *not* dogfight with the Zeke 52.
Do not try to follow a loop or half-roll with pull-through.
When attacking, use your superior power and high-speed performance to engage at the most favourable moment.
To evade a Zeke 52 on your tail, roll and dive away into a high-speed turn.

To fight by night

In this section we shall examine the evolution of a quite different genre of fighter that emerged during the Second World War: the nightfighter.

In May 1941 the German night blitz on Britain ended as the bulk of the Luftwaffe moved east for the attack on the Soviet Union. The damaging raids on the cities had forced the RAF to give the highest priority to developing means to counter the night raider. As a result, when the blitz ended, Britain possessed the only really effective night air defence system anywhere. Borne of trial and error, foresight and much hard work, the elements of that system remained in place for the rest of the war.

Before describing the nightfighters themselves, it is important to understand how they fitted into the system. For, compared with day fighting, night fighting was more of a team effort. As during a daylight interception process, the long-range, low-precision Chain Home radar provided early warning of the approach of raiders. This enabled nightfighters to take off in good time and head for the general area under threat. When the raiders

The Bristol Beaufighter, when fitted with AI Mark IV radar, was the most effective nightfighter of all in the late spring of 1941.

neared the coast they came within range of one or more of the medium-range, medium precision Ground Controlled Interception (GCI) radars. GCI operators 'talked' the nightfighter pilot to a point in the sky about two miles behind the bomber and at the same altitude. That put the bomber in the field of view of the nightfighter's short-range, high precision Airborne Interception (AI) radar. When the fighter's radar operator had the bomber on his screen, he 'talked' the pilot into a position where the latter had visual contact with the prey. From there on the pilot carried out a visual attack, usually closing to short range – about fifty yards – before opening fire.

To operate within this system, the nightfighter required attributes different from those of the day fighter. It ideally needed a roomy fuselage to accommodate the AI radar and its operator, armament powerful enough to destroy or cripple a bomber with a few short bursts, and, since its patrols often lasted several hours, it needed a much longer endurance. Because of these requirements a nightfighter needed to be a fairly large aircraft, which meant it required the power from two engines.

In mid-1941 the most effective nightfighter type in service anywhere was the RAF's Bristol Beaufighter. This two-seater carried an armament of four 20mm cannon and six 0.303in machine-guns. On the power of two 1,400hp Bristol Hercules engines it had a maximum speed of about 300mph (about 480km/h). The AI Mark IV radar fitted to the Beaufighter was a first-generation equipment, working on frequencies in the 150 MHz band. The radar's maximum range was just under three miles (4.8km) or the fighter's height above the ground, whichever was less.

The Beaufighter was not the only nightfighter type then in use by the RAF, as single-engined Hurricanes and Boulton Paul Defiants flew 'catseye' patrols,

RAF Nightfighters					*Figures for initial production version of each type*
Type	Entered service	Engine power	Max. speed	Weight (normal loaded)	Radar range
Bristol Beaufighter I	Sep 1940	2 × 1,400hp	300mph 480km/h	20,800lb 9,433kg	3 miles 4.8km
De Havilland Mosquito II	Mar 1942	2 × 1,480hp	370mph 596km/h	18,547lb 8,411kg	3 miles 4.8km
Mosquito 30	Apr 1944	2 × 1,690hp	424mph 682km/h	21,715lb 9,848kg	10 miles 16km

attempting to engage enemy bombers illuminated for them by searchlights or found visually. A two-seater, the Defiant carried its armament of four 0.303-in machine-guns in a power operated turret mounted behind the pilot's cockpit. Since it lacked AI radar, the Hurricane could not achieve much at night, although AI sets were fitted in Defiants which served in this role until mid-1942.

The next significant nightfighter type to enter service in the RAF, at the beginning of 1942, was the Mosquito. It had its share of teething troubles, but within a few months these were sorted out. The Mark II version carried the same type of radar and a similar armament to the Beaufighter. Its maximum speed was 370mph (596km/h). As the war progressed the Mosquito, later fitted with more advanced types of radar, equipped the entire RAF nightfighter force.

In building up the nightfighter defences of Germany the Luftwaffe trod a generally similar path to that taken by the RAF. Because initially the pressures were less, however, the process took a bit longer. After much trial and error the Luftwaffe developed its own technique for an 'all-radar' interception, having also found the catseye nightfighting methods to be relatively ineffective. In 1942 the main German nightfighter type was the Messerschmitt Bf 110F, with a performance generally similar to that of the Beaufighter I. This three-seater carried an armament of two 20mm cannon and four 7.9mm machine-guns. On the power of two 1,350hp Daimler Benz DB 601 engines the German fighter had a maximum speed of about 500km/h (310mph). Its 'Lichtenstein' AI radar worked in the frequencies in the 440 MHz band and it had a similar performance to the British AI Mark IV.

The Boulton Paul Defiant, pressed into use as a night fighter, carried its four-gun armament in a turret mounted behind the cockpit. The type was far less effective than the Beaufighter, however.

A de Havilland Mosquito 30 of No 85 Squadron, one of the units assigned to No 100 Group, warming its engines before take-off in the winter of 1944/5.

By the time the Bf 110F was in large-scale service, several RAF nightfighter squadrons had re-equipped with the faster and more effective Mosquito II. Initially these types operated only in the home defence role, however, so the lower performance of the Messerschmitt was not an important factor.

The so-called 'Himmelbett' system of close control for Luftwaffe nightfighters was more rigid than that used in Britain. It employed a line of ground radar stations in France, Belgium, Holland, northern Germany and Denmark. These formed a barrier through which the raiding forces had to pass, to reach their targets in Germany. Individual Luftwaffe nightfighter units operated with the same few ground control stations, each time they went into action. Aircraft rarely ventured more than 100km (60 miles) from their base airfields, and the Bf 110 was quite adequate for this relatively undemanding task. Operating in this way, the German nightfighter caused heavy attrition among RAF raiding forces.

Had matters been allowed to continue, the Himmelbett system might have remained in use for the rest of the war, but the RAF produced a countermeasure in the form of 'Window' (now called 'Chaff'), aluminium foil strips measuring 30cm long and just over 1.5cm wide. These strips were designed to jam the precision radars on which Himmelbett depended, the 'Würzburg' and

A Messerschmitt Bf 110G nightfighter, fitted with a Lichtenstein radar aerial array on the nose.

'Giant Würzburg' ground radars and the Lichtenstein airborne equipment. At the end of July 1943 RAF bombers began dropping large quantities of Window to fill the German radar screens with hundreds of false targets.

With the Himmelbett system of close ground control neutralised, the Luftwaffe was forced to make a radical change in tactics. As a temporary expedient it employed single-engined fighters at night, flying catseye patrols.

For twin-engined nightfighters the Luftwaffe introduced a new system of control. As the incoming raiding force was detected on early-warning radar (the long-wavelength sets were not affected by this type of Window), scores of nightfighters took off and assembled over designated radio beacons. Then, operating under radio broadcast control, the packs of nightfighters were directed to fly from beacon to beacon to bring them progressively closer to the bombers. From there they 'stepped off' to join the stream, the crews searching for the bombers visually and with radar. Throughout this time the fighter controllers broadcast a running commentary on the progress of the bomber stream. The aim was to set up long-running battles lasting throughout the time the bombers were over Germany or occupied territory.

In the autumn of 1943 the Luftwaffe introduced a new AI radar, the 'SN-2', with a range of four miles. This operated on frequencies in the 90 MHz band, and its longer wavelength rendered it almost immune to the types of Window then in use. Also, to assist in locating bomber streams at long range, German nightfighters carried 'Naxos' and 'Flensburg' equipment to home, respectively, on emissions from the 'H₂S' bombing radar and the 'Monica' tail warning radar.

A further innovation at this time was the fitting of the so-called 'schräge Musik' installation in some nightfighters: one or two 20mm cannon in the cockpit or rear fuselage firing upwards at an angle of 60°. This enabled

Luftwaffe Nightfighters					*Figures for initial production version of each type*
Type	Entered service	Engine power	Max. speed	Weight (normal loaded)	Radar range
Messerschmitt Bf 110F-4	Aug 1942	2 × 1,350hp	500km/h 310mph	9,285kg 20,474lb	4.8km 3 miles
Junkers Ju 88G-6	Oct 1944	2 × 1,608hp	626km/h 389mph	13,106kg 28,900lb	4.8km 3 miles

A Junkers Ju 88G nightfighter with SN 2 radar aerials on the nose and Flensburg homer aerials mounted on the leading edges of the wings.

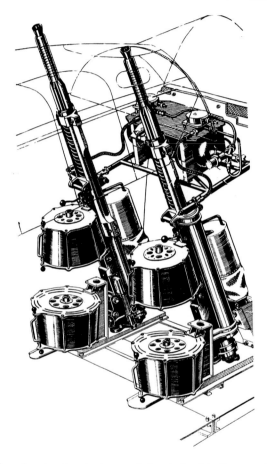

Drawing showing the layout of the schräge Musik upward-firing cannon installation fitted to the Bf 110 night fighter, with two 20mm cannon.

the fighter to engage the bomber from below, from outside the field of fire of its rear gunner.

The new nightfighting tactics were challenging for the Bf 110; when fitted with all of the extra new equipment, plus external tanks to give it the necessary extra endurance, it suffered a major drop in performance. It was not fast enough for the long pursuit operations that were now the order of the day – but it remained in service. Some units began to re-equip with the latest night-

fighter versions of the Junkers Ju 88. Larger and more powerful than the Bf 110, the Ju 88G had a loaded weight of 13,000kg (28,900lb) and a maximum speed of 622km/h (389mph).

The thrust, parry and counterthrust battle of the night war over Germany did not end there, however. In mid-1944 No 100 Group of RAF Bomber Command began operations in support of the night bombing raids. As well as using specialised jamming aircraft to disrupt the German radar network, the Group employed six squadrons of Mosquito night fighters to harass their German counterparts in the air and on the ground.

During the final months of the war the Mosquito Mark 30 was, by a wide margin, the most effective nightfighter type in service anywhere. Its maximum speed was 424mph (678km/h) and it carried the latest AI Mark 10 centimetric-wavelength radar, with a range of up to ten miles (16km). The Mosquitoes of No 100 Group had to search for the German nightfighters in a sky full of friendly bombers, but homing on radar emissions from enemy aircraft was a game that two could play. The RAF fighters carried the 'Serrate' and 'Perfectos' equipments to enable them to home, respectively, on emissions from the SN-2 radar and the IFF sets carried by their prey.

The nightfighters' war lacked the panache and spectacle of that fought by day. Single nightfighters stalked individual bombers and, later, individual enemy nightfighters. Success in this type of action often went to

A 250lb (113kg) bomb mounted on the wing rack of a Spitfire.

Spitfire IXs of No 73 Squadron, each carrying two 250 pounders, taxy out for a dive-bombing sortie at their base at Prkos in Yugoslavia.

the side with the better electronic equipment and the crews best able to use it effectively. Throughout the war the RAF and the Luftwaffe remained the main players in the night air defence battle. Although the other contestants also dabbled in this art, none of them was able to achieve any great success at it.

The rise of the fighter-bomber

The Luftwaffe pioneered the use of fighter-bombers, interceptor fighters fitted with bomb racks, during the Battle of Britain in 1940, when it sent Messerschmitt Bf 109s and Bf 110s to carry out small-scale attacks on targets in southern England. There were obvious advantages to using fighters in this way. They are much cheaper than bombers and they required a smaller crew. In engineering terms the installation of bomb racks was a relatively simple matter. Once the aircraft had released its bombs it could revert to the fighter role and it was well able to take care of itself in combat. In speed and altitude performance the fighter-bomber was far superior to most of the specialised bomber types. Indeed, if it was not possible to establish temporary air superiority over a target area, the fighter-bomber offered the only chance of delivering attacks without incurring prohibitive losses.

These clear advantages tended to blind people to the shortcomings of the fighter-bomber, however. These aircraft carried a relatively small weight of bombs, and if the latter were to have any useful effect they needed to be delivered with great accuracy. Moreover, since the carriage of bombs usually precluded the use of drop tanks, the radius of action of fighter-bombers was usually rather short.

Initially the fighter-bombers carried normal types of bombs weighing around 250 or 500lb (around 110 or 250kg). Getting these weapons to explode close to the

chosen targets proved to be difficult under operational conditions. If a fighter-bomber delivered a low-altitude horizontal attack from around 60ft (18m), its bombs needed a fusing delay of at least ten seconds after impact. Otherwise the aircraft was liable to suffer splinter damage – or worse – when they detonated. Such an attack could be effective only against a target bulky enough to stop a bomb ramming into it at speeds up to 300mph (480km/h), and those were rare, especially in a battle area. If the bomb failed to stop at the target, the rest of its travel was fraught with unpredictabilities. During one RAF trial, fighter-bombers flying at 300mph (480km/h) released 250lb (110kg) bombs from 60ft (18m), aiming at vehicle targets on flat ground. Ciné photography revealed cases where, after striking the ground, bombs bounced to twice the height of the releasing aircraft and often maintained disconcertingly close formation on it. During the ten seconds following the initial impact these bombs continued on, often tumbling end over end across the ground, as they exhausted their huge momentum. The distance they covered varied greatly, depending on the type of surface. In some cases the bombs finally came to rest more than half a mile (800m) from their initial point of impact (fortunately for the people involved in the trial, the bombs were not live!).

High-altitude horizontal attacks by single-engined fighter-bombers were even less accurate. Such aircraft usually had the cockpit over the wing, which meant that the pilot's view downwards varied between poor and non-existent. Since he could not see the target at the time of release, it was impossible to aim the weapons using a bombsight. This type of attack could have only a nuisance value.

The only reasonably effective method of attack available to the fighter-bomber, when it carried normal types of bomb, was to release the weapons in a dive, but the accuracy of such attacks compared poorly with those by purpose-built dive-bombers. Almost all the interceptor fighters converted to this role lacked dive brakes, so in their dives they gained speed rapidly. Even in a relatively shallow dive of 60° they built up speed rapidly and often exceeded 450mph (725km/h). Because of their high diving speed, and because their airframes were not stressed for a tight pull-out manoeuvre, fighter-bombers usually released their bombs from altitudes above 4,000ft (1,200m). Even when flown by well-trained pilots, the accuracy of attack of a converted fighter was considerably less than that by a specialised dive-bomber type. The latter delivered its bombs flying steeper and slower, and bomb release was at about 2,000ft (about 600m). This is not to say that fighter-bombers did not carry out many effective attacks using normal bombs, but it required more aircraft and many more bombs than if a specialised dive bomber had done the job. Of course the specialised dive-bomber was far more vulnerable to fighter attack than a fighter-bomber, but in this business one cannot have everything.

To increase the effectiveness of the low-flying fighter-bomber, specialised weapons were needed. In June 1941 the Luftwaffe introduced the first of these, the SD 2 anti-personnel bomb, weighing only 2kg (4.4lb). Although the weapon proved extremely successful against battlefield targets and aircraft on the ground, the Luftwaffe soon discovered that it had a serious shortcoming. Occasionally a bomblet failed to leave its container and remained lodged in place, and the crew of the aeroplane had no way of knowing it. When the aircraft landed, the jolt freed the weapon, which then dropped to the ground and detonated on the runway. After several German aircraft were destroyed or damaged in this way, the SD 2 was withdrawn from service until a solution was found.

The answer was to fit the SD 2s into a streamlined container that could be aimed and dropped in the same way as a normal bomb. Once it was safely clear of the aircraft, the container split open along its length to disgorge its load of bomblets. Thus was born the first cluster-bomb, a weapon designed to produce an area of destruction on the ground rather like the blast of a shot-

The SD 2 Fragmentation Bomb

The SD 2 fragmentation bomb weighed only 2kg (4.4lb), and was much smaller than any air-dropped weapon previously in general use in the Second World War. In the stowed condition the weapon was a cylinder 7.5cm (3in) in diameter and 9cm (3½in) long – about the size of a small beer can. After release, the bomb's casing opened to form 'wings' which caused it to decelerate rapidly. It then descended to the ground relatively slowly.

The SD 2 bomblets were carried in special containers which fitted on the aeroplane's normal bomb racks. The type of container carried by the Bf 109 held 96 of these bomblets, while that fitted to the Bf 110 held 360.

Designed for release during low-altitude attacks, the SD-2 was highly effective against 'soft skinned' vehicles, troops and aircraft on the ground. From the attacker's point of view there were several advantages to releasing a large number of small bombs rather than one or two large ones. The rapid deceleration of the SD-2 after release, and its small explosive charge, meant that when the weapon detonated the fighter-bomber was safely clear of any flying splinters. Also, since it could be delivered in low-altitude attacks, the SD 2s could be laid very accurately across small targets.

The SD 2 fragmentation bomb, weighing 2kg (4.4lb), was the first free-fall weapon specially designed for release from low-flying aircraft. After release the bomb's casing opened to form 'wings', causing it to decelerate rapidly and descend to the ground relatively slowly.

An AB 250 cluster-bomb being loaded on the bomb rack of a Fw 190. This container could hold up to ninety-six SD 2 bomblets.

gun. From the summer of 1942 the Luftwaffe made large-scale use of SD 2s as cluster munitions.

Tanks were among the most difficult targets for air attack, being small and often well armoured. It required a direct hit, or else a very near miss with quite a large warhead, to put them out of action. Generally speaking any weapon carried by a fighter that was accurate enough to have a good chance of hitting a tank, for example a 20mm cannon, was insufficiently powerful to destroy it, and any weapon powerful enough to destroy a tank, for example a bomb of 50kg (110lb) or larger, was insufficiently accurate to stand much chance of hitting it.

The first serious attempt to break out of that circle, using a converted fighter type, came with the introduction of the Hurricane Mark IID. This aircraft carried a Vickers 'S' 40mm cannon under each wing and two 0.303in machine-guns loaded with tracer ammunition to assist aiming. The pilot approached the tank flying horizontally at a height of about 50ft at 240mph (about 15m at 385km/h), and commenced firing at 600 yards (540m). The cannon were single-shot weapons, and each loosed off a round with each press of the firing button. A well-practised pilot could get off ten pairs of aimed rounds during the firing pass.

The Hurricane IID was at its most effective against tanks that had broken through a defensive line and had outrun their AA gun protection. In North Africa, where the Hurricane IID first saw action, such conditions occurred rarely after the summer of 1942. Certainly it was reassuring for the army commander to know that he had this capability on call, however, in case such an emergency should arise. If they went against tanks in a defensive position with AA protection, the low-flying Hurricanes often suffered heavy losses.

At the end of 1942 the German Army introduced its powerful new Panzer VI (Tiger) tank, much of whose thick armour was impervious to rounds from the Vickers S gun. Thereafter the RAF lost interest in the heavy cannon as an anti-tank weapon, in favour of the rocket projectile.

During the war the air-launched rocket was touted as a highly effective weapon for use against tanks. The Hawker Typhoon, the main RAF fighter-bomber type to employ this weapon in the ground-attack role, carried eight of them on launching rails under the wings. When employed against ground targets, the British 3in rocket carried a 60lb (27kg) warhead containing 17lb (7.7kg) of high explosive. After launch the rocket accelerated rapidly. It reached its maximum speed of about 1,000 mph (1,600km/h) in 1.5 seconds, having covered about 550 yards (500m). At that point the motor burned out and from then on the missile lost speed rapidly owing to air resistance. During a typical rocket attack the Typhoon established itself in a 30° dive and fired the projectiles from a range of 1,000 yards (900m). The aeroplane's dive angle and firing range were critical, and required very fine judgement at the time when the pilot might himself be under fire. Even slight deviations from the ideal would cause fairly large miss distances at the target. If the reflector sight was set up for the above figures and rockets were fired in a 27° dive from 1,150 yards (1,035m), the errors amounted to only 3° in angle and 15 per cent in range, yet they would cause the rockets to impact 17 yards (15m) short of the target, far enough to allow an armoured vehicle to escape without serious damage.

Despite the enthusiastic claims made for it at the time (and later), there is clear evidence that during the Second World War the air-launched rocket projectile was not very effective against tanks or armoured vehicles. The weapon was just not accurate enough. According to RAF records on operational rocket strikes during 1945, the chance of scoring at least one hit on a tank from eight rockets was a derisory two per cent. The M.10 rockets carried by USAAF fighter-bombers performed no better against tanks. That said, the rockets were very effective against unarmoured vehicles, artillery positions and other soft targets where a near-miss could cause serious damage. And against large targets such as U-boats or ships, salvoes of rockets were often lethal.

Hawker Hurricane IID delivers a training attack on a tank with its 40mm cannon. The need to make a straight-and-level firing run at very low altitude made the aircraft extremely vulnerable to AA fire.

A Hawker Typhoon of No 198 Squadron, fitted with eight 60lb rockets, taxies out at an airstrip in northern France in 1944. Although the rockets were effective against soft targets, they were not accurate enough to have a good chance of scoring a direct hit on a tank.

One problem common to all converted interceptor fighters operating in the fighter-bomber role was that most of their protective armour was in the wrong place. Air superiority fighters did not carry much armour, and most of it was positioned behind the pilot to give protection against rounds from enemy fighters attacking from behind. Also, in front of his head, there was a toughened glass windscreen to give protection from rounds from a bomber's rear guns. During a low-level attack on a ground target, however, the enemy rounds usually came from below and from ahead or the sides. The normal armour fitted to a fighter afforded little protection against these.

The Focke-Wulf Fw 190F, the main ground-attack version of the famous German fighter, was one of the finest ground-attack aircraft of the Second World War. Although in its external appearance it was little different from the fighter version, internally it had important changes. To suit it for the low-level, ground-attack role it carried about 360kg (about 800lb) of armour along the underside and lower sides of the fuselage, and each side of the cockpit. Thus the pilot and the internal fuel tanks were well protected against rounds coming from ahead and below. At the front of the aeroplane the rugged air-cooled BMW 801 engine gave added protection to the pilot, and it could take heavy battle damage and continue to run. The Fw 190F carried two 20mm cannon and two 13mm machine-guns, plus an ordnance load of up to 550kg (1,100lb) of bombs. Its maximum speed carrying full ordnance load was about 520km/h (325mph) at

low altitude, making it the fastest armoured attack aircraft of the Second World War. Such was the importance of this aircraft that, despite the competing requirement for fighters, during 1944 more than a third of all Fw 190s were built as ground-attack variants. In the closing stages of the war the Fw 190F went into action carrying twelve 8cm 'Panzerblitz' air-to-ground rockets. There is no evidence that these proved any more effective against armoured vehicles than their British or American counterparts.

In the next section we shall examine the development and service careers of the final generation of fighter designs in the Second World War, those powered by turbojet engines and rockets.

The Focke-Wulf Fw 190F was the fastest armoured ground attack aeroplane of the Second World War. This example from Schlachtgeschwader 2, based at Sopoc, Hungary, in January 1945, carries an AB 250 cluster-bomb container under the fuselage.

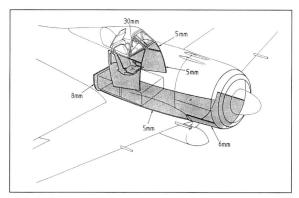

Although its external appearance was similar to the fighter version, the Fw 190F was extensively modified for the ground-attack role. This drawing shows the additional armour fitted along the underside and sides of the fuselage and on each side of the cockpit.

Flame belches from the rear of a Jumo 004 turbojet during start-up. This temperamental engine, two of which powered the Me 262, required careful handling in flight or it was liable to flame-out or catch fire.

The Messerschmitt Me 262 was the most effective jet fighter type to enter service in the Second World War, but due to the short running life of its engines it was able to achieve little.

Enter the jet fighter

By the spring of 1943 two fighter types powered by turbojet engines were undergoing tests, the German Messerschmitt Me 262 and the British Gloster Meteor I. Owing to the low power levels generated by the early turbojets, both aircraft employed two engines. Of the two fighters, the Me 262 was the more advanced. It had an excellent performance when the engines developed their full thrust, but they did not do so for long (see box overleaf 'German Problems with the Turbojet Engine'). In a new condition each of the two Jumo 004 turbojets delivered 900kg (1,980lb) of thrust, giving the fighter a maximum speed of 870km/h (540mph). Its nearest Allied rival, the Meteor I, was powered by two 1,700lb (770kg) thrust Rolls-Royce W2B/23 engines and had a maximum speed of 410mph (660km/h).

In the spring of 1943 Luftwaffe senior officers regarded the Me 262 as an interesting novelty, but one that met no immediate need. The main battlefronts were in North Africa and the Soviet Union, and from time to time there were daylight attacks on peripheral targets in Germany. Provided there were enough of them available, the latest versions of the Fw 190 and the Bf 109 were well able to deal with the enemy air opposition.

A Gloster Meteor I fitted with a belly tank to increase its range.

Moreover these rugged and well-proven machines could operate from primitive forward airfields and were easy to maintain in action. Any diversion of industrial resources to build jet fighters would be at the expense of the conventional fighter types the Luftwaffe really needed. In the type of war then being fought, what use was a temperamental, if fast, short-range jet fighter that required long runways and constant nursing from its maintenance

crews? Nevertheless, to keep abreast of the latest technological developments, the Luftwaffe placed an order for thirty pre-production Me 262s.

Interestingly, RAF senior officers felt the same way about the Meteor when it was first considered for production. The early British jet engines were more reliable and had longer running lives than their German counterparts, but as yet the Service had no requirement for an aircraft with the Meteor's unique capabilities. Early in 1943 the Ministry of Aircraft Production produced comparative performance curves for versions of the Meteor planned to appear in 1944, and the Mk 21 Spitfire scheduled to appear at the same time. These

---

Rationale for the Turbojet Engine in Fighters

The concept of the turbojet engine had been known as an engineering possibility since the early part of the twentieth century, but not until the late 1930s did work begin to produce a practical unit of this type to power aircraft. The main factor driving the work in this field was the dawning realisation, in several countries, that there was a finite limit to the maximum speed that an aircraft could attain on the power from a piston engine driving a propeller. That limit, imposed by the immutable laws of physics, lay somewhere very close to 500mph (805km/h).

The problem centred on the use of the propeller to convert the engine's rotational power into thrust. As the aircraft's forward speed neared 500mph, the efficiency of the propeller fell away drastically. A few figures will serve to illustrate the point. In round terms, the Spitfire Mark I attained a maximum speed of about 300mph (about 480km/h) at sea level on the 1,000 or so horsepower from its Merlin engine. At that speed the propeller was about 80 per cent efficient, and the 1,000lb (450kg) of thrust thus produced equalled the drag from the fighter's airframe.

Now consider the engine power that would be needed to propel the Spitfire at twice that speed, 600mph (960km/h). Drag rises with the square of speed, so if the speed is doubled the drag is quadrupled. Thus the 1,000lb of drag at 300mph becomes 4,000lb (1,814kg) of drag at 600mph. To overcome that amount of drag the aircraft would need 4,000lb of thrust. But at 600mph the efficiency of the propeller was reduced to about 50 per cent, so to drive the aircraft at that speed would have required a piston engine developing about 12,000hp. During the Second World War the best piston engines produced a fraction over one horsepower for each pound of weight. Thus the piston engine needed to propel our notional fighter at 600mph would have weighed about 11,000lb (4,990kg), about double the all-up weight of the early production Spitfire. For high-speed flight the turbojet was a far more efficient power unit than the piston engine. The former produced its output in the form of thrust, without the conversion losses caused by the propeller.

German Problems with the Turbojet Engine

The problem facing the designers of the early turbojet engines was that these ran at far higher temperatures, and at much greater rotational speeds, than previous aircraft engines. In Germany these difficulties were exacerbated by shortages of nickel, chromium and other steel-hardening ores needed in the production of high-temperature-resistant alloys. Because of this, Junkers engineers had to develop substitute materials for use in the critical parts of the Jumo 004.

The hottest part of the turbojet is inside the flame tubes. An ideal material for these would have been a nickel-chrome-steel alloy with small amounts of silicon, manganese and titanium as hardening elements. In the Jumo 004, however, the flames tubes were fashioned from mild steel sheet and had a spray coating of aluminium baked in an oven to prevent oxidation. This inelegant material did not survive long at extreme temperatures. As a result, throughout the time the 004 was running, its flame tubes were slowly buckling out of shape.

Another critical area was the turbine blades. These worked in temperatures often exceeding 700°C, and the centrifugal forces imposed tremendous stresses on the blades. The turbine blades on the Jumo 004 were manufactured from a steel-based alloy containing 30 per cent nickel and 15 per cent chromium, which was not up to the task. During running the blades developed 'creep', that is to say the metal deformed and slowly the blades increased in length. When blade 'creep' reached a laid-down limit the engine had to be changed.

Curtailed by flame tube buckling and blade 'creep', the running life of pre-production Jumo 004 engines rarely exceeded ten hours. The Me 262 then had to be grounded for an engine change. Production engines were a little better in this respect, with a notional running life of 25 hours – still a very low figure.

showed that although the Meteor had a higher maximum speed at the extremes of low and high altitude, this was offset by its inferior rate of climb and its relatively short endurance and radius of action. The only role in which the Meteor I was superior to the best piston-engined fighter types was that of short-range daylight home defence interceptor, operating against targets at very high or very low altitude. The RAF had no requirement for an aircraft with those capabilities. Nobody doubted that the jet fighter had enormous potential, however. It was decided to continue development of the Meteor and get it ready for production, in case the war took an unexpected turn. Both in Germany and Britain, the war took that 'unexpected turn' much sooner than expected.

In the summer of 1943 US heavy bombers began mounting deep-penetration daylight attacks on targets in Germany itself, and escort fighters accompanied them progressively deeper into Germany. For the Me 262 this change in the war situation brought about a reversal of its fortunes. With its excellent turn of speed and powerful armament, the Me 262 was seen as a fine home defence fighter. Suddenly the Luftwaffe had a clear operational requirement for a fighter with those capabilities. In the summer of 1943 the Luftwaffe ordered the

Me 262 into large-scale production, confident that Junkers would soon solve the Jumo 004 turbojet's reliability problems. The schedule called for initial production aircraft to be appear in January 1944, with output rising to sixty aircraft per month by the end of May. From now on the Me 262 was the white hope for the future of the Luftwaffe fighter force.

In Great Britain the mood changed just as abruptly, and at almost the same time. Disturbing intelligence reports from Germany told of novel types of air weapon under development there, including high-speed fighters powered by turbojet engines and rockets. Following a directive from Prime Minister Winston Churchill, the Meteor was ordered into production with an order for 120 aircraft. Later this was increased to 300.

Thus, by the beginning of 1944, the RAF and the Luftwaffe each had a turbojet-powered fighter type in production. Both were ordered for use as home defence fighters, however, so the chance of their meeting in action was small (in fact, they never did). In the event, however, neither the Me 262 nor the Meteor was the first jet-propelled fighter to go into action. That honour went to the Messerschmitt Me 163, a small rocket-propelled target defence fighter. The development of the rocket

Wearing a special suit to give protection from contact with the volatile T-Stoff *fuel, a pilot boards a Messerschmitt Me 163. The small dimensions of the rocket-powered fighter are readily apparent in this photo.*

fighter outpaced that of the two turbojet powered types, and the Me 163 began flying practice interceptions against Allied aircraft in May 1944.

Power for the Me 163 came from a Walter 509A bi-fuel rocket motor. This ran on two liquid chemical fuels, code-named 'T-Stoff' and 'C-Stoff' by the Germans. T-Stoff was highly concentrated hydrogen peroxide, an unstable and highly corrosive compound liable to decompose on contact with copper, lead or almost anything combustible. When it decomposed, the chemical produced heat at a rate similar to that of gunpowder. Not least of its unendearing qualities was that it would decompose violently if it came into contact with human flesh. At take-off the Me 163 carried more than 1.5 tonnes of the vile liquid, which must have done little for the pilot's peace of mind. The other fuel carried by the fighter, C-Stoff, was a relatively stable combination of methyl alcohol, hydrazine hydrate and a little water. The two fuels came together in the rocket's combustion chamber in the ratio of about three parts of T-Stoff to one part of C-Stoff. This caused a violent chemical reaction that produced a jet of superheated steam and nitrogen with a velocity of 1,980m/sec (6,500ft/sec) and a temperature of 1,800°C. That gave a thrust of 1,700kg (3,750lb).

When an Me 163 took off, just over half of its weight was fuel. At full thrust the Walter 509A consumed about 8kg (18lb) of fuel *per second*. That was *fifteen times* more than a pair of contemporary turbojet engines developing the same level of thrust. Because of this voracious appetite, the Me 163 carried sufficient fuel to run the

rocket motor at full power for only four minutes. Once the fighter had reached its operational altitude and accelerated to fighting speed, the pilot would shut down the motor and deliver his attack coasting along at high speed. As the fighter slowed, the pilot fired the rocket in short bursts to restore his fighting speed. In this way he could extend the Me 163's endurance at high altitude to about eight minutes, giving the fighter an effective combat radius of action of about 40km (25 miles) from base. Because of the explosive nature of the T-Stoff, it was important to exhaust the fuel before landing, and the rocket fighter returned to base as a glider. However, as some Me 163 pilots discovered to their cost, gliding could be an unhealthy activity in areas where American escort fighters were on the prowl.

The Me 163 had a sparkling speed and climbing performance, yet it operated too close to the limits of what was possible for it to achieve much in action. Moreover, the T-Stoff was rather too exciting for general service use, and the fighter's formidable rate of fuel consumption gave it a very restricted radius of action. At the peak of its deployment there were just under a hundred Me 163s in service with two front-line Gruppen, yet there were never more than thirty of them serviceable, and on no day did more than ten of the rocket fighters go into action. On its most successful day the Me 163 shot down only four enemy aircraft. In its service career lasting almost a year, it is doubtful whether the rocket fighter accounted for more than sixteen enemy aircraft in total.

It will be remembered that the Meteor I had been placed in production to counter the threat from the novel

Trailing smoke from its exhaust, an Me 163 begins its take-off run.

During the final six months of the war the Luftwaffe had no shortage of Me 262 fighters, but providing pilots with adequate training and supporting the type in service gave severe problems.

Problems Common to all Early Turbojet-powered Aircraft

All of the early turbojet engines were temperamental and required very careful handling. Moreover, as speed was reduced the ram effect of the air lessened and the engine's power dropped away. Once speed had fallen beyond a certain point, for example on the landing approach, the turbojet responded very slowly to any movement of the throttle. In that event the pilot was committed to continuing the landing even if he had misjudged his approach. If he advanced the throttles and tried to overshoot, the aircraft was likely to strike the ground before it gained sufficient speed to commence a climb away. This limitation became particularly important for the Luftwaffe during the final months of the war. Marauding Allied fighters often caught German jet fighters on the landing approach, where they were unable to take any evasive action and fell as easy prey.

Another problem with the early jet fighters was that they had a short endurance, of the order of 45 minutes. Since they cruised much faster than the piston-engined machines the pilots had flown previously, navigation was far more difficult. Several of the early jets were wrecked because their pilots became lost, ran short of fuel and were forced to bale out. Clearly, those early jet fighters were not suitable mounts for inexperienced pilots.

types of attack weapon being developed in Germany. On 13 June 1944 the first of these, the V1 flying bomb, went into action. Between then and the end of the month more than 2,400 of these missiles were launched against London. About a third of the flying bombs smashed into the City, where they caused widespread destruction.

Distinctly underpowered, the Meteor I was certainly no great performer, yet it had a significant advantage over the available piston-engined fighters. Between sea level and 4,000ft (1,220m), the band of sky inhabited by flying bombs, its maximum speed of 385mph (620km/h) was about 30mph (48km/h) faster than anything else. That was sufficient to spell the difference between the success and failure in the interception of a V1. A single squadron of Meteors was hastily formed and sent into action against the robot weapons. During August 1944 the Meteors accounted for thirteen flying bombs, most of which fell to cannon fire. However, on one famous occasion a Meteor with jammed guns manoeuvred into formation alongside a V1 and the pilot nudged up the flying bomb's wing to flip it out of control. Towards the end of August Allied ground forces overran the V1 launching sites in northern France, and the main bombardment ended.

Meanwhile, what of the Me 262? In May 1944, as a means of countering the expected Allied seaborne invasion of north-west Europe, Adolf Hitler ordered that all new Me 262s coming off the production line be modified to serve as fighter-bombers rather than fighters. Some writers have made too much of this edict, asserting

Early Jet Fighters					*Figures for initial production version of each type*
Type	Entered service	Engine thrust	Max. speed	Weight (normal loaded)	Armament
Messerschmitt Me 163B	Mar 1944	Rocket 1 × 1,700kg 1 × 3,750lb	953km/h 592mph	4,308kg 9,500lb	2 × 30mm
Messerschmitt Me 262A	Apr 1944	Turbojet 2 × 900kg 2 × 1,984lb	870km/h 540mph	4,417kg 9,740lb	4 × 30mm
Gloster Meteor I	Jul 1944	Turbojet 2 × 1,700lb 2 × 770kg	410mph 660km/h	11,800lb 5,351kg	4 × 20mm

that it played a serious part in delaying the Me 262's entry into action as a fighter. In fact, the Jumo 004 engine was still not reliable enough for the design to be 'frozen' for large-scale production. Although it caused consternation in the Luftwaffe at the time, Hitler's order made remarkably little difference.

In September 1944 Hitler rescinded his edict and, coincidentally, the nominal running life of the Jumo 004 engine finally reached twenty-five hours. Its 'life' was still painfully short, but at last the turbojet could enter mass production.

At the end of September the Me 262 underwent its first operational deployment as a fighter, when Kommando Nowotny deployed with twenty-three of the jets to airfields in northwest Germany. The venture ended in failure. Poor serviceability dogged the jet fighter, imposing severe constraints on its effectiveness. Although the new production Jumo 004 engines had longer nominal running lives than their predecessors, they still gave a lot of trouble. Also, the airframe of the Me 262 had its share of 'bugs' that needed to be ironed out.

For their part, the Allied fighter pilots soon discovered the Achilles' heel of the jet fighter. If it could be caught flying at low speed, immediately after take-off or on the landing approach, it was extremely vulnerable. To counter the jets, Allied fighters began mounting standing patrols over the airfields they used.

During just over a month of operations on the western front, Kommando Nowotny claimed the destruction of four American heavy bombers, twelve fighters and three reconnaissance aircraft. In achieving this meagre total, the unit lost seven Me 262s in combat, while seven more were destroyed and nine damaged in accidents or following technical failures. Worst of all, fighter ace Major Walter Nowotny, the unit's commander, was killed in action. It had not been an auspicious start to the Me

262's combat career. In mid-October the Kommando withdrew from operations so that its pilots could receive further training and its jet fighters could be modified. Nowotny had been given an impossible task; to introduce a revolutionary new fighter into combat in an area where the enemy held almost total air superiority. The unit's general level of training was low, and serviceability of the Me 262 was so poor that rarely could it put up more than five aircraft at the same time.

By the beginning of 1945 Me 262s were coming off the assembly lines at a rate of about thirty-six per week. Following the earlier débâcle it was decided that when the jet fighter next went into action it would do so in strength, as a fully working system and flown by fully trained pilots. Owing to poor weather and the all-pervading Allied air superiority, however, pilot conversion training in the winter of 1944/5 took much longer than expected. Only in February 1945 were the Me 262 fighter units ready to re-enter the fray, and not until the following month did they start to launch large-scale attacks on American bomber formations. During the final two months of the war the jet fighter units waged a losing battle against enemy air forces with vast numerical superiority. The cold statistics highlight the Me 262's lack of effectiveness under such conditions:

Total Me 262s delivered to
the Luftwaffe by May 1945:   more than 1,200
Greatest number of Me 262
fighters in service (April 1945):   about 110
Greatest number of Me 262 fighter
sorties in a day (7 April 1945):   59
Greatest number of Me 262 victories
in a day (31 March 1945):   16

Several postwar writers have derided Luftwaffe leaders for failing to get the Me 262 into large-scale

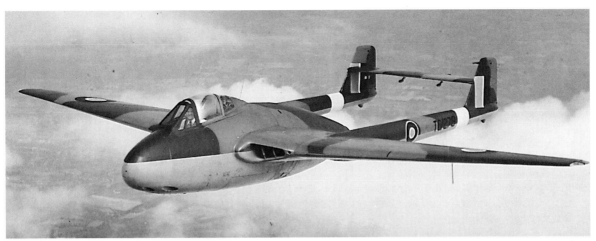

The de Havilland Vampire I jet fighter outclassed the Spitfire XIV, one of the best air superiority fighters at the end of the Second World War, in almost every aspect of combat performance.

production early enough. Yet, as we have seen, if anything the production of the aircraft was initiated too early, and Me 262 airframes started coming off the assembly lines before the engine to power them was ready for mass production. Nor did Adolf Hitler's order regarding the initial use of the Me 262 as a fighter-bomber cause any appreciable delay in the type's operational introduction as a fighter. First and always, the main factor

---

How they Compared:

De Havilland Vampire I *versus* Spitfire XIV

During the Second World War the jet fighter types that went into action produced uniformly disappointing results in terms of the number of enemy aircraft they shot down. However, there can be no doubt that, had the war continued a few months longer, this picture would have changed radically. In 1946 the RAF flew a comparative trial in which it pitted a de Havilland Vampire I with a Goblin II engine against a Spitfire XIV. As has been seen elsewhere, the Spitfire XIV was one of the most effective piston-engined fighters at the end of the war. Yet as these excerpts from the official report show, the Vampire outclassed the Spitfire in every aspect of combat performance that really mattered.

Maximum level speed The Vampire is greatly superior in speed to the Spitfire XIV at all heights. Its speed advantage is shown below:

Altitude			
ground level		140mph	(225km/h)
5,000ft	(1,500m)	120mph	(193km/h)
10,000ft	(3,000m)	110mph	(177km/h)
15,000ft	(4,600m)	110mph	(177km/h)
20,000ft	(6,100m)	105mph	(169km/h)
25,000ft	(7,600m)	85mph	(136km/h)
30,000ft	(9,100m)	70mph	(112km/h)
40,000ft	(12,200m)	90mph	(145km/h)

Acceleration and deceleration With both aircraft in line-abreast formation at a speed of 200mph (322km/h) indicated, on the word 'Go' both engines were opened up to a maximum power simultaneously. The Spitfire initially drew ahead, but after a period of approximately 25 seconds the Vampire gradually caught up and quickly accelerated past the Spitfire. The rate of deceleration for the Spitfire is faster than the Vampire even when the Vampire uses its dive brakes. This shows that the Vampire's dive brakes are not as effective as they should be.

Dive The two aircraft were put into a 40° dive in line-abreast formation with set throttles at a speed 250mph (indicated, 400km/h). The Vampire rapidly drew ahead and kept gaining on the Spitfire. *continued*

---

continued

Zoom climb The Vampire and Spitfire XIV in line-abreast formation were put into a 45° dive. When a speed of 400mph (indicated, 644km/h) had been reached, a zoom climb at fixed throttle settings was carried out at approximately 50°. The Vampire showed itself vastly superior and reached a height 1,000ft (300m) in excess of the altitude of the Spitfire in a few seconds, and quickly increased its lead as the zoom climb continued. The same procedure was carried out at full throttle settings and the Vampire's advantage was outstandingly marked.

Climb The Spitfire XIV climbs approximately 1,000ft per minute (5.08m/sec) faster than the Vampire up to 20,000ft (6,100m).

Turning circles The Vampire is superior to the Spitfire XIV at all heights. The two aircraft were flown in line-astern formation. The Spitfire was positioned on the Vampire's tail. Both aircraft tightened up to the minimum turning circle with maximum power. It became apparent that the Vampire was just able to keep inside the Spitfire's turning circles. After four or five turns the Vampire was able to position itself on the Spitfire's tail so that a deflection shot was possible. The wing loading of the Vampire is 33.1lb sq ft (1.39kg/m²) compared with the Spitfire XIV's 35.1lb sq ft (on the aircraft tested, 1.48 kg/m²).

Rates of roll The Spitfire XIV has a faster rate of roll at all speeds. The higher the speed the faster the Spitfire rolls in comparison with the Vampire. At speeds of 500mph (indicated, 805km/h) there is a feeling of overbalance and aileron snatch when attempting to roll the Vampire.

Combat manoeuvrability The Vampire will outmanoeuvre the Spitfire type of aircraft at all heights, except for initial acceleration at low speeds and in rolling. Due to the Vampire's much higher speed and superior zoom climb, the Spitfire can gain no advantage by using its superior rate of climb in combat.

---

limiting the Me 262's capabilities in combat was the short running life and general unreliability of its Jumo 004 engines. Despite imaginative efforts by the Junkers engineers, even in the spring of 1945 the 004 was not a fully reliable unit. As a result, the Me 262 never came close to living up to its original promise.

At the beginning of 1944 it had seemed that the side which was first to bring into service large numbers of jet aircraft would gain a huge advantage in the battle for air supremacy. Certainly the jets had the potential to win that supremacy for, particularly in the case of the German aircraft, their performance was far in advance of anything previously achieved. Yet due to poor serviceability these aeroplanes went into action only in relatively small numbers. In a large-scale conflict a few aeroplanes, no matter how brilliant their flying performance, cannot and did not secure decisive results.

In the event the German and British jet fighters achieved remarkably little in action. Had they not seen combat, the outcome of the war would not have been different in any material respect.

Bibliography

Ethell, J, and Price, A, *World War II Fighting Jets* (Airlife, Shrewsbury, 1994). Account of the development and service careers of the nine jet-propelled aircraft that entered service before the end of the Second World War.

Francillon, R J, *Japanese Aircraft of the Pacific War* (Putnam, London, 1970). Standard reference work on Japanese military aircraft during the Second World War.

Green, W, *Warplanes of the Second World War*, Volumes 1 to 4 (Macdonald, London, 1961). Useful general reference work on fighter aircraft during this period.

Green, W, *Warplanes of the Third Reich* (Macdonald, London, 1970). A standard reference work on German aircraft before and during the Second World War.

Gunston, W, *Aircraft of the Soviet Union* (Osprey, London, 1983). Standard reference work on Soviet aircraft from 1917 to 1982.

Price, A, *Battle over the Reich* (Ian Allan, Shepperton, 1973). Account of the air attacks on Germany during the period 1939 to 1945, and the development of the German air defence system.

Price, A, *Blitz on Britain* (Ian Allan, Shepperton, 1977). Account of the air attacks on Great Britain during the period 1939 to 1945, and the development of the British air defence system.

Price, A, *Fighter Aircraft* (Arms & Armour Press, London, 1989). Account of the development of the day fighter aircraft before and during the Second World War.

Price, A, *The Spitfire Story* (Arms & Armour Press, London, 2nd Edition 1995). Detailed and comprehensive account of the development of the Spitfire.

4

The Bomber Revolution

M J F Bowyer

When hostilities commenced in September 1939, it took hundreds of bombers and thousands of bombs to wreck a major city. When hostilities ceased, one bomber using one bomb could cripple, indeed almost destroy, an entire nation. Such was the bomber revolution.

Eleven minutes before Germany declared war on Poland, three Junkers Ju 87Bs of 3./StG 1 screamed down to pulverise the approaches to the river Vistula's Dirshau bridge. The brutish, spine chilling Stuka terror had been unleashed to start what their crews termed 'the easy war', only the weather preventing their friends in Heinkels from smashing Warsaw. However, they had miscalculated; in a year's time they would be fighting a very tough war with very inadequate bombers.

The spatted-undercarriage 4,350kg (10,000lb) Ju 87B carried a 500kg (1,100lb) bomb on a centreline cradle, supplemented by four 50kg (110lb) bombs beneath each wing, in which a 7.9mm (0.3in) MG 17 machine-gun was installed. All was finely tuned in the most effective, lightest mainstream bomber, which had a top speed of about 370km/h (230mph) at 4,115m (13,500ft), and a cruising speed of 187km/h at 4,572m (175mph at 15,000ft). A weakness the Ju 87 shared with many German bombers was its limited fuel capacity, giving a mere 595km (370 miles) normal range. That mattered little until the easy war turned hard and the distances increased.

In September 1939 nine Stuka Gruppen nominally fielded 335 aircraft – mostly Ju 87B-1s – which ruthlessly dive-bombed Polish communications, preventing reinforcements from reaching the front. Heinkel He 111s, of which 800 were operational, soon carried out massive raids upon Warsaw's worthwhile targets with little regard for collateral damage. Dornier Do 17s assisted others attacking encircled Polish forces and carried out interdiction raids. With German air superiority quickly established, armoured forces with air support raced forward in the first blitzkrieg; slowly the world came to terms with the fact that Germany had caused a major war. Could it muster the resources and supplies needed to win? How could Britain be hit hard from the Fatherland without long-range bombers? What about the RAF – was it really able to bomb Germany effectively from bases in Britain?

The British experience

Britain's bomber force, quite different from that of Germany, had been assembled to carry out a strategic campaign intended to destroy the German capacity to wage war and to help sink its navy. For those purposes it was using long-range, twin-engine bombers, and a second generation was emerging, bigger and necessarily four-engined because pairs of available engines no longer provided sufficient power. All would spend much time over hostile territory, and because long-duration fighters were not available, defensive guns in heavy power-operated turrets would, hopefully, fully protect them. These turrets added nothing to offensive results, which was one reason why German bombers were generally defended by a few single or paired guns in light mountings, usually manually trained.

At the outbreak of war Bomber Command's six Vickers-Armstrongs Wellington squadrons were rearming with the Mk 1a, fitted with Frazer-Nash two-gun

The Junkers Ju 87B-2 of 1940, a traditional form of 'Stuka' dive bomber.

Between 1939 and 1941 the Heinkel He 111H was the Luftwaffe's principal medium bomber.

The Vickers-Armstrongs Wellington Ic's nose and tail turrets were typical of those fitted to 1940s British bombers. This machine, R3175, wears the codes of No 149 Squadron.

nose and tail turrets. On the first day of war Wellingtons searched in vain for German naval ships until storms and darkness closed in. Next day, fourteen aircraft of Nos 9 and 149 Squadrons, operating off Brunsbüttel, met fierce AA fire which claimed two Wellingtons. Such operations were mounted up to the end of 1939. On 3 December twenty-four Wellingtons were sent in daylight to attack naval ships near Heligoland. German radar, its

Slim lines and a slender boom carrying the tail surfaces reduced the Handley Page Hampden's surface area and drag. These are No 408 Squadron aircraft.

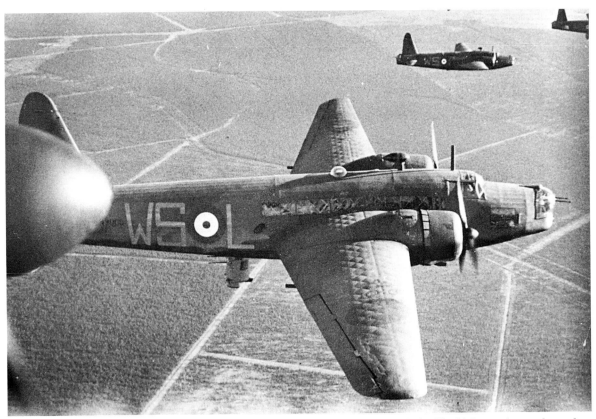

A Vickers Wellington Ic of No 9 Squadron near Honington in 1940, with its drag-inducing 'dustbin' ventral turret lowered.

presence unknown, tracked them, intense accurate AA fire greeted them and cloud cover helped to protect them. Two badly damaged Wellingtons crash-landed on return.

With only nose and tail turrets defending many Wellingtons, the Air Staff on 6 December 1939 decided that seventy-seven must be fitted with retractable belly turrets. A dozen Wellingtons of No 99 Squadron so equipped set off in daylight on 13 December for the Schillig Roads. An 800ft (244m) cloudbase did not stop AA guns firing and German fighters being vectored on to the bombers, which, despite holding their formations, fought a disastrous battle. Five were shot down, another later crashed, and only one fighter was destroyed. In Bomber Command's opinion it was the cloudy weather that made the operation difficult.

Stubborn belief remained that bombers could hold their own in daylight, and not until 18 December 1939, when twenty-four Wellington Ias of Nos 9, 37 and 149 Squadrons headed for warships reported off Wilhelmshaven, was reality accepted. Flying in four formations at about 14,000ft (4,267m), they skirted 'flak-ships' and then German fighters pounced. Easily evading turret fire by bearing down upon the Wellingtons' blind beams, they shot down ten bombers,

and two more later ditched. German pilots of JG 1 reckoned that by keeping formation, giving ineffective crossfire, the bombers actually made interception easier.

Between 3 September and 18 December 1939 RAF Bomber Command's Handley Page Hampdens, Wellingtons and Bristol Blenheims flew 861 daylight sorties and dropped 61 tons of bombs for a loss of forty-one bombers and highly trained Regular air force crews. That amounted to ten per cent of Command average daily strength. Ten German fighters had been shot down and three warships damaged.

Protection of bombers could only come with concealment, something which darkness could provide. That generated many problems, not the least of which would be target acquisition at night. The Germans had been working on that problem, making use of radio beams, and soon the British would need to do likewise. Bomber Command, with no choice, switched to mainly night operations in February 1940. Operational flying in darkness emphasised needs for much technical development including new equipment, improved signals and homing systems and airfield lighting. General agreement was reached on 10 January 1940 that four-gun tail turrets, first suggested by Vickers in October 1936, must be fitted to Wellingtons, although it was mid-1941 before

Had the Fairey Battle been smaller and Griffon engined, it might have proved very useful. These three belong to No 226 Squadron.

that came about. On 7 February orders were given to fit additional armour and self-sealing fuel tanks. A lowered belly turret cut the Wellington's speed by 15mph (24km/h), so on 15 May 1940 the decision was taken to replace it with beam guns, saving 500lb (225kg), and the idea was extended to new bombers. Beam guns were a transient feature, all British 'heavies' by 1942 having two-gun dorsal turrets.

Whereas Germany updated its bomber designs throughout the war, Britain introduced completely new types, upgrading only the Wellington. A potentially faster Merlin-engined Mk II for tropical use made its first flight on 3 March 1939, but tailplane troubles caused development to continue mainly with the Pegasus-powered variant. A stronger undercarriage allowed increased weight, and a 24V electrical system improved equipment performance. When, in August 1940, supplies of Pegasus engines were in doubt, pick-up points on Wellington nacelles, designed to cope with a variety of engines, led to an order to fill the gap with Merlin Xs in 200 airframes. The Air Ministry insisted that a Pratt & Whitney Twin Wasp 1,830hp version should go ahead as the Mk IV, although the Mks Ic and III (Bristol Hercules) would remain standard versions. On 31 March 1941 two Wellington IIs became the first bombers to drop a 4,000lb (1,810kg) bomb each, Emden being the target.

The need for heating, ample oxygen and extra crew comfort were evident during long night flights, as was the need for navigation aids over blacked-out areas. All aircraft needed ready escape exits for use after ditching, along with dinghies; crews required ample training and an air/sea rescue service.

Dropping largely ineffective bombs and avoiding civilian targets, Bomber Command was going to find it difficult to penetrate heavily defended areas, especially in poor weather. But some hard lessons had been administered in good time, for to have launched large bombers in daylight during the German western offensive would have been catastrophic. Instead, the planned strategic night bombing offensive against the Ruhr and Rhineland began when ninety-six bombers set out on 15/16 May 1940. Only twenty-four crews even claimed to have found their targets. The task ahead, to wage an effective strategic bombing offensive, was daunting; how bad things might have been was shown by the RAF's light bomber squadrons.

To support the British Army

Britain's two other bomber types were regarded by Bomber Command as irrelevant, as they were developed for army support to a 1,000lb (454kg) bomb load, 1,000-mile (1,609km) range requirement. Larger than a Ju 87, the 10,900lb (4,940kg), 54ft-span (16.4m) single-engine Fairey Battle carried the prescribed bomb load for 1,000 miles (1,610km) but failed on other counts. The intention had been to power it with a 1,500hp Rolls-Royce Griffon engine based upon the 'R' engine used by the 1931 Schneider Trophy winners. Non-availability forced Fairey to turn to its 1,700hp 24-cylinder Prince double engine driving contrarotating propellers, but its complexity caused the company to fit a 1,000hp Rolls-Royce Merlin. The Battle was thus seriously underpowered, its cruising speed falling to a mere 148mph (238km/h) at 15,000ft (4,570m). French-based Battles

Four 250lb General Purpose bombs formed the internal load of the Bristol Blenheim Mk I.

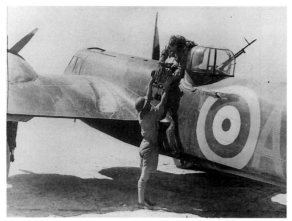

An F.24 camera is taken aboard a Blenheim I of No 211 Squadron in 1940. Many Blenheim sorties were for reconnaissance purposes.

proved useless for stemming the German invasion despite the great courage and sacrifice of their crews, mauled during futile shallow-dive and medium-level bombing escapades. Between 10 May and 20 June 1940, 115 Battles were destroyed during operational flying, the highest loss rate for any British bomber.

The Bristol Blenheim fared little better. Defended by a fixed wing gun and another in a manually traversed turret, it was vulnerable to fighter interception but tough enough to take considerable punishment. Survival came mostly through defensive tactics worked out in 1939 by Wg Cdr Basil Embry; a formation embracing vics of three aircraft, stepped up and if possible having other vics on the flanks, provided maximum protective crossfire. The need for well-conceived bomber formations and finely executed fighter protection was a lesson all air forces bought dearly.

Like the Battles, 2 Group Blenheims were hurled into action in May 1940, usually fatally, without fighter cover. Gunfire broke apart their formations, allowing Bf 109 fighters to pick off the bombers. No longer 'faster than a fighter', the Blenheim IV (two 920hp Bristol Mercury radials) had a top speed of 227mph (365km/h) at sea level and 266mph (365km/h) at 11,870ft (3,618m). At 15,000ft (4,572m) it cruised at 180mph (290km/h), carrying a 1,000lb (454kg) bomb load for a creditable 1,460 miles (2,349km). Until 1943 the Blenheim IV remained an army support aircraft, although it was much used as a mainstream bomber for daylight 'nuisance' raids. At night Blenheims bombed Channel ports and heavy guns, then during the 1940–41 winter they took part in Bomber Command's main night offensive before intensively operating against shipping; tasks for which the type was never intended.

Another easy war?

On 1 April 1940, 1,726 of the Luftwaffe's 5,178 operational aircraft were bombers and 419 were dive-bombers, many shortly to be committed to the invasion of Norway, an operation undertaken to secure iron ore supplies from Sweden and provide bomber bases from which Britain could be attacked. By capturing the Benelux countries and northern France, more suitable bases were obtained. Junkers Ju 87s had supported rapid troop advances, particularly at the Meuse

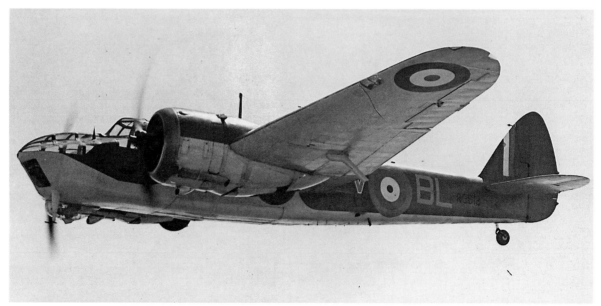

The unusual geometry of the Blenheim IV's nose improved the navigator/bomb aimer's accommodation. Beneath it is a rearward-firing, periscopically sighted gun. This is a No 40 Squadron aircraft.

river crossing. The Luftwaffe protected and supported the army, Do 17s and He 111s mainly carrying out day and night raids on cities, airfields, industrial premises, troops, transport and rail targets. When surrender negotiations were under way and the 9th Panzer Division was at the edge of the city, KG 54's He 111s took out the heart of Rotterdam, killing 800 and making 80,000 citizens homeless in a menacing and cruel five-hour onslaught. By mid-1940, with France vanquished, the Luftwaffe could look back with satisfaction upon its war work, albeit at a cost of 491 bombers and 113 Stukas lost in action during May and June; this total was thirty per cent of the entire bomber force.

Italian interlude

When Italy declared war in June 1940 a very different aspect of the bombing campaign was immediately dis-

Long-span, high-aspect-ratio wings gave the Vickers Armstrongs Wellesley lengthy duration. The underwing panniers housed the bomb load. This is L2654 of No 14 Squadron.

played. The Italians held Abyssinia, Eritrea and Somaliland, and the RAF faced them with four squadrons holding many of the 80 Vickers Wellesley bombers dispatched overseas out of 176 built. The Wellesley's size belied its general-purpose light bomber role, sailplane-like wings making it appear frail. In reality, geodetic construction conferred great strength, allowing Wellesleys to accept heavy punishment and still reach home. Spanning 74ft 6in (22.7m), those high-aspect-ratio wings had an exceptionally low wing loading of 19lb/ft², and ideally supported the aircraft during arduous sorties involving eight hours' flying over the wild East African mountains. Not surprisingly, the two-man crew needed strong faith in their machine and especially its single 925hp Bristol Pegasus XX engine. Only 39ft 1in (12m) long, weighing only 6,812lb (3,090kg) empty and 11,128lb (5,048kg) loaded, the Wellesley carried up to 496.5gal (2,257 litres) of fuel, and, cruising at about 180mph (290km/h) at 15,000ft (4,572m), its range was 1,340 miles (2,156km). At full throttle the Wellesley could reach 200mph (322km/h) at 20,100ft (6,126m).

In 1938 modified Wellesleys set a world long-distance record by flying non-stop from Ismailia (Egypt) to Darwin – a journey of 7,162 miles (11,525km) completed in just over forty-eight hours. Such exceptional range came not by chance, British bombers having been conceived with needs to reinforce garrisons in overseas territories where distances were enormous.

Wellesleys proved ideal for East African operations, No 14 Squadron on the first day of war mounting a long-distance raid on Massawa. Facing heavy anti-aircraft fire, the slow-flying, unwieldy bombers repeatedly bombed airfields, railways, dumps and in particular the two very busy Eritrean Red Sea ports of Assab and Massawa. Their meagre 1,377lb (625kg) bomb load was carried within two large panniers slung beneath the wings.

A lesson for Britain

Such African activity was utterly different and remote from the ferocious fight about to break out over England for, at the start of July 1940, the Luftwaffe was to unleash its Stukas again. So powerful would be the blows that full-bloodied invasion would be unnecessary. Shipping, ports, industry and the remnants of the RAF would be obliterated, and the civilian population blasted into submission.

Brazenly the Ju 87s sallied forth across the English Channel and immediately encountered something unexpected. Their short range, even with an external long-range tank beneath each wing producing the Ju 87R (R for 'Reichweit', or range) was insufficient, but a far greater shock came when the Stukas encountered, for the first time, radar controlled, skilfully assembled and highly effective fighter defences against which their almost non-existant self-defence rendered them easy prey. All German bomber crews discovered during the Battle of Britain that only plentiful fighter protection could ensure survival, and it was not always to hand.

A hard war

On 4 July thirty-three Ju 87Bs of III./StG 51 attempted the first dive-bombing of Portland, where they encountered strong defences. By 20 July 1940 battle casualties had cut the Ju 87 force by a third, to 248 aircraft out of its intended holding of 316, and by the time the Luftwaffe launched its main Battle of Britain offensive the Stuka's superiority was ousted by revolutionary change.

At about 0830 on 12 August a group of Messerschmitt Bf 110s roared along the English Channel, sections peeling away. They were were no ordinary Bf 110 escort fighters, but fighter-bombers. Delivering fast, shallow-dive and low-level bombing attacks on south coast radar stations, they replaced the tactical light bomber and then reverted to being fighters.

Changing the Messerschmitt Bf 110 fighter into a fighter-bomber was a novel idea with everlasting consequences.

Germany's most ubiquitous warplane, the Junkers Ju 88, carried its offensive load externally.

Long range made the Martin Maryland valuable for photographic reconnaissance. This Maryland I was under test in Britain in November 1941.

Developed from the Maryland, the less cramped Baltimore served with the RAF in North Africa. This aircraft, Baltimore I AG688, was evaluated at the A&AEE in late 1941.

Strike and support aircraft would never be the same again, a point re-emphasised when, at midday, Bf 110 fighter-bombers hit RAF Manston, paving the way for a Dornier Do 17Z medium-level raid. The Ju 87s were left behind to annoy Channel shipping.

That protected Ju 87s could still inflict serious damage was proven when forty smashed Detling. On 15 August others closed the major RAF anti-invasion base at Lympne for two days, and on 16 August Stukas effectively dive-bombed Tangmere, Ventnor radar station and Lee-on-Solent's hangars. But the Tangmere raid alone cost nine Ju 87Bs, almost half the attacking force. Two days later, when Ju 87s and Ju 88s attacked Ford, Thorney Island and Poling Chain Home (CH) station, RAF fighters shot down sixteen Ju 87s. Another two were write-offs and four were seriously damaged. With thirty-nine Ju 87s shot down in two weeks of operations against England, their raids halted and they moved, congregating in the Pas de Calais, awaiting to support their army in an invasion which was impossible to mount.

The lessons the Battle of Britain gave to the Luftwaffe bomber force were blatant. Heinkel He 111s, Dornier Do 17s and even the newer Junkers Ju 88s were very poorly defended, and there were insufficient fighters, all with inadequate range, to protect them completely. Now, like the RAF, the Luftwaffe was forced into a night-bombing campaign. It started officially on 16 September 1940, which greatly increased accident rates, especially as winter closed in, but radio-guided blind bombing led to more accurate night attacks.

When the cost of the battle between July and September was counted it showed an overall loss of 78 Ju 87s and 621 medium bombers. That rate was unsustainable. The RAF, desperately defending its homeland, not only fought well but drew upon reserves cleverly and safely mustered by Air Chief Marshal Sir Hugh Dowding well beyond reach of the raiding forces.

The American input
Before the war, Europeans had shopped across the Atlantic, France for bombers and Britain for advanced trainers. One purchase was the Lockheed 14 airliner. Displaying modern features and the comfort typical of US combat aircraft, it was easily modified into the Hudson reconnaissance bomber.

In July 1940 more American-built combat aircraft began arriving in Britain, mainly fugitives from the contracts of vanquished nations. Although they had modern items such as variable-pitch propellers, flaps, good air-cooled engines, nosewheel undercarriages and high standards of personnel comfort, most were ill-equipped for the European conflict. Their duration and speed were acceptable, but not their poor armament and small bomb loads. They had been designed either to drive off America's southern neighbours or defend the USA by attacking the Japanese navy.

Rated highly was the three-seat Glenn Martin Model 167F Maryland bomber, 75 of the French order for 215 ultimately reaching the British. The 61ft 4in (18.6m) span aircraft, with a loaded weight of 17,890lb (8,115kg), had a respectable top speed of 294mph at 13,000ft (473km/h at 3,962m) and a maximum range of 1,870 miles at 179mph (3,009km at 288km/h). Unfortunately its maximum bomb load was only 1,800lb (816kg), and that for short-range operations. For defence the Maryland relied upon two 0.30in (7.62mm) guns, making it quite useless. As with many other US aircraft, the British used them for purposes other than intended, the Maryland undertaking long-range photographic reconnaissance. Among other coups, it secured the photographs upon which the Royal Navy's Taranto raid of 11 November 1940 was based. The British ordered 150 Maryland Mk IIs which, with speed boosted by more powerful engines, were used for formation level bombing raids over North Africa, where opposing fighters included Italian biplanes.

The Maryland's 1940 successor, the Model 187 Baltimore, drew upon combat feedback. The view through the additional nose glazing was improved, a deeper fuselage allowed crew contact, and self-sealing fuel tanks, bulletproof glass, additional armour and

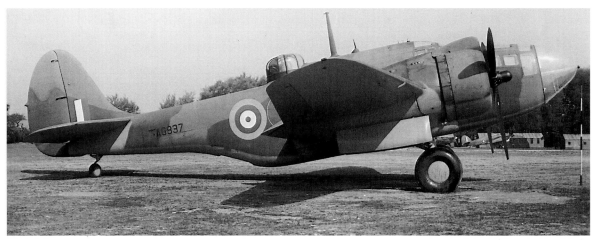

As the lightly defended Baltimores proved easy prey to fighters, the Mk III featured a dorsal turret.

400hp more power from two 1,600hp Wright Double Cyclone GR-2600-A5B engines were all useful changes. Increasing the bomb load even to 2,000lb (910kg) was not easy, but armament was much improved, at one stage totalling eleven guns. Four, ventrally mounted, were to administer a parting gesture after low-level bombing. Wing-mounted fixed guns, of little value in a bomber, were replaced in other US aircraft such as the Douglas A-20, North American B-25 and Martin B-26 by gun packs on the sides of the nose, or by guns in a 'solid' nose for ground strafing.

When the Baltimore went into action on 23 May 1942, its poor manually traversed gun defence was only too obviously inadequate, for fighters shot down three

bombers. A four 0.303in (7.69mm) turret version, the Baltimore III, had an all-up weight of 23,000lb (10,430kg), attained 302mph (486km/h) at 11,000ft (3,350m) and had a range of 950 miles (1,530km) when carrying a 2,000lb (9078kg) bomb load.

The first American bomber to see combat in Europe was the shapely all-metal, stressed-skin Douglas DB-7 with nosewheel undercarriage and radial air-cooled Pratt & Whitney Wasp engines. The prototype, flown in December 1938, was by early 1939 showing a creditable top speed of 314mph (505km/h) and a climb rate of half-a-mile a minute. Only thirty reached France before it collapsed, the residue beginning to arrive in England during July 1940. Although fast, the 105 ex-French

The most effective US light bomber was the short-range but speedy Douglas A-20G Boston IV, which was ideal for low-level attacks as well as formation daylight raids. Seen here is BZ403 under test.

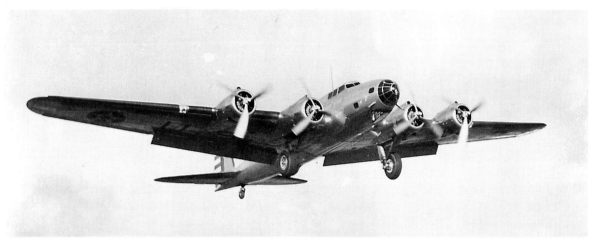

A sound design, Boeing's Model 299, the predecessor of all B-17 Flying Fortresses, first flew on 28 July 1935.

DB-7s, supplemented by sixteen from a Belgian order, were poorly armed and too short of range to reach Germany. Special training was needed because of the nosewheel gear, so the first nineteen examples were after modification set aside as Boston I trainers. Major improvements soon followed. The Pratt & Whitney Wasps were replaced by Wright double-row Cyclones and more aerodynamically satisfactory nacelles were fitted to the DB-7A. Stability was improved by increased-area vertical tail surfaces, but the type's short duration remained a drawback.

The US Army had ordered the DB-7 as the A-20, the engine change from Pratt & Whitney to Wright R-2600-3 being a feature of 143 A-20As, each able to carry a 1,100lb (500kg) bomb load. The A-20B/DB-7A, the first effective version for the USAAC, had two 1,690hp R-2600-11 engines and seven guns, all of 0.50in (12.7mm) calibre.

Not until late 1941 did the longer-ranged DB-7B/Boston III emerge, powered by two 1,600hp R-2600-23 engines. Here at last was a top performer whose shoulder wing sat upon a slender fuselage, whose pilot had an excellent forward view and in which the navigator or bomb aimer sat in an ideal glazed nose. Amidships the gunner had two guns and the pilot could operate four 0.30in (7.62mm) machine-guns fitted on either side of the nose. The bomb load was 2,600lb (1,180kg). In RAF Boston IIIs six 8th USAAF crews on 4 July 1942 mounted the AAF's first bombing operation over western Europe. By 1944 the A-20G version was in service, sporting a dorsal turret and a clear-vision or sold nose.

As the night blitz was ending, a new shape entered European skies when a Boeing B-17C Flying Fortress landed at Prestwick, Scotland, after a direct 8hr 20min flight from the USA. Ultimately this bomber would have a profound effect upon the war. With turbosupercharged engines, the four-engined B-17C was one of twenty purchased by Britain.

The B-17 originated in a 1934 competition for a four-engined bomber, Boeing copyrighting the trade name 'Flying Fortress' for the aircraft. Of all-metal construction, it initially had four 750hp Pratt & Whitney Hornet R-1690-E nine-cylinder radial engines, a retractable undercarriage, a shapely 103ft 9in-span wing and a crew of eight. Defence comprised four single-gun positions and a solitary nose gun. Fully loaded it weighed 43,000lb (19,500kg) and carried up to eight 600lb (270kg) bombs. It first flew on 28 July 1935. Its top speed was around 250mph (400km/h), cruising speed 200mph (320km/h), and service ceiling about 24,000ft (7,300m), but uncertainties arose because the prototype crashed on 30 October 1935.

Thirteen YB-17s with more suitable 930hp Wright Cyclone GR-1 820-39 (G2) engines followed, and one important static airframe. Arguments arose because the US Navy viewed the 'flying battleship' as a threat to its building programme, and funding methods caused the new examples to be redesignated Y1B-17s, the first flying on 2 December 1936. All thirteen went to the 2nd Bombardment Group (BG) whose lengthy flights tested an aircraft which formed the nucleus of US strategic air power. By the 1938 Munich crisis they had flown 1,800,000 miles (2,897,000km) without serious accident.

Turbosuperchargers in the static test machine improved all-round performance so much that, as the only Y1B-17A (37-369), it began flight tests in April 1938 and revealed a ceiling exceeding 30,000ft (9,150m) and a top speed of 311mph (500km/h), way ahead of the 256mph (412km/h) shown by the others. Averaging 238mph (383km/h), it could carry an 11,000lb (4,990kg) load for 620 miles (1,000km), or more realistically 2,400lb (1,090kg) for 1,500 miles (2,415km). Not

Although it was less nimble than the A-20, North American's B-25C Mitchell carried a heavier bomb load. Forward firing gun packs made later versions useful for low-level strikes.

surprisingly, an order for thirty-nine B-17Bs (1,000hp R-1 820-65) followed. These had an enlarged rudder, a flat nose panel for use with the Sperry bomb sight, and more flap area. All were delivered by March 1940.

Then came thirty-eight B-17Cs, somewhat different in appearance because the gun positions had been replaced by a ventral bath and large side panels which the gunner removed before using his guns. Power was provided by 1,200hp GR-1820-65 (G-205A) engines. The B-17C's weight had risen to 49,650lb (22,521kg), and the first example flew on 21 July 1940. Further refinements were incorporated in forty-two subsequent B-17Ds.

A belief that high flying afforded safety from interception (something the Germans also believed) aroused a British desire to acquire turbosupercharged B-17s to see whether they were suitable for high-level operations. The reluctance of the USA to release them was tempered by American interest in what could be achieved under combat, so it was agreed to sell Britain twenty B-17Cs. Known as Fortress Is, the RAF aircraft had two waist, two dorsal and a single ventral 0.50in guns and one or two 0.30in free guns in the nose. British testing showed the B-17C's top speed to be 325mph (523km/h) at 29,000ft (8,840m), and its cruising speed 230mph

(370km/h). With four 1,110lb (500kg) US bombs the operational radius was 450 miles (725km). To operate at around 28,000ft (8,630m), the seven men aboard the bomber drew for hours upon oxygen supplies during long, cold and exhausting sorties. They wore electrically heated clothing, layers being added as the aircraft climbed to a regime where the temperature could fall to −50˚C. From 10,000ft (3,050m) a bombing error of only 450ft (140m) was claimed when using the Sperry sight, but only on clear days, of which there were few.

Such a day was 8 July 1941, when B-17Cs operated for the first time. No formation flying was undertaken by the trio running up on Wilhelmshaven to bomb from 27,000ft (8,230m). One, with an inch of frozen oil covering its tailplane, had to unload near Nordeney. The most disastrous operation occurred on 8 September, when four Fortress Is set out for Oslo. Messerschmitt Bf 109s intercepted one at 27,000ft (8,230m), and another, badly shot up, had wounded aboard. A third found cloud covering the target, and the fourth never returned. The last sortie took place on 25 September, and was the twenty-fourth abortive sortie out of fifty-two flown.

The Fortresses showed how difficult it was to mount high-level raids needing clear weather that was rarely present. Poor gun defences confirmed that even high flyers unprotected by fighters were ready prey, and easily seen contrails revealed the precise position at altitudes where a pressure cabin was desirable.

Back in the USA reworking of the B-17 was under way in the belief that sufficient defensive guns would make it impregnable. In the B-17E a forward dorsal two-gun turret was added and twin ventral guns were replaced by a 'ball turret' for manning by the short of stature. A twin-gun rear turret covering a major blind spot was faired into an enlarged tail unit fitted to improve the aircraft's stability. The weight rose to 54,000lb, seven tons above the original, the first example flying on 5 September 1941. The B-17E reached a top speed of 317mph (510km/h), and production totalled 512.

Japan's Pearl Harbor assault immediately preceded the operational introduction of the B-17E and a new generation of US bombers, the Consolidated B-24 Liberator, North American B-25 Mitchell and Martin B-26 Marauder. All, during development, benefited from the fighting in Europe.

Named after Billy Mitchell, the B-25 became America's most widely used bomber, proving adaptable and very stable. Twenty-four were ordered off the drawing board in 1939, the first flying on 19 August 1940 and serving as the prototype. Production deliveries began in February 1941, and to improve handling the wing centre section from the tenth example retained dihedral whereas outer mainplanes were horizontal, as on all subsequent B-25s. The forty B-25As, also lightly defended by four 0.50in (12.7mm) guns, had self-sealing tanks and extra armour. Weighing 17,870lb (8,106kg) empty and 25,322lb (11,486kg) loaded, the B-25A could carry 3,000lb (1,360kg) of bombs for 1,350 miles (2,170km), more than many aircraft in its class, and attained 315mph at 15,000ft (507km/h at 4,570m). Improved defence came with the B-25B's dorsal and belly turrets in lieu of waist and tail guns. As a penalty the weight rose to 26,208lb (11,887kg), and speed fell to 300mph at 15,000ft (483km/h at 4,570m). By December 1941 130 B-25Bs had been delivered.

The Mitchell's good endurance was first exploited during anti-submarine patrols off the US coast. Early in 1942 the 3rd BG moved to Australia, from where the first operation involved ten B-25s island hopping to the Philippines and then attacking Japanese shipping. In April 1942 operations against targets in New Guinea began, and B-25s were subsequently active in the Pacific region throughout hostilities.

One highlight of the Mitchell's career followed successful trial launching of the 67ft 6in (20.5m)-span bomber from the aircraft carrier USS *Hornet*, no mean feat. The 17th BG then provided twenty-four B-25Bs for a carrier-launched attack on Japan. Their lower turrets and Norden bombsights were removed, and additional fuel tankage allowed 1,141gal (5,187 litres) to be carried.

Aboard each aircraft were ten 5gal (19-litre) fuel drums to 'top up' if needed. Each B-25B carried four 500lb (228kg) bombs, and two had wooden 'scare guns' protruding from the tail. Sixteen prepared B-25Bs were aboard the *Hornet* when it sailed for the launch 440 miles off Japan. Unfortunately small enemy ships were encountered, so to save the operation it began at 0800 on 18 April 1942, 714 miles from Japan.

Leading was Lt Col James Doolittle aboard 40-2344, typically heavily laden at 31,000lb (14,060kg), but all sixteen Mitchells were launched within an hour and bombed from 1,500ft (460m) without loss, other targets being Kobe, Yokohama and Nagoya. Finding designated landing airfields in China in very bad weather was so difficult that four crews crash-landed, eleven baled out and 40-2242 landed at Vladivostok, only to be promptly interned.

The B-25C – loaded weight 33,500lb (15,200kg) – could with additional fuel deliver 3,200lb (1,450kg) of bombs during a 1,525-mile (2,450km) sortie. It had a top speed of 264mph (424km/h) at sea level, and 284mph at 15,000ft (457km/h at 4,570m). On short missions external racks increased the load to 5,200lb (2,360kg). Production ended in May 1943 with the 1,619th example. A new plant to build B-25s opened in Kansas City, where between February 1942 and March 1944 2,290 B-25Ds, similar to the B-25C, were completed.

The B-25's stability rendered it ideal for medium-level, strongly escorted formation bombing in Europe, where most losses were caused by AA fire. In the Pacific theatre 'solid-nose' adaptations included packages of machine-guns and a hefty 75mm cannon , making the B-25G and H models good for low-level strike. More conventional bomber B-25s of the 28th Composite Group operating from the Aleutians raided targets in Japan's Kurile island chain for a second time on 10 July 1943.

At the time of the Tokyo raid the other twin-engined US medium bomber, the controversial B-26 Marauder, was available for operations. Originating in a plan for a 2,000-mile (3,219km) range bomber with a 20,000ft (6,100m) ceiling and able to fly at 350mph (563km/h), it had a 56ft (17m) long fuselage mated to wings of only 65ft (20m) span, giving a 50lb/ft² (244kg/m²) wing loading. That helped to produce a hazardous landing speed of 130mph (209km/h). The circular-cross-section fuselage reduced bomb bay size, the load being only 2,000lb (910kg). Initial defensive armament was again poor, comprising only one 0.30in (7.62mm) nose gun, a 0.30in tail gun and two 0.50in guns (12.7mm) in the dorsal Martin turret. Two 1,850hp Pratt & Whitney R-2800 Double Wasp eighteen-cylinder, two-stage supercharged engines fitted with ejector exhausts drove four-bladed propellers.

Martin's shapely B-26 Marauder proved too vulnerable for low-level attack. Formations of US 9th Air Force B-26s attacked airfields and bridges in the weeks before the invasion of northern Europe.

The first of 1,100 Marauders ordered in September 1939 flew on 25 November 1940, rapid production resulting in 200 by mid-1941. After taking off loaded at 26,625lb (12,077kg) the B-26 reached 315mph (507km/h), but landing accidents during crew training with the 'very fast ship' raised calls for cancellation. Production was halted in early 1942 and resumed in May, the B-26B-10 introducing a larger wing, of 71ft (21.6m) span.

The 22nd Bombardment Group at Muroc in California introduced the bomber to operations with B-26 anti-submarine patrols. In February 1942 the Group moved to Australia, joining the 5th AF and resuming operations in April with anti-shipping sorties and raids on New Guinea. Torpedo-bomber Marauders operated during the Battle of Midway but no sinkings were achieved. Although B-26s were active over the south-west Pacific in 1942-1943, they really needed Europe's firm, long runways. There, the Marauder was highly effective. It operated in large formations at medium altitudes, often carpet-bombing airfields, well protected by shoals of fighters.

Arguably America's best wartime bomber was the B-24 Liberator. Had it not been for European interest it might never have proceeded, as the USAAC was firmly committed to the B-17. Designed in 1939, the four-engined aircraft was planned to fly faster and further than the B-17 and carry an 8,000lb (3,620kg) load. Its high-aspect-ratio Davis wing conferred exceptionally long

range on an aeroplane with transport potential. Exhaust turbosuperchargers boosted its speed and rate of climb. When the XB-24 (four 1,200hp Pratt & Whitney R1830-33s) flew on 29 December 1939 it was clearly a good performer, but was defended by only by six 0.30in (7.62mm) guns. Britain ordered the LB-30 variant with a 2,000-mile (3,219km) range and 3,000lb (1,360kg) bomb load for its maritime reconnaissance potential. In 1940 the British expressed reservations about the very poor defences, and the Americans responded with the LB-30A (first flown in January 1941) with two tail defence guns, but this was still unacceptable for European operations. Britain's first Liberators were converted into transatlantic transports.

There was no doubt of the design's potential. The XB-24B tested oval cowlings which improved cooling, and the B-24A had twin 0.30in (7.62mm) tail guns and six 0.50in (12.7mm) guns. The RAF acquired twenty LB-30B Liberator Is and fitted them with a four 20mm gun pack. Cruising at 150kt carrying a 2,000lb load, the Liberator I could patrol for an amazing sixteen hours. Using the forward firing cannon a Liberator shot down a Focke-Wulf Fw 200 on 4 October 1941 in an unusual bomber-versus-bomber combat. Additional tankage allowed convoys to be met by Condors 800 miles (1,290km) out in the Atlantic.

Curiously, the USAAC ordered only seven YB-24s, nine B-24As and only nine B-24Cs, whereas the British continued to back the Liberator by ordering 165 Mk II

A combination of high-aspect-ratio wings and turbosupercharged engines gave Consolidated's B-24 Liberator longer range and better all-round performance than the B-17. The B-24M depicted, like the H and subsequent Liberators, had nose, tail, dorsal and ventral turrets.

bombers with two-gun rotating tail turrets, available from October 1941. Soon after the Japanese attack on Pearl Harbor the US acquired some of the British order, their value over the Pacific being only too obvious.

The B-24 had phenomenal range, ample speed, fast climb and fairly good load potential. Vital increased defence came with the B-24D (Liberator III), which had tail and forward upper turrets along with waist positions from which 0.50in (12.7mm) guns could be fired, as in the B-17. For an 11.6-hour ocean patrol the B-24D (of which 2,696 were built) could carry a 3,000lb (1,360kg) bomb or depth-charge load, so the US Navy as well as the RAF ordered it. The USAAF began operating B-24Ds from Britain in October 1942, but their stay was shortlived, for they moved to North Africa and in 1943 made the famous low-level raid on the Ploesti oilfields in Romania. Not until summer 1943 were B-24s again a going concern in the 8th Air Force.

In autumn 1942 a newer Flying Fortress, the B-17F with frameless Plexiglas nose, 400 modifications and additional guns, replaced the B-17E. It entered production in April 1942 and 3,405 were built. The loaded weight was 56,000lb (25,402kg), and eventually the maximum permissible take-off weight was 72,000lb (32,659kg). The B-17F with a possible 9,600lb (4,186kg) bomb load partly carried on external racks became the standard USAAF bomber in Europe until the B-17G, featuring a prominent chin turret to discourage frontal attacks (8,680 built), was introduced in 1943. B-17Fs made the

first raid on Germany on 27 January 1943. On 17 August their vulnerability became very evident when 60 out of 376 raiding Regensburg and Schweinfurt were shot down. On a second Schweinfurt raid enemy fighters shot down 60 out of 305 operating. The lesson the RAF had learned in 1939 was being taught to the Americans, who clearly did not heed any warning. During raids on Germany B-17s carried bomb loads of 4,000–5,000lb (1,814–2,268kg), compared with the 10,000lb (4,536kg) average load of the RAF's Avro Lancaster.

Early B-17 Flying Fortresses were defended from open gun ports, using hand-held weapons. The B-17G, shown here, had improved defences including mechanically driven turrets.

Soon after the B-24Ds returned to Britain in summer 1943 they were replaced by the B-24H (3,100 built) and B-24J (6,778 built), both of which had new, power-operated twin 0.50in (12.7mm) nose gun turrets, and better waist positions. The slab-sided B-24 was easier to mass produce than the B-17, and a huge Ford complex at Willow Run churned out B-24s at an amazing rate. Twin 0.50in (12.7mm) guns were in the tail turrets of the 1,667 B-24Ls and 2,593 of the lighter B-24M. The B-24 was usually faster than the B-17, but the 'Flying Fortress' was long established and more charismatic. Two-thirds of the US 8th Air Force went to war in B-17s; the rest had B-24s.

Russia's Bombers

At dawn on 22 June 1941 German troops stormed the USSR from the Baltic to the Black Sea. Junkers Ju 88s, He 111s and Do 217s raced in high to pulverise airfields clandestinely reconnoitred by Dorniers, and by noon the USSR had lost 528 aircraft on the ground and 210 in the air in the Western District. German records claim that by mid-afternoon 1,200 Russian aircraft had succumbed. Ill-trained and poorly organised, the Soviet Air Force undoubtedly suffered a reeling blow and is thought to have lost 3,808 aircraft within five days.

Built in large numbers, the Tupolev SB-2 'fast bomber' of the late 1930s stemmed from the ANT-40.

Soviet military policy recognised two threats; one from the east and one from the west. Therefore its forces were organised to fight independently and simultaneously, the Western and Eastern Air Forces each even having their own sources of production. Both Air Forces comprised four main elements: Air Forces of the Air Armies or Military Districts, Fighter Defence Force defending special rear areas, the Long Range Bomber Force or Independent Strike Force under the Supreme Command, and the Air Force of the Red Fleets or Naval Commands. Prewar control was entirely through Military Districts, then during the war each Army

Steady development of the ANT-42 led to the Petlyakov Pe-8, the Soviet Union's only wartime heavy bomber.

Conceived before the war, but not in service until 1941, the Ilyushin Il-2 was a heavily-armed and well armoured light attack bomber. Production began with the single-seater version in 1941, the two-seater following in mid-1942.

Group had its own Air Army, there being three main Groups, North, Central and Southern, which much improved the air forces. Within each Air Army were Air Divisions comprising three Air Regiments, whose task was to support the Red Army. The Long Range Bomber Force raised during the war attacked targets well behind the battle line and its bombers, with no sophisticated night bombing aids, carried out operations deep into hostile territory including Poland, Germany and Hungary. As the Germans advanced eastwards they overran many of the Western District factories. Rapid establishment of new production sources well to the east allowed a turnaround in Russia's air force strength, and by the end of 1943 the Soviet Air Forces were fighting back strongly. By then aircraft were being known by their designer or factory name, whereas previously they merely had classification titles: BB for close-range bomber, DB for long-range bomber, SB for fast bomber and TB for heavy bomber; Il for Illyushin, Pe for Petlyakov, Tu for Tupolev and so forth, preceding bomber design numbers.

The three-man, Tupolev designed SB-2 was in use for much of the war. Two 830hp M-100 inline engines were set far forward and its huge wings, spanning 20.33m (66ft 8in), were supplemented by a giant triangular tailplane. It had a top speed of about 393km/h (244mph) and a limiting range of 1,250km (777 miles). Defended by two nose guns and single dorsal and ventral guns (replaced by turrets) later versions were powered by two 960hp M-103 engines. Owing to their vulnerability, SB-2s usually operated at night. Some were fitted with skis, a special variant being the Arkhangelskii Ar-2, powered by 1,100hp M-105Rs and intended for close support and dive bombing.

The backbone of the Russian bomber squadrons was the 1937 Ilyushin DB-3 with twin 1,000hp M-88 radial engines, in production by 1940 as the DB-3f or Il-4. Used also in the Russo-Finnish war, the DB-3 had a 21.35m (70ft 3in) span, and, with a top speed of about 370km/h (230mph), could carry a 907kg (2,000lb) load

for 2,607km (1,620 miles). Normally loaded, the DB-3 weighed 7,938kg (17,500lb) (10,025kg/22,100lb maximum), and it was defended by three 7.3mm (0.30in) guns. Early DB-3s had a nose turret, but by 1940 the DB-3f had a more pointed nose with additional glazing. With a top speed of 418km/h (260mph) and a range of 4,023km (2,500 miles), its normal bomb load was 998kg (2,200lb), although it had room for 2,495kg (5,500lb). It was used as a tactical or strategic bomber, and Capt Alexandr Molodchy of the long-range bomber force, flying a DB-3f, claimed on 7 August 1941 to be the first Soviet bomber pilot to attack Berlin. That flight involved a round trip of some 2,000 miles (3,220km).

The USSR's great strategic advantage was the depth of its territory, and the Pe-8 (or TB-7), Russia's only four-engined strategic bomber, was built well inside the USSR. With primitive nose, tail and dorsal turrets, it carried a crew of six, the pilots sitting in tandem. Machine-guns poked from the rear of the inner engine nacelles, underneath each of which was one radiator for two 1,350hp AM-35A engines. A large aeroplane, it spanned 40m (131ft 3in), was 24.5m long (80ft 6in) and weighed over 22 tons when loaded. With a top speed of 427km/h (265mph) it had a range of 4,700km (2,920 miles) when carrying a 2,000kg (4,400lb) load.

At the other extreme was a Russian equivalent to the Stuka, not ready when the Germans invaded. Ilyushin had devised a tough, single-engine ground-attack aircraft. It began as the BSh-2, a two-seat armoured assault aircraft, and effectiveness increased with modification into the famous Il-2. With a wingspan of 14.6m (47ft 11in) and length of 11.6m (38ft 3in), it weighed 5,556kg (12,250lb) loaded and could carry a 599kg (1,320lb) bomb load. Much weight was ascribed to extensive armour protecting the crew and the engine from ground fire. Two 7.62mm ShKAS machine-guns and two 20mm ShVAK cannon were fitted in the wings, below which were racks for four 25.4kg (56lb) RS-132 rockets. Alternatively it could have two 37mm (1.4in) or two 57mm (2.24in) wing cannon for tank busting. In the rear cockpit was a 12.7mm (0.5in) machine-gun or 20mm (0.78in) cannon for ground strafing. The top speed was 426km/h (265mph) and cruising speed around 322km/h (200mph), achieved using an AM-38F inline engine giving 1,700hp for take-off and 1,550hp for cruise. Like the Stuka, the Il-2 had a range of some 612km (380 miles), which meant basing it vulnerably close to the front line.

Typical of Soviet aircraft of the period was Vladimir M Petlyakov's Pe-2 twin-engine light bomber for ground support, medium-level dive bombing and tactical reconnaissance. With a span of 17.1m (56ft 4in) and thus similar in size to the Douglas DB-7, it appeared to owe some of its origin to the French Potez 63. Of the crew of three, the rear gunner was dangerously separated from the others by a large fuel tank. As well as a dorsal 7.62mm

The Tupolev Tu-2 300mph bomber entered service in late 1942.

(0.30in) gun, replaced on later versions by a dorsal turret, the rear gunner also controlled a ventral gun aimed through a periscope. Bombs were carried in small cells within the fuselage and the rear nacelles of the 1,100hp M-105R inline engines. The usual load totalled 598kg (1,320lb), but could be increased to 998kg (2,200lb), for there was provision for additional weapons below the wing centre section. Two 7.62mm (0.30in) forward firing guns were usually fitted in the nose. The Pe-2 weighed 5,851kg (12,900lb) empty and 7,679kg (16,930lb) loaded. Its low-level top speed was 460km/h (286mph), and the maximum attainable was 537km/h at 4,998m (334mph at 16,400ft). It had a normal range of about 1,126km (700 miles). A longer-range version carried an additional navigator.

Mid-war development to maintain the effectiveness

The Petlyakov Pe-2 was the USSR's principal wartime tactical bomber.

of the Il-2 resulted in the 6,350kg (14,000lb) all-up weight Il-10 of 1944. The wing and tail unit were modified, thicker armour was installed and engine power rose to 2,000hp with the fitting of an AM-42, boosting the top speed to 455km/h at 2,133m (283mph at 7,000ft). Range was much enhanced, to about 1,239 (770 miles), for which a 1,002kg (2,210lb) weapon load could be carried. Soviet fascination with rocket weapons was evident under the wings, where the aircraft carried a hefty load. There were two 23mm cannon in its mainplanes and a 12.7mm or 20mm free gun in the rear cockpit. The pilot had two forward firing 7.62mm machine-guns.

Although its design began in 1938, the Tupolev Tu-2, of which over 3,000 were eventually built, did not fly until June 1941 and came into use in late 1943 as a Pe-2 replacement. With two 1,750hp Ash-82/83, its loaded weight was 12,802kg (28,224lb) and late examples attained 557km/h at 5,791m (348mph at 19,000ft). Defended by four 0.50in guns and a 20mm cannon, it had a span of 2.3m (69ft 10in), reached a ceiling of 10,972m (36,000ft) and had a range of 2,494km carrying 1,497kg (1,550ml carrying 3,300lb), which made it the best Russian bomber of the war.

Germany and the heavy bomber

Germany's strategic heavy bomber programme originated in May 1933, when the air force supported a study suggesting that it should acquire sufficient

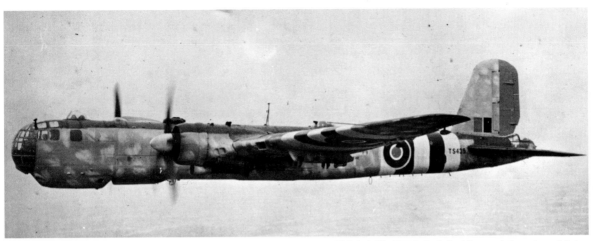

Germany's only dedicated long-range heavy bomber, the troublesome Heinkel He 177A, had double coupled engines driving huge four-bladed propellers. This captured example was tested at RAE Farnborough in 1944.

deterrent force to prevent France and Poland from stopping Germany re-establishing itself as a great power. A fleet of 400 four-engined bombers was proposed, to destroy enemy means of production and break civilian morale. The army, opposing this concept, believed that it invited retaliation, and pointed out that German industry lacked the capacity to build such aircraft.

The Luftwaffe's first chief of staff, Oberst Walter Wever, favoured a broader based strategy in which the air force complemented the army and navy and did not operate independently. Although Wever expressed the view that 'the decisive weapon of air warfare is the bomber', he pointed out that a strategic bomber fleet could not destroy an enemy air force. He contended that Germany needed ample fighters and AA guns for defence and the provision of air superiority for the army and navy. While the destruction of enemy industry might be sound policy, it could take a very long time. Nevertheless, he agreed that it made sense to have a fleet of long-range bombers.

The four-engine Dornier Do 19 and Junkers Ju 89 were steadily going ahead when, in June 1936, the far-sighted Wever was killed in an accident. His successor was Gen Albert Kesselring, a military leader rather than a strategist, who questioned the heavy bomber plan. Cancellation of both large bombers came about because design and production of engines to provide the required performance was beyond achievement within the necessary timescale. The Luftwaffe then pursued the 1936 short-range medium bomber programme because its aircraft were suitable for the likely restricted sphere of operations covering Czechoslovakia, France and Poland. Ernst Udet began parading his belief that, because dive bombing gave the most accurate results, all bombers should have that capability.

Nevertheless, a firm decision was taken in 1937 to build a long-range bomber able to reach as far as all parts of the UK from Germany. The Reichsluftfahrt-ministerium (RLM) drafted a specification that was sent only to Heinkel. Naval backing was given on the understanding that the aircraft would be used to co-operate with U-boat activity. It needed to carry 907kg (2,000lb) for 6,600km (4,100 miles) at a speed of 539km/h (335mph). Aided by Daimler-Benz, Heinkel offered a novel four-engine bomber made possible by coupling two twelve-cylinder liquid-cooled DB 601 engines to make a duplex DB 606 driving one propeller through elaborate gearing. Having only two nacelles would cut drag and save development cost and time. Large radiators would obviously be needed. Fuel consumption could be high, and there was no doubting the overall complexity. Guns in barbettes would have reduced drag, but turrets proved easier to develop. The undercarriage geometry was unusual, both pairs of legs parting, one to retract inwards and one outwards before being covered by doors. Heinkel's He 177 bomber seemed likely to have an all-up weight of 26,998kg (59,520lb) and to be able to reach 550km/h at 5,486m (342mph at 18,000ft). Design work was well under way when Heinkel was told to apply Udet's dive-bomber policy to the He 177. The 31.39m (103ft) span bomber would need to dive at up to 60°, which meant restressing, adding much useless weight and delaying the project by more that a year. The first flight took place on 19 November 1939.

Future war, it was reckoned, would be total, thereby making the destruction of industry, cities and the morale of their people legitimate objectives. If new bombers became unstoppable and were the heart of air power, then the means to retaliate were essential. Many Luftwaffe officers wrongly believed that the Do 17 and He 111 were quite suitable for strategic operations, but neither had sufficient range to reach any part of Britain from

Germany. In the event of war, bases in France and the Low Countries would need to be seized to achieve that, unless a long-range bomber was available.

Chief of Staff Kesselring was replaced by Hans Jeschonnek, who, driven by the belief that Hitler could do no wrong, staunchly followed his leader's ideas, proposing air force policies that were economically impossible and which gave little support to a long-range bomber. By 1939 Wever's carefully conceived plans had become submerged in daily reaction to the existing situation, making a coherent strategic bombing policy impossible to implement. The Luftwaffe was virtually sidelined into supporting a ground war, and became increasingly tied to the army.

Experience in Spain had shown how hard it was to find a target, let alone hit it. At night that would be exceedingly difficult, so research was instigated to develop radio bombing aids to support the He 177 force when it became effective. In August 1939 Hermann Göring claimed to place great importance on the He 177 and the new high-speed Messerschmitt Me 210 multi-purpose types. Then he ordered that concentration be directed upon producing existing types, not on entirely new designs and experimentation, a policy little changed until 1942. Future bombers became steady improvements of the Do 17 (the Do 217) and the Ju 88 (Ju 188). Only Heinkel would develop a major new type while it kept the He 111 in production until 1944.

A low-powered, limited-performance four-engine Focke-Wulf Fw 200 Condor reconnaissance bomber adapted from a transatlantic airliner design and ordered by the Japanese was nearing completion. Could a strengthened, BMW 132H-powered version be adapted to become an interim long-range bomber, at least to satisfy the navy? From a prewar batch of ten Fw 200C-0s (modified Fw 200Bs) six were completed with defensive guns early in 1940, and soon the Fw 200s of I./KG 40 commenced bombing shipping during the Norwegian campaign. By July 1940 the Condors were based at Bordeaux/Merignac, from where they carried out anti-shipping operations over Biscay, and off Ireland and Norway. They also made a few bombing sorties over the UK in late August 1940, becoming the first four-engine Luftwaffe bombers to raid Britain, but were quite unsuitable for employment as strategic bombers.

Against undefended merchant ships, though, Condors had success far beyond that implied by their small numbers, and during August and September 1940 sank over 90,000 tons (91,500 tonnes) of Allied shipping. On 26 October a Condor set on fire the 42,378-ton (43,000-tonne) Canadian Pacific *Empress of Britain* northwest of Ireland, the burning liner being subsequently torpedoed by the U-32. Could the He 177 soon play a similar part?

The answer was a resounding 'no', for its complex engines vibrated badly, ran at very high temperatures, overheated quickly and readily caught fire. Connecting rods were breaking, tearing open oil tanks. Tightly packaged engine parts received insufficient lubrication, and with no firewalls between the powerplant bays and the mainplane, fires spread easily. Tail surfaces had insufficient area, and the second prototype disintegrated owing to control flutter.

Early trials showed that a loaded He 177, carrying a mere three guns, weighed 23,920kg (52,734lb), had a top speed of only 460km/h (286mph) and a 4,855km (3,017-mile) range. By comparison, the 1940 Fw 200C-0 bomber now had three 7.9mm guns, and the Fw 200C-1 also featured a forward-firing MG FF 20mm cannon in a gondola. A 250kg (550lb) bomb was carried beneath each outer engine nacelle and another on an outboard rack; four in all. Before 1940 was out Winston Churchill was calling the Condor 'the scourge of the Atlantic', yet only twenty-six Fw 200Cs had been built, and on average only eight were serviceable. Between August 1940 and February 1941 they were credited with sinking eighty-five ships totalling 363,000 tons (368,800 tonnes), making them an exceptionally successful investment.

The same could not be said of the He 177 Greif (Griffon). Each troublesome example became heavier, and the sixth prototype reached 28,070kg (61,883lb), giving it a very high wing loading of 280kg/m² (57.49lb/ft²). For take-off the DB 606A-1 could provide 2,700hp, but the engines gave constant trouble. Airframe, equipment, combatting fires in the air, aerodynamic problems, worries about structural strength and repeated modifications – not to mention coping with all the ingenuity – resulted in a disastrous programme. Two prototypes planted among the Condors for trials in late 1941 were immediately pronounced useless.

Not until November 1941 did the first He 177A-0 pre-production aircraft fly. With a crew of five and an all-up weight of 30,000kg (66,139lb), it relied for defence upon five machine-guns and a cannon. Its offensive load was a mere 2,340kg (5,290lb).

Had the Germans known, they might have derived slight comfort from problems besetting RAF 'big bombers'. The Avro Manchester's Rolls-Royce Vulture engines suffered overheating and crankshaft troubles, while the Short Stirling's engines peaked so low that its ceiling was around 13,000ft (3,962m). But whereas the Germans had no heavy bomber in prospect, the RAF was looking forward to receiving the superb Avro Lancaster, which inherited the spacious bomb bay of the Manchester, the world's first bomber conceived as a weapons system. This newcomer, with room for 12,000lb (5,440kg) of bombs, could convey much of that weight deep into Germany, and regularly deliver to Berlin's factories and offices around 9,000lb at 20,000ft

Britain's second-generation bombers, the Halifax, Stirling and Manchester, were designed to accommodate 2,000lb bombs which the Hampden could also carry. Here a Manchester is about to receive its 2,000-pounder.

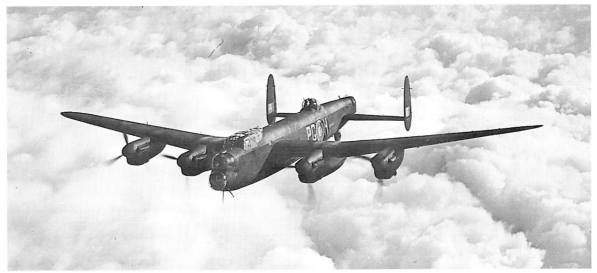

The Manchester's huge bomb bay, able to contain bombs larger than 2,000-pounders, formed the nucleus of its four-engined derivative, the Lancaster, an aircraft of No 619 Squadron being seen here.

Bremen under RAF night attack, photographed on 2/3 July 1942 from a Lancaster of No 97 Squadron. Aircraft movement, drifting flares and markers, and the seats of fires all contribute to the horrific beauty of this picture.

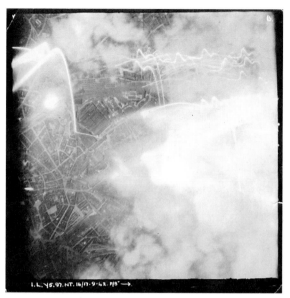

On 16/17 September 1942 369 crews claimed to have made a highly effective raid on Essen. Among them were those aboard the No 97 Squadron Lancaster, one of 93 involved, from which this night photograph was secured. More than 100 large fires were started.

at 200mph (3,630kg at 6,100m at 320km/h). No other mid-war bomber could equal that.

As Britain's champion bomber prepared for its 1942 operational debut, the first production He-177A-1s also appeared, with a top speed of 510km/h at 5,800m (317mph at 19,030ft) and the ability to cruise at 430km/h (270mph), provided there was no engine fire. Some improvement was expected from mating two DB 605s to produce the DB 610, forecast to provide 2,950hp for take-off and over 3,100hp above 7,000ft. That was largely hypothetical, the He 177A-3 settling for the DB 606, a succession of modifications, differing guns and various weapon loads, with little prospect of successful bomber or maritime operations.

Meanwhile, the Condors of I./KG 40 moved to Norway, bent on monitoring and attacking Russian-bound convoys. When the full extent of the Stalingrad debacle became apparent, the Germans began ferrying troops out of their encirclement. So desperate did they become that He 177s participated, five being variously lost during such activity between November 1942 and 2 February 1943, along with nine Fw 200s, 169 He 111s and a Ju 290 transport derived from the ill-fated Ju 89.

February 1943 saw delivery of the first He 177A-5, the most effective of its breed. Whereas Germany still had no strategic force, RAF Bomber Command could, on 1 March 1943, call upon 330 Lancasters, 237 Wellingtons, 214 Halifaxes, 147 Stirlings and 74 Mosquitoes in its squadrons. Of the latter, twenty-two

The best-known RAF special attack of the war breached the Mohne Dam. Water can be seen pouring through the wall in this picture, taken from a Spitfire PR.XI.

were Oboe pathfinders which, within a week, were to mark the Krupp works at Essen so accurately in darkness that it was devastated. Even by the end of 1943 only 261

He 177A-5s had been built, primarily for anti-shipping operations. That left the Ju 88, Ju 188 and updates of the Do 217 to continue sparse bombing of the British Isles while awaiting New Year's Eve, when Operation Capricorn, a combined V1 flying bomb, V2 rocket and bomber onslaught, would burst upon London with teutonic ferocity. Instead, the V-weapons were, like the bombers, not ready.

The DB 610A-1-engined He 177A-5 had a service ceiling of 8,000m (26,250ft) and a top speed of 488km/h at 6,100m (303mph at 20,000ft), where it cruised at 415km/h (258mph). Its range was 5,480km (3,400 miles) at a starting all-up weight of 25,840kg (59,970lb), the maximum overload permitted being 31,000kg (68,340lb). Its 31.39m (103ft) wingspan was close to the Lancaster's 102ft (31.08m), and its length a similar 19.4m (67ft).

In November 1943 twenty He 177s of II./KG 40 carrying Hs 293 glider bombs attacked a Biscay convoy in daylight, sinking a ship and losing three of their number. Of another fourteen attacking shipping five days later, four were shot down and three crash-landed. On 21 January 1944 some thirty A-3s and A-5s drawn from I./KG 40 and I./KG 100 based at Chateaudun and Rheine took part in the postponed 'Baby Blitz' on London. This was hardly successful, KG 100 alone losing six aircraft between 21 January and 2 March, four of them to nightfighters.

The He 177A-3s fielded were hardly glittering performers. Operating at 30,844kg (68,000lb), 32,886kg (72,500lb) overloaded, they proportionately carried very small loads, some bringing to London only twelve 250kg (550lb) bombs. The average load for a 885km (550-mile) flight could total 7,690kg (16,950lb), which could comprise two 1,800kg (3,968lb) and two 1,000kg (2,200lb) bombs internally and two external 1,000kg bombs. The first He 177A-3 shot down in Britain had carried an 11,000lb load, and set out for a 645km (400-mile) flight carrying 4,245kg (9,360lb) of fuel. The average top speed for the aircraft being employed was around 450km/h at 3,960m (280mph at 13,000ft). For defence there were five MG 131s, an MG 81 and a 20mm MG 151 in the tail, where lack of power traverse limited its usefulness. The DB 610 in the He 177 A-5 was now giving 2,580hp for take-off, 2,468hp at 5,791m (19,000ft). It was possible to shut down one of its DB 605s, which usually led to trouble, as the remaining power unit tended to overheat.

The He 177s continued operating into March, suffering from attacks by Mosquito nightfighters, day strafers and more from mechanical malaise. They withdrew from operations that month, as the Allies massed in southern England for the D-Day assault. How useful 400 effective 'heavies' would have then been, for they could have incinerated the gliders, knocked out loading ports, battered troop concentrations and might have prevented the invasion. Instead, a few He 177s played a minimal part during the nights following the Normandy landings by attacking Allied shipping in Caen Bay with advanced weapons.

But the He 177's engine problems were never completely cured, merely adjusted. Four conventional engines were later fitted to the He 277, the wings of which were extended to 39.95m (131ft 3in) to improve the range. A high-altitude version, the He 274 (four DB 603A), wingspan 44.19m (145ft), carried an 4,006kg (8,832lb) bomb load. Its all-up weight was 36,010kg (79,388lb), its range 4,248km at 11,000m (2,640 miles at 36,100ft) and the top speed was 579km/h at 10,990m (360mph at 36,060ft). However, these were only experimental versions flown too late to be of any value.

On 3 July 1944 Germany's conventional bomber programme was largely halted in order to concentrate resources on fighter production and a handful of advanced types, particularly jets. But that same month the ill-fated He 177 found some 'eleventh hour' success. With about ninety aircraft on hand, three Gruppen of KG 1 flew the Grief against Russian tactical targets while dwindling fuel stocks lasted. This single unit's strength was by a significant margin the most powerful Luftwaffe striking force on the Eastern Front. Operations were mainly successful, with little sign of the engine fires that had so plagued the type previously. They culminated in a series of daylight formation bombing raids by eighty-plus He 177s to demonstrate what might have been.

Japan's bombers

In common with other types, Japanese Air Force bombers had a chronological 'Ki' number, and when orders were placed the aircraft were given a manufacturer's name, a type number indicating the year in the Japanese calendar in which production began, a function and model or mark number. Up to 1939 the type number used the last two digits of the year, i.e. '99' came from 2599 and 1940 was denoted by 100, after which 1941 and 1942 used Type 1 and Type 2. Navy systems were more complex, and three styles were used. An experimental number was replaced by a type number followed by year, function and model identity figures. After mid-1943 the type number was replaced by a name. The Navy model number had two figures, one for the airframe and one for the engine.

An ageing Army design frequently updated was the Kawasaki Ki-48 (Army Type 99), codenamed 'Lily' by the Allies. Carrying a crew of four, it had two 1,000hp Ha 25 engines. Close in size to a Blenheim, it weighed 4,050kg (8,930lb) empty and 6,085kg (13,417lb) loaded and was quite agile. Its bomb load was only 299kg (660lb), and the top speed of 479km/h (298mph) was linked with a 2,398km (1,490-mile) maximum range for

Kawasaki produced the Ki-48 'Lily' reconnaissance bomber.

Manchurian border operations. Widely employed as a light bomber, the Ki-48 readily fell to fighters if unescorted, its only protection being four 7.7mm (0.30in) or 12.7mm (0.50in) free guns. Like the Hampden and the Bf 110, the Ki-48 had a slender, cut-away, drag reducing fuselage to improve the gunner's view. Between July 1940 and 1942 550 Ki-48s were built. The Model 2a followed, with 1,130hp Ha 115 radial engines increasing the top speed to 315mph while the bomb load remained only 453kg (1,000lb). Another 1,450 examples were built before production ceased in late 1944.

When war began the Army made much use of the Mitsubishi Ki-21 Type 97 'Sally' although it was obsolescent. Schemed in 1936 and operated between 1937 and 1945, this long-range four-seat bomber was also intended for use over the Russo-Manchurian border region. Carrying a 748kg (1,650lb) load and cruising at 306km/h (190mph), it had a top speed of 402km/h (250mph) at 3,048m (10,000ft) and was powered by two 14-cylinder two-row engines. The armament of three 7.7mm (0.30in) guns, one each in the nose, ventral and dorsal positions, was later increased when a remote tail-cone gun was installed. Production of the Ki-21-I began in 1938. Spanning 22m (72ft 10in) and 116m (52ft 6in) long, it had a top speed of 433km/h (269mph). In December 1941 Ki-21s bombed Hong Kong, Burma and the Philippines.

The Ki-21-II had 1,400hp engines, more armament, and in IIb form a 12.7mm (0.50in) gun in a dorsal turret. Extra power gave a top speed of 478km/h (297mph) at 3,999m (13,120ft) and carrying a maximum load the aircraft had a range of 2,172km (1,350 miles) when cruising at 283km/h (176mph). Production ended in September 1944, nearly 2,000 Ki-21s having been built within eight years. On 24 May 1945 nine Ki-21s were dispatched in a spectacular attempt to disrupt B-29 activities on Okinawa. Seven reached the island but six were shot down, leaving one to land troops who destroyed seven B-29s and much ammunition and fuel in a courageous but futile suicide attack.

Japan's heaviest land attack bomber, based on operational experience gained in China, was the navy's Mitsubishi G4M1 Type 1 Rikko, known to the Allies as 'Betty' and possessing exceptional range of trans-Pacific proportions. As with other Japanese bombers, this was gained at the expense of defensive armament, which made it highly vulnerable if unescorted, especially so because the 5,000-litre (1,100gal) wing tanks were unprotected. Design work started in 1937, the Japanese by then relying upon their indigenous aircraft industry. The navy required a bomber with a 3,701km (2,300-mile) range when carrying a torpedo or a 798kg (1,760lb) bomb load. That meant a light airframe, and the G4M1 had two Mitsubishi Kasei 1,530hp 14-cylinder radial engines. With a top speed of 428km/h at 4,200m (266mph at 13,780ft), and cruising at 315km/h at 2,999m (196mph at 9,840ft), the seven-man G4M1, defended by four hand-held 7.7mm guns and a 20mm tail cannon, became operational in May 1941. Carrying a 998kg (2,200lb) bomb load or an 807kg (1,760lb) torpedo, it weighed 6,758kg (14,900lb) empty and 9,500kg (20,944lb) loaded. Of the 180 delivered by December 1941, the navy held 120 ready to bomb Malaya, the Philippines and Dutch East Indies. From Formosa on 8 December they very effectively struck at Clark Field. When the battleships HMS *Prince of Wales* and *Repulse* were discovered, twenty-seven 'Bettys' based in Indochina were ordered to make the fateful torpedo attack.

The Mitsubishi G4M, codenamed 'Betty' by the Allies, served throughout the conflict.

Mitsubishi's Ki-21 'Sally' was rapidly outclassed during the Far East war.

A late entry into battle was the Mitsubishi Ki-67 Hiryu, alias 'Peggy'.

Subsequently G4M1s operated over the Marianas, the Marshall Islands, New Guinea and the Solomons, and sank the USS *Langley* during a very successful but costly phase of the war.

The G4M2, with laminar-flow wing and Kasei 21 engines with methanol injection, carried 330gal more in a protected tank in the fuselage. It first flew in November 1942. The prominent flank observation blisters had been replaced, and additional nose glazing and a dorsal turret with a 20mm cannon were added, along with two more 7.7mm (0.30in) guns. The weight of the 24.9m (81ft 8in) span, 19.5m (64ft 5in) long aircraft rose considerably to 7.994kg (17,624lb) empty and 12,500kg (27,557lb) loaded. In 1943, 660 were built. An improved version, the G4M3, appeared in May 1944, powered by 1,850hp Kasei 25s which gave it a top speed of 438km/h at 4,599m (272mph at 15,090ft) and an enhanced range of 3,640km (2,260 miles) when cruising at 315km/h (196mph). A revised wing layout, along with crew and fuel-tank protection, turned the 'Betty' into a short-range maritime patrol bomber. In all 2,479 were built.

The finest Japanese bomber was the late-war Mitsubishi Ki-67 Hiryu, 'Peggy', a 1941 army design introduced to operations in October 1944 as a torpedo bomber and Ki-21 replacement. Here at last was a Japanese bomber with good defence to revitalise, potentially, an outclassed force to tackle US Navy units. The slim, clean form, carrying a crew of six or eight and defended by four 12.7mm (0.50in) and one 20mm guns, incorporated Western ideas mixing combat needs and crew safety. The prototype Ki-67 flew in December 1942, with two 18-cylinder, two-row, two-speed supercharged, fan-cooled Mitsubishi Ha-104 radials delivering 2,000hp for take-off. Easy to build and maintain, the Ki-67, with a wing span of 22.5m (73ft 9¾in) and a length of 19m (621ft 4in), was progressing well. Then the Services asked for more and more modifications, to such an extent that production was seriously retarded. Only 251 were delivered in 1944, yet the Ki-67 was then one of the few bombers Japan could depend upon. By this time B-29 raids were badly damaging Japan's aircraft factories.

Its speed and range allowed the Ki-67 to attack US bases on the Marianas and Okinawa, carrying a 798kg (1,760lb) bomb load. With a top speed of 537.5km/h at 5,815m (334mph at 19.080ft) it stood a reasonable chance of evading fighters. Cruising at 399km/h (248mph), it possessed a normal range of 2,800km (1,740 miles) and a service ceiling of 9,470m (31,070ft), and was clearly the type of bomber Japan should have developed sooner.

The Unarmed Bomber

The concept was simple. A bomber would fly much faster if shorn of defensive guns, gunners and the structure and fuel conveying them. Overall it would be safer, and operationally far more efficient. Whether it was multi-piston or even jet-engined, the hypothesis still made sense. Expenditure would be less and tactical flexibility greater, but getting such ideas accepted was very difficult, especially in 1938, for the RAF's Blenheim was faster than opposing fighters, though they were only biplanes. De Havilland, which in the First World War had produced the D.H.9 bomber, faster than existing fighters, was planning another, to reach 400mph.

Within three weeks of its D.H.88 Comet racer winning the speed prize in the 1934 Mildenhall to Melbourne McRobertson Air Race, de Havilland had applied its clean aerodynamics to the four-engine D.H.91 Albatross airliner. With war clouds gathering, the company pointed out that the Albatross could convey a 6,000lb (2,721kg) load to Berlin in a non-stop return flight. When Specification P.13/36, outlining a twin-engined bomber, arrived at Hatfield in August 1936 it aroused interest. Could the wooden D.H.91 be adapted? Turrets, bombs and torpedoes were all required for this 275mph (443km/h) bomber able to transport 4,500lb for 3,000 miles (2,040kg for 4,830km). De Havilland proposed a twin-Merlin wooden bomber in which speed was paramount, but this idea from a company inexperienced in bomber design was dismissed by the Air Ministry.

In the first week of war de Havilland again approached the ministry, presenting ideas for a small, two-man, unarmed bomber. Sceptical officials requested more details, so the company reminded them that Berlin was two hours away! Estimates were carefully studied and different engine installations considered, with the Merlin always best. A turret and gunner added 915lb (415kg), clipping a vital 20mph (32km/h) off the speed. Keeping the aircraft small was likely to give a top speed of 409mph (654km/h), and by November 1939 work was concentrated on a 54ft-span twin Merlin-engined bomber to carry a 1,000lb (453.6kg) load for 1,500 miles (2,414km) at a speed approaching 400mph (644km/h). Although its surface area was twice that of the Spitfire, it would have twice the power. A very

Unarmed and made of wood, the de Havilland Mosquito IV was the fastest light bomber of its time. Its speed and efficiency allowed it to fly two sorties to Berlin in one night, usually immune to attack, delivering a 4,000lb 'cookie' each time.

smooth, aerodynamically refined wooden structure and ducted radiators would further compensate for size, making it at least 20mph faster than the Spitfire.

The Commander-in-Chief, Bomber Command, said on 12 December 1939 that he had 'no use' for the unarmed bomber, but that the newcomer showed promise for high-altitude reconnaissance. Eventually, after strong arguments put forward by Sir Wilfrid Freeman, the Air Member for Research, Development and Production, an order for fifty such aircraft was agreed, giving de Havilland a foot in the door. Design went ahead on a wooden photographic-reconnaissance (PR) machine weighing about 17,000lb (7,710kg) and having a top speed of 397mph at 23,700ft (639km/h at 7,220m). On 1 March 1940 a contract for fifty D.H.98 reconnaissance aircraft for the RAF was confirmed.

On 25 November 1940 the prototype (W4050) made its maiden flight, almost immediately confirming performance estimates. By February 1941 it had flown at 386mph (620km/h) – 20mph (32km/h) faster than the current mark of Spitfire. Official trials at Boscombe Down confirmed the high performance, luckily before the tailwheel jammed on a rough surface and the Mosquito's fuselage fractured. De Havilland brought along a replacement unit from the PR prototype,

W4051, and carpenters armed with saws, glue and skill demonstrated the ease of repair.

By May 1941 the 16,000lb (7,257kg) prototype had reached 392mph at 22,000ft (631km/h at 6,706m), making it faster than any existing fighter. An order for bombers followed, and a contract amendment now called for ten PR/Bomber Conversion Type equivalent to the later Mk IV. On 15 November W4064 became the first Mosquito bomber to join the RAF.

The true bomber prototype was W4057, the Mosquito B Mk V. Bomb-bay measurements showed that double the load could be carried if telescopic fins could be fitted to bombs. Instead, their tails were shortened so that the bomber could carry four 500lb (227kg) high-explosive (HE) bombs. With emphasis on high flying for protection, the next stage in Mosquito development came when W4050 was grounded in October 1941 for fitment of two-stage supercharged Merlin 61s.

Not until 31 May 1942 did the bomber conversion go into action, as a PR aircraft flying high to assess the effectiveness of the previous night's 'Thousand Bomber' raid on Cologne. The sixth flight that day was undertaken by Sqn Ldr Channer, who, for safety and to try for better photographs, decided to fly W4069 very low to escape radar and fighters. He thereby initiated a tactic now standard in the RAF. In September 1942 came a headline-grabbing low-level attack on the Gestapo HQ in Oslo. Four bombers, in Channer style, flew low across the North Sea to avoid radar detection. So low did they attack that some bombs went through the front windows of the building and out through the back. One bounced on a table at which a clerk was working.

Further proof of the Mosquito's bite came on 30 January 1943, when Nazi leaders broadcasting speeches in Berlin were twice rudely interrupted. Between February and May 1943 Nos 105 and 139 Squadrons, holding up to thirty-two aircraft between them, delivered highly spectacular and accurate combined low-level and shallow-dive attacks culminating in calls on Zeiss Optics at Jena and the nearby Schott glassworks deep in Germany.

A Bomber Command survey showed that losses during day raids reached about eight per cent. Dog-legged tracks were often flown, confusing defenders as to the target. Crews reckoned they had a five mph advantage over the Fw 190A fighter. Between 31 May 1942 and 31 May 1943 726 day sorties were flown for a loss of forty-eight aircraft. A third squadron, No 109, was using Mk IVs fitted with special blind bombing radio equipment codenamed 'Oboe' which entailed a 'cat' station measuring an aircraft's range and directing its track. A 'mouse' station signalled to the crew the precise moment for bomb release. On 20 December 1942 No 109 Squadron conducted an Oboe trial operation, relying upon the operators to give instructions as to when to release bombs on Lutterade power station in the Netherlands. Alongside was a cemetery, and when German radio announced that bombs had fallen upon it, the RAF knew that Oboe was accurate enough to revolutionise night bombing accuracy. From March 1943, Oboe Mosquitoes led Bomber Command in raids up to a radius of 278 miles (447km), beyond which it was impracticable – so far.

Summer 1942 brought a new high-flying Mosquito with a 2 psi (0.14kg/cm²) pressurised cabin. Specially modified, the bomber prototype was first flown on 8 August 1942. A week later it was carrying guns and ready to tackle high-flying Junkers Ju 86R nuisance raiders. Weighing 22,350lb loaded, this was the heaviest Mosquito yet.

The two-stage supercharged Merlin Mosquito was produced as the Mk IX, the first bomber flying in March 1943. Within weeks a Mk IX carrying a 500lb (227kg) bomb below each wing was tested. The 23,000lb (10,433kg) weight at which it was flying confirmed that a Mosquito could lift a 4,000lb (1,815kg) bomb load; a single 'cookie' if there was room in the bomb bay. Mosquito capacity was explored, and a 4,000lb 'cookie' was fitted in the swollen bomb bay of Mk IV DZ594, which first flew in July 1943. A lot of 'refining' followed,

Specially supercharged Rolls-Royce Merlins and a pressurised cabin enhanced the Mosquito XVI's high-altitude performance.

and on 9 October 1943 the decision was taken to modify more Mk IVs rather than interfere with Mk IX production. The first operational 4,000-pounders were dropped on Dusseldorf by Mk IVs on 23 February 1944.

The first production B Mk XVI pressure-cabin bomber was rolled out in October 1943. After twelve had been built, Mk XVIs came off the production lines able to carry 4,000lb (1,815kg) bombs.

A typical Mosquito Mk IX had a top speed of about 424mph at 26,200ft (678km/h at 7,860m), a figure which compared favourably with that for the Merlin 66-powered North American P-51 Mustang, which, on tests at Boscombe Down, reached 430mph at 22,000ft (688km/h at 6,600m), after which its performance fell away. Even German jets had a tough task to catch 'Mossies'. De Havilland had the potential answer; a jet-engined Mosquito.

Did the Mosquito live up to the forecasts? Many factors influence comparisons with other Bomber Command aircraft, but total sortie/overall loss relationships show: Stirling 18,440/3.81 per cent, Blenheim 12,214/3.62 per cent, Lancaster 156,192/2.13 per cent, and Mosquito (all versions including 100 Group fighters) 39,795/0.63 per cent, suggesting that de Havilland was right to push its idea. Amazingly, this small aeroplane dropped 8,386 huge 4,000lb (1,815kg) bombs. On 20/21 February 1945, and on the following thirty-five consecutive nights, Mosquitoes bombed Berlin, suffering a 0.58 per cent loss rate. During 1945 3,988 night sorties were dispatched to the capital for a loss of fourteen aircraft, a rate of 0.99 per cent. The largest number attacking in one night was 139 on 21/22 March. Of those, twenty made two calls in the one night. Yes, the Mosquito was unique.

The kamikazes

Volunteering for any wartime mission might result in death; becoming a Japanese kamikaze, kikusui or suicide pilot made it virtually certain. On 26 July 1944 two Aichi D3A1 'Val' dive-bombers approached the British East Indies Fleet at 8,000ft (2,400m), their purpose uncertain. Although HMS *Ameer* destroyed one, the other, hit by fire from HMS *Sussex*, bounced on to the ship, causing little damage. A third 'Val' then crashed on to, and seriously damaged, the minesweeper HMS *Vestal*, which had to be sunk by gunfire. It is believed that these were the first kamikaze attacks, following a suggestion in May 1944 to pack obsolescent aircraft with bombs, explosives and specially fused additional fuel, and to ask for volunteer pilots of the Special Air Corps to ram them into Allied warships.

During a special ceremony celebrating their flight to final glory, the first kamikaze pilots wore white robes. Later, many settled for a white scarf, the traditional symbol. Their chosen title of kamikaze, or 'divine wind', recalled a typhoon which frustrated a Mongolian invasion of Japan in 1280, the hope being that it might again come to the rescue. Pilots were drawn from varied backgrounds, some being deferred university students in

Most kamikaze assaults, including this attack on the carrier HMS Formidable *on 4 May 1945, involved the use of obsolescent aircraft. The effectiveness of a kamikaze hit upon a highly combustible aircraft carrier is obvious here. although a surprising number of attackers missed their targets.*

An effective hit on a carrier deck usually meant disposing of many aircraft, like these Corsairs aboard Formidable. *The ship could thus become useless for many hours, and sometimes far longer.*

their early twenties, prepared to repay a cultural debt by calmly sacrificing their lives. Performing for honour (bushido), not hatred, and eager to fly an obsolescent fighter or bomber to mutual destruction, a pilot's final spartan days would bring a pure, noble end to life. Some waited for months, even sleeping soundly in the hours preceding the final call.

Most of the aircraft used were ageing and single-engined, including the Aichi D3A 'Val', Mitsubishi A6M 'Zeke' (or 'Zero') and Nakajima Ki 43 'Oscar' fighters, and the Nakajima B5N2 'Kate' and B6N2 'Jill' and Yokosuka D4Y2 'Judy' dive bombers. Fully laden for a one-way flight they often carried a 250kg (550lb) bomb. Twin-engined aircraft also used included the Kawasaki Ki-48 'Lily', Mitsubishi Ki-21 'Sally', Nakajima J1N1 'Irving', the 30,500lb (13,835kg) Mitsubishi Ki-67 'Peggy' and Yokosuka P1Y1 'Frances', but these were more vulnerable to interception.

Suicide bombers had to elude extensive US fighter defences. Once that was achieved it was difficult to thwart their intent. The first attacks involved groups of aircraft which separated about thirty miles from the target area and then attacked singly to make themselves difficult to detect and distinguish. Some wave-skimmed to evade radar detection.

Off Leyte on 7 December 1944 kamikazes displayed a new tactic. A dozen or more grouped over one target and delivered a co-ordinated attack. No armoured ship was ever sunk by suicide bombers. Against very steep dives, quick reaction by a ship and a positive course change were sometimes effective. Although the pilot usually aimed his machine to its demise, controls became

very stiff at high speeds, making any manoeuvre by a ship worthwhile. If the aircraft was badly damaged by gunfire and its controls destroyed, engine damaged or pilot killed, inertia and the aircraft's characteristics tended to keep it on course unless a wing or other essential control surface was shot away. In some instances the aircraft continued to dive after both wings came away, changing it into a bomb.

Nothing except heavy, accurate gunfire could stop a suicide aircraft once the dive had begun. Mutual support was needed, with no ship being left on its own. Starting from outside automatic weapons range, a suicide aircraft reached its target in about twenty seconds. In a dive it was constantly accelerating, making it difficult to track. To counter massive suicide attacks, destroyers and escorts were positioned as outlying early warning radar pickets which made them highly vulnerable.

The full-scale kamikaze campaign began during October 1944. The dubious distinction of being the first ship to be hit fell to HMAS *Australia*, a distinctive three-funnel cruiser lying off Leyte, when, at dawn on 21 October, a low-flyer approaching from land and hit by AA fire turned and then crashed into the ship's foremast, setting fire to the bridge. Thirty officers and men lost their lives in the ensuing explosion and fire. On 9 January the battleship *Mississippi* was hit and *Australia* suffered for the fifth time, forty-four of the crew dying and the injured totalling sixty-five. Between 21 November and 13 January 1945 kamikazes sank 22 ships and damaged 126.

Next, the operations to take Iwo Jima initiated intensive kamikaze activity. The nightfighter carrier *Saratoga* soon came under attack, two bombs or torpedoes being followed by four suicide aircraft. Nevertheless, fires were under control within an hour, the ship maintaining 25kt. Forty-five minutes later another kamikaze attack was launched, two raiders being destroyed before a third placed its bomb on the flight deck, clouted the carrier then tumbled overboard. *Saratoga* had by now lost forty-nine aircraft and suffered 350 casualties, and had to withdraw.

Action leading to the seizure of Okinawa saw kamikazes reach their zenith, the first mass suicide attack developing during mid-afternoon on 6 April, when nearly 700 aircraft, 355 of them kamikazes, left Kyushu to sink shipping off Okinawa. About 400 penetrated outer defences, although again many vented their wrath upon the picket screen. Another huge force of attackers followed two hours later, quickly mauling two screening destroyers. Six ships were sunk and eighteen damaged, nearly all by suicide bombers, and 300 enemy aircraft were claimed destroyed.

Although it was spectacular, the small one-man Yokosuka MXY7 Ohka (Cherry Blossom), which began operating in April 1945, was a simply constructed

Japan's dedicated kamikaze manned rocket bomb, the Yokosuka MXY7 Ohka (Cherry Blossom), was used in relatively small numbers.

rocket-propelled piloted bomb. With a 5m (16ft 5in) wingspan, it weighed 1,895kg (4,718lb) loaded, and usually had a 816kg (1,800lb) tri-nitro-aminol warhead fitted to its 6m (19ft 10in) cylindrical fuselage. First used against shipping off Okinawa, it posed less of a threat than might be supposed because its slow launch aircraft was easy to intercept. Designed by naval ensign Mitsuo Ohta, the MXY7 was known to the Allies as the Baka (Idiot), it first flew in summer 1944, production of 755 examples of the Model 11 (the only operational version) starting in September. Carried in the belly of a Mitsubishi G4M2e land attack bomber, Ohka was launched from about 8,240m (27,000ft) at 280–320km/h (175–200mph) and could glide at 5° on a run of 83km (52 miles) at 368km/h (230mph). The electrically fired 588lb s.t. Type 4 Model 20 solid-fuel rocket motors would then start accelerating the bomb to 856km/h (535mph) before the terminal dive on to the target at 990km/h (620mph).

During April 1945 1,400 kamikaze sorties were dispatched from Kyushu alone in operation 'Ten-Go', the defence of the homeland. The first night kikusui attack took place on 28/29 April, over half of the attackers being destroyed. A serious error was the decision to make suicide operations compulsory, a crusade off the Philippines degenerating into an event devoid of all humanity.

Over 5,000 pilots died in suicide attacks. Long after the campaign failed, pilots were still being herded to death in the knowledge that the Emperor, regarded as a Supreme Being, along with their country, had not the slightest consideration for them as human beings.

Superfortress, scourge of Japan

Boeing's B-29 Superfortress will always be remembered as the aeroplane which dropped the first two atomic bombs, which rapidly ended the war with Japan. From Pacific islands, 'Superforts' of the US XXth Air Force had already wiped out many Japanese industrial cities, upon which they rained fearsome incendiary loads. Millions of close-packed, earthquake-frail Japanese buildings succumbed completely to the B-29s.

In 1938 Boeing had produced a study for a pressurised B-17 in which a large-diameter circular-section fuselage was mated with normal wing and tail components. Owing to problems regarding sealing the pressurised sections while retaining gun positions, no order was placed. Boeing, anticipating that such an aircraft might later be required, worked on the armament problem, eventually producing a layout having two pressurised sections linked by a small tunnel, and this was a feature of subsequent projects. Convinced it was on to a winner, Boeing built a mock-up as a private venture,

Boeing's B-29 Superfortress could deliver heavy loads to distant targets. Using mainly incendiaries, B-29s incinerated many of Japan's largest population centres – and then delivered the atomic bombs.

adding their new high-lift aerofoil section to a high-aspect-ratio wing. A top speed of 405mph at 25,000ft (652km/h at 7,620m) was estimated for the 'super-bomber', which was fitted with the smaller, lighter Pratt & Whitney R-2800 engines of 2,000 hp. At an all-up weight of 85,672lb (38,861kg) a range of 7,000 miles (11,265km) was estimated when carrying a ton of bombs. The maximum feasible load was 10,000lb (4,540kg).

In January 1940 a specification for such a 'super-bomber' was issued to the Boeing, Lockheed, Douglas and Consolidated companies, outlining a 400mph (640km/h) bomber with a range of 5,333 miles (8,530km) when carrying 2,000lb (900kg). When news was received of the RAF's day bombing losses, the specification was amended to call for increased defensive armament, self-sealing fuel tanks and extra armour. To cope with the additional loading, Boeing increased the Model 341's overall size and reverted to more powerful Wright R-3350s. Details of this design, the Model 345, submitted in May 1940 showed a 141ft 3in (43.05m) wing and a double-wheeled nosewheel undercarriage. While the range was unchanged, the maximum bomb load had risen to 16,000lb (7,260kg), but the estimated speed had fallen to 382mph at 25,000ft (615km/h at 7,260m). Greatly increased defensive armament was

mainly responsible, having risen from six manually operated 0.50in (12.7mm) guns to ten of the same calibre in Sperry periscopically controlled retractable power-operated turrets above and below the fuselage. Twin tail guns were supplemented by a 20mm cannon.

As the most favoured submission, the Boeing XB-29 received a go-ahead in June 1940, funding for two prototypes and a static test airframe following in August. May 1941 brought production authorisation and an order for 250, doubled the following January. By the time the XB-29 (four 2,200hp Wright R-3350-13s) flew, on 21 September 1942, 1,664 B-29s were on order. Major changes had previously been incorporated. The fuselage was slightly lengthened, engine cooling and turbosuperchargers were improved, a large fin fillet was added, the turrets were no longer retractable and the bomb bay was modified to carry 20,000lb (9,070kg). That new estimated all-up weight was 114,500lb (51,940kg), and the predicted maximum range was about 5,330 miles (8,580km) when carrying only a ton of bombs. The narrow-chord mainplanes raised concern, but they gave the aircraft its long range. Large Fowler flaps would take care of take-off and landing.

The second prototype, first flown on 28 December 1942, developed an engine fire during a landing approach on 18 February 1943 and crashed into a factory,

121

killing eleven top B-29 people and many in the building. Attention was at once concentrated on the fire problem, modifications being made to the third XB-29, which was also lost in a crash, but not before it had shown a need for different propellers and a revised General Electric system of turrets controlled from astrodomes. These changes delayed the fourteen YB-29s.

On 1 June 1943 the first Superfortress unit, the 58th Bombardment Wing (VH), was activated at Marietta, near Bell's Superfortress plant. With 150 Superfortresses promised for early 1944, the first operational Wing comprised five bombardment groups, the 40th, 444th, 462nd, 468th and 472nd, the last of which acted as a training unit at Smoky Hill Field, Salina, where, on 27 November 1943, the XXth Bomber Command was formed to control B-29 units. A second Very Heavy Wing, the 73rd, comprised four more groups to absorb the next batch of 150 Superfortresses.

By the end of 1943 the Bell-Marietta and Boeing-Renton plants also began turning out Superfortresses, which now had a maximum permissible weight of 138,000lb (62,597kg) and a normal gross weight of 133,500lb (60,556kg), figures that indicated the huge size of the B-29.

The Superfortress was the first production aircraft to make extensive use of remotely-controlled armament. Four barbettes, each housing two 0.5in (12.7mm) guns with 1,000 rounds per gun, were installed, two on top and two underneath the fuselage, controlled remotely through a complex fire control system operated from stations in the pressurised sections of the fuselage. Additionally, the tail turret gunner controlled two 0.50in machine-guns and a 100-round 20mm M-2 Type B cannon. Fourteen outer-wing, eight inner-wing and four bomb-bay tanks provided a maximum fuel capacity of 6,801gal (30,917lit) until four more were added to the wing centre-section, giving a total of 7,896gal (35,892lit). That gave the B-29 a normal range of about 3,700 miles (5,954km) when carrying 12,000lb (5,443kg) of bombs.

On 2 April 1944 the first B-29 for Far East operations landed at Chakulia, and on 24 April, only eighteen months after the XB-29 first flew, a Superfortress arrived at Kwanghan to start an operational China-based force.

About 100 Wichita-built B-29s of the 58th BW set out from India to attack Bangkok on 5 June 1944, many equipped with 'bombing through overcast' (BTO), H$_2$X and Loran, along with electronic countermeasures (ECM). The force bombed through the clouds using radar. On 15 June forty-seven B-29s operating from Chengtu bombed the steel mills at Yawata by night in the first raid upon Japan proper since 1942. The build-up of Superfortress missions was slow until the capture of the Mariana Islands of Saipan, Guam and Tinian in July and August 1944 allowed the construction of five extensive airfields, each holding a Wing of 180 Superfortresses and 12,000 men. B-29 groups began arriving in the Marianas during October. On 24 November 111 B-29s set out in daylight on a high-altitude mission led by Gen O'Donnell aboard *Dauntless Dotty*. This was the first operation by Marianas-based B-29s, eighty-five of which bombed targets in Tokyo. The first mass release of incendiaries took place on 18 December, when Hankow docks suffered under eighty-four B-29s while another sixty-three raided Mitsubishi at Nagoya on 3 January 1945. Fighters were active, 400 attacks being made on B-29s raiding the latter target, and five bombers subsequently being reported missing.

Major-General Curtis E LeMay took command of the Marianas-based B-29s in January 1945. Keen to launch incendiary attacks on Japanese cities, he decided to switch B-29s to low-altitude night bombing, which increased the bomb load without increasing vulnerability, and daylight attacks ended with the Tokyo raid of 4 March. The first night fire raid, flown on 9 March, involved 334 Marianas-based B-29s. Marker lead ships each released 180 70lb (31.8kg) M.47 napalm bombs before the main force attacked, each bomber dropping twenty-four 500lb (227kg) clusters of M.69 oil incendiaries intended to total 8,333 per square mile. The force, strung out in three 400-mile-long streams (640km), carried out a three-hour raid and incinerated 15.8 square miles of the heart of Tokyo, killing 83,793 people and injuring 40,918. A million lost their homes and 267,171 buildings were destroyed. Over the next eight days similar incendiary attacks were launched, twice upon Nagoya and on Osaka and Kobe. Superfortresses were soon partly stripped of defensive armament to allow maximum bomb loads to be carried.

Massive raids were launched throughout May, and the terrifying onslaught raged into June. On the 17th each of the four Wings visited a city; Omuta, Amamatsu, Yokkaichi or Kagoshima. Operations were mounted at a rate of two a week, LeMay targeting three or four towns each time following leaflet warnings. Eventually sixty urban centres were laid waste, Toyama being almost completely destroyed. Almost untouched were Hiroshima, Kokura, Niigati and Nagasaki.

When B-29-45-MO 44-86292, *Enola Gay*, released the atomic bomb over Hiroshima on 6 August 1945, it surely marked the climax of the Superfortress's fame. There was never any doubt that the weapon would be very large, and fifteen B-29s were modified to carry it. In mid-1944 the 393rd Bombardment Squadron (VH), part of the 509th Composite Group, was taken over by Col Paul W Tibbets to plan for the drop, and after much training it moved in May to North Field, Tinian. Two operational bombs arrived on Tinian and Hiroshima was chosen as primary target. The 9,790lb (4,170kg) 'Little

To extend the flying-bomb campaign against Britain, Heinkel He 111 bombers were adapted to carry a V1 'cruise missile' for release over the North Sea, usually towards London. The campaign extended from summer 1944 to early 1945.

Boy' cylindrical atomic bomb, 129in (3.27m) long and 31.5in (0.8m) in diameter, contained 137.3lb of uranium-235. *Enola Gay* left Tinian at 0245hrs on August 6 1945, and at 0915hrs the nuclear weapon was released from 31,600ft (9,630m). At 800ft (245m) above Hiroshima an explosion equivalent to 20,000 tons (20.3Mkg) of TNT devastated 4.7 square miles of the city, killing more than 70,000 people. Three days later a second atomic bomb was released over Nagasaki from Capt F Bock's B-29-35 MO, 44-27297 *Bockscar*. In all, 3,970 Superfortresses were built.

Although the nuclear weapons heralded a revolution in warfare, mercifully they did not necessarily give a glimpse of the future. That was displayed by the advanced aircraft and weapons available to Germany by 1945, which would form the basis of aerial bombardment during the rest of the 20th century.

A Glimpse of the Future

As the war drew towards its conclusion, weapons for future decades were emerging. One was the Fieseler Fi 103 FZG-76, or V1 flying bomb, intended for a massive New Year 1944 onslaught on London. Henschel's self-propelled glider bombs were launched against shipping in 1943, and in 1944 radio controlled PC 1400 bombs were aimed at warships off Plymouth. The V1 was quite different, being a ground launched 'cruise missile' which made its own way to the target. It relied on a simple pulse jet, its range being determined by the rate of fuel consumption. A small aeroplane with wings and a tail, its guidance was mainly governed by the orientation of its launch ramp. Fired from France in large salvos, flying

bombs came in at a few hundred feet, ending their flights by diving upon the target area and exploding to produce maximum blast effect.

The only way to halt the attacks was to destroy the launch sites, weapon dumps and factories, or force the launchers out of range, which was ultimately achieved. The Germans then started air-launching V1s from Heinkel He 111H-22s, a risky affair involving hazardous low flying and dangerous launching. They were, however, introducing the idea of stand-off air launched cruise missiles. Perhaps because V1s could be seen and heard until the fuel ran out, they were considered more disturbing than the V2 or A4 ballistic missile, forerunner of the ICBMs and moon rockets of later decades. The first V2 fell without any warning at Chiswick in September 1944. No warning of a V2's approach was possible, although launch trails from sites around the Hague were often visible. Postwar estimates stated that 26 million AA shells bursting in close proximity were needed to destroy a V2 in flight.

More general concern might have arisen had it been realised that jet-propelled bombers were available for raids on Britain. Germany expected a short war until the Luftwaffe's failed assault in 1940, and then to obtain victory German scientists, aerodynamicists and engineers made a great effort to devise war-winning weapons, but lacked sensible direction from the top. The Arado Ar 234B, the world's first operational jet bomber, was a typical advance which came too late to affect the war's outcome.

In 1940 a fast, medium-range reconnaissance aircraft operating at altitude to evade interception was called for,

The unreliability of jet engines curbed their use in bombers during the war. Arado Ar 234s flew some operational sorties, and the four engined Ar 234C version shown here was under extensive development.

with a top speed of 700km/h (435mph) and a range of 2,000km (1,242 miles). Arado's submission was a shoulder-wing monoplane powered by two gas turbines under the wings. Originally the Ar 234 was to have a jettisonable three-wheel trolley for take-off and retractable skids for landing, saving the weight of an undercarriage. The extensively glazed pilot's cockpit was in the fuselage nose.

The first machine was completed before 1942, but development of the Junkers Jumo 109-004 turbojet did not keep pace with airframe construction, the engines needing a year to reach a reasonably reliable state. Not until March 1943 did a pair of pre-production Jumo 004As reach Arado. After troublesome trials with the take-off trolley, the prototype first flew on 15 June 1943, from Rheine. Landing on skids was not very successful either, and a conventional nosewheel undercarriage be-

came favoured. A second Ar 234 flew on 27 July. The third, first flown on 25 August, had a pressure cabin and an ejector seat for the pilot. Flight trials showed the third aircraft to have a top speed of 750km/h (466mph), a ceiling of 12,500m (41,000ft) and a range of 1,200km (750 miles). Early prototypes exceeded the specification in several respects. The airframe was able to accept more power, and the aircraft flew much faster before encountering serious compressibility effects.

Another 'first' followed when two Ar 234 prototypes were fitted with four lighter 1,760kg (798lb s.t.) BMW 003A jet engines, these becoming the world's first four-engined jet bombers. One had four turbojets in individual underwing nacelles, while the other had them paired in two nacelles. The first, ready to begin flight trials on 1 February 1944, was beset by cowling contour problems and airflow through the narrow space between fuselage and nacelles caused severe shock waves. Both aircraft flew reconnaissance sorties during early summer 1944, Allied fighter pilots often finding themselves incapable of intercepting the Ar 234s.

Trolley and landing skids were proposed for some postwar jets, but those fitted to the Ar 234 showed their impracticability. After landing, aircraft had to be lifted on to a trolley before removal to a dispersal bay for turn-around. Landing areas would become cluttered with aircraft, so the Ar 234B had a narrow-track retractable nosewheel undercarriage. Powered by two Jumo 004B turbojets, it had a pressurised cabin and a braking parachute (a common postwar item) to reduce an emergency landing run. Production of the Ar 234B was well under way by autumn 1944, about 150 being delivered before 1945, by which time it had become one of four highest-

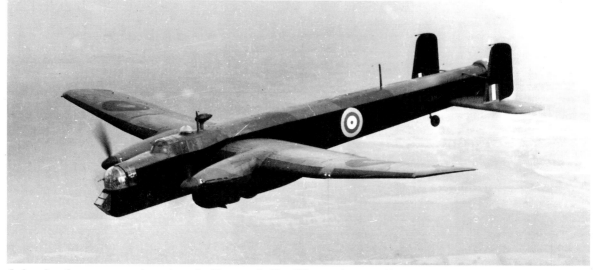

In less than four years amazing progress had been made. The differences between this ambling Armstrong Whitworth Whitley V and the Arado jet bomber, which flew almost four times as fast and twice as high, provide ample evidence of spectacular advances.

The Ar 234C four-engined BMW 003A-1 powered reconnaissance version of the Ar 234B was in production when hostilities ceased. It had maximum speeds of 829km/h (515mph) at sea level and 872km/h (542mph) at 6,004m (19,700ft), a range of 1,480km (920 miles) and could climb to 9,997m (32,800ft) in 11min 54sec. The Ar 234C-1 and -2 were abandoned in favour of the multi-role C-3. Other versions were to carry a Fieseler Fi 103 flying bomb on a cradle, the weapon being lifted by hydraulically-operated arms to clear the top of the aircraft for firing. Nineteen production Ar 234C-3s were completed before the war's end, but Ar 234Bs, of which 210 were completed by VE Day, were the only jet bombers to undertake operational missions. When the 'hot war' ceased in August 1945 the main ingredients for the Cold War were available; the jet bomber, the cruise missile and 'the bomb'. The bomber revolution was complete.

In 1939 a well-wrapped Whitley crew member in darkness pushes a load of propaganda leaflets down a chute – hopefully over the right place after map reading and dead reckoning had played their parts. By 1945 sophisticated radar, radio aids and assorted electronic devices were beginning to take control of operations.

priority types. Deliveries were made to KG 76, but many training accidents retarded operational activity until late summer 1944, when Ar 234s flew a number of reconnaissance flights over battle areas and, from Norway, over the northern British Isles.

Arado planned many far more advanced versions, one for high-speed research having two BMW 003A-1 turbojets and a BMW 718 bi-fuel rocket motor to augment thrust briefly by 2,700lb. Various wings and tail surfaces, some swept back, were planned, but none were completed.

Bibliography

Air Ministry, Weekly Intelligence Summaries (unpublished)

Craven, W E, and Cate, J L, (eds) *The Army Air Forces in World War II, Vol 5, The Pacific: Matterhorn to Nagasaki* (Chicago University Press, USA, 1948)

Glines, Lt Col C V, *The Doolittle Raid* (Orion Books, USA, 1988)

Jane's All the World's Aircraft 1945-1946 (Sampson Low, London, 1946)

PRO Air 22/203 Bomber Command Operations Statistics

Richards, Denis, *The Royal Air Force 1939–1945*, Vol 1 (HMSO, London 1953)

Sharp, M C & Bowyer, M J F, *Mosquito* (Crecy Books, 1996)

War with Japan, Vol VI (HMSO, London 1995)

Williamson, Murray, *Luftwaffe* (Grafton/Collins, London 1988)

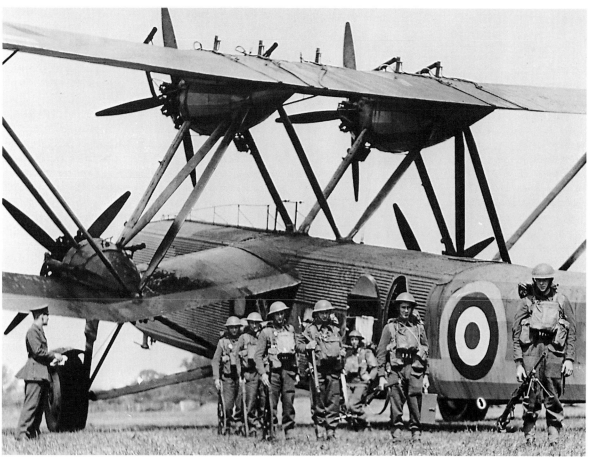

With no aircraft designed specifically for transport, at the outbreak of the war the RAF relied on converted bombers or requisitioned airliners, such as this Handley Page H.P. 42, for aerial movement of troops and supplies.

The Douglas C-47, known as Dakota to the British forces and Skytrain to the American, was derived from the DC-3 airliner and became the transport workhorse of the Allied forces.

5
Airmobility
Peter Hearn

Fallschirmjager

They had expected dive bombers. They had expected artillery fire. They had expected the distant rumble of armour. But the few lookouts in their emplacements on Belgium's fort Eben Emael had not expected these grey, bat-like figures swooping gracefully and silently from a dawn sky. Mesmerised, they watched in the half-light as the flying vehicles ploughed into the grass amongst them; vehicles that bore on their flanks – they realised too late – the black cross of Germany.

From each glider poured nine close-helmeted figures, firing as they came. The few defenders on the surface of the fort were overwhelmed by smallarms fire, grenade and flame. Others fled to join the main body of the fort's garrison in the supposed safety of the underground maze of tunnels, shelters and gun emplacements, there to be trapped and further stunned as specially prepared hollow charges tore through the six-foot-thick reinforced concrete of the emplacements to destroy the great guns intended to dominate this vital stretch of the border between Belgium and Germany. Within minutes, a fort manned by 1,200 men and considered impregnable had been neutralised by seventy-eight troops who had swooped upon it from dawn skies, at the cost of only six of their number.

Thus began the German assault on the Low Countries on 10 May 1940.

Further west, other glider-borne troops were taking the bridges of Vroenhofen and Velchrezelt. Paratroops were spilling from their Junkers Ju 52s from heights as low as 100m (300ft) to seize other river crossings at Moerdijk and Dordrecht. In Rotterdam itself, 50 paratroops jumped into a sports stadium, and 120 men were landed on the river Maas in 12 Heinkel He 59 seaplanes. A larger force of paratroops seized the airfield at Waalhaven, while further north others were dropping on to three airfields around The Hague, battling to secure them for the airlanding of reinforcements and supplies.

Although the assault on The Hague was fiercely resisted and losses of aircraft were heavy, Rotterdam was held by German airborne troops until the 9th Panzer Division entered the city on 14 May, having rolled along the carpet of intact bridges and neutralised strongpoints laid for it by the 'Fallschirmjager' – Germany's young 'hunters from the sky'. Holland surrendered to the invaders that evening. Belgium followed suit two weeks later.

This assault on the Low Countries was the largest and most dramatic airborne operation of the Second World War so far, but not the first. In February 1939, and again in November, small groups of Russian paratroops jumped near Summa and Petsamo to cut communications in support of the invasion of Finland. On a much larger scale, in September 1939, 4,000 paratroops and 12,000 airborne infantrymen had stood in readiness on Silesian airfields for operations against Poland at the outbreak of the war, but so devastatingly swift had been the advance of Germany's Panzer divisions that there had been no call for airborne assault – although the 16th Regiment of the 7th Air Division had been airlifted to forward battle positions north of Lodz to fight as ordinary infantry.

In April 1940 over 500 transport aircraft, mostly Ju 52s, with smaller numbers of heavy Ju 90s and Focke-Wulf Fw 200s, had spearheaded and then supported Germany's invasion of Denmark and Norway. Initial assault from the sky had achieved immediate results, largely through audacity and surprise rather than by weight of arms. During the brief and victorious campaign that followed, the Germans airlifted 29,280 men, 2,376 tons (2,414 tonnes) of supplies and 259,300 gal (980,000 litres) of aviation fuel into the combat zone.

This combination in 1940 of assault by parachute and glider, airlanding by transport aircraft and subsequent resupply and reinforcement from the air, was the first major demonstration of the concepts of airmobility and airborne operations conceived and developed by Italy, Russia, and above all by Germany during the years between the two world wars. The support of ground forces from the air had become an integral part of the German doctrine of 'Blitzkrieg': surprise assault by fast-moving columns of tanks, artillery and motorised infantry to break through or bypass the linear defence still favoured by traditional military thinking. The role of air support in this novel method of warfare was:

1　To gain air superiority
2　To provide reconnaissance
3　To bomb and strafe in close support of the advance
4　To deliver troops from the air ahead of or on the flanks of the advancing mechanised columns
5　To resupply and reinforce the ground assault.

This doctrine had a vigorous and far-sighted proponent in Generalleutnant Kurt Student, commander of Germany's fledgling airborne forces. It also had the personal backing of Hitler, and of Goering as commander of the Luftwaffe.

Germany's startling use of paratroops in 1940 relied upon the Junkers Ju 52, which remained the backbone of German airmobility throughout the war.. Jumps were made from as low as 400ft, using the RZ-1 parachute with its distinctive single suspension point.

Student enjoyed the benefits of single command of the men and of the aircraft that were to carry them; the whole force was part of the Luftwaffe. This centralised command was an advantage that would not be enjoyed by Student's British and American emulators.

Not only did Student so aptly match his own ideas on airborne support to the overall doctrine of Blitzkrieg; encouraged by Hitler, he purposely fostered the aura of élitism that has ever since been the stamp of the paratrooper of all nations. It is a creed that represents the supreme confidence and audacity of men who are prepared and expect to fight against great odds and win. It was a mystique reinforced by the assaults on Scandinavia and the Low Countries, where the purely physical blows dealt by the airborne invasion had been augmented by the devastating psychological impact on the enemy. The confusion and disruption caused by the Fallschirmjager had struck at the heart of civilian, political and military willpower.

To back a well-defined policy, integrated command, and high-calibre troops, Kurt Student had the tools for the job. He had an aircraft well suited to the task, gliders specifically built for it, and a reliable parachute. The tri-motor, low-wing Ju 52/3m with its distinctive corrugated metal skin had been developed by Ernst Zindel from the single-engine Ju 52 of 1930. The Ju 52/3m first flew in 1932, intended as a civilian airliner but with its potential as a bomber and troop carrier barely disguised. The military version produced in 1934 found employment in both roles with Germany's Condor Legion during the Spanish Civil War. Readily converted to the parachuting role in 1936, the Ju 52 could deliver eighteen fully equipped men to a range of 620 miles. It was an excellent glider tug, and its ruggedness, reliability and short-take-off-and-landing capability commended it for an airlanding role in forward battle areas. Affectionately known to the first generation of Fallschirmjager as 'Tante Ju', it attracted an alternative nickname of 'Corrugated Coffin', not through any inherent fault, but because of the extreme battle situations into which it was flown. Of the 475 Ju 52s committed to the assault on the Low Countries, 170 were lost, mainly during the heavily opposed airlandings on airfields, roads, fields and beaches around The Hague.

By far the most widely used German assault glider was the DFS 230, which could carry eight heavily-armed troops. It was used to capture the Belgian fort of Eben Emael on 10 May 1940, and took part in the invasion of Crete in May 1941.

The Ju 52/3m would remain the mainstay of German air transport throughout the war, but the four-engined types, the Ju 90 and structurally less reliable Focke-Wulf

The Messerschmitt Me 321 Gigant glider could deliver a massive load of 130 troops or 26,000lb of freight; provided it could be encouraged into the air. This could be achieved by two or three tugs or by using a Heinkel He 111Z, a composite of two He 111s with a fifth engine added.

Fw 200B Condor, would provide heavier lift. A small number of Dornier Do 24 and Do 26 flying boats would provide a transport and communication facility, as they had done effectively during the Norwegian campaign. Development and production of the promising Ju 252 Herkules, a thirty-five-seater equipped with a rear loading ramp, would be cancelled in 1944 as Germany's priority for dwindling resources concentrated mainly on fighters.

The gliders that swooped with such devastating effect on to Eben Emael were DFS 230s, each carrying eight troops in the fabric-covered, steel-tube fuselage. As Germany's most numerous battle glider, over 2,200 would be built during the war. Later versions had enlarged doors for the loading of anti-tank guns and motorcycles, but the real 'heavy-lift' would be provided by 1,500 vehicle-carrying Gotha Go 242s, small numbers of the 30-seat DFS 330, and the Messerschmitt Me 321 glider, which deserved its name of Gigant (Giant) by swallowing through its nose-mounted clamshell doors a heavy tank or an 88mm gun, or up to 200 troops, who

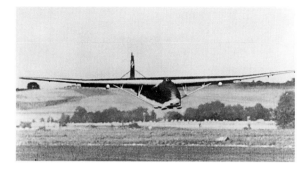

With the addition of six engines the Me 321 (top left) *became the Me 323. Its huge nose doors allowed rapid unloading for its cargo of troops, freight or vehicles.*

were to be carried on two decks. The main problem was hauling this 24-ton load into the air, which required a 'troika' of three aircraft before a special five-engined tug consisting of two Heinkel He 111s joined together, was produced for the task. More than 200 of these Messer-schmitt monsters were converted into six-engine aircraft as the Me 323, also known as the Gigant. Larger still but a failure and not entering service was the Junkers Ju 322 glider, whose suitability was questioned when a tank fell through its wooden floor during trials.

Germany's RZ-1 parachute derived its single-point suspension and harness from study of Italy's Salvatore parachute, and its 8.5m (28ft) circular canopy from meticulous trials at the Luftwaffe test site at Rechlin. The performance of the RZ-1, particularly its stability, was to be improved in subsequent models, culminating in 1943 in the RZ-36 with a triangular canopy. Thus equipped, Germany had demonstrated forcibly during the early

years of the war the effective exercise of airpower to achieve a ground force objective.

It was a lesson waiting to be copied.

The British reaction

The first to copy it were the British. Winston Churchill, ever an admirer of the audacious and the unconventional in warfare, even when at the receiving end of it, was much impressed by Germany's use of airborne assault, and on 6 June 1940 had the foresight to ask the Joint Chiefs of Staff to form 'a corps of at least 5,000 para-chute troops'. At a time when they were desperately preparing to repel a likely invasion, not launch one, the Chiefs cast a sour eye upon this directive. British military thinking had in any case rejected the concept of para-chute assault when demonstrated to observers by the Russians in 1936. It had neither the knowledge nor the will to set about it now. Nor did it have any suitable aircraft for such a task. Although Britain had pioneered air mobility through its use of aircraft to transport freight and troops, particularly in the Middle East, the nation had entered the war in 1939 with only a few outdated remnants of that force in the form of small numbers of Handley Page Harrows, Bristol Bombays and even older Vickers Valentia biplanes, still operating mostly overseas. The RAF had no modern, custom-built transport aircraft. The emphasis during the rearmament phase of the 1930s had been on air defence, in which air transport had little part to play.

To fill the transport gap in 1939, and also to provide aircraft for various training roles, Britain's airlines were brought under government contract. These airlines and charter companies tried to persuade the Air Ministry that they should be allowed to maintain their identities, their aircraft and their personnel to provide an 'Air Merchant Service' similar to that given by their seafaring colleagues. Instead, the private companies and their assets were requisitioned and their personnel conscripted. Some of the 'assets' found their way to RAF Hendon to be operated by the RAF's only transport squadron at the time, No 24. To the squadron's Avro Ansons and de Havilland Tiger Moths were added impressed D.H. Rapides and Dragons, Armstrong Whitworth Ensigns, Percival Proctors, Airspeed Envoys, Lockheed Lodestars, and even three Italian Savoia-Marchetti S.73s. An equally diverse array of airline pilots was welcomed into the RAF Volunteer Reserve to fly these aircraft on communication flights throughout Britain and Allied Europe. In 1940, as the British Expeditionary Force retreated in confusion towards the Channel ports, this motley collection of unarmed airliners and freighters flew ammunition and other essential supplies into forward airfields and strips, often under the guns of the enemy.

The support of military operations by British airlines and their machines would reach further afield when Imperial Airways airliners and flying boats were employed to ferry personnel and small-bulk freight, primarily to the Middle East, India and the Far East, following where possible the established routes through central Africa. An alternative to the use of civilian air transport lay in the conversion of bombers to a passenger or freight role. It was to this resource that the RAF turned when, as a result of Churchill's directive, it was tasked with the training of Britain's first paratroopers.

To establish a Central Landing School at Manchester's Ringway Airport in June 1940, came a renowned flyer from the First World War and civilian aviation, now returned to uniform in the RAFVR, Sqn Ldr Louis Strange, and a Major of the Royal Engineers, John Rock. They had one thing in common – neither knew anything about parachuting. Yet within a month of their arrival, and with no great encouragement from their superiors in either Service, they began the training of Britain's first paratroops. Instruction was given by a hastily gathered band of RAF parachute technicians and Army physical training instructors, with an element of parachuting know-how being provided by two former exhibition jumpers from the travelling flying circuses of the 1930s, Bruce Williams and Harry Ward, soon to be joined by a third, Bill Hire.

The parachute first used for British airborne training was a manually operated aircrew training type converted for 'static line' operation. When, on the fourth day of training, one failed to open and a man fell to his death, the canopy-first deployment was changed to rigging-line first, and the pack modified accordingly, to create the 8.5m (28ft) 'X' Type parachute that was to give Britain's paratroops good service throughout the war and for almost twenty years beyond.

The bomber that the Air Ministry reluctantly made available for conversion to parachute training was the Armstrong Whitworth Whitley; six of them. The all-metal Whitley Mk V first flew in 1936 but was obsolete as a bomber by 1940. Paratrooping gave it a new lease of life, even though it was unsuited to and desperately uncomfortable for the job. A narrow fuselage described by Harry Ward as 'a sewer-like passageway connecting the tail to the nose' could accommodate ten jumpers, who would shuffle on their bottoms to drop through an aperture where the ventral gun-turret had once been, hoping not to smash their faces on the far side of the 'hole', an injury known as the 'Whitley Kiss'.

The main drawback to British development of an airborne force was, and would long remain, this lack of an air transport fleet and the reluctance of the Air Ministry to provide one. Louis Strange made strenuous but

Britain's pioneer paratroopers emplane in an Armstrong Whitworth Whitley Mk V, converted to carry ten paratroopers to drop through an aperture in the floor.

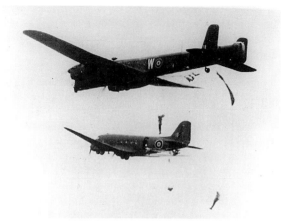

For British airborne forces, the Dakota with its side-door exit provided a welcome replacement in 1942 for the cramped and aged Whitley, nearest.

unsuccessful bids for Douglas DC-3s. Not until America entered the war would this eminently suitable aircraft be made available to Britain's airborne forces (see photo above, and also page 126). Meanwhile, British paratroops would continue to train and to go to war through the dreaded 'hole in the fuselage' of the Whitley and other converted bombers such as the Short Stirling, Armstrong Whitworth Albemarle, Handley Page Halifax and Lockheed Hudson.

For training purposes an unusual 'flying machine' would supplement the Whitleys from mid 1941, a tethered barrage balloon. From a 'cage' suspended beneath the balloon, trainees would make their first two jumps under well-controlled but silently terrifying conditions. The balloon was not well liked, but it would serve airborne forces as a basic training vehicle for more than fifty years.

Soon after its formation, the Central Landing School was renamed the Central Landing Establishment and divided into three sections: parachute training, technical development, and gliding.

Early trials of military gliding were carried out by a handful of former sport flyers including Robert Fender, Peter Davis, Laurence Wright and Douglas Davie. When it was concluded that there was potential in the concept (already well proven by the Germans!) the training of pilots began, using civilian sailplanes, mostly Kirby Kites, while production of a military glider was put in hand. This was the General Aircraft Hotspur. An unnecessarily elegant glider that reflected its sporting origins, the Hotspur could deliver seven troops. Its small capacity was determined by uncertainty at the time as to the type of aircraft that might be available to tow it. If bombers could not be converted to the role, the only other available aircraft were old biplane bombers such as the Hawker Hart, used during the early trials at Ringway. Although some 1,000 Hotspurs were built, they never went to war but

Britain's first military glider, the General Aircraft Hotspur, shows its elegant lines. It could carry seven troops, but was used mainly for the training of pilots and never went to war.

were used solely for training. Other gliders, larger and more functional, would fill the operational role.

Who was to fly the glider into battle? The RAF did not want to; gliding was a one-way ticket. The Army, on the other hand, was keen to do so. Nor would it confine its pilots simply to flying others into the combat area. On landing, they too would join the battle as infantrymen. So was born the Parachute Glider Regiment, formally established in February 1942 as part of the recently formed Army Air Corps, which was also responsible for Air Observation Posts.

Despite the lack of knowledge, inadequacy of equipment, high-level indifference and rivalries, not to mention a disturbing casualty rate, Britain's embryo airborne force was created, and went to war in a small way in February 1941. Flying out of Malta in six Whitleys, forty men of 11 Special Air Service Battalion parachuted at night into Southern Italy to attack the Tragino aqueduct. Material damage was slight and all the men were captured when attempts to recover them by submarine failed, but Operation Colossus demonstrated Britain's ability to strike deep into enemy territory, and Italy was frightened into diverting large numbers of troops to home defence. This 'tying up' of forces in a defensive role against surprise attack has been an often underestimated function of airborne forces.

In March 1941 Winston Churchill visited Ringway to see how his brainchild was faring. Instead of the 5,000 paratroops he had asked for, he found fewer than 400 drawn up on the parade ground for his inspection, watched a mere forty-four others parachute on to the airfield from their ancient Whitleys, and saw one lonely Hotspur looking very unwarlike as it swooped elegantly to earth. Disappointed by the numbers, he was, however, much impressed by the enthusiasm and spirit of the airborne pioneers. In a testy note to the Chiefs of Staff he subsequently asked for an immediate expansion of the force. In this he was also influenced by another awesome demonstration of airmobility and airborne potential by Germany's Fallschirmjager.

Crete
On 20 May 1941, having battered his enemy with almost unopposed bombing and strafing, Kurt Student launched the first wave of 8,000 airborne soldiers from a force of 500 Ju 52s and 74 DFS 230 gliders against the Allied-held island of Crete. The immediate aim of Operation Mercury was to capture and hold airfields and docks for subsequent reinforcement by airlanded and seaborne forces.

Once the defenders had recovered from the immediate shock of seeing their skies suddenly filled with parachutes and gliders, they fought back so viciously that by nightfall of the first day, with none of their objectives taken, the Germans seemed to be pinned down. But a tactical error by the defenders of Maleme airfield let the invaders through, and, despite heavy losses of aircraft from artillery and mortar fire, into this base Student poured his airlanded reinforcements. The tide of battle turned, and even the destruction of their seaborne force by the Royal Navy could not now stop the Germans. On the very day that Churchill again urged the expansion of his airborne force upon his Chiefs of Staff, Gen Freyburg, commanding the Allied forces on Crete, began to evacuate his men from the lost island. It was the first – and only – major battle to be won entirely by airborne forces.

While Churchill – and other distant observers – were again impressed, Hitler was not. Although he was pleased at the victory, he weighed it against the cost; 56 per cent of his 8,100 paratroops were killed or wounded, the airlanded Mountain Division suffered 34 per cent casualties, and 258 of the 500 Ju 52s were destroyed. The price had been too high, Hitler decided. And he needed his Ju 52s to haul supplies to his new and greater battle area, his Eastern Front. Furthermore, he believed that airborne assault was losing the element of surprise. He personally cancelled a well-planned airborne invasion of Malta because he feared a repeat of the heavy losses sustained in Crete. There would be no more mass assaults by his beloved Fallschirmjager.

But he did not disband them. Expansion and training of the airborne units continued, and their technical capability was improved. Night jumping techniques were evaluated and practised; parachutes were improved; new methods of carrying weapons into war were developed; and glider technology was advanced with the introduction of 'Piggy-back' gliders carried aloft by converted fighter-bombers, and 'dive gliders' that would spend less time in the air providing targets for ground fire. Few of these innovations went into battle, however, for never again would German paratroops descend *en masse* upon a startled foe. Thus an operation that spurred the development of Allied airborne forces spelt the end for the victors themselves.

The Americans
Winston Churchill was not the only one impressed by the capture of Crete by airborne forces alone. So were the Americans. During the 1930s the USA had shared Britain's indifference to the airborne concept. However, in 1939 the US Army undertook an appraisal of 'air infantry' which concluded that certain tasks could be undertaken by infantrymen landed by aircraft or parachute. But as America girded for likely war, the project was temporarily shelved in favour of more pressing requirements, until the combat use of paratroops by Russia and more emphatically by Germany, spurred the USA towards the formation of its own airborne force.

In early 1940 the task was given to Maj William Lee,

An American Waco CG-4A is towed aloft by a C-47. It could accommodate thirteen troops.

destined to become revered as 'father of the US Airborne'. Like his British counterparts, he had to learn from scratch. He had a new parachute made – the T-4, whose canopy-first opening delivered a severe shock. His jumpers, however, had the comfort of a reserve parachute carried on the chest. He gathered instructors from the test-jumpers of the Air Corps, and had no lack of volunteers from the Army for a Parachute Test Platoon. And he had a highly suitable aircraft.

Early jumps were made from a C-33 (the military designation for the DC-2), but it was the Douglas C-47 that was to become the mainstay of air support for the Americans and their allies. In 1932 the Douglas DC-2 had introduced a new breed of sleek, low-wing transport craft to the world's airlines, and its development culminated in the DC-3. With a reinforced metal floor, a strengthened undercarriage and a large loading door, the military version of the DC-3 entered service with the US Army Air Corps in 1941 as the C-47 Skytrain, offering a capacity to carry 6,000lb (2,722kg) of freight or twenty-seven troops over a range of 6,000 miles. Like the Ju 52, its side door provided a far safer, more convenient and quicker mode of exit than the 'holes' through which British pioneer paratroops went to war. Rugged, durable, and with a capacity to well exceed that 6,000lb of freight, as long as the maxim 'shove everything as far forward as it will go' was obeyed, the C-47 became a remarkable workhorse. Over 10,000 would emerge from America's vast manufacturing capacity during the war, of which 1,900 would go to the RAF under Lend-Lease arrangements. To the thirty-three RAF squadrons equipped with the C-47 it became the Dakota. As an indication of the extent to which Britain had fallen behind in the production of transport aircraft, when the Dakota was issued to No 31 Squadron in India it replaced the Vickers Valentia.

The evaluation of methods and equipment by William Lee's Parachute Test Platoon culminated in the

formation of the 501st Parachute Infantry Unit and plans to form three more airborne battalions. These plans were accelerated and extended following the German victory in Crete, and within a year of the USA entering the war in December 1941 it had two airborne divisions, the 82nd and the 101st. These divisions included a glider regiment and two parachute regiments.

The USA did not have a glider policy until early in 1941, and when it did decide that it had a need for such a force, procurement of an appropriate aircraft did not run smoothly. It was given a low priority, to the extent that major aircraft manufacturers were not allowed to bid for glider design and construction contracts lest they interfere with their more important task of aeroplane production. The small companies who gained the orders then subcontracted to a total of 150 other businesses to provide components. The result was administrative chaos and flawed workmanship – sometimes fatally flawed.

However, out of this chaos came the Waco CG-4A, to become the busiest American glider of the war, with a production total of 14,000. Of these, 700 were supplied to the British, who called it the Hadrian and did not like it. 'Burn the bloody gliders and fly the bloody crates,' suggested a sergeant-major of the Glider Pilot Regiment as he watched Waco machines being uncrated and assembled. The CG-4A could carry thirteen troops or light vehicles and guns, and had a nose door. It was small enough for two at a time to be towed by a C-47, usually in tandem.

Of a further 2,000 gliders built in America, the largest was the Waco CG-13A, with a capacity for forty troops. The Douglas CG-17 was a light, cheap and engineless version of the C-47.

As in Britain, the US development of airborne forces out of few resources and no pre-knowledge was marred and confused by much apathy, a general lack of under-

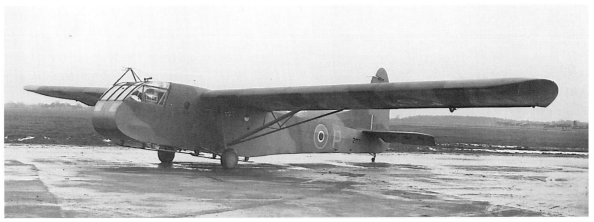

In Britain, the Waco was known as the Hadrian.

standing of the potential of the new arm, and inter-Service differences of opinion and priority. Even those dedicated to the airborne concept in principle differed on the implementation of that concept in detail. There was, for example, much argument about the relative merits of glider and parachute. Each had its particular advocates. Germany had pioneered a concept that favoured glider assault backed up by parachute troops, as Student had employed at Crete, and before that in the assault on the Corinth Canal. America's doctrine, enshrined in its 1942 *Tactics and Techniques of Airborne Troops*, put the paras in first, reinforced by glider landings. British planners tended to adapt the 'batting order' to specific circumstances.

It was with the exact role of its airborne force undecided and its potential poorly understood at higher levels of command that America first sent its paratroops into battle.

The Middle East

Elements of America's airborne forces were parachuted into North Africa in late 1942 in a combined operation with troops of the British 1st Parachute Battalion, to support the Operation Torch seaborne invasion. The airborne operation was poorly conceived and planned, was largely unopposed, and through no fault of the paratroops, contributed little to the success of the invasion. In a pure infantry role the airborne soldiers subsequently fought with immense distinction, justifying the élitism they had inherited from their German counterparts and from their distinctive method of going to war.

This was not the first use of paratroops in North Africa, for its deserts had been the birthplace of David Stirling's Special Air Service. Self-trained with 'acquired' parachutes and ancient Vickers Valentia and Bristol Bombay aircraft, sixty of Stirling's men had been launched against targets in the Tobruk area, at night, on to rocky ground, in a 45mph sandstorm. The painful

results decided Stirling to go overland in future, but the parachute would later take a much-expanded SAS into Europe on numerous clandestine missions.

Later in the North African campaign, groups of Italian paratroopers of the 'X' Regimenti Arditi would be dropped on similar small-scale sabotage raids against Allied positions, with varying success.

Also in this theatre of great distances and poor surface communications, air freighting in both a strategic and a tactical mode played an increasingly important role.

Suffering losses of almost 40 per cent of seaborne supplies destined for Rommel's Afrika Korps, Germany was forced in late 1942 to establish a Mediterranean 'air bridge'. This, too, was costly, seventy Ju 52s being lost to Allied fighters in November alone. This battered fleet was reinforced with Ju 90s, Focke-Wulf Fw 200s, twenty six-engined Me 323s and large numbers of gliders. In two months this combined force lifted 9,000 men and 5,000 tons of supplies across the Mediterranean, but all in vain. The aircraft that had supplied the ground forces were now called upon to fulfil another role of air support: the evacuation of a defeated army from the battle zone.

For the Allies, air transport provided a strategic link between North Africa and bases in England, Gibraltar and Malta, and tactical support within the combat area, provided largely by Lockheed Hudsons converted from their bombing and sea-reconnaissance roles, and later by similarly adapted B-24 Liberator bombers. An example of particularly audacious use of air support was Operation Chocolate, which involved the establishment and resupply of a desert base, LG125, for a Wing of Hurricanes fifty miles behind enemy lines and destructively close to the enemy airfields and supply routes that were its targets.

The Far East

Air transport both strategic and tactical played an important role in the Far East and Pacific, although direct assault by paratroops was carried out on a relatively small scale; audacious raids rather than the massive airborne operations of the European theatre were the norm.

Japan entered the war with a variety of modern transport aircraft, some of indigenous design (such as the licence-built Mitsubishi Ki-57 Type 100), others built under licence such as the DC-3 derivative Showa L2D1 and the Nakajima Ki-34 Type 97, inspired by the Douglas DC-2. With these aircraft, Japanese paratroops, trained by German instructors, captured airfields in the Celebes and Timor and oilfields in Sumatra in 1942. But Japan failed to develop the strength of airlift for larger-scale operations, and loss of air superiority in the later stages of the conflict deterred any airborne assaults at all, apart from two desperate raids launched in the Philippines in late 1944.

In India, Britain established a Parachute Training School manned by instructors from Ringway to train an Indian Parachute Brigade, but the only large-scale operation by elements of this force came in 1945, with a largely unopposed drop outside Rangoon as part of the reoccupation of Burma.

American paratroops mounted imaginative and largely successful assaults in the Pacific theatre, notably to capture airfields along the northern coast of New Guinea, and most spectacularly against the island fortress of Corregidor, where they completely surprised the Japanese defenders by parachuting from low-flying C-47s on to the parade ground and a narrow strip of cratered land on the very crown of the island, instead of on to the more obvious but very vulnerable lower ground. Shortly afterwards, a classic *coup de main* by 125 paratroops rescued, without loss, 2,000 civilian captives under threat of execution in the Los Banos prison camp in the Philippines. These and similar operations may have been low in numbers but were high in the basic ingredient of successful airborne assault, audacity and surprise. The only glider-borne assault in the Pacific came in 1945, towards the end of the war, when seven US gliders landed troops in northern Luzon to hasten the capture of the island.

It was through resupply and reinforcement that the transport aeroplane best served the ground forces in the Far East and Pacific. In retrospect it can be argued that not enough use was made of airmobility in a military theatre of vast distances, most of them scattered over the sea or rugged terrain. However, limited resources and in some cases an uncertainty of vital air superiority undoubtedly influenced air transport operations in these areas.

With few hospitable airfields, the seaplane came into its own as a means of communication in this zone. Across the Pacific (and across the Atlantic) Pan-Am's giant Boeing 314 Clippers provided a long-range mili-

Japan developed an airborne capability based on German methods, but made only limited use of gliders, mainly owing to a lack of towing aircraft. The Kokusai Ku-7, seen here, was the largest assault glider built in Japan and could hold thirty-two troops or an eight-ton tank. By the time of its first flight, in August 1944, Japan was losing the war, and it did not progress beyond the experimental stage.

tary passenger service for the Allies similar to that provided by Imperial Airways flying boats via the African routes. Within the war zone, US Army Air Force and US Navy flying boats such as the Martin PB2M-1 Mars and the smaller Catalina and Mariner were used for supply and communications. Britain's Short Sunderland flying boats provided both strategic and in-theatre support.

The China-Burma-India theatre saw two outstanding examples of air transport support. From 1942 to 1945 US and Chinese forces operating out of southern China were sustained by massive airlift from bases in India and Burma. Pushed westwards by threat of Japanese fighters, this route had to surmount the Himalayas; 'Crossing the Hump' it was called. The operation began with C-47s, each carrying three tons of supplies. As the C-47s were progressively replaced by Curtiss C-46 Commandos and smaller numbers of Douglas C-54s and Consolidated C-109s, the monthly airlift rose from 2,800 tons (2,840 tonnes) in February 1943 to 7,000 tons (7,110 tonnes) by December of that year, then to 12,000 tons (12,200 tonnes) in early 1944.

A more direct use of air support was provided in Burma for Orde Wingate's 'Chindits' in their long-range penetrations of Japanese-held territory east of the Chindwin river. Wingate had previously employed RAF transport support in a successful campaign against the Italians in Ethiopia. Now, this 'genius for unorthodox and novel warfare' as his commander, Gen Wavell, called him, inspired an operation that presaged modern concepts of air mobility with its total integration of air and ground forces employing an ingenious variety of techniques and airborne operations. His first infiltration of Japanese territory in 1942 involved 3,000 men in eight separate 'columns' moving by foot through hazardous terrain where their success and very survival depended

The 'Chindit' campaigns in Burma saw the Second World War's best example of air transport in support of a ground campaign, including the early use of helicopters for communications and casualty evacuation. A Sikorsky R-4 is seen here.

upon supply from the air by RAF C-47 Dakotas and Lockheed Hudsons. Wingate's more ambitious operation in 1944 was more generously supported by an integrated USAAF force of bombers and fighters, gliders, Stinson L-1 and L-5 light aircraft, and seven squadrons of C-47s, all under the command of the equally inspirational Lt Col Phillip Cochran, USAAF. His force of support aircraft became the 1st Air Commando Group, whose successors have continued to give dedicated air support to clandestine operations to this day.

Of the 12,000 Chindits committed to Operation Thursday in 1944, 10,000 were airlifted (with 1,300 mules) into rough airstrips and jungle clearings that had been seized by glider-borne assault troops then prepared by glider-borne engineers. The troops who struck out from these forward bases were further supplied by air-

Designed for army co-operation, the Westland Lysander provided an air-drop capability for ground forces and air-sea rescue, and a clandestine delivery and retrieval system for Allied agents, usually under cover of darkness.

drop and glider, and at the end of the operation were mostly airlifted out of the battle zone. An increasingly valued aspect of air support, the recovery of the wounded, was demonstrated in the Burma campaign. Mostly they were flown out of the forward areas by light aircraft. Some were actually returned by glider, for among the ingenious innovations in concept and technique born of this campaign was a system whereby Waco gliders that had delivered their load could subsequently be 'snatched' from the ground by a low-flying C-47. The helicopter also made an appearance in support of the Chindits, the Sikorsky R-4 and later the R-5 being used for communications and casualty evacuation.

Orde Wingate died in an air crash before the end of his campaign, but not before his vision, well supported by colleagues and by senior commanders, had inspired a major advance in the concept of airmobility.

Special operations

Britain's second airborne operation had been more successful than its ill-fated attack on the Tragino aqueduct. On 27 February 1942 120 men of the 2nd Parachute Battalion made a daring night drop from their Whitleys on to the French coast at Bruneval, near Le Havre, to overcome the defences of a German radar installation, not to destroy it but to enable a radar expert specially trained for the mission to examine, dismantle, and take parts from it. The force was recovered from a nearby beach by a naval flotilla. It was a classic *coup de main*; a clandestine raid rather than a full airborne assault.

Throughout the war and in most of its theatres the support of covert operations was an important but understandably less apparent function of air transport, ranging from the dropping or air landing of single 'agents' to the delivery of 'special forces' in groups of various strengths. A total of 420 men and women of Special Operations Executive (SOE) alone entered France during the war, mostly by parachute or air-landing. For the latter, the Westland Lysander was well suited. Evolved as a two-seat army co-operation aeroplane, it found wider use during the war for air-sea rescue and for the transport of agents into and out of hostile territory. Four such passengers could be crammed into its fuselage, and its short-take-off-and-landing capability made it ideal for the small fields, roads and rough moorland that it used for missions in occupied Europe.

An aircraft offered the obvious advantage of lifting people out of as well as into hostile territory. A fine example of a 'lift-out' was Germany's rescue in 1943 of the deposed Benito Mussolini from imprisonment in what was thought to be an impregnable hotel 9,000ft up in the Abruzzi mountains, served only by a funicular railway. Led by self-styled 'air commando' Otto Skorzeny, eighty men were landed in twelve DFS gliders on a narrow outcrop of rock alongside the hotel, while others dropped by parachute into the valley below to secure the funicular. The stunned defenders offered little resistance. A small Fieseler Storch communications aeroplane landed, and flew out Mussolini and Skorzeny by simply trundling off the ledge and picking up flying speed as it dived into the valley.

Britain's first use of gliders to mount a covert operation ended in tragedy. In November 1942, Operation Freshman sought to land thirty airborne engineers in two Horsa gliders in southern Norway, to sabotage a hydro-electric plant that was providing Germany with 'heavy water', an essential element for atomic research. At night and in a snowstorm, and unable to locate the radio beacon set up on the ground by four members of the SOE who had previously parachuted into the area, both gliders crash-landed. Eleven men were killed outright, and the remainder were captured by German troops and summarily executed. One of the Halifax glider tugs crashed into a mountainside, killing the whole crew.

The parachute provided a more certain and usually more covert means of clandestine infiltration than the glider, and was used for the purpose by most of the warring nations. For the Allies it provided a delivery service for SOE in Europe; for Force 133 operating in Yugoslavia; for Force 136 in the Far East; for their US counterparts of the Office of Strategic Services (OSS); and of course for the Special Air Service (SAS), which included not only British troops but strong elements from France, Belgium and other European allies. SAS missions in Western Europe reached their peak in the months before and after the Allied invasion of the mainland in June 1944, and again during the 'mopping-up' operations towards the close of the war. In April 1945,

for example, 700 men of the French SAS dropped in fifty separate parties to disrupt German communications in north-east Holland.

The dropping of Allied agents and 'special force' groups was largely vested in RAF Special Duty Flights or US Air Commando units, using the full range of available aircraft.

Allied expansion

Churchill's hectoring of his Chiefs of Staff in 1941 led to immediate plans to expand the airborne force to a full brigade of four battalions, and to put the training of paratroops entirely in RAF hands, instead of it continuing as a joint task. To the overall command of British airborne forces Churchill personally appointed General 'Boy' Browning. Under his elegant and forceful leadership and against considerable opposition, particularly from the Air Ministry, the force was to expand into two divisions. To operate the British transport support for these divisions, RAF Transport Command was formed in March 1943. Operational control of its fleet of converted bombers, C-47 Dakotas and gliders was vested in 38 and (later) 46 Groups.

The British glider force now had a less attractive but more workmanlike vehicle than the Hotspur; the Airspeed Horsa, of which 700 were built during the war. This all-wooden machine could carry twenty-eight troops or a gun crew with howitzer and light truck. To unload the latter, many Horsas were equipped with cordite charges known as 'surcingles' to blow off their tailplanes, or with a system of quick-release nuts and wire cutters to achieve the same result. A larger version and a powered version of the Horsa were projected but not produced. The heavier lift was provided by the

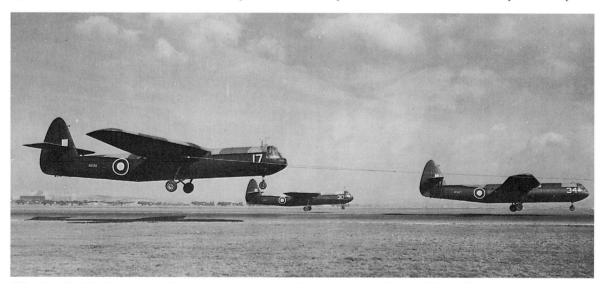

When British gliderborne troops did go to war, it was primarily in the Airspeed Horsa, which could carry twenty-eight troops or a howitzer with a light truck.

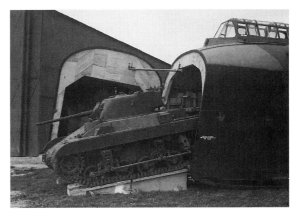

Heavy lift for British airborne forces was provided by the General Aircraft Hamilcar, capable of carrying sixty troops or a tank specially designed for it, which was unloaded through the hinged nose door.

General Aircraft Hamilcar, which could carry sixty troops or a light tank (specially built for it) into battle. It had clamshell doors in the nose for ease of loading and unloading. Over 400 were built. A handful of fifteen-seat Slingsby Hengist paratroop-carrying gliders had been produced, but changing Service requirements rendered them obsolete.

This force of powered aircraft and gliders would never be enough to lift the whole of British airborne forces into battle, and reliance would have to be placed on additional American airlift resources, which were vast.

The advance of the status and strength of air transport during the Second World War was most apparent in the USA, where it was supported by a manufacturing capacity well beyond that of its Allies – and its enemies. By 1943 the USA had over 1,900 transport aircraft, more than all the rest of the world's transport aeroplanes combined. Furthermore, these aircraft were designed as transports, not converted from bombers, and were operated by an appropriate command structure. In July 1942 Air Transport Command was formed as part of the USAAF, with the US Navy and Marine Corps retaining their own independent transport forces, and their own airborne units. In March 1943 USAAF Troop Carrier Command was also formed, to give specialist support for airborne operations and for airlift of troops between major theatres and battle zones.

The first large-scale airborne operation mounted by the Allies, combining assault by glider and parachute, came close to total disaster. The planning of the invasion of Sicily by sea and air had been notable for disagreements between most of the commanders, poor communications at all levels, and inadequate training of the American aircrews who were to deliver the airborne forces. Most were former airline pilots, accustomed to flying fixed routes with beacons to guide them, not to delivering troops across seas at night into unknown terrain against enemy guns.

On the night of 9 July 1943 British and American airborne troops were lifted from bases in Tunisia to spearhead the invasion. Of 147 Waco and Horsa gliders carrying Britain's 1st Airlanding Brigade, only twelve reached their landing zones. Sixty-nine were released early and landed in the sea, drowning 600 men. One landed in Malta, one in Sardinia. The remainder were littered about southern Sicily. The first wave of paratroops fared no better. Of 3,400 American troops delivered into southern Sicily that night, only some 200 were dropped on target; some landed as far as sixty miles from their drop zones. The following night an attempt to reinforce the Americans with a further 2,000 men came under intense fire from 'friendly' naval guns which killed 20 per cent of the paratroops. On 13 July the British 1st Parachute Brigade joined the battle and suffered the same treatment. Of their 116 aircraft, twenty-nine failed to drop at all, and only thirty-nine dropped their men on or within half a mile of their drop zones.

Determined fighting and plenty of 'airborne initiative' helped to retrieve the situation, but the immense shortcomings in planning and delivery threw the whole future of airborne forces into question. Gen Eisenhower ordered an inquiry which only narrowly concluded that airborne forces did have a part to play, provided they were given realistic tasks, adequate support, and proper training, particularly of aircrews.

The Allied invasion of Europe

Doubts and differences of opinion about the effectiveness and the purpose of airborne operations still lingered at high levels of command as the Allies prepared for the invasion of mainland Europe in June 1944. The enthusiasts favoured a deep penetration by four airborne divisions to establish an airhead midway between the Normandy beaches and Paris. At the other extreme, Air Chief Marshal Leigh-Mallory, as Gen Eisenhower's Air Commander, forecast 80 per cent casualties and advised against an airborne assault at all. Eisenhower chose the middle path, with plans to protect the flanks of the seaborne invasion with airborne landings in strength. The US 82nd and 101st Divisions were to create a defensive block on the right flank; the British 6th Airborne Division to seize vital bridges and destroy selected strong points on the left.

The drops took place in darkness on 5 June. The Americans were again poorly dropped, being spread over an area twenty miles wide instead of being concentrated on their intended drop zones. But, fighting numerous isolated battles in small groups, they created even more confusion amongst a surprised enemy than they experienced themselves, and by dawn were on their way to achieving their objectives.

With some exceptions, the British were dropped with greater accuracy by their more experienced crews. Glider-borne troops captured vital bridges over the Caen Canal and the River Orne and held them until reinforced by ground troops advancing from the beaches. Paratroops destroyed other bridges then fought a holding action against German forces trying to launch a counterattack against the beach landings. A classic *coup de main* by only 150 men out of a very scattered 750 dropped by glider and parachute silenced the heavy guns of the Merville battery.

Despite the scattered dropping of the Americans, the airborne assault was fully justified, and the troops then remained in position and fought on the flanks through much of the battle to consolidate the beach-head.

Supply of the beach-head by air became crucial. As soon as a toehold on the coast had been achieved, Airfield Construction Companies hacked out rough airstrips known as Temporary Staging Posts (TSPs) into which poured essential supplies, and out of which poured the wounded – over 50,000 of them from British strips alone during the first three months of the battle for Europe. The great force of Allied C-47 Dakotas was the mainstay of this mighty airlift.

After the breakout from the beach-head, supply lines became critically stretched by the rapid Allied advance through France and into Belgium. Before the Channel ports could be taken and repaired, the aeroplane was a vital link between supply bases in Normandy and the forward positions, particularly when the road supply of the British armies suffered from the withdrawal of 1,400 lorries to which wrong gearbox components had been fitted. The TSPs and the Dakotas kept hard on the heels of the advancing armies. Louis Strange, now commanding a Wing of TSPs in Europe, remembered watching 435 Dakotas land at Evere, offload, then take off again in the space of six hours.

Arnhem

The epic struggle for the bridge at Arnhem is perhaps the best-known of all airborne battles, purely through the heroic nature of the fight against great odds that is the hallmark of the paratrooper.

Operation Market Garden, of which Arnhem was but a part, was a bold concept, tragically flawed in its de-

Halifax tug aircraft and their Hamilcar gliders are marshalled at Tarrant Rushton in prepration for the airborne invasion of Normandy on D-Day

Heavily-laden troops of Britain's 1st Airborne Division on board a Dakota heading for the drop zones outside Arnhem, and the brave but poorly planned 'Battle for the Bridge'.

tailed planning. Just as Kurt Student had laid a 'carpet' to Rotterdam for Hitler's Panzers in 1941, the Allies sought to lay a seventy-mile carpet of neutralised defences and captured bridges across the Low Countries, along which would roll the British 2nd Army to gain a foothold beyond the lower Rhine at Arnhem, then wheel right and strike into the heart of Germany. But if it had Student's vision, Market Garden scorned the basic ingredients of successful airborne operation as pioneered by him: boldness, surprise and concentration of force upon the target.

The Americans, after their painful experiences of night dropping, insisted on a daylight assault even though it would lessen surprise. Surprise at Arnhem disappeared altogether in tactical terms when the RAF then decided that if the assault was to be in daylight, it would not fly against the flak barrage that would surely protect the bridge; instead it would deliver the troops to suitable dropping zones seven miles to the west of the town. Concentration of strength even in the wrong place might have compensated for the lack of surprise, but such concentration was denied by spreading the delivery of the total force over three days. To these major faults were added differences of opinion at high level, an inadequate plan for close air support, poor communications, underestimation of the time that it would take the ground forces to reach Arnhem, and an intelligence report that completely failed to acknowledge the presence in Arnhem of heavily armed Panzer units. All stemmed from a gross underestimation of the enemy, written off by some as already defeated.

The outcome was the military disaster known to the world. The airborne delivery on 17 September 1944 went well. The US 101st Airborne Division took the southernmost river and canal crossings in the Eindhoven area. The 82nd Airborne Division captured the bridge over the Waal at Nijmegen, but only after some delay. At Arnhem, although well delivered outside the town, the 1st British Airborne Division soon met unexpected and fully alerted opposition, and only one battalion was able to fight its way to the bridge. Its northern end was held by 750 men of John Frost's 2nd Battalion for over three days, a day longer than ordered; a day longer than it should have taken the British 2nd Army to reach and relieve them. The rest of the division were pressed back against the Rhine by far heavier enemy forces. Bad weather delayed resupply and reinforcement by the 1st Polish Parachute Brigade, and the British 2nd Army failed to appear until after the battle was over. Of the 10,095 men who had landed at Arnhem, only 3,000 came back over the Rhine.

It was not the airborne soldiers nor the aircrews who flew them into battle who failed at Arnhem. It was the planners. The solution? With not too much hindsight, a direct assault on the bridge by gliders backed by paratroops, preferably at night, reinforced when local defences had been wiped out, might have been costly in immediate terms, but it would not have cost 7,000 men.

The unforeseen

Towards the end of 1944 an operation was forced upon Allied airborne forces that was to presage one of their more modern roles: rapid reaction to the unforeseen. The unforeseen in this case was an unexpected attack by eight Panzer divisions on weakly held positions in the Ardennes, in an attempt to break through Allied lines and strike in 'Blitzkrieg' style for Antwerp. As part of this bid, Hitler ordered his Fallschirmjager into battle once more. Fewer than 700 paratroops could be mustered in sixty-seven Ju 52s, flown by inexperienced pilots in poor visibility and 30kt winds. The drop was widely scattered and the airborne operation a complete failure. However, in what was to be called 'The Battle of the Bulge', the Panzers broke through the American lines and slammed the defenders back upon the town of Bastogne, there to be reinforced by the US 82nd and 101st Airborne Divisions, trucked into battle only two weeks out of the fighting in Holland. At Bastogne they were immediately surrounded by the Germans and cut off from ground supply. A group of Pathfinders parachuted into the battleground to guide in an airdrop by C-47 Dakotas from British bases. Essential fuel and artillery ammunition could only be carried by glider, so in a series of flights, fifty Waco gliders manned by US crews were launched into the area. Thirty-five of them landed within the perimeter; fifteen were destroyed by ground fire, as were thirteen of the tow aircraft. The losses were heavy, but the supplies, and the volunteer surgical teams, that they brought to beleaguered Bastogne played an important part in the eventual Allied defeat of Hitler's last bold attempt to turn the tide of the battle for Europe.

From 1943 until 1945 the Curtiss C-46 Commando provided valuable airlift of fuel and other supplies across the Himalayan ranges from India to Southern China. It proved vulnerable when used during Operation Varsity, the crossing of the Rhine.

The Rhine – the last great airborne assault

Still reeling from the defeat at Arnhem, the planners got it right to the point of over-caution for the last great airborne operation of the war, Operation Varsity. The intention was to use airborne troops to support the crossing of the Rhine by seizing high ground beyond the river and blocking possible counterattacks. On 25 March 1945 21,680 airborne troops of the British 6th and the American 17th Airborne Divisions were carried over the Rhine near Wessell in 1,696 transport aircraft and 1,348 gliders, flying in three columns each of nine aircraft across, with escorting fighters above and fighter-bombers on the flanks to suppress anti-aircraft fire. There may have been some in that aerial armada who recollected the six ancient Whitleys and the single Hotspur glider that demonstrated the full might of British airborne forces to Churchill in 1941.

The paratroops went first, saturating the target area in less than twenty minutes. Then came the gliders, taking longer to land yet still concentrating the whole one-lift assault into less than two hours. The main ingredients for success were there: concentration of force in the shortest possible time, on top of the targets, with air superiority and close air support. Success it was, with all objectives achieved, and a link-up with ground forces within twenty-four hours.

But the cost of Varsity was high. Most losses were from anti-aircraft fire on the approach and ground fire from German troops on the landing zones, 25 per cent of the airborne troops being killed or wounded, and 240 troop-carrying aircraft shot down. Particularly vulnerable was the C-46 Commando, used for the first time in combat. It proved to be a fire-trap. With fuel running down the fuselage from ruptured tanks, the machine would explode in flame if hit by tracer. Twenty-four of the seventy-two that flew across the Rhine that day crashed in flames. The Horsa and Hamilcar gliders suffered heavily, too. Released as high as 2,500ft (750m), they lingered far too long in the sky as choice targets for German gunners. The Waco gliders, released as low as 500ft (150m) for their more shallow approach, fared slightly better.

There were those who said that the costs were too high, and the achievements of the airborne assault too small to justify such massive application of effort and material. Even at this late stage of the war the arguments over the effectiveness of massive airborne assault went on.

But if Varsity lacked boldness, other operations planned for the closing months of the war certainly did not. Operation Arena envisaged the delivery of six airborne divisions (the USA now had four) and four air-landed infantry divisions to create an 'island' stronghold and airhead midway between the Rhine and Berlin, and it was no coincidence that this concept echoed Orde Wingate's long-range massive-penetration theories, for his Air Commander, Col Phil Cochran, was now on the planning staff for airborne operations in Europe. Operation Eclipse was a planned assault on Berlin itself.

essential supplies of food were dropped to starving civilian populations, as a precedent for a modern function of air supply. Most notable was Operation Manna, in which Allied aircraft flew to the relief of the population of northern Holland, starved by German denial of food and the flooding of their polder-lands. During ten days in April 1945 the RAF alone mounted 3,156 sorties by 145 de Havilland Mosquito light bombers and 300 Avro Lancasters to drop 6,685 tons of food, mostly by free drop.

With the ending of the war in Europe, attention turned to the movement of aircraft and men to reinforce Allied operations in the Far East and the anticipated invasion of Japan, in which airborne forces were expected to feature. The atomic bombs dropped on Hiroshima and Nagasaki cancelled such moves.

Conclusions

The Second World War prompted immense advances in the use of air transport in support of ground forces, notably in the delivery of troops into battle from the air, and in the reinforcement and supply of combat areas.

Mistakes were made, particularly among the Allies, who suffered throughout the war from having begun it without a clear air transport policy, and then continued it without resolving differences of opinion over the role of air transport in general and airborne forces in particular.

Of the major combatants, only Germany entered the war with a well-prepared transport force and an agreed doctrine for its use. The USA was able eventually to provide the material resources, but suffered from lack of an agreed policy as to how those resources might best be employed. Britain, too, failed to integrate adequately its command and control of the air and ground forces.

Technical improvements to the transport fleets continued throughout the war, though not as fast as development of the fighter and bomber, and generally with a lower priority in construction. The tendency was to rely upon the Junkers Ju 52 and the C-47 Dakota as well-tried workhorses, and to supplement them with newer aircraft with increased payload. Throughout the war Britain relied on civilian air transport, converted bombers, and American aircraft.

What of Russia, that great pioneer of airborne assault? Small groups of paratroops jumped into Finland in 1939, and later parachuted behind the advancing German armies to act in a partisan role. Gliders were used on a few occasions in similar small-scale actions. The only Russian airborne operation of any size mounted during the war failed dismally when 5,000 men were dropped on the western side of the River Dneiper to hamper the retreating Germans, but were so widely scattered that they fought only in defensive pockets and were virtually wiped out. The 'Locust Warriors' who had once promised so much, now suffered from lack of leadership,

One of the final air-supply operations of the war was Operation Manna, the dropping of food to starving Dutch civilians by a variety of British aeroplanes, including Lancaster and Mosquito bombers.

Neither plan was implemented; Varsity remains the last of the great airborne battles in Europe.

Some of the final airmobility operations of the war in Europe were of a more humane nature. SAS parties were parachuted in to protect prisoners of war and some of the inmates were airlifted from their camps. And

Although Russia pioneered the concept of assault gliders during the 1930s, it made little operational use of the Antonov A-7 during the war.

143

A wave of C-47s drops Allied troops beyond the Rhine during the last of the great airborne assaults of the Second World War. More than 20,000 men were landed by parachute and glider in less than two hours.

lack of a doctrine, lack of an adequate transport fleet and, for much of the war against Germany, lack of air superiority. It is also likely that, in a totalitarian society that encouraged a belief that all are equal and no man better than another, the Russian paratroops themselves lacked that spark of élitism without which a paratrooper is not fully armed.

From the developments, from the mistakes and from the successes, derived several pointers towards the potential for airmobility in support of the ground forces:

1 The aeroplane now had the 'reach' and the reliability for strategic deployment of men and material, as shown by the airlift over the Himalayas into China and the establishment of an 'Atlantic bridge' for the ferrying of aircraft to Britain.

2 The conventional transport aircraft had established a tactical role within the battle area, and the newly introduced helicopter promised to extend and ultimately alter this role immensely.

3 The massive airborne assaults against a prepared enemy had become increasingly costly. Would further advances in ground-to-air defences sweep them from the sky altogether? On the other hand, smaller-scale operations making full use of boldness and surprise had generally been more successful and less expensive in men and material.

4 Transport aircraft designed for the job, with good load/range ratio, rugged performance and preferably wide-door loading, now had a definite place in the air force inventory.

5 The optimum use of air transport in support of ground forces required integrated command and control of air and ground elements and an agreed doctrine of usage; rarely were either achieved by the Allies during the Second World War.

Whether these pointers would be followed remained to be seen.

Appendix:

Principal Transport Aircraft and Gliders

GERMANY

Junkers Ju 52/3m

The mainstay of Germany's air transport fleet, derived from early Junkers civil airliners. Rugged performance made it an ideal front-line support aircraft for freighting, paratrooping, and troop-landing roles.

Engines	3 × 830hp BMW 132A-3 radials	
Maximum speed	276km/h	(172mph)
Range	998km	(620 miles)
Span	29.26m	(95ft 11in)
Length	18.90m	(62ft)
Load	18 paratroops or	
	4,536kg	(10,000lb) of freight.

Junkers Ju 352

An all-wooden version of the cancelled Ju 252 project, produced only in small numbers as a freighter with rear loading doors. Not usually employed in an assault role, but used for reinforcement and supply.

Engines	3 × 1,000hp Bramo 323R-2 radials	
Maximum speed	437km/h	(272mph)
Range	3,970km	(2,473 miles)
Span	34.05m	(111ft 10in)
Length	25.11m	(82ft 4in)
Load	35 troops or	
	5,670kg	(12,500lb) of freight.

Messerschmitt Me 323

High-winged, six-engine monoplane, Germany's main heavy-lift aircraft, valuable on the Eastern Front but an easy prey to fighters elsewhere. Later versions mounted defensive 20mm cannon in four power-operated turrets.

Engines	6 × 990hp Gnôme-Rhône 14N 48/49 radials	
Maximum speed	214km/h	(137mph)
Range	1,121km	(696 miles)
Span	55.15m	(181ft)
Length	28.35m	(93ft 4in)
Load	130 troops or	
	9,752kg	(21,500lb) of freight.

Fieseler Fi 156 Storch

A communications and liaison aircraft with outstanding STOL performance, ideal for clandestine support.

Engine	1 × 240hp Argus AS10C-3 in-line	
Maximum speed	175km/h	(109mph)
Range	385km	(240 miles)
Span	14.25m	(46ft 9in)
Length	9.9m	(32ft 6in)
Load	2 passengers.	

DFS 230 (glider)

Germany's main tactical assault glider. Later versions used a braking parachute to shorten the landing run, and had a forward-firing machine-gun to keep defenders' heads down.

Loaded weight	2,090kg	(4,630lb)
Maximum tow speed	209km/h	(130mph)
Span	21.98m	(72ft 1in)
Length	11.24m	(36ft 10in)
Load	9 troops or	
	1,236kg	(2,750lb) of freight.

Messerschmitt Me 321 (glider)

Heavy transport glider, one of the largest aircraft of the Second World War. Used rocket-assisted take-off and special tug aircraft.

Loaded weight	39,404kg	(86,860lb)
Maximum tow speed	218km/h	(137mph) with He 111Z tow
Span	55m	(180ft 5in)
Length	28.15m	(92ft 4in)
Load	130 troops or up to	
	12,196kg	(26,896lb) of freight.

Gotha Go 242 (glider)

A twin-boom freight glider well suited to the carriage of guns, small vehicles or light tanks. Introduced in early 1942 and used mainly for supply missions on the Russian Front. Twin engines were added to create the unsuccessful Gotha Go 244.

Loaded weight	7,296kg	(16,094lb)
Maximum tow speed	209km/h	(130mph)
Span	24.36m	(80ft 4in)
Length	15.76m	(51ft 10in)
Load	22 troops or	
	2,721kg	(6,000lb) of freight.

ITALY

Savoia-Marchetti SM.81 and SM.82

Military development of the tri-motor SM.73 civil transport, and Italy's predominant paratrooping, troop transport and freighting aircraft.

Engines	3 × 750hp Alfa-Romeo RC35 radials	

Maximum speed	326km/h	(196mph)
Range	1,311km	(932 miles)
Span	22.96m	(78ft 9in)
Length	18.33m	(60ft 1in)
Load	16 paratroops or	
	4,761kg	(10,500lb) of freight.

GREAT BRITAIN

Armstrong Whitworth Whitley Mk V

Converted from its original bombing role for parachute training and operations by replacing the ventral gun turret with an aperture for troops to drop through. Tug for Hotspur glider only.

Engines	2 × 1,145hp Rolls-Royce Merlin X in-lines	
Maximum speed	230mph	(370km/h)
Range	2,400 miles	(3,863km)
Span	84ft	(25.58m)
Length	69ft 3in	(21.17m)
Load	10 paratroops.	

Armstrong Whitworth Albemarle

Conceived as a fast bomber, it served almost exclusively as a glider tug and special transport, fitted with underwing panniers for dropping supplies. Paratroops exited through a floor aperture.

Engines	2 × 1,590hp Bristol Hercules radials	
Maximum speed	250mph	(403km/h)
Range	1,300 miles	(2,092km)
Span	77ft	(23.45m)
Length	60ft	(18.29m)
Load	10 paratroops.	

Handley Page Halifax

A converted bomber used extensively as a glider tug as well as for dropping paratroops, agents and supplies. Specification for Mk II.

Engines	4 × 1,390hp Rolls-Royce Merlin in-lines	
Maximum speed	285mph	(458km/h)
Range	3,000 miles	(4,823km)
Span	98ft 10in	(30.09m)
Length	71ft 7in	(21.83m)
Load	16 paratroops	

Short Stirling

First of RAF's new generation of four-engine bombers, converted to troop carrying, parachuting and supply dropping from its retained bomb cells.

Engines	4 × 1,600hp Bristol Hercules XVI radials	
Maximum speed	280mph	(449km/h)
Range	3,000 miles	(4,823km)
Span	99ft	(30.17m)
Length	87ft 3in	(23.92m)
Load	40 troops as passengers, or 24 paratroopers.	

Westland Lysander

The Mark IIIA was used for clandestine landing of agents in enemy territory.

Engine	1 × 870hp Bristol Mercury 30 radial	
Maximum speed	212mph	(342km/h)
Range	500 miles	(805km)
Span	50ft	(15.24m)
Length	30ft 6in	(10.69m)
Load	4 passengers.	

General Aircraft Hotspur (glider)

The first British glider built to a military specification, but used only as a trainer. A twin-fuselage version was produced but difficult to fly and did not enter service.

Loaded weight	4,300lb	(1,948kg)
Maximum tow speed	120mph	(193km/h)
Span	62ft	(18.90m)
Length	36ft 3in	(11.08m)
Load	8 troops.	

General Aircraft Hamilcar (glider)

Designed to carry a variety of loads including the light 'Tetrarch' tank or two Bren Carriers; loaded and unloaded through hinged nose door.

Loaded weight	36,000lb	(16,326kg)
Maximum tow speed	150mph	(241km/h)
Span	110ft	(35.52m)
Length	68ft	(20.72m)
Load	25,000lb	(10,337kg) freight or vehicles.

Airspeed Horsa (glider)

Britain's main battle glider, carrying troops or freight.

Loaded weight	15,500lb	(7,028kg)
Maximum tow speed	150mph	(241km/h
Span	88ft	(26.8m)
Length	67ft	(20.4m)
Load	25 troops or	
	7,200lb	(3,259kg) of freight.

UNITED STATES

Douglas C-47 Skytrain (Dakota)

'Skytrain' to the Americans, 'Dakota' to the British, the most widely produced transport aircraft of the war, derived from the DC-3 airliner.

Engines	2 × 1,200hp Pratt & Whitney	
	R-1830 Twin Wasp radials	
Maximum speed	230mph	(433km/h)
Range	1,600 miles	(2,575km)
Span	64ft 5in	(19.65m)
Length	95ft	(28.96m)
Load	27 troops, or	
	6,000lb	(2,721kg) of freight.

Curtiss C-46 Commando

Military version of the commercial airliner, used primarily for freighting in the Far East and Pacific, and occasionally for paratrooping, for which it provided the first instance of simultaneous jumping from doors on both sides.

Engines	2 × 2,000hp Pratt & Whitney	
	R-2800-51 Double Wasp radials	
Maximum speed	269mph	(433km/h)
Range	1,200 miles	(1,931km)
Span	108ft	(32.9m)
Length	76ft 4in	(23.3m)
Load	30 paratroopers, 40 passengers, or	
	10,000lb	(4,536kg) of freight.

Waco CG-4A (glider)

Only glider used in any number by US airborne forces, for troops and freight, including light guns and vehicles, loaded through hinged nose door. Also used by British as the Hadrian. Other versions produced in small numbers, such as the CG-13A, capable of lifting 30 troops.

Loaded weight	9,150lb	(4,151kg)
Maximum tow speed	125mph	(201km/h)
Span	83ft 8in	(25.48m)
Length	48ft 4in	(14.74m)
Load	13 troops or	
	4,000lb	(1,814kg) of freight.

Bibliography

Arthur, M, *Men of the Red Beret* (Hutchinson, London, 1990). A chronicle of personal experiences narrated by men of Britain's airborne forces. Low in technology.

Cole, C and Grant R, *But Not In Anger* (Ian Allan, London, 1979). Subtitled 'The RAF in the Transport Role', this is a selection of illustrative episodes rather than a comprehensive history of the subject.

Devlin, G M. *Paratrooper* (Robson Books, London, 1979). The story of American parachute and glider combat troops during the Second World War.

Farrar-Hockley, A, *The Army in the Air* (Alan Sutton Publishing, Stroud, 1994). The history of the British Army Air Corps, including the Glider Pilot Regiment.

Gavin, J M, *Airborne Warfare* (Infantry Journal Press, New York, 1947). Review of airborne operations and policies during the Second World War by commander of the US 82nd Division.

Gregory, B and Batchelor, J, *Airborne Warfare 1918–1941* and *Airborne Warfare 1941–1945* (Phoebus Publishing, London, 1978). Illustrated treatment, with selective technical details of aircraft and weapons.

Hart, L, *History of the Second World War* (Cassell, London, 1970). Puts airborne operations into a wider perspective.

Hearn, P, *Flying Rebel* (HMSO, London, 1994). Biography of Louis Strange, who in the Second World War was heavily involved in the training of British airborne forces, air resupply and the planning of airborne operations.

Heydte, Von Der, *Daedelus Returned* (Hutchinson, London, 1958). Personal account of experiences with Germany's Fallschirmjager, including an evocative account of the battle for Crete.

Hickey, M, *Out of the Sky* (Mills & Boon, London, 1979). Comprehensive history of air transport in support of ground forces, with emphasis on development of airborne forces.

Kuhn, V, *German Paratroopers in World War Two* (Ian Allan, London, 1978). Concise and authoritative treatment of the history of the Fallschirmjager until the end of the war.

Middlebrook, M, *Arnhem 1944* (Viking, London, 1994). A recent examination of the Arnhem battle, adding nothing new but concisely gathering in the previous material.

Mrazek, J E, *The Glider War* (Robert Hale, London, 1975). Written by one who was there; expresses the spirit of the glider men as well as the history.

Tugwell, M, *Airborne to Battle* (William Kimber, London, 1971). Well-presented history of airborne warfare from 1918 to 1971.

Whiting, C, *Slaughter Over Sicily* (Leo Cooper, London, 1992). No-punches-pulled examination of the Sicily operation.

Wigan, R, *Operation Freshman* (William Kimber, London, 1986). An account of Britain's ill-fated glider raid into Norway in 1942.

Wragg, D, *Airlift* (Airlife, Shrewsbury, 1986). A comprehensive history of military air transport.

Wright, L, *The Wooden Sword* (Elek, London, 1967). Personal account of author's involvement with glider development and training during the Second World War.

6
Naval Aircraft in the Second World War
Norman Friedman

As in all other spheres, aircraft enormously affected the course of the Second World War at sea. Three countries, Britain, Japan and the United State of America, operated large aircraft carrier forces; Germany and Italy began work on carriers but did not complete them during the war. All the major combatants operated land-based aircraft and seaplanes assigned to maritime operations, and most battleships and cruisers operated floatplanes or seaplanes.

The roles of these aircraft reflected some important differences between land and sea warfare. Surely the single greatest fact of naval warfare is mobility. A ship, however large, is a very small speck even on a relatively small sea such as the Mediterranean. Except for the important case of an attack on a fixed base (such as Taranto or Pearl Harbor), naval warfare begins with, indeed is almost dominated by, reconnaissance.

Aircraft originally entered into naval warfare because they offered far better coverage of the sea around a moving fleet than any combination of surface ships. Indeed, initially the only real issue was the extent to which air scouting could be made available in bad weather. The advent of true carriers launching wheeled aircraft solved that problem. However, the carriers soon became strike platforms, supporting torpedo and then level and dive bombers. Strike warfare, particularly against ships but also against shore targets, was the main Second World War carrier role, although the fighter defence of a fleet or convoy was also extremely important.

Scouting did not disappear, however, and radar made scouts much more effective. That was particularly the case in the British and US navies. For example, from 1943 on Grumman TBM Avengers were normally equipped with simple anti-ship radars. Beginning in

Naval aircraft design must always be adapted to limits imposed by carriers. Seafire NF627 on the lift of HMS Ravager *has its wings double-folded to fit within a limited hangar deck height. US-built Hellcat Mk I JV215, visible on deck, was designed for carrier operations, with wings folding backwards specifically to limit folded height.*

1942, the US Navy worked on an extension of this theme, Project Cadillac, in which a high-powered microwave radar on board a modified bomber could transmit a good-resolution radar picture down to a ship from well beyond the horizon. In 1944 Project Cadillac was reoriented towards detecting and tracking low-flying enemy aircraft. It resulted in both carrier- and land-based forms of airborne early warning, a very important postwar theme.

Many navies placed their scouting aircraft on board battleships and cruisers. By the Second World War such aircraft were typically launched by catapults developing an end speed of about 60kt. Catapult-launched aircraft were also important for spotting the fall of shot from large-calibre guns. Naval guns only rarely scored hits with the first salvo. More usually they missed, and the second and later salvoes were corrected by 'spotting' the position of the splashes (the misses) relative to the moving target. Aircraft clearly offered advantages in spotting, since observers on board could see well beyond a ship's horizon, and clearly see by how much shells had missed. This role faded as radar came into service during the war. Radar could measure range quite accurately, and its beams even penetrated beyond a ship's horizon. That was a relief, since catapult-launched aircraft could be difficult and cumbersome to recover, and catapults were often subject to damage by the blast from a ship's guns. In the Royal Navy, space originally provided for catapults was often filled with light anti-aircraft weapons.

Carrier (and land based) anti-submarine warfare was also an important theme throughout the war. Second World War submarines were essentially surface ships capable of diving to hide. A submerged submarine could remain down for up to about 48 hours, but only by moving extremely slowly; endurance at high speed was limited to about an hour. Merely by appearing, then, an aeroplane could in effect immobilise a submarine by forcing it down. If the aeroplane caught the submarine on the surface, it could drop a depth bomb as the boat dived, with a very fair chance of causing serious or even fatal damage.

For example, only a surfaced submarine could close with a convoy or a naval formation. Air patrols around that formation could keep submarines down and thus prevent them from attacking. Initially, submarine commanders were relatively safe at night, and had to lie low only during daytime, or beyond the ship's or formation's horizon. The effect of wartime aircraft radar in Britain and in the USA was to keep submarines down during the night, limiting them to lying in wait ahead of their targets. One German counter was the snorkel, which allowed a submarine to run diesels while submerged and thus largely restored mobility. The Allied counter was higher-frequency radar capable of detecting a snorkel.

Thus the mere presence of aircraft near a convoy could drastically reduce the effectiveness of submarines. Hence the intense interest in adapting long-range bombers to the convoy escort (maritime patrol) role, and also the conversion of many merchant ships to escort carriers.

Aircraft were not always the answer. Land-based bombers enjoyed enormous endurance and considerable capacity, but once on station they could not easily be reinforced or relieved before the scheduled time. For example, a Consolidated B-24 Liberator assigned to a March 1943 Atlantic convoy spotted a group of U-boats closing in. Unfortunately a series of attacks on the U-boats failed. The bomber ran out of depth bombs long before it was time for another bomber to appear, so it began to make dummy attacks, to force down the U-boats. For a time the dummies worked. Then the U-boat commanders realised that the bomber had run out of bombs. They closed in, and the bomber crew could only watch in horror as the attack progressed.

In contrast, an escort carrier would have been able to rearm aircraft for repeated attacks. Clearly she, too, would have suffered from limited magazine capacity, but that would not have been nearly so limited as the bomb load of the hapless Liberator.

Submarines could generally expect to be safe once underwater. However, in the very clear waters of the Mediterranean submerged submarines were sometimes so visible as to be quite vulnerable to air attack. After several losses of boats to Italian seaplanes, the Royal Navy had to repaint Mediterranean submarines for better concealment.

Until 1943 the aircraft could attack the submarines only when they were surfaced or when they were diving. Then the Allies introduced a homing torpedo, the Mk 24 (Fido), which could be dropped as the submarine dived and could follow it down. About this time they also introduced the first sonobuoys, which permitted an aeroplane to estimate a submarine's course once underwater (the search began at the point at which the submarine dived).

There was also magnetic anomaly detection (MAD). It proved useful in the Strait of Gibraltar, where flows between the Atlantic and the Mediterranean rendered conventional sonar nearly useless. Consolidated PBY Catalinas flying over the Straits could, however, detect the metal mass of a submarine, and they could drop bombs (actually retro-bombs, whose rockets cancelled out the aeroplane's forward motion) as they passed.

The other side of mobility is the need to shift forces to meet unexpected demands. The navies of the Second World War favoured flying boats for long-range patrol because those aircraft required so little in the way of preparation for their bases; often no more than sheltered coves. The US and Japanese navies built specialised seaplane tenders specifically to support very mobile

The sea is vast; even the largest ship is a small speck upon it. Almost all naval operations begin with finding the enemy, and from the outset aircraft offered an important means of reconnaissance. For the US Navy, long-range sea-based aircraft like this Catalina were a key to locating the Japanese fleet. The great perceived advantage of sea-basing was that the flying boats could move rapidly to any sheltered-water area, where they would be serviced by tenders. One of the surprises of the Pacific war was that airstrips could be built so rapidly that this sort of mobility proved less vital than had been imagined.

The way in which maritime air power developed in different countries during the period leading up to the war depended on politics. In Britain, the RAF sought to replace the other Services almost completely. One consequence was that it thought of its big flying boats as maritime attack aircraft rather than scouts. The Short Sunderland shown here was a late expression of this concept.

Aerial mining could deny an enemy key waters. During the Second World War a British pressure-mine campaign destroyed many U-boats on training runs in the Baltic, killing off numerous crews before they could become operational. The US aerial mining campaign of 1945, prosecuted largely by heavy bombers, contributed significantly to the strangulation of Japan. Here a British Hampden, operating as a land-based torpedo bomber, is loaded with an aerial mine (of which the parachute retarder is visible), in 1941.

operations. One of the surprises of the Pacific war was the ease with which airfields could be built on islands as they were seized. That surprise largely explains the adoption of large numbers of land-based patrol aircraft, such as Consolidated PB4Y Privateers, by the US Navy.

Every country except Japan was much affected by the politics of air control. In Britain, the Royal Air Force was established in 1918 as the single air service. In practice, the Royal Navy continued to control carrier-based aircraft (although the RAF tried to limit their numbers). The RAF controlled all land-based aircraft, including those assigned to maritime missions. One consequence was a rivalry between the two Services for the role of defending important bases such as Singapore, the RAF exaggerating the prowess of its land-based torpedo bombers as alternatives to coastal fortifications and ships. Another was that, instead of providing a reconnaissance service to the fleet, RAF flying boats were conceived as an *alternative* to the fleet, with parallel anti-ship responsibilities. A third was that the Royal Navy was not allowed to develop its naval aircraft for land attack, except in the exceptional circumstances of raids on enemy naval bases.

In the USA, an important agreement with the army limited the navy to carrier aircraft and water-based aircraft (floatplanes and seaplanes), to the point that in 1941 the navy planned to buy small seaplanes (to be based in coastal coves and bays) to provide anti-submarine patrols off the US coast. Then the navy was permitted to buy a few twin-engined maritime patrol aircraft (Lockheed Hudsons), of a type already being bought for the RAF. For a time it competed with army anti-submarine units, then, in 1942, the decision was taken to transfer all maritime patrol aircraft, whether land- or water-based, to the navy. By that time the Marine Corps, an arm of the navy, was already operating land-based bombers in the Pacific.

Japan was very different. In most wartime spheres the almost absolute separation of army and navy had disastrous consequences. However, in this one case the navy was able to operate whatever types of aircraft it liked, including land-based bombers and even the land-based fighters which defended its bases. That made for considerable duplication of effort, which strained the weak Japanese industrial base.

In Germany and Italy the land-based air arms were

Throughout the Second World War, shore-based anti-ship aircraft had a considerable effect on naval operations within their range limits. The Italian air force achieved some considerable successes with S.M.79-II torpedo bombers like this one

Dive bombing, developed by several navies between the wars, dramatically improved a carrier's ability to attack enemy warships because the dive bomber could in effect be aimed at a moving ship. US Navy Dauntlesses like this one, shown with dive brakes extended, won the Battles of the Coral Sea and Midway, the first in history in which the ships involved never came within visual contact.

dominant. The Luftwaffe controlled all land-based aircraft and seaplanes, and only grudgingly helped the navy with such essential services as reconnaissance in support of U-boats. The Italian navy did operate aircraft based on board its battleships and cruisers, but it could not control the much more important land-based reconnaissance and strike aircraft. Nor could it force the Italian air force to provide strike aircraft (the land-based *Aerosilurante*) in sufficient numbers.

The Soviet Navy did control its own land-based aircraft, whose assigned roles included attacks on enemy naval bases as well as on enemy ships. Thus the naval air arm included conventional land-based bombers which were expected to carry mines and torpedoes; they were organised in mine-torpedo regiments. The later missile-carrying regiments were their direct descendants.

Some important facts of life limited the effectiveness of aircraft at sea. Bombing was of limited value against a manoeuvring ship. The development of dive bombing from the 1920s onwards made it possible to hit manoeuvring ships (essentially by pointing the aircraft at them),

but the technique severely limited bomb weight, as the aeroplane had to be able to manoeuvre violently while carrying its load. Thus a dive bomber could wreck the upper works of a capital ship, but probably could not expect to inflict fatal damage. The sort of bomb which could do the job could not be dropped in a dive, and most likely would not hit. Of course, dive bombers could and did sink anything short of a battleship.

Part of the problem was the bomb had to be dropped from a great height to gain sufficient momentum to penetrate armour, yet in that case hits were quite unlikely. Bombs dropped from hitting altitudes tended not to arrive at sufficient speed. Thus, for example, it seems unlikely that any of the converted battleship shells dropped by Japanese aircraft at Pearl Harbor actually penetrated deck armour. This problem was only solved in 1943, with the advent of guided bombs, one of which was used by the Germans to sink the Italian battleship *Roma* that September. In the Pacific, the Japanese kamikazes achieved similar accuracy, but not deck penetration; the combination of bomb and aeroplane could not attain anything like the terminal velocity required.

On the other hand, dive bombers proved extremely difficult to shoot down because they moved so fast. Conventional anti-aircraft fire control techniques, in which the motion of the air target was measured and projected ahead, could not deal with them. The only solution seemed to be light automatic weapons (typically 20mm and 40mm in Allied navies, 25mm in the Japanese Navy) which could, in effect, fill with fire the area through which the bomber had to dive.

Wartime developments included the adoption of glide bombing (in effect, shallow dive bombing) by aircraft not stressed for full, near-vertical dives, and also the invention of skip-bombing, in which a very low-flying aircraft dropped a bomb to skip along the surface of the water and hit a ship almost horizontally. In Britain a variety of bouncing anti-ship bombs were developed during 1943–44, but they were not used operationally.

Capital ships certainly could be stopped and sunk by torpedo attack. However, to deliver torpedoes seemed to require a low, relatively slow approach which was itself quite hazardous. Any violent pre-launch manoeuvre would throw off the delicate mechanism of the torpedo. There were various attempts to solve the problem, the best probably being the British 'monoplane air tail' (MAT), in effect a gyro-controlled glider which carried the torpedo through the air, and thus allowed launch at a greater range. The US Navy tried spoilers which slowed the torpedo both in the air and once it hit the water, in theory allowing launching at higher speed. The Russians developed a generally unsuccessful technique of high-altitude launches of patterns of torpedoes.

Throughout the war, battleships sunk by aircraft generally fell victim to torpedoes, even though in many cases they also suffered serious bomb damage. The exceptions were the Italian *Roma* (see above), USS *Arizona* (which seems to have exploded after a fire touched off by a bomb penetrated a hatch in the armour deck and set off black powder inside a magazine), and the German *Tirpitz* (sunk by several very heavy bombs while at anchor).

The main addition to Allied air-launched anti-ship weaponry was the rocket, initially adopted to attack surfaced submarines (it could penetrate the submarine's pressure hull from a distance, thus precluding diving). By about 1944 rockets were commonly being used against surface ships, and the US Navy had adopted an 11.75in weapon alongside its more conventional 5in rockets. These unguided missiles were effective, but they also added to the amount of explosive on a carrier's hangar deck, as the US Navy found to its cost when carriers were hit by kamikazes in 1945.

Carrier operation imposed stiff limitations on aircraft. Although deck catapults existed well before 1939, aircraft were generally expected to make rolling take-offs. Thus they had to be able to take off within a few hundred feet into, say, a 20kt wind generated by the ship's motion. Landing into arresting gear limited allowable stalling speed and thus wing loading. Aircraft also had to be able to cover distances greater than those common on land. The Royal Navy believed that really long range required specialist navigators, so it generally used two-seat aircraft.

There were other limits. The carrier deck has a finite strength; it can accommodate only so much weight. Much the same goes for the lift, which also limits overall airframe dimensions, at least when the wings are folded. Arresting gear is rated for a given maximum aircraft speed and weight.

On the other hand, existing aircraft could operate from relatively small decks. Catapults could make up for limited deck length and low ship speed. Arresting gear could be installed on small decks. It even turned out that standard land-based fighters could be launched by catapult, for delivery directly into combat. Merchant ships could therefore be converted into simple low-

Before the war most Western designers apparently believed that the combination of long range and relatively low stalling speed demanded of carrier fighters limited their performance compared with contemporary land-based aircraft. The Mitsubishi A6M Zero (a designation taken from its year of service entry, 2600 [zero] in the Japanese calendar) represented an alternative, in which structural (including armour) weight was drastically pared to achieve high performance and range. This is a late-war A6M5. By the time it had entered service, the advent of higher-powered engines had allowed US designers to combine performance, range and a heavy structure in aircraft such as the Hellcat and Wildcat.

performance escort carriers (in two important cases, the US *Casablanca* and *Commencement Bay* classes, ships were built intentionally as carriers, but they were based on standard merchant hulls). Numerically, escort carriers formed the bulk of wartime fleets. They did not, however, carry the bulk of wartime carrier aircraft, since (on a ton-for-ton basis) they were quite inefficient (most of their hulls were filled with ballast).

Within the limits set by carriers, aircraft performance depended on engine performance. A typical fighter engine of the late 1930s, such as the British Rolls-Royce Merlin or the US Pratt & Whitney R-1830, generated about 1,000 to 1,200hp. The designer had to choose between speed and range, which was why the sparkling Supermarine Spitfire (navalised as the Seafire) had very short legs, whereas the US Grumman F4F Wildcat had relatively poor speed. The Japanese choice was to cut structural weight to achieve both speed and range, in the famous Mitsubishi A6M 'Zero'.

At this time, engines were developing extremely fast. Thus a typical fighter engine of about 1942, such as the later Merlins or the Griffon, or the US R-2800, developed something closer to 2,000hp. Although piston-engine fighter speed was ultimately limited (by aerodynamics) to about 400 or 450mph, the extra power allowed a much heavier aeroplane to attain that speed, and thus allowed naval aircraft the combination of high speed and long range. Ultimately they were quite the equals of land-based piston fighters which did not need anything like their range.

Not all navies could enjoy that combination. Much depended on industrial capacity. Britain mobilised in the late 1930s. That froze many designs. Although new designs were developed continuously during the war, it was difficult to place them in production, and some aircraft, such as the Fairey Firefly, conceived as early as 1939, did not see service until 1943. Blessed with much greater industrial capacity, the USA did not mobilise until about 1941, and such new aircraft as the Grumman F6F Hellcat could progress very quickly from design to service (in this case, between 1941 and 1943). The Royal Navy was fortunate in being able to exploit this US capability.

As for Japan, limited industrial capacity made a shift from prewar designs extremely difficult. The A6M was still in production at the end of the war, although by that time it was clearly outclassed. New carrier bombers had been introduced, but not new carrier fighters. To some extent, the fighter-making capacity which might have been important during the decisive 1944 Battle of the Philippine Sea seems to have gone instead into land-based naval fighters, a type inspired by the success of US carrier raids conducted from 1942 onwards.

A fourth factor was the perceived ability of naval aircraft to protect carriers and other ships. About 1930 it seemed obvious that observers on surface ships could spot approaching enemy aircraft early enough to warn a carrier to launch interceptors. Then the situation changed dramatically as bomber speed increased. Within about five years, interception seemed hopeless. Not only would warning time be too short, but bombers could spend much of their time above cloud. It could not, of course, be assumed that an enemy would fail to launch fighters. That seemed to leave bomber escort as the main valid naval fighter role; the fighters might also strafe enemy air defence weapons to help the bombers.

The fleet would have to rely on its anti-aircraft guns and its armour for protection in the face of enemy air attack. Hence, for example, the British choice in 1936 to build carriers with armoured hangars, whose aircraft would be struck below (and thus protected) at the approach of enemy bombers.

Ironically, just as it seemed that the naval fighter was more or less finished, radar was invented simultaneously in Britain and in the USA. Suddenly there was a real prospect of gaining sufficient warning time to react effectively, and indeed of vectoring fighters out to attack incoming bombers.

It is not clear to what extent the Imperial Japanese Navy ever accepted these ideas. Certainly it lacked radar in 1941, but equally certainly the radar-less Japanese carriers put up a fighter defence at battles such as Midway in 1942. It appears that by concentrating multiple ships together the Japanese were able to maintain a standing patrol of fighters over their force, without having to rely on warning. US and British thinking was much more wedded to single-carrier operations, in which limited numbers would have prohibited standing patrols. The Japanese may also have believed that their underwater sound equipment would provide sufficient early warning of the approach of large groups of aircraft (sound from aeroplanes travels into and through the water).

In any case, it was generally agreed that a carrier loaded with aviation fuel and bombs was an accident waiting to happen. Thus, at least at the outset of war, it was assumed that whichever carrier force located the other first would enjoy a decisive advantage, the ability to gain air superiority by wiping out the opposing carrier force.

That made the situation in narrow European seas radically different from that in the central Pacific, where the USA and Japan expected to fight. British carrier forces operating either in the North Sea or in the Mediterranean faced land-based rather than carrier-based aircraft. It was likely that no strike they could make would suffice to wipe out the opposing air arm.

Prewar treaties limited the size and number of carriers. Just how those limits affected aircraft numbers varied from navy to navy. British operating practice was apparently formed after 1918, when the land-oriented

RAF imagined a carrier as literally a floating airfield. An aeroplane had to be struck below into the hangar before the next one was allowed to land. Carrier aircraft capacity was therefore equated to hangar capacity. Moreover, the standard British operating practice made for a lengthy interval between landings. Japanese carrier operating practice seems generally to have followed British practice, probably because of the enormous influence of a 1921 British official mission.

British practice had an interesting indirect effect. When the British naval staff calculated the number of aircraft the fleet needed, it far exceeded the capacity of the carriers. Interwar economics precluded large-scale carrier replacement. One alternative was to place combat aircraft on board battleships and cruisers. They would be launched with full combat loads (e.g., torpedoes), and would crash-land on their return. The requirement that all aircraft be suitable for catapult launching (at an end speed of 60kt) further constrained aircraft design.

Limited carrier capacity also encouraged the Royal Navy to demand multi-purpose designs, in hopes that a carrier's aircraft could swing from role to role in the course of a battle. That in turn limited performance, as will be seen below.

The Imperial Japanese Navy made similar assumptions but was less limited, largely because it had larger carriers. That was partly a matter of luck. The key 1922 Naval Arms Limitation Treaty allowed each signatory to convert two existing capital ships to carriers. Largely because Britain had laid down almost no such ships during the First World War, the ships she chose were two relatively small battlecruisers, HMS *Courageous* and *Glorious*. The other British carriers of the interwar period were ships conceived during the First World War, when the key importance of large hangars was not yet understood. Thus they carried few aircraft per ton compared with postwar designs.

Because Japan started later, in 1921 she had only a single small carrier under construction. However, she also had a very large capital ship construction programme. The two ships selected for carrier conversion, *Akagi* and *Kaga*, were much larger than the two British ships. Successors had large hangars.

The US Navy benefited from a very different carrier operating practice. Early studies at the US Naval War College showed that very large numbers of aircraft would be needed to secure vital tactical advantages. To accommodate large numbers on board even small carriers, a barrier was installed. Instead of striking an aeroplane below after it landed, it was pushed forward beyond the barrier. The next aircraft, landing into arresting gear, stopped well short of the barrier (which protected the parked aircraft stowed forward). Once the whole air group had landed, all the aircraft were moved aft, into position to fly-off again. This practice

was clearly dangerous (a pilot might well be killed while hitting the barrier), but on the other hand it allowed a relatively small carrier to accommodate a very large air group.

One peculiarity of US practice was that it was difficult to fly small numbers of aircraft, e.g. for patrols, since one or the other end of the flight deck was generally full of aeroplanes. To solve that problem, just before the Second World War US carriers were provided with arresting gear at the forward end of the flight deck. Their machinery was designed for high astern speed. In theory, then, a single aeroplane on patrol could take off over the forward end of the flight deck and then, at the end of its patrol, land back over the same part of the deck. Alternatively, if all the aircraft were parked forward, the same aircraft could be launched using an athwartships catapult, then land over the usual arresting gear. These rather exotic capabilities were little-used during the war, and the hangar catapults were removed about 1943.

Unlike the Royal Navy and the Japanese Navy, the US Navy did not build its hangars integral with its carrier hulls. They were open-sided, often with rolling doors to close them in rough weather. One consequence was that aircraft engines could be run up while aircraft were still in the hangar. Aircraft could then be brought up to deck warmed up, ready for take-off. The alternative, as in British practice, was not to warm up any aircraft before they had been 'ranged' at the after end of the flight deck; the area of that after end, leaving enough length for a rolling take-off, in effect decided how many aircraft a carrier could launch at one time.

Large US carriers of the standard wartime *Essex* class had one other peculiarity; the deck-edge elevator just forward of amidships. They also had the usual centreline lifts at the ends of the hangar. For much of the time these lifts were covered, by aircraft parked aft ready for take off, or by aircraft parked forward having landed. Using the deck-edge lift, a damaged aeroplane could be struck below after landing without disturbing the parked aircraft in the bow. Alternatively, an aeroplane could be brought up from below and fed to the take-off zone forward without disturbing parked aircraft aft.

Germany

Germany entered the Second World War with a Luftwaffe high command firmly convinced that all naval operations were peripheral. On the other hand, the large tactical bomber force proved quite adaptable. The major theatres of maritime air operations were the Norwegian Sea (the convoy routes to Russia), the Mediterranean, and the Eastern Atlantic.

Except for the Focke-Wulf Fw 200, a four-engine converted airliner, the Germans mainly used conventional level bombers (Junkers Ju 88s, Dornier Do 217s and Heinkel He 111s) and dive bombers (Ju 87s) against

Although the prewar Luftwaffe showed little interest in maritime warfare, wartime Allied convoys in both the Arctic and the Mediterranean were badly damaged by German aircraft, both torpedo- and dive-bombers. They were an important reason for the development of British escort carriers. This Heinkel He 111 carries a pair of aerial torpedoes.

surface ships. Their main contribution to anti-ship weaponry was a series of guided bombs (Fx-1400) and missiles (mainly Henschel Hs 293). The former was used in the Mediterranean in 1943–44, the latter initially in the Bay of Biscay. Although Allied jamming is sometimes credited with ending the Fx-1400 problem, apparently the destruction (by bombing) of the specialist squadron involved was more important (the Luftwaffe high command was unwilling to replace it).

Both in the Norwegian Sea (against convoys to Russia) and in the Mediterranean German dive and level/torpedo bombers sank numerous Allied merchant ships and some warships. Ironically, this contribution to Allied losses was relatively little appreciated, to the point where, after 1945, shipping protection seemed often to mean protection against submarines but not against air attack.

At the outbreak of war the German navy had a small force of floatplanes and flying boats, some of which were equipped with aerial torpedoes. They came under the authority of Führer der Luftstreitkräfte (FdL) within the Luftwaffe. During 1940–43 FdL units gradually changed over to conventional land-based bombers.

The main anti-shipping force of Fliegerkorps X comprised KG 26 and KG 30 (the first unit to be equipped with the Ju 88 bomber). These units specialised, respectively, in level and dive bombing. As the Germans conquered Europe, Fliegerkorps X was moved to Norway for anti-shipping work (although it was active on a wider scale during the Battle of Britain). In January 1941 it was moved to the Mediterranean specifically to attack warships such as aircraft carriers. For example, Fliegerkorps X aircraft hit and disabled HMS *Illustrious*. In Norway, Luftflotte 5 retained a residual anti-ship role.

When Germany invaded Russia, Fliegerkorps X moved to the Eastern Mediterranean and changed into a more conventional air unit. However, its sub-command continued to specialise to some extent. Thus KG 26 (He 111s) converted partly to a torpedo-bomber unit, ultimately using torpedoes developed with Italian help (the FdL torpedoes, which were of Norwegian origin, had to be dropped at low speed and low altitude). KG 26 also contributed pathfinders using sophisticated radio navigational aids, presumably as an outgrowth of its experience navigating over the sea. Parts of KG 30 specialised in anti-ship bombing.

Meanwhile, in March 1941 a new command, Fliegerführer Atlantik, was formed to help fight the

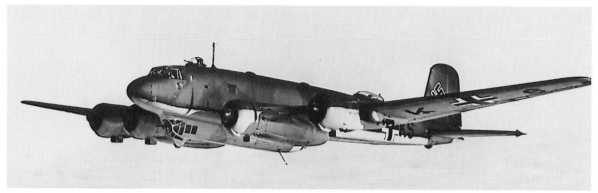

The Fw 200 Condor, a converted airliner, was used for both reconnaissance and anti-ship attack at low level.

Battle of the Atlantic. Its Fw 200s provided some reconnaissance in support of U-boats; for that matter, U-boats sometimes provided targeting support for the aircraft, which dropped their bombs at low altitude.

Elements of KG 26 and KG 30 moved back to Norway to attack convoys to Russia. Others operated in the Mediterranean.

KG 100, the pathfinder unit in the Battle of Britain, became a specialist anti-ship missile unit; III./KG 100 was responsible for attacks using the Fx-1400 guided armour-piercing bomb; and II./KG 100 used the Hs 293 missile. The first successes with these weapons were, respectively, against the Italian battleship *Roma* on 9 September 1943 and against the British sloop *Egret* (in the Bay of Biscay) on 28 August 1943. Together these two weapons claimed 68 victims up to 15 August 1944.

The Germans launched a carrier, *Graf Zeppelin*, and developed plans for numerous conversions of cruisers and merchant ships. They also developed carrier versions of the Messerschmitt Bf 109 fighter and the Junkers Ju 87 dive bomber. However, no carrier ever entered service; after the war the Soviets seized the incomplete *Graf Zeppelin*, expending the hull in weapons tests.

Italy

Under a 1923 law, Italian military aviation was centralised under an air force. Like other air forces, the pre-war Italian service had little interest in naval operations, and it resisted the formation of land-based attack units (*Aerosilurante*). At the outbreak of war the standard torpedo bomber was the three-engine Savoia-Marchetti S.79 Sparviero. It was successfully tested with torpedoes in 1938, and the first torpedo-bomber, the S.79-II, carrying two 45cm torpedoes, was delivered in September 1939. At the Italian declaration of war in 1940 there were 200 Aerosiluranti aircraft. By the Italian capitulation in September 1943 they had been reduced to 61, in 5 Aerosilurante Gruppi (2 squadrons each) with a strength of 9 to 14 aircraft each.

Naval units were equipped with Cant Z.501s (reconnaissance flying boats), Z.506s (tri-motor reconnaissance-bomber floatplanes), and Fiat RS.14s (bomber floatplanes, including ASW).

Like Germany, Italy flirted with aircraft carrier construction, but the two ships, *Aguila* and *Sparviero*, were never completed.

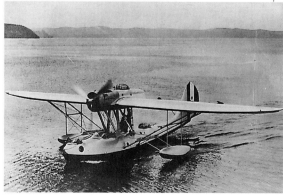

The wartime Italian Navy used the four- or five-seat Cant Z.501 Gabbiano (Gull) for patrol, including ASW.

The Italian Navy operated all sea-based Italian aircraft. In 1940 the Cant Z.506B Airone (Heron) was its long-range bomber, capable of carrying a torpedo or two 1,100lb bombs. Initially the Service's Airones operated mainly as bombers, but after mid-1941 all Airones were switched to reconnaissance, including convoy escort and ASW.

Japan

The Imperial Japanese Navy designated its aircraft by mission, sequence number, and manufacturer number. Thus the Zero was A6M; A for fighter, 6 for the sixth fighter, and M for Mitsubishi, the maker. The main mission letters were: A for carrier fighter, B for torpedo bomber, C for carrier reconnaissance, D for dive bomber, E for floatplane reconnaissance, F for floatplane observation (spotting), G for land-based bomber, H for flying boat, and J for land-based fighter.

Carrier air group composition emphasised attack, on the theory that numerical inferiority could be overturned only by aggressiveness at the outbreak of war. Thus in 1936 the large *Kaga* accommodated 72 aircraft: 24 dive bombers, 36 torpedo bombers, and only 12 fighters. At about the same time the new *Shokaku* was designed to carry 27 dive bombers, 27 torpedo bombers, and 18 fighters. At this time the Japanese Navy also operated light carriers such as *Soryu* (18 of each type of bomber plus 9 fighters). Like the US Navy, by 1944 the Japanese Navy needed many more fighters, and it tried to maintain its striking power by using fighter-bombers, in this case modified A6Ms. Typical (May 1944) large-carrier air groups consisted of 27 A6Ms, 27 Yokosuka D4Y dive bombers, 18 Nakajima B6N torpedo bombers, and 3 D4Y scouts. Light carriers had on board the same 27 A6Ms (9 of them fighter bombers) and 6 B6Ns.

The prewar treaties left Japan with only 60 per cent of the carrier tonnage of the USA or Britain. Although Japan renounced the treaties in 1934 (effective at the end of 1936), the Japanese Navy was well aware that it could not win an arms race with its most likely enemy, the USA. It therefore sought equalisers.

One was the long-range land-based bomber. In theory such an aircraft could attack the approaching US fleet long before it came within attacking range of Japanese fleet units, and long before it expected any sort of attack. These bombers were first used to attack Chinese cities during the war which began in 1937 – indeed, their need for long-range fighter escorts inspired some of the requirements for the Zero fighter. The first operational aircraft of this type was the Mitsubishi G3M, which helped sink HMS *Prince of Wales* and HMS *Repulse* off Malaya in December 1941 in company with its successor, the Mitsubishi G4M. The latter was used throughout the war against US ships, often in lone night attacks. In 1945

Like the prewar US Navy, the prewar Imperial Japanese Navy needed long-range reconnaissance and attack aircraft. Unlike its US counterpart, the Japanese navy was not hampered by any requirement that all its aircraft be sea-based. Admiral Isoroku Yamamoto, then chief of the Japanese Bureau of Aeronautics, saw this as an opportunity: it might be possible to build long-range land-based bomber/reconnaissance aircraft, capable even of scouting over the major US base at Pearl Harbor. The Mitsubishi G3M was the first successful aeroplane of this type. Thanks to its long range it was used to bomb distant Chinese cities during the war beginning in 1937. It turned out to need escorts of similar range; hence the development of its stablemate, the A6M Zero. Again, thanks to long range, G3Ms were able to locate, attack, and sink the British capital ships Prince of Wales *and* Repulse *when the commanders of the latter might quite reasonably have thought themselves outside air attack range.*

The Mitsubishi G4M superseded the G3M during the Second World War, and was used throughout the conflict. Late in the war these aircraft were used to launch rocket-propelled suicide aircraft ('Bakas') at US warships.

The wartime Imperial Japanese Navy also used flying boats. Its Kawanishi H8K is usually considered the best of all Second World War flying boats.

G4Ms carried rocket-powered kamikaze bombs ('Bakas'). As in the case of the Zero fighter, these aircraft achieved their extremely long ranges largely through the use of very lightweight structure, i.e., by avoiding armour of any kind.

Another equaliser was the long-range flying-boat bomber. In 1942 Japan had the best in the world, the four-engined Kawanishi H8K. That year H8Ks raided Pearl Harbor, using submarines to refuel them *en route*.

To some extent the Zero fighter was also an equaliser. It was the first Japanese naval fighter to have an enclosed cockpit and retractable landing gear. In most equivalent fighters high speed was achieved partly by shrinking the wings, and hence accepting high wing loadings and sharply reduced manoeuvrability. Japanese pilots apparently demanded manoeuvrability, which the Zero's designer, Jiro Horikoshi, supplied using special combat flaps. The result was a unique combination of speed, range, and manoeuvrability – at a cost in structural strength, particularly armour. Apparently the Zero also could not dive with contemporary US fighters (which it could outrun in level flight).

Perhaps the most important equaliser was the very high level of training accorded naval pilots and other aircrew. Whenever confronted by the obvious disparity in sheer weight of numbers and material between Japan and the Western powers, the Japanese answer was that human differences, both in training and in sheer fighting spirit, would overcome them. Unfortunately for Japan, once large numbers of pilots had been lost at Midway and in the Solomons campaign which followed, it was impossible to train their successors to anything like the pre-war standard. The combination of obsolescent aircraft (which a limited Japanese industrial base could not replace with more modern types available in prototype

form) and less-trained pilots proved fatal at the Battle of the Philippine Sea in June 1944. Without trained pilots, the carriers which survived that battle could function only as decoys at the Battle of Leyte Gulf that October.

By that time it was clear to the Japanese high command that conventional air tactics were largely pointless. The solution adopted at the time was suicide warfare, the ultimate exploitation of the supposed superiority of Japanese fighting spirit. As it happened, the kamikazes fared better than their conventional counterparts partly because they did not fly tight formations, and hence could not be tracked and intercepted as easily by the fleet's radars and fighters. Allied countermeasures included adding fighters to air groups and attacking Japanese aircraft on the ground, before they could be launched. The latter tactic explains the intense US interest in fighter-bombers at the end of the war.

At the outbreak of war in 1941 the standard Japanese strike aircraft were the Nakajima B5N and Aichi D3A, the latter having won a 1936 competition. They were roughly parallel to, but somewhat later than, the US TBD and SBD. The corresponding fighter was the Mitsubishi A5M, which was no longer in large-scale service by 1941.

A 1937 competition for a new trio of carrier aircraft produced the Zero, the Yokosuka D4Y Suisei dive bomber, which appeared in small numbers at Midway, and the Nakajima B6N torpedo bomber, which did not enter service until 1943. The new dive bomber was intended to equal the new fighter in speed, exceed its range, and carry the standard Japanese 250kg (550lb) bomb. By 1941 the Imperial Navy had decided to unite the dive and torpedo bomber categories; the winner of this last pre-war competition was the Aichi B7A, which did not enter production until 1944 and had little effect upon the war.

In 1941 the standard Japanese carrier-based torpedo bomber was the Nakajima B5N2.

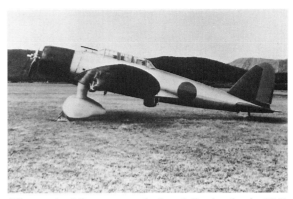

The standard Japanese carrier-based dive bomber in 1941 was the Aichi D3A.

In 1937 the Japanese Navy introduced the world's first modern monoplane carrier fighter, Mitsubishi's A5M, at about the same time that it issued a specification for the aeroplane's much more modern successor, which became the A6M. Like its predecessors, the A5M was lightly-loaded for extreme manoeuvrability in dogfighting. The faster A6M could not be as handy, but it was accepted on the theory that very-highly-trained Japanese pilots could make up for the difference in performance. The slaughter of many of those pilots at Midway and in the Solomons eliminated any such advantage at just the time the Allies were fielding much more powerful aircraft, such as the Hellcat.

Japan also developed a superb specialised carrier scout, the Nakajima C6N Saiun, but it appeared too late for the major carrier battles of 1944. As in the US Navy, the standard wartime scout was a dive bomber, the D4Y.

Soviet Union

The pre-1941 Soviet Union flirted with the idea of building one or more aircraft carriers, but none was ever laid down. Both during and after the war, Soviet naval aviation was almost entirely shore-based, the only exception being a few floatplanes flying from battleships and cruisers. They saw very little action.

All Soviet aircraft were united in a single air force in 1920, but on 5 May 1935 naval aircraft were placed

The fast D4Y Suisei (Comet) was one of two new attack aircraft intended to replace the pair with which Japan began the Pacific War. There were both radial- and in-line-engined versions. In effect the D4Y was equivalent to (and probably more successful than) the US SB2C Helldiver. A few D4Ys fought at Midway in 1942.

Nakajima's B6N2 Tenzan was intended as the standard wartime torpedo bomber, replacing the earlier B5N2. It entered service in 1943.

under naval control as an arm of the navy (they were briefly returned to a unitary air force between 23 July 1937 and 1 January 1938). It appears that initially only floatplanes and seaplanes of various types were taken over by the navy, but certainly by 1941 there were also substantial numbers of land-based bombers, including

Ilyushin's DB-3 was a standard wartime Soviet land-based torpedo bomber.

versions of the Ilyushin DB-3 (Il-4) and the Tupolev SB-2 medium bomber, and the Petlyakov Pe-2 light bomber. Fighters defending ports and naval bases were also under naval control.

Of the bombers, the DB-3T was a specialised torpedo bomber produced in 1937–38 specifically for the navy, and thus probably the first fruit of the return to naval control. It could carry a single 45cm torpedo (which could be dropped by parachute from a considerable altitude) or a conventional bomb or mine, and it could also be used for long-range reconnaissance. As the first mass-produced Soviet torpedo bomber, it formed the initial strength of the new mine-torpedo formations raised in 1939–40. One *minno-torpednye aviapolki* (MTAP) was assigned to each of the Baltic, Black Sea, and Pacific Fleets. A floatplane version, the DB-3PT, was developed for the Northern and Pacific Fleets, which had limited airfield facilities, but it was never produced in quantity. Instead, additional airfields were built. Baltic Fleet DB-3Ts were the first Soviet aircraft to bomb Berlin, on the night of 7–8 August 1941.

In June 1941 a total of 2,581 aircraft were reported in naval service, of which 1,445 were in the three Western fleets (Northern, Baltic and Black Sea) facing the German attack. Of these aircraft, about half (763) were fighters.★

The Northern Fleet air component was particularly important because it helped defend the convoy terminus. Thus in July 1941 it received a regiment of Tupolev SB-2 bombers from the Baltic Fleet, at the end of the year a regiment of Hurricanes, and in January 1942 a regiment of Petlyakov Pe-2 light bombers. Baltic and Black Sea air components seem to have concentrated more on the land battle.

Modernisation began in 1943, with Ilyushin Il-4 and Douglas A-20G (Boston) torpedo bombers, Pe-2 dive bombers, Ilyushin Il-2s and Yakovlev- and Lavochkin-series fighters coming to predominate. In 1943 the Baltic Fleet air component began to attack German sea lanes of communication.

At the beginning of 1944 strengths were 298 aircraft in the Northern Fleet, 313 in the Baltic, and 429 in the Black Sea. As the general offensive against Germany accelerated, the Baltic Fleet air component grew; by the end of the war it alone of the three Western fleet air components was heavily engaged in land operations, and it had 787 aircraft.

In August 1945 the Pacific Fleet was part of the force which crushed Japanese forces in Manchuria. At that time its air component amounted to six air divisions (torpedo, bomber, two mixed, two fighter), ten separate air regiments and fourteen separate squadrons; about 1,500 aircraft in all. By way of comparison, in 1941 there were no air divisions at all. The Northern Fleet had two regiments and a separate squadron; the Baltic Fleet had three brigades, three separate air regiments and seven separate squadrons; and the Black Sea Fleet had two brigades, two separate air regiments, thirteen separate squadrons and two air detachments.

No new specialised naval aircraft were developed during the war, although it appears that the Soviet navy was the sole user of the hybrid piston-jet fighters made in 1945. At that time a new torpedo bomber, the Tupolev Tu-2T, was being tested. Production began in 1947, and this aeroplane was standard until jets replaced it in the 1950s.

★ According to a history published in 1984, at this time seaplanes (scouts) amounted to 25 per cent of total strength, fighters to 45.3 per cent, bombers to 14 per cent, and torpedo aeroplanes to 9.3 per cent of effective combat strength. Standard types were the Ilyushin DB-3 torpedo bomber; the Tupolev SB-2/Arkhangelskii Ar-2 and Tupolev TB-3 bombers; the Polikarpov I-15bis, I-16 and I-153, Yakovlev Yak-1 and Mikoyan and Guryevich MiG-3 fighters; and the Beriev MBR-2, Tupolev MDR-2 and MTB-2, Amtorg GST (Catalina) and Chyetverikov Chye-2 flying boats.

United Kingdom

The Royal Navy of 1939 had been designed mainly to fight Japan. From about 1919, the British feared that their Far Eastern ally might turn on them to seize the riches of the Eastern part of the Empire. There was initially some hope that the alliance could be maintained (the British actually sent a mission to Japan in 1921 to help the Japanese establish their naval air arm), but most British naval strategic thinking seems to have gone into solving the problem of a major fleet action in the Far East. The concept was that the base at Singapore would be held until the fleet arrived. Resources on hand would include submarines and land-based RAF torpedo bombers. To deal with the arriving British fleet, the Japanese would have to steam so far south as to be out of the cover of their own shore-based aircraft. A decisive fleet engagement would leave Japan open to a fatal blockade.

From an aviation point of view, this outlook meant that British naval aircraft procurement concentrated on the problems of the decisive fleet battle. For example, the British fleet would have to locate and to shadow the opposing fleet. For that purpose, special low-speed carrier aircraft were designed in the late 1930s (they never entered service, however). Given the limitations of dive and level bombing, the British assumed through the interwar period that their aircraft could not sink the enemy's capital ships; that would have to be left to battleship gunfire. However, the enemy's fleet would probably be a good deal faster, partly because the Royal Navy had never had enough money to rebuild its elderly battleships. Aircraft would, therefore, be essential to slow down the enemy's fleet. They would achieve that with torpedoes.

The British fleet could not be based at Singapore for several reasons. One was fear of uncovering home waters; another was the sheer cost of keeping so large a force so far from home. The compromise adopted between wars was to keep a large fleet in the Mediterranean, from where it could swing either north or east, through the Suez Canal.

The late 1930s brought a series of unpleasant surprises. Without any reduction in the Japanese threat, two European threats emerged, Germany and Italy. It soon became obvious that Germany was rebuilding a U-boat arm, and both countries were building battleships. They were outnumbered by the Royal Navy (particularly since France was a British ally), but to face them down the Royal Navy would have to abandon its plan to fight the decisive battle in the East.

In particular, many British officers recalled that the Germans had tied down the British fleet during the First World War simply by refusing to give battle. Aircraft offered a solution, since they alone could penetrate an enemy's harbour to attack the ships inside. The culmina-

tion of this thinking was the dramatic attack which crippled the Italian fleet at Taranto in November 1940. By that time the balance had worsened because France had been knocked out of the war. Thus, despite considerable success in the Mediterranean, there could be no question of sending the fleet east the following year; all that could be spared was a pair of capital ships (the accompanying carrier grounded in the West Indies, and could not be sent).

The lesson drawn from the loss of *Prince of Wales* and *Repulse* was that henceforth battleships could not operate freely without accompanying carriers. Unfortunately the Royal Navy carrier force suffered badly during the first three years of war, and the large carrier construction programme begun prewar (six ships, the largest of any contemporary navy) took some considerable time to complete.

Limited in the total number of aircraft its carriers could accommodate, the Royal Navy sought to combine multiple functions in each of its aeroplane types. The Fairey Swordfish, one of which is shown landing aboard the 'MAC' carrier Empire McAlpine *in June 1943, typified the compromises adopted. The relatively slow biplane design was accepted because it offered the slow landing and take-off speeds required of aircraft which might have to be catapulted from battleships and cruisers with full combat loads, and which would land on board carriers without arrester gear. Low speed was also the price of long scouting range, which was vital to a fleet which could not benefit from sea-based scouts. Long endurance was vital in the gunfire spotting role which the Royal Navy hoped would help assure it victory in the decisive battle it sought. The torpedo role was also vital, since only torpedo hits could slow a fast enemy fleet enough for the British battle fleet to catch it. Indeed, the compromises made in the Swordfish design show just how many different air requirements the Royal Navy had, rather than (as is often suggested) how little it understood aircraft.*

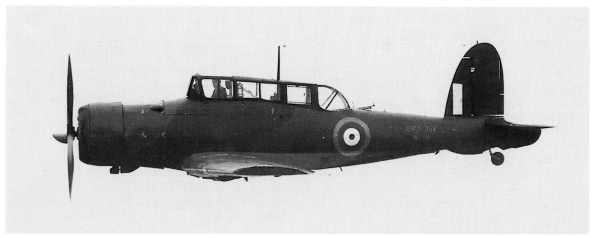

Like other navies of the interwar period, the Royal Navy was fascinated by the potential of dive bombing. Many initially called this form of attack strafing, so it is not altogether surprising that the Royal Navy's first dive bomber, the Blackburn Skua, was also considered a fighter. The US Navy flirted with much the same concept at about the same time, ordering prototype two-seat fighters which soon became scouts and then scout-bombers.

Aircraft also promised to help solve the U-boat problem. As long as the Allies controlled the exits from the North Sea (the English Channel and the route around Scotland), U-boats had to travel carefully to their patrol areas west of the British Isles, submerging during the day. Since a U-boat could spend only so many days at sea, any such limitation (imposed mainly by air patrols) would drastically reduce the extent of its operating area, and hence the area through which the Royal Navy would have to convoy ships. Thus the Royal Navy could economise on escorts, building ships intended to operate within about 500 miles of their bases. This logic collapsed with the loss of the French and Norwegian coasts, which placed the U-boats much closer to the central Atlantic. Once there, they could operate out of range of

shore-based aircraft, remaining surfaced and mobile until they sighted their targets. The extension of air coverage to the central Atlantic became an important theme of wartime Allied air policy.

The Royal Navy needed several different carrier or catapult aircraft capabilities: dive bomber (B), fighter (F), reconnaissance (R), spotting (S), and torpedo bomber (T). Given limited carrier capacity, it had to combine them in multi-purpose aircraft. Dive bombing first became important about 1934. At that time the planned combination was a fighter/dive bomber (FB), the Blackburn Skua, and a torpedo/spotter/reconnaissance aeroplane (TSR), the Fairey Swordfish. Neither had a particularly sparkling performance, and the Skua could not carry a heavy enough bomb. Nor was it

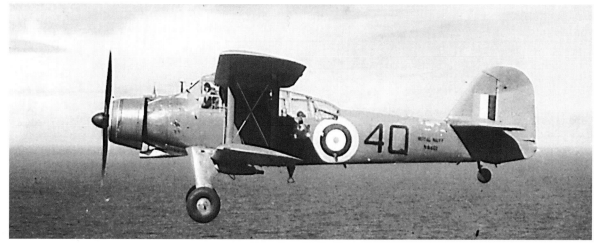

The Fairey Albacore was much more than a cleaned-up and modernised Swordfish; it was a heavy dive-bomber, too, and the demands entailed in dive-bombing badly retarded its development.

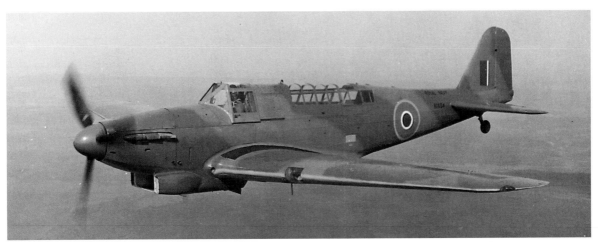

With the dive-bombing role shifted from fighter to torpedo bomber, the Royal Navy could buy a fighter whose structure was not stressed for dive bombing, the Fairey Fulmar.

altogether clear that spotting was worth the load it placed on the Swordfish. The Royal Navy began the Second World War with the combination of Skua and Swordfish, and in 1940 Skuas sank the German cruiser *Königsberg* in Norway.

In 1936 the armoured-deck carriers were designed. It was no longer so clear that fighters were worthwhile; the whole point of the deck was to help the ship absorb the inevitable bomb hits when the enemy bombers arrived. Although nothing in the records suggests as much, it seems reasonable to associate this shift with the crisis with Italy in 1935–36, when it became obvious that the fleet might well have to fight in the Mediterranean. The

aeroplane associated with this shift was the Fairey Albacore, conceived as a TBR, a torpedo- and dive-bomber.

By 1938, however, the Royal Navy was again interested in carrier-based fighters. Although no surviving records suggest as much, it seems likely that by this time radar and radar fighter control were clearly in sight. Radar would also eventually make it very difficult for low-performance reconnaissance aircraft to approach an enemy fleet. In addition, a new engine, the Rolls-Royce Merlin, was now available. A new pair of carrier aircraft, the two-seat Fairey Fulmar fighter and the Fairey Barracuda bomber, were designed. As it turned out, only

Like the Swordfish and Albacore, the wartime Fairey Barracuda had to satisfy several conflicting demands, including both torpedo bombing and dive bombing (note the dive-brake flaps). The demand for observation capability led to the adoption of a high wing with windows beneath it. The somewhat awkward result is represented by this aircraft of 814 Squadron on board HMS Venerable *in 1945.*

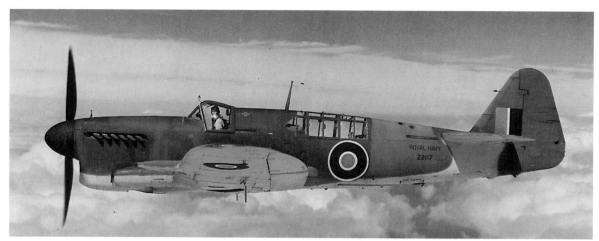

As in the USA, the advent of engines in the 2,000hp class solved many problems. However, it was much more difficult for the British aircraft industry to switch to new types in wartime. As a result, aircraft which should have entered service about 1941, like this Fairey Firefly I, did not appear in numbers until the end of the war.

the Fulmar soon entered service. Its performance was indeed limited, but when guided by radar it could beat off bomber attacks quite effectively.

Pending the availability of the Fulmar, the navy placed a few ex-RAF Gloster Gladiators on board Mediterranean Fleet carriers. The ships carrying them lacked radar, so they cannot have been of very great use in combat.

By this time several new engines in the 2,000hp class were in prospect, notably the Rolls-Royce Griffon and the Napier Sabre. A follow-on Griffon FR specification, which produced the Fairey Firefly, was issued. Eventually a Griffon-engined version of the Barracuda would also be built. For the moment, the Barracuda was condemned to low performance because other types of aircraft claimed much higher priorities for the new engines.

There was much grumbling in British aeronautical circles at the low performance of existing aircraft. Many felt that the second-seat requirement was to blame. As a consequence, a specification was issued for a Sabre-engined single-seat fighter. As expected, it could not offer a really impressive performance because, like the other naval aircraft, it still had to land and take off at limited speeds. Ultimately it became a single-seat torpedo bomber (officially a torpedo fighter), the Blackburn Firebrand.

Then the war began, and radar made its immense impact on carrier operations. Suddenly carrier-based interceptors were clearly worthwhile. Experience in Norway showed that Hurricanes could be accommodated on board carriers, and somewhat later Seafires also operated from British carriers. It may be objected that these fighters had exactly the sort of performance the Royal Navy thought, in 1939, it could not have, with

very high wing loadings. However, they both lacked range, and the Seafire was clearly quite fragile.

None of the Griffon- or Sabre-engined aircraft was available in 1942–44. Fortunately for the Royal Navy, US aircraft powered by equivalent engines were provided in large numbers: Hellcats, Corsairs, and Avenger torpedo bombers. Because so much power was available, they could be quite sturdy without sacrificing performance (fortunately the Royal Navy never got the large number of Curtiss Helldivers it wanted).

By the latter part of the war, Britain had large air-cooled radial engines quite equal to the big US engines, and a very new generation of naval aircraft was on its

Until the advent of radar, the Royal Navy had little use for short-range single-seat interceptors, so none was adopted. Then the situation changed dramatically. Unfortunately, the high-performance British type adopted in wartime, the Supermarine Seafire, had been designed at a time when range and ruggedness had to be traded off to gain performance. Here, a Mark III is shown in Pacific markings.

Not all the aircraft bought in the prewar British mobilisation proved successful. The Saunders-Roe Lerwick failed so badly that it was cancelled, despite the desperate need for aircraft. Even so, it seems fair to say that the production decisions taken in 1936-39 determined most of what the Royal Navy and the RAF had available to them as late as 1944.

way. In the Hawker Sea Fury the Royal Navy finally had a high-performance naval interceptor with adequate endurance. The new Firebrand and Fairey Spearfish seemed to offer adequate strike performance. However, none of these aircraft was available in time for the war.

For its part, the RAF had specialist torpedo bombers, albeit obsolete Vickers Vildebeests, at the outbreak of war. They were soon superseded by torpedo-armed Bristol Beauforts and Beaufighters, both of which enjoyed much higher performance and were used extensively.

On the other hand, the RAF seems to have had little prewar interest in maritime patrol It planned to use a combination of small landplanes (Avro Ansons) and flying boats (big Short Sunderlands as well as the new but unsuccessful twin-engined Saunders-Roe Lerwick). Unfortunately, the Anglo-Irish agreement of 1938 denied Irish bases to both the RAF and the Royal Navy, so there was no continuous air cover in much of the Eastern Atlantic. A Royal Navy attempt to fill this gap using carrier aircraft led to the loss of HMS *Courageous* in 1939, and the attempt was not repeated.

United States

At the outbreak of war the US Navy bought three kinds of carrier aircraft: fighter (VF), scout/dive bombers (VSB), and torpedo/level bombers (VTB). In each case the initial 'V' stood for heavier-than-air, in contrast to Z (for airships) and later H (for helicopters). The V is dropped in actual designations. Battleships and cruisers carried scout/observation aircraft (VSO and VOS, the order indicating priority). Flying boats were VPB, the bombing role having been added owing to the perceived high performance of the pre-war Catalina (PBY). There were also utility aircraft (VJ), generally floatplanes.

In 1941 the new carriers were being designed to ac-

commodate five eighteen-aircraft squadrons: one of scouts, to find the enemy before being found; one of dive bombers; one of torpedo bombers; and two of fighters. The number of fighters had only recently been doubled, probably with radar fighter control in mind. Earlier four-squadron carriers had their fighter squadrons enlarged to twenty-seven aircraft. By 1943 it was clear that fighters would be needed in much larger numbers, and the new *Independence*-class light carriers operated two reduced fighter squadrons plus a torpedo squadron.

At the end of the war many more fighters were needed to counter kamikazes. Thus in 1945 an *Essex*-class carrier normally accommodated a fighter squadron, a fighter-bomber squadron, and reduced (fifteen-aircraft) dive- and torpedo-bombers had made it possible to gain fighter strength at a minimum cost in strike power. Even so, it can be argued that a pilot cannot be trained effectively for both roles.

Aircraft development was shaped by engine development, new engines appearing at roughly two-year intervals up to 1940. Typically later versions of an engine first used in large aircraft gained power (i.e., had better power-to-weight ratios) and were used in smaller ones. In the USA engines were rated in cubic inches of displacement, e.g. R-2800 or R-3350, the R standing for radial (air-cooled), the navy's preferred type. In 1932 the latest powerplants fitted into multi-engined types were the Wright R-1820 and the Pratt & Whitney R-1830 (which was used in the new PBY Catalina). Such engines were rated at 700 or 800hp. A few were used in fighters, but engines such as the Wright R-1510 or the Pratt & Whitney R-1535 were more common in single-engine aircraft. They powered the bombers of the 1934 competitions and the fighters of the 1936 competition. By 1938 the R-1820 and R-1830 were approaching 1,000hp output, and they were used in a new generation

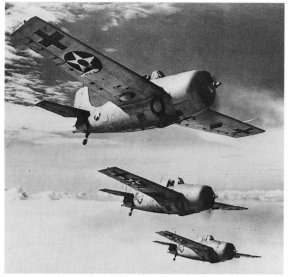

Like the Royal Navy, the US Navy of 1941 paid a performance penalty for carrier operation. These early Grumman F4F Wildcats show an important US Navy feature; light bomb racks bought so that aircraft could support landing operations. The crosses under the wings indicate participation in prewar exercises. The red circles in the stars of the national insignia were eliminated during 1942 for fear of being mistaken for the Japanese rising sun 'meatball'. For the same reason, many British and Commonwealth aircraft operating in the Pacific Theatre had the red centres of their roundels eliminated, and later had US-style horizontal white bars added. Although quite outclassed by the Zeros, Wildcats were retained through the war because they could operate from small escort carriers. (Oddly, the Royal Navy managed to operate Hellcats and Corsairs from much the same decks at this time.)

of fighters and bombers (Grumman F4F Wildcat, Douglas SBD Dauntless, and Douglas TBD Devastator). However, a further new generation was in prospect, the Wright R-2600 and the Pratt & Whitney 2800, offering about twice the output of the earlier engines. They powered the aeroplanes which entered service from 1942 on. By that time a further new generation was represented by the Wright R-3350 and Pratt & Whitney R-4360. They were incorporated in wartime designs, including the Douglas BT2D, which became the postwar AD Skyraider.

The main prewar fighter competition (1935) produced the Grumman Wildcat and the unsuccessful Brewster F2A Buffalo. Although outperformed by the Japanese Zero, and hence replaced in first-line units by the next-generation Grumman Hellcat and Vought Corsair, the Wildcat survived in production for use on board escort carriers. A heavily redesigned version, the F2M, was developed for this important duty..

A 1938 competition for a higher-performance fighter powered by the new R-2800 engine produced the Vought F4U Corsair, Grumman failing to convince the navy to buy its alternative. However, after the fall of France in June 1940 the company managed to convince the navy to buy a redesigned, uprated version of the F4F, powered by the new R-2600 engine. Shifted to the R-2800, it became the very successful F6F Hellcat. Its appearance was fortunate, because by 1942 the Corsair was not yet considered entirely acceptable for carrier operations. By 1944 both the Hellcat and Corsair were in service in very large numbers, and both proved quite successful. Both were modified in wartime as single-seat nightfighters, at a time when all other Allied nightfighters had a separate radar operator.

A further fighter competition was held in 1940. It was

Through the interwar period, like other air arms, the US Navy ran competitions to choose the aircraft it would buy. The Brewster Buffalo (shown in British markings as a Buffalo I) beat a Grumman biplane design in 1935. Fortunately Grumman was permitted to offer a rather different monoplane, which became the Wildcat; the Buffalo was less than successful in service.

As in the case of the 1935 competition, Grumman was able to recoup its 1938 loss. Work on a Corsair alternative began in 1940, and the result, the Hellcat, entered combat in 1943. This example is in British markings. Despite its wartime success the Hellcat did not offer performance matching that of the Corsair, and it was withdrawn from US combat service after 1945. It did, however, fight in Indo-China in French service. Probably its last US combat role was as a drone, attacking targets in Korea in 1952.

The Vought F4U Corsair won the next US Navy fighter contest, in 1938, but initially seemed poorly suited to carriers. Fortunately the Royal Navy found it extremely effective. By 1945 it was clearly the best US Navy fighter, and it was retained in production postwar. This is a Marine Corps AU-1, an attack version of the final fighter version.

not, as many writers have suggested, connected with the *Midway*-class carriers, which had not yet been designed. This time Grumman won with a radical twin-engine design, the F7F Tigercat. Grumman's argument was that careful streamlining of the fuselage would reduce drag dramatically, allowing the aeroplane to make full use of its doubled horsepower (two R-2800s). As it happened, the F7F was only rarely used aboard carriers. It missed the war.

During the Second World War the US Navy commissioned numerous small escort carriers. In 1943 Leroy Grumman proposed a stripped-down interceptor specially suited to them. It became the F8F Bearcat, shown here.

The USA mobilised in 1941, freezing designs for production (the Hellcat nearly missed its chance). Production of the existing F4F was switched to General Motors (Eastern Aircraft), the fighter being redesignated FM. The Corsair was licence-produced by Goodyear as the FG. Late in the war, when the kamikazes became a major threat, Goodyear produced a much more powerful redesigned Corsair, the F2G, using the new R-4360 engine. It was never produced in numbers.

Grumman's other wartime design, the F8F Bearcat, seems to have originated as a private proposal to build a fighter particularly suited to small carriers, which were limited to advanced versions of the Wildcat. It was also an interceptor, with much better climb than a Hellcat or Corsair. The F8F just missed war service. Small-carrier requirements probably also led to the design of the Ryan Fireball (FR), which combined a small piston engine with a jet in the tail. This also just missed war service, and unlike the F8F it was not produced in any numbers postwar. Curtiss also produced a mixed-power fighter, the F14C.

There were also a variety of experimental projects, perhaps most notably the Vought F5U 'Pancake', which was shaped almost like a flying saucer and which was expected to have a very low stalling speed. It never flew,

The Curtiss SB2C Helldiver was the planned successor to the prewar Dauntless. Aside from higher performance, it could carry a torpedo instead of a bomb. That attracted the Royal Navy, with its strong interest in multipurpose aircraft. Unfortunately, probably due to necessary compromises in its design, the Helldiver lacked lateral stability and also structural strength. In the US Navy it survived almost by default, as there was no way to reinstate the early SBD. Perhaps fortunately for the Royal Navy, production never sufficed for many to be transferred.

In the early 1930s the US Navy almost abandoned torpedo bombing altogether, on the theory that aeroplanes capable of lifting torpedoes were far too heavy to achieve sufficient performance to survive enemy fighters. The torpedo bombing role was saved by the advent of the navy's first modern monoplane, the Douglas TBD-1 Devastator, shown here on the USS Saratoga *in January 1938. Ironically, this same high-performance aeroplane was massacred at Midway in June 1942. To a large extent the problem was not the aeroplane but the difficulty inherent in its tactics, which called for torpedo and dive bombers and supporting fighters (all with different cruising speeds) to come together at the target. As it happened the torpedo bombers arrived first, but by their sacrifice the defending fighters were drawn to the surface, letting the dive bombers attack unhindered.*

although a low-powered, piloted scale model, the Vought V-173, did.

The bureau held its first post-1940 fighter competition in 1944. For the first time, aircraft could be designed primarily to be catapulted, so their stalling speeds could exceed 90mph. All were to be interceptors. Out of this competition came the first postwar US naval jet fighters, the Grumman F9F Panther and Cougar, North American FJ Fury (which evolved into the Sabre), the McDonnell Phantom (FH), and the Vought Pirate (F6U).

In 1934 the Bureau of Aeronautics held competitions for new scout bombers (5,000lb aeroplanes to carry 500lb bombs) and heavy dive bombers (6,000lb aeroplanes to carry 1,000lb bombs). Northrop proposed a single aircraft to do both jobs, the BT, and it developed into the SBD Dauntless. The following year the other two competitors, the Curtiss SBC and the Vought SB2U, were also modified for the dual-purpose role, and the heavy dive bomber disappeared. Both the SB2U and SBC were used in small numbers at the outbreak of war. Brewster's SBA was produced in small numbers but did not see action.

By that time the dominant scout bomber was the Douglas SBD Dauntless. More than any other aeroplane, it was responsible for the decisive victory at Midway. By 1941, however, the Dauntless seemed dated. A 1938 competition had produced a successor, the Curtiss SB2C Helldiver (as well as the abortive Brewster SB2A). One important requirement had been that two Helldivers fit a standard carrier elevator. That proved unfortunate, the Helldiver being too short for sufficient

longitudinal stability. It also turned out to be overweight. In service, the Helldiver also proved to be too weak structurally, many losing their tails when stressed. After a weak debut in November 1943, the fleet asked to keep the reliable SBD. However, by that time only the Helldiver was in production, and it ended the war as the standard US dive bomber.

A further competition in 1941 resulted in two more designs, the Curtiss SB3C and the Douglas SB2D, but the former was never built and the latter was soon dropped as too large and too complex. The failure of the SB2D led Douglas to develop the very successful postwar Skyraider.

The other major bomber at the outbreak of war was the Devastator (TBD), which was also the result of a 1934 design competition. It had been the first US Navy monoplane, and by 1941 was considered dated. However, Devastators performed well as level bombers during the carrier raids conducted early in 1942. At Midway, working as torpedo bombers, they were massacred. It is only fair to say that plans had called for a joint attack by dive and torpedo bombers screened by fighters, but that the different elements of the attack failed to arrive simultaneously. The appearance of the TBDs pulled defending Japanese fighters down to the surface, leaving the higher-altitude approach of the SBDs unchallenged. One might ascribe the disaster to a

The Grumman TBF Avenger was the higher-performance successor to the TBD; these aircraft are probably General Motors-built TBMs. Like the TBD, they were level bombers, not stressed for dive bombing, but they could make shallow glide attacks.

lack of Japanese radar, as a radar-equipped force would have been aware of the threat represented by the approaching SBDs.

Grumman had already won a 1939 competition for a replacement VTB, producing the very successful Avenger (TBF). The same competition produced Vought's Seawolf (TBU). Although technically superior to the TBF, the Seawolf was dropped so that Vought could concentrate on the more vital Corsair fighter, although a few were produced by Consolidated as TBYs. Production of the TBF shifted to Eastern Aircraft so that Grumman could concentrate on Hellcats (the aircraft were designated TBM).

A variety of follow-on attack aircraft were developed during the war. It turned out that multi-seaters had uninspiring performance, and many of them seemed too heavy for easy carrier operations. About 1944 the US Navy's Bureau of Aeronautics became interested in single-seaters with near-fighter performance, capable of attacking and then fighting their way home. By this time, too, it seemed less and less attractive to separate attack aircraft into dive and torpedo bombers. The new, very powerful engines allowed both roles to be combined. There was also pressure to do so, as carriers needed more fighters on board to cope with kamikazes.

The new class of aircraft was designated VBT. Eventually it produced the Douglas Skyraider, initially designated BT2D but then redesignated AD (A for attack).

Patrol aircraft were extremely important to the US Navy of 1941. Given the vast spaces of the Pacific, they were needed to provide the fleet with early knowledge of enemy movements. Quite aside from the agreement with the army, such scouts had to be seaplanes because so few airfields existed. The main type in service in 1941, the Consolidated PBY Catalina, arose out of a 1932 design competition, which the company won with an aeroplane designated XP3Y, i.e., a pure patrol aircraft. The Bureau of Aeronautics was sufficiently impressed with its performance to add a bomber role, redesignating a modified version of the XP3Y the PBY. This served very successfully through the Second World War, and was also given to US Allies, including Britain and the Soviet Union.

The PBY served in the Second World War at least partly because attempts to develop a new generation of scouts took much longer than expected. In 1935 the Bureau of Aeronautics let a contract which it hoped would produce an aeroplane carrying twice the bombload of the PBY over twice its combat range. The result was an unsuccessful Sikorsky four-engine flying boat, the XPBS; the bureau almost immediately let a contract to Consolidated for an alternative, the PB2Y, which became the wartime Coronado. It flew in 1938. These aeroplanes used developments of the R-1830 engine; the PBY was powered by earlier versions.

As in the single-engine aircraft, the next step was due to the appearance of new engines, in this case the R-2600. The bureau announced competitions for four- and twin-engine seaplanes in the autumn of 1936. Martin won the 4,000-mile twin-engine competition with its PBM Mariner, which served alongside the Catalina throughout the war. By 1937 the bureau had three aeroplanes under development, the PBS, PB2Y, and PBM. It immediately ordered the PBM, on the basis that it would be easiest to maintain and offered the best performance. Development proved more difficult than had been

expected, but by 1941 the Martin Mariner was in service, along with the Catalina.

The new four-engine flying boat became the huge Martin PB2M Mars; it was soon redesigned as a long-range transport. Like most Coronados, the Mars was also used as transport rather than a patrol bomber.

The most striking wartime patrol bomber development was the shift towards land-based aircraft. The US Navy flew its first Second World War ASW patrols out of Iceland in the summer of 1940, using PBYs. That autumn and winter it became obvious that such aircraft could not operate reliably, and in October 1941 the navy received 20 Lockheed Hudsons, essentially small airliners converted to maritime patrol aircraft for the RAF. One of them sank the first U-boat credited to a US aircraft. In US service the PBO Hudson developed into the PV-1 Ventura (first delivered December 1942) and, late

Experience with flying boats in rough Northern waters convinced the US Navy to renegotiate its agreement not to operate land-based aircraft. It began to buy Lockheed bombers, ultimately Lockheed PV-1 Venturas (shown here) and PV-2 Harpoons. Quite successful during the war, they inspired the postwar development of the P2V Neptune (later P-2) and then of the Orion (P3V, changed to P-3).

The wartime US Navy needed high-endurance aircraft. It received B-24 Liberators, which it designated PB4Ys. Late in the war a special single-tail version, the PB4Y-2 Privateer, seen here, appeared. These aircraft were used during and after the war for electronic reconnaissance (hence the numerous small radomes forward), and carried the US Navy's first air-launched guided missile, the Bat.

in the war, into the PV-2 Harpoon (first delivered in August 1944).

Although these aircraft were bought for ASW, they were soon valued for general anti-shipping patrol work, and the Pacific forces demanded them. The first squadron arrived in the summer of 1943. At sea level the Ventura was faster than many contemporary fighters, so it could be used aggressively in daylight sweeps into enemy territory. Many Venturas were used in the Aleutians where, as in Iceland and elsewhere in the North Atlantic, seaplane operations were hazardous at best.

At this time the US Army Air Force operated heavy bombers, mainly B-24 Liberators, on anti-submarine patrol. The pre-war Army Air Corps had claimed a coast defence responsibility, hence a need for anti-ship capability. This was actually an RAF-style attempt to supersede the navy. It was most spectacularly manifested in

1938, when Boeing B-17s intercepted the Italian liner *Rex* well out to sea. One consequence was that the standard US medium bombers, the North American B-25 and Martin B-26, could carry torpedoes. Wartime army aircraft in the South Pacific conducted numerous anti-shipping attacks, generally skip-bombing rather than using torpedoes. When the navy took over the Liberators at the end of 1942, they were redesignated PB4Ys (a PB3 flying boat flew in 1943, but was unsuccessful). A heavily modified version with a single tail appeared late in the war as the PB4Y-2 Privateer, and continued in US service postwar. Although the RAF used Boeing B-17s for coastal operations, the US Navy did not. The PBs taken over late in the war were used for initial experiments with airborne early warning, under Project Cadillac.

The PVs were clearly interim aircraft. In December 1941 Lockheed began work on a follow-on, which

Well before carrier aircraft could expect to do much damage to major enemy warships, spotter aircraft offered a potentially decisive degree of improvement in heavy-gun fire control. Carrier fighters soon followed, as it was essential to protect friendly spotters and drive off those of an enemy. By 1939 most of the world's battleships carried catapult-launched spotters (cruisers carried similar aircraft, which served as scouts). One problem, never fully resolved, was how to recover spotters during a battle so that they could be refuelled (the only realistic answer, to move them to aircraft carriers, on to which they could land, was generally impractical, given the other carrier roles). This is a US Vought OS2U-1 Kingfisher, the standard wartime type, on floats.

became the P2V Neptune, the principal postwar patrol bomber through the mid-1960s.

There were also battleship and cruiser floatplanes. In 1941 the standard was the Curtiss SOC biplane, the prototype of which had been ordered in 1932. It was primarily an observation aircraft, its original designation having been O3C. The combination designation reflected a decision to combine the scouting role (for cruiser aircraft) and the gunnery observation role (for battleship aircraft). Vought designed the monoplane OS2U Kingfisher as a replacement, and it proved quite successful. Its intended successor, the Curtiss SO3C Seamew, was, however, a failure, and some were replaced by SOCs reinstated into service. In 1942, as the SO3C was entering service, the navy circulated a specification for a much faster catapult-launched scout. Curtiss won this competition with its single-seat SC Seahawk, which entered service in 1944.

Finally, the US Navy seems to have been unique in using airships for anti-submarine patrol. Prewar interest in very-long-range rigid airship scouts lapsed after a disastrous crash, but the non-rigid 'blimps' survived, and indeed were retained in service for more than a decade after the war. Compared with conventional aircraft, they were very attractive because they could slow down to something like convoy speed, and they enjoyed something approaching surface ship endurance.

Select Bibliography

(Standard books on aircraft of this period are not listed here.) There are no full-length accounts of several important Allied aircraft: the Barracuda, Helldiver, and the Ventura/Harpoon series. Apart from the Zero fighter, there are also no book-length English-language accounts of the major Japanese aircraft. Many of these aircraft were, however, covered by *Profiles* and/or by booklets in the Squadron/Signal 'In Action' series.

Abrams, R, *F4U Corsair at War* (London and New York, 1981).

Belote, J H and W M, *Titans of the Seas* (New York, 1975).

Bowyer, C, *Coastal Command at War* (London, 1979).

Brown, E, *Wings of the Navy* (London and Annapolis, 1987). Evaluations of sixteen wartime carrier aircraft; includes large keyed cut-away drawings.

Brown, E, *Duels in the Sky: World War II Naval Aircraft in Combat* (London and Annapolis, 1988). An attempt to compare aircraft in each major category.

Brown, J D, *Allied Carrier Fighters of World War II* (London, 1975).

Brown, J D, *Carrier Operations in World War II* (2 vols., London, 1974).

Brown, J D, *The Seafire: The Spitfire that Went to Sea* (London and Annapolis, 1989 [second edition]).

Brown, J D, *Aircraft Carriers of World War II* (London, 1977).

Chesneau, R, *Aircraft Carriers of the World* (London and Annapolis, 1984).

Creed, R R, *PBY: The Catalina Flying Boat* (Annapolis, 1985).

Friedman, N, *Carrier Air Power* (London, 1981).

Friedman, N, *US Aircraft Carriers: An Illustrated Design History* (Annapolis, 1983).

Friedman, N, *British Carrier Airpower* (London and Annapolis, 1988). Treats the aircraft as well as the ships, giving design and operational rationales.

Fuchida, M and Okumiya, M, *Midway, The Battle that Doomed Japan* (Annapolis, 1955, revised edition 1992). The story of the key Pacific naval air battle, told from the Japanese point of view.

Hanson, N, *Carrier Pilot* (Cambridge, 1979).

Harrison, W, *Fairey Firefly* (Shrewsbury, 1992).

Hendry, A, *Flying Cats: The Catalina in World War II* (Annapolis, 1988).

Hezlet, VADM Sir Arthur, *Aircraft and Sea Power* (London and New York, 1970). One of a trilogy on major influences on modern sea power; the other volumes concern submarines and electronics.

Ikuhiko, H, *Japanese Naval Aces and Fighter Units in World War II* (Annapolis, 1989).

Inoguchi, R and Pineau, R, *The Divine Wind* (Annapolis, 1958). The first full account of the kamikazes.

Lundstrom, J, *The First Team* (Annapolis, 1984). US naval fighters from Pearl Harbor to Guadalcanal.

Lundstrom, J, *The First Team and the Guadalcanal Campaign* (Annapolis, 1994). US naval fighters in combat, August through November, 1942.

Mikesh, R C, *Zero* (Osceola, 1992).

Miller, N, *The Naval Air War, 1939–45* (Annapolis, 1991).

Nesbit, R C, *The Strike Wings: Special Anti-Shipping Squadrons 1942–45* (London, 1984). RAF land-based anti-ship units formed from November 1942 onwards, using Beaufighters and Mosquitos.

Poolman, K, *The Catafighters and Merchant Aircraft Carriers* (London, 1970). Describes two wartime British expedients to bring aircraft to sea, catapults for one-way fighter missions and semi-conversions of merchant ships which retained their freighter or tanker capabilities.

Poolman, K, *Allied Escort Carriers* (London and Annapolis, 1988).

Price, A, *Aircraft vs. Submarine* (London and Annapolis, 1973).

Reynolds, G, *The Fast Carriers* (New York, 1968; second edition: Annapolis, 1992).

Smith, P C, *Dive Bomber!* (Ashbourne and Annapolis, 1982).

Sturtivant, R *Fleet Air Arm at War* (London, 1982).

Sturtivant, R, *The Swordfish Story* (London, 1993).

Till, G, *Air Power and the Royal Navy 1914–1945* (London, 1979).

Tillman, B, *Wildcat: the F4F in World War Two* (Annapolis, 1983; second edition 1990).

Tillman, B, *Hellcat* (Annapolis, 1979).

Tillman, B, *The Dauntless Dive Bomber in World War Two* (Annapolis, 1976).

Tillman, B, *Avenger at War* (London, 1979 and New York, 1980).

Tillman, B, *Corsair* (Annapolis, 1979).

Vaeth, J G, *Blimps and U-Boats* (Annapolis, 1992).

Warner, D and P, *The Sacred Warriors* (New York, 1982). The kamikaze story, including a score card of ships hit and sunk in 1944–45. This book also includes other Japanese suicide weapons.

Y'Blood, W T, *Red Sun Setting* (Annapolis, 1981). The Battle of the Philippine Sea, in which the Japanese naval air arm was destroyed.

Y'Blood, W T, *Hunter-Killer* (Annapolis, 1983). The story of US escort carriers in the Battle of the Atlantic.

Y'Blood, W T, *The Little Giants* (Annapolis, 1987). Escort carriers against Japan.

Ten Cierva C.30A Rota I Autogiros were delivered to the RAF in the mid-1930s for evaluation by the army co-operation squadrons. The survivors were integrated into No 5 Radio Servicing Section in 1940 for radar calibration work. This example, K4235, is seen coded as KX-B of No 529 Squadron.

Almost rejected by the RAF in its intended role as an aerial observation post, the C.30A proved indispensable during the war as the only accurate means of calibrating the then-secret defence radar chain.

7

The Helicopter's First War

Elfan ap Rees

At the outbreak of the Second World War only three countries, France, Germany and Great Britain, could claim to have successfully flown a controllable helicopter, and even these machines were still very much experimental. Consequently it was the helicopter's predecessor, the autogyro, to which the warring nations first looked for military potential. This slow moving, short take-off / vertical landing machine seemed ideal for reconnaissance and artillery-spotting, replacing the existing fixed-wing aerial observation posts (AOPs) supporting the army, and introducing a similar role aboard larger ships where space for a flight deck might be possible. Beyond that the autogyro seemed limited in its capabilities.

In the 1930s the Cierva C.30A Autogiro and its variants were dominant. The Spanish Navy was actually the first service to use a rotary-wing aircraft on military operations, using a C.30A in Asturias during a rebellion in October 1934. Over the next five years a small number of C.30As were supplied to the French Air Force and Navy, Britain's Royal Air Force and the Soviet government, whilst in the USA derivatives built by Kellett were delivered to the US Army Air Corps and to the Japanese Army. A second US licensee, Pitcairn, worked with the US Navy. In Germany the local licensee, Focke-Wulf, built about thirty C.30As out of a planned production run of forty. Single C.30As were also delivered for military evaluation to several other governments, which did not progress their use further. Despite this apparent wide interest, September 1939 saw only the British, French and German services using the autogyro operationally, although the Soviet Army and Japanese military were to use them later in the war.

In France, the delivery of twenty-five military Cierva C.30A Autogiros, mostly built under licence by Lioré et Olivier (LeO), began in October 1935 with the handover of the first of four aircraft to the Aeronavale. Deliveries to l'Armée de l'Air (AdA) followed between January and July 1936. The AdA later received a further thirty-four LeO-built C.30As. The primary role envisaged by the French generals for the Autogiro was artillery observation along the expected front of the Maginot and Siegfried lines. The plan was to equip up to thirty AdA Flights, each with three C.30As, to work in conjunction with front-line army artillery units. The Aeronavale was less ambitious, seeing the Autogiro mainly of value in tracking torpedoes during peacetime training exercises.

By the beginning of September 1939, immediately before the outbreak of war, eight AdA units were equipped with a total of twenty-eight C.30As, with a further twenty-one in storage or under repair and three operating at Sommesous in a training role. The Aeronavale was operating six aircraft, divided between 3S-2 Flotille at Cuers-Pierrefeu and the training school at Hyeres. Two more Autogiros were in storage. Over the next nine months, as the 'phoney' war period gradually deteriorated, the French Autogiro force changed relatively little, with forty-seven C.30As still on AdA charge at the beginning of May 1940 and thirteen in service with the Aeronavale. More than thirty artillery observation pilots had been trained during the intervening period, along with a small number of naval pilots.

However, when the long-expected German attack on France and the neighbouring Low Countries began in May 1940, the French generals were taken by surprise. The 'Blitzkrieg' assault rapidly saw the Maginot and Siegfried lines and their fixed artillery made redundant, and the intended role of the autogiro units changed. As the German advance continued, the surviving AdA C.30As were forced to retreat to Tonneins, and by early June 1940 had been reduced to eighteen aircraft. While reconnaissance missions to report on the positions of German forces continued for a short while, by 24 June the last survivors had finally been withdrawn to Biard, near Poitiers, and their crews dispersed.

Meanwhile, the Aeronavale 3S-2 Flotille had relocated to Le Havre at the beginning of April 1940 to patrol the harbour approaches, and this was followed by patrols of the Seine estuary from a base at Cherbourg during May. On 3 June the seven remaining aircraft retreated to Lanveoc-Poulmic where, with the German advance coming closer, they were burned on 18 June. The crews escaped by sea.

Following the French surrender on 25 June 1940, seven C.30As remained on strength in Vichy, but six of these were taken over by Italian forces when the Axis invaded the region in November 1942. All remained serviceable for only a very short period. The seventh remained hidden until the end of the war, and is now displayed at the Musée d l'Air. Although there is no evidence of German forces using any of the French C.30As during their occupation, it has been suggested that two aircraft were later resurrected by the AdA and operated by French forces in Germany during the latter months of the war. However, this has not been positively

At the outbreak of war in 1939 the French Services had some sixty LeO-built C-30A Autogiros available, mostly for artillery spotting. Seen here are C.30s of French Navy Escadrille 352 at Deauville, Normandy, in 1940. Machine number 6 is a LeO C.301, the developed version distinguished by its dihedral tailplane and revised fin surfaces.

confirmed. Some 5,000 flight hours had been accumulated by the AdA and Aeronavale C.30 fleet by the end of operations.

French manufacture of the C.30A was due to be followed by the modified LeO C.301 which introduced several improvements, including irreversible controls and eradication of the longitudinal stability that made instrument flying in the C.30A very risky. In the event, German bombing of the LeO factory, and the subsequent occupation, saw C.301 production ended after completion of only five aircraft. One of these was flown at Marignane for the benefit of a German armaments delegation in October 1940, but no further manufacture or service operation was undertaken.

On the far side of the world, in Japan, military interest in rotary-wing aircraft was sharpened during incidents along the Manchurian/Mongolian border in 1939, when a large number of captive artillery observation balloons were shot down. As a result, in late 1939 – early 1940, an imported Kellett KD-1A Autogiro was evaluated by the Army Air Force, and this was followed by a decision to develop a local variant for the artillery observation and liaison role. With the declaration of war against the USA and the forming of a partnership with Germany, the first Japanese autogyro, the Kayaba Ka-1, introduced the Argus inverted-vee powerplant rather than the Jacobs radial engine which powered the KD-

1A. Two Ka-1s were built, in late 1942, but engine overheating problems delayed flight trials until mid-1943.

In the meantime an order for 300 Ka-1A production aircraft was placed by the Japanese Army, with the first sixty due to be produced by March 1944. The first was completed by Kayaba in June 1943 but, in the event, only about thirty-five were built, and at least ten of these were destroyed in an American air raid before delivery. In mid-1944 the first Ka-2 variant was produced, with a licence-built Jacobs radial engine, and production begun alongside the Ka-1A. Engine shortages hindered completion, however, and fewer than sixty Ka-2s were delivered.

Of the estimated ninety-five Ka-1A and Ka-2 autogyros delivered to the Japanese military, about fifty entered service before the war ended. Some of these were operated by artillery units, although there is no record of any front-line service. Others were given the capability to carry depth charges to combat the growing threat of Allied submarines in Japanese coastal waters. Operating from about six coastal bases, they covered the Korean, Tsugara and Eastern Channels and other vulnerable areas. All such autogyro operations ended with the Japanese defeat in August 1945.

Helicopter development in Japan progressed no further than some brief experimental flights in mid-1944, although low-priority research continued until the end of the war.

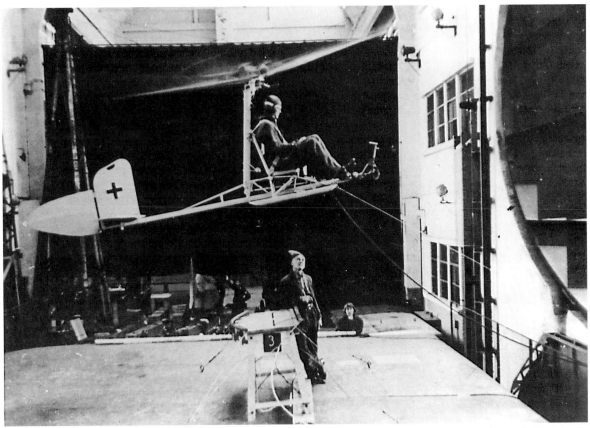

The Focke-Achgelis Fa 330 was a remarkably simple gyroglider, designed as an over-the-horizon surveillance platform for the German Navy's U-boat fleet. This one is undergoing full-scale windtunnel tests at Chalais-Meudon, Paris.

In Russia, autogyro development had advanced from a straightforward copy of the early Cierva C-8 by Kamov and Skrzhinskii in 1929 to the TsAGI A-7 in 1934, which copied features from the Cierva C-19. A two-seat autogyro, powered by a 480hp M-22 radial engine and with a distinctive steerable nosewheel undercarriage, the A-7 retained short wings and a tail unit with conventional aileron and elevator control surfaces and was much larger than the C-19 or later C-30. Development of the A-7 continued into mid-1938, when five A-7-3a production aircraft were ordered. These were built in a factory at Smolensk in 1939 and delivered to the Soviet Air Force early in 1940. Armed with one fixed and two movable machine-guns, the A-7-3a was used operationally for reconnaissance missions against the advancing German forces on the Smolensk front later that year.

Further autogyro development in the Soviet Union, now being led by Kamov at the Smolensk works, was interrupted in mid-1941 when the factory had to be relocated east to a new site in the Lake Baikal area, out of reach of the Luftwaffe. However, all Russian autogyro development had been abandoned by the end of 1943 in favour of developing the more versatile helicopter, although none of the latter entered service until the postwar period.

In Germany few, if any, of the thirty C.30s built by Focke-Wulf entered military service, although some may have been requisitioned for second-line operations following the outbreak of war. Instead, the Luftwaffe relied on the highly efficient and slow-flying Fieseler Storch fixed-wing reconnaissance aircraft for artillery observation, while Professor Focke and others successfully pursued the development of practical helicopters.

However, Focke did not entirely abandon the autogyro, developing in 1942 the Focke-Achgelis Fa 330 Bachstelze (Water Wagtail). This easily dismantled, one-man gyroglider was specifically designed for use by the German navy U-boat fleet. Capable of being stowed below decks when the submarine was submerged, the various components of the Fa 330 could be brought up through the conning tower hatch when the vessel was operating on the surface and quickly assembled on deck, the machine then being flown as a towed kite behind the U-boat. By thus extending the visible horizon, the Fa 330 was expected to offer a unique observation

The Cierva C.40 introduced a side-by-side two-seat cockpit and a jump take-off capability, but was only a limited operational success. This one, L7589, was the first of three originally intended for the Royal Navy.

platform, and could even be used to carry a radio aerial to enhance communications. Some 200 Fa 330s were built by Focke-Achgelis from 1942 onwards, and an unknown number were embarked operationally on U-boats. However, they were not universally popular with the U-boat commanders, who felt that the hovering autogyro betrayed the presence of the submarine and delayed the ability to escape when detected.

Having been closely involved with development of the Cierva Autogiro from the mid 1920s, the British Air Ministry had eventually ordered ten C.30As for army co-operation duties as the Rota Mk I. Built by Avro in 1934, these aircraft were mostly delivered to the RAF School of Army Co-operation at Old Sarum, where they were used for artillery observation, reconnaissance and liaison operations.

By 1939, however, the RAF had concluded that the Autogiro was less effective in these roles than light, fixed-wing aircraft and, with the outbreak of war, the surviving Rotas were withdrawn from the army co-operation role. Instead, successful trials with a single C.30A, which was used to help calibrate the new and secret British defence radar chain along the east and Channel coasts, led to all available Rotas and civil C.30As being pressed into service in July 1940 to equip eight radio servicing units. Subsequently amalgamated into No 1448 Flight, with up to seventeen Autogiros on strength and based at Dux-ford, Hendon and Odiham, the unit continued in the radar calibration role into June 1943, when the Flight became No 529 Squadron, with bases at Halton and Henley-on-Thames. The squadron finally disbanded on 20 October 1945, after accumulating over 9,000 operational flight hours.

Following deck landing demonstrations with a C.30 in

September 1935, the Royal Navy also showed some interest in the Autogiro, seeing a possible role for fleet spotting and 'night shadowing'. In 1937 five examples of the C.40 Autogiro, a new side-by-side two-seat Cierva design with a jump take-off capability, were ordered by the Air Ministry. Three of these were intended for the Royal Navy and two for the School of Army Co-operation. In the event only two C.40s entered naval service, and these only for evaluation at Lee-on-Solent between December 1939 and April 1940. These trials helped confirm the unsuitability of the Autogiro in the roles envisaged, and the aircraft were transferred to the RAF where they were issued to the radar calibration unit.

Meanwhile, three other C.40s were flown to France in October 1939 to support the short-lived British Expeditionary Force. With the fall of France, two managed to escape back to England, where they served out their days with No 1448 Flight and later No 529 Squadron. The third was destroyed in France to prevent it being captured by the advancing German forces.

By late 1940 it was evident that the importance of the radar defence network was such that the procurement of further autogyros needed to be considered to counter any losses among the radar calibration fleet. With almost all rotary-wing manufacturing in Great Britain at a standstill, the only alternative was to go to the USA, and in particular to the Pitcairn Autogiro Company, which had become a Cierva licensee in 1929. Pitcairn had been responsible for manufacturing a series of Autogiro variants, some of which had been successfully sold on the American market. To meet the British request the company bought back seven civilian PA-18 Autogiros and remanufactured them as the PA-39, with the more modern direct-control jump take-off rotor system,

Seven Pitcairn PA-39 Autogiros were manufactured in the USA during 1941 for radar calibration duties in the UK, but none entered operational service, BW834, seen here, being one of only two to reach England.

incorporating irreversible controls. Seven PA-39s were constructed, the first being flown in February 1941 and all being completed by the year end. In January 1942 five of the PA-39s were shipped to Canada for onward transportation, but only two were to arrive intact in the UK, the others being sabotaged on the Canadian dockside.

In the meantime, and despite previous pessimism, Royal Navy interest in the use of autogyros suddenly revived following the successes being recorded by the U-boat fleet against Allied shipping convoys. Accordingly it was decided to evaluate the PA-39 for shipboard operations and investigate the development of a more powerful variant for anti-submarine operations. The PA-39 had already demonstrated an ability to carry out a vertical jump take-off of 25ft (7.6m) and almost-vertical landings, making it much more suited to small-deck operations than earlier Autogiros. To follow up the apparent potential, two PA-39s were retained with Pitcairn for development trials, to include actual shipboard flying at sea. Initial trials took place aboard the escort carrier HMS *Avenger*, sailing in Chesapeake Bay in April 1942, using a dummy landing platform marked out on the flight deck, complete with arrester wire. The PA-39, fitted with an arrester hook, completed the tests satisfactorily and repeated them in May 1942, flying on and off a short flight deck built over the stern of a requisitioned British merchant ship *Empire Mersey*. No further trials took place, and British interest in the PA-39 and autogyros in general lapsed.

In part this was due to a mechanical weakness found in the rotor drive system of the two PA-39s actually delivered, during their evaluation in Great Britain. This resulted in further use being abandoned. However, the lack of operational success accorded to the PA-39 and the various other Cierva derivative Autogiros during the war was not entirely due to the limitations in performance and control associated with autogyro design. The fact was that, by the early 1940s, the main warring factions were each beginning to recognise the advantages of the helicopter, and development of this had finally eclipsed the autogyro in military minds.

The helicopter arrives

While the autogyro had entered service in a number of countries by September 1939, the impact of the Second World War was to both accelerate and retard the development and entry into service of the autogyro's successor, the vertically-capable helicopter.

Pre-war France was the first to see a successful controllable helicopter, with development centred around the single-seat Breguet-Dorand Laboratory Gyroplane, first flown in June 1935 and featuring a coaxial, contra-rotating rotor layout. By 1938 this helicopter was demonstrating speeds of 105km/h (65mph) at altitudes up to 158m (518ft), and even autorotative landings with the engine at idle. It continued to fly almost right up to the outbreak of war, when development was shelved to concentrate on the production of fixed-wing aircraft. The aircraft itself was destroyed during an Allied bomber raid on the Breguet factory at Villacoublay, and further original French helicopter development was not revived until the end of hostilities. However, the Breguet manufacturing facilities did become involved in the construction of the uncompleted German Focke-Achgelis Fa 284 crane helicopter in 1944–45.

In Great Britain the pattern of domestic development was similar. Initially Cierva and the parent Weir Group co-operated with Dr Focke in Germany, with a

The second Focke-Achgelis Fa 223, D-OCEW, was one of two airframes originally laid down with commercial operations in mind, but completed instead to a military specification.

cross-licensing agreement that saw Focke being able to use the patented Cierva cyclic/collective pitch hub control system in return for the production of Focke-derived helicopters in Great Britain. This liaison obviously became impossible as Nazi intentions became clearer, and Weir was forced to go it alone. Following the first successful flights with the Weir W5 in 1938, the company went on to develop the larger two-seat W6. Flown in October 1939, this used the same side-by-side lateral rotor layout as the W5 and Focke design, and was succeeded by a scaled-up design project in 1940, intended to meet the Royal Navy requirement for a 'fleet shadower'. Further development was shelved in July 1940 as a result of the deteriorating war situation, and the W6 was dismantled. Essential design data was subsequently passed to the USA where, together with patented Cierva work, it was to contribute to the first successful US heli-

The Weir W6, the world's first helicopter to carry a passenger, was intended to act as a prototype for a scaled-up antisubmarine variant for the Royal Navy. The deteriorating war situation forced abandonment of the project in 1940.

copter flights from 1940 onwards. Although British design development continued at a very low level of priority throughout the war, it was to be many years before a British-designed helicopter entered military service.

German helicopter development was more advanced than that of any of the other countries involved in such research by September 1939. From the original and very successful single-seat Focke-Achgelis Fa 61 of 1936, using the Cierva cyclic/collective pitch control hubs, Professor Focke had gone on to design the larger Focke-Achgelis Fa 266, which retained the same side-by-side rotor configuration but with a six-passenger cabin layout for potential commercial operations with Lufthansa. A prototype Fa 266 was built at Delmenhorst-Hoyencamp in September 1939, but was almost immediately commandeered for military development. Powered by an 800hp BMW132 radial engine, and with a design gross weight of 3,200kg (7,055lb), it was redesignated Fa 223 and used for a series of tethered ground tests to iron out various control problems before making its first free flight in August 1940. Two months later this aircraft, the V1, reached an altitude of 7,100m (23,300ft), far exceeding the previous height record achieved by any helicopter, but it was written off in February 1941 in a heavy autorotative landing.

Two more prototypes followed in 1941, by which time the type had already been ordered into production for the Luftwaffe as the Fa 223E Drache (Kite) powered by the uprated 1,000hp Bramo 323 radial engine which allowed an increased gross weight of 4,300kg (9,500lb). The Luftwaffe saw a requirement for up to 121 Fa 223s, in roles including anti-submarine operations armed with two 250kg (550lb) bombs or depth charges, external load carriage and recovery, and rescue. The increased power made the Fa 223E capable of lifting external loads of up to 1,100kg (2,245lb), although 800kg (1,760lb) was more usual. The helicopter was capable of achieving speeds of 185km/h (115mph), despite high vibration levels which normally kept it down to a more sensible 120km/h (75mph).

Initially the Luftwaffe ordered a batch of thirty pre-production Fa 223Es for service evaluation, and these were laid down at the Focke-Achgelis Delmenhorst factory. However, an Allied bomber attack in June 1942 destroyed the production line and the two surviving prototypes before any aircraft could be completed, bringing all flight testing to a halt. The line was moved to Laupheim, where production resumed in early 1943. Service trials, originally planned for the spring of 1943, had to be delayed until new aircraft were available.

In June 1943 the first Fa 223E completed at Laupheim, the V11, carried out a series of external loading and lifting trials to demonstrate the type's potential, including the carriage of a 900kg (1,984lb) engine a distance of some 32km (20miles). Later that year the second aircraft built at Laupheim, the V12, was earmarked to rescue Mussolini from imprisonment in Italy atop the 1,700m (5,600ft) Gran Sasso Massif northeast of Rome. In the event the helicopter became unserviceable at the last moment and the operation was carried out using a Fieseler Storch. The Fa 223 V11 was subsequently written off in a crash near Osnabruck in the spring of 1944, while trying to recover the major components of a downed Dornier Do 217 from the Vehnier Moor. To recover both the Do 217 and the Fa 223E, a second helicopter, the V14, was flown to the site in May 1944 and successfully recovered all the major parts of both aircraft in a two-day operation which provided a very practical demonstration of the Drache's capabilities.

Continuing production disruptions meant that by mid-1944 only seven Fa 223Es had been completed at Laupheim before the production line was again destroyed in a second Allied bomber raid in July. Indeed, as a result of the Allied attacks, only a very small number of Fa 223s entered service, and then mostly on a trials basis and flown by Focke-Achgelis test pilots.

In September 1944 the Fa 223 V16 (with the V14 as a back-up), was flown to the Alpine town of Mittenwalde, north of Innsbruck, for trials with the Mountain Warfare School, where the helicopter carried out a series of general transport and external load tests in the nearby mountains. These included moving the ammunition and supplies for a complete German mountain brigade, a task normally carried out by forty or fifty mules, and carrying a 75cm (30in) mountain infantry gun and ammunition in a cargo net, from a mountain valley to a site some 1,800m (5,900ft) below the Wornergrant peak. Using a 16m (52ft) cable the Fa 223E then lifted the battery even higher, to a position where a landing was impossible. These successful series of trials were completed

In June 1943 an Fa 223E carried out a series of external load lifting trials, including this carriage of a 900kg engine, to demonstrate the helicopter's potential for army support.

on 5 October, but unexpectedly all further testing of the Fa 223 was forbidden a few days later and the Focke-Achgelis staff were all ordered to the Messerschmitt factory. This order was reversed soon afterwards and the organisation was sent to Berlin Tempelhof with a contract to manufacture Fa 223s at a rate of 400 per month. Needless to say, the requirement was impossible to meet at such a late stage in the conflict.

At this time, towards the end of 1944, there were only five Fa 223 helicopters operational, the V12 having been lost in the Alps while attempting to rescue seventeen people trapped in snow on Mont Blanc. A mechanical failure resulted in a disintegrating rotor and the crew were killed in the ensuing crash. Early in 1945 three of the five surviving Draches were allocated to Luft-Transportstaffel 40, the first dedicated Luftwaffe helicopter unit, set up at Muhldorf in Bavaria. The other two helicopters were retained for development work with Focke-Achgelis at its new Tempelhof site.

In late February Wr Nr 00051, the first Fa 223E from the Tempelhof line, was accepted and immediately assigned 'by order of the Fuhrer' to fly to Danzig on a secret rescue mission. Russian advances made it

Six prototype Flettner Fl 265s were built, retaining the nose mounted engine installation of their autogyro forebears but introducing the intermeshing rotors which became the Flettner trademark.

impossible to achieve the objective, but the crew successfully rescued a wounded Bf 109 pilot instead and, having flown him back to base, returned over the sea to Swinemunde in a three-hour operation which included manual refuelling in flight from a 200 litre (44 gal) drum stowed in the cabin. The helicopter eventually reached its assigned destination at Werder after an epic three-day flight and 16 hours 25 minutes flying time, having covered a total distance of 1,675km (1,041 miles) with no mechanical problems. By April 1945 only three Fa 223s appear to have been still airworthy, and Wr Nr 00051 and the V14 were assigned for the training of pilots with Luft-Transportstaffel 40, now based at Ainring, to support the planned 'Defence of the Alpine Stronghold'. On 30 April the squadron personnel left for Aigen in Austria, the two Fa 223s following on 2 May. Then, with the war rapidly ending, the two Fa 223 crews decided to fly the helicopters away from the advancing Russians and towards the Allies, whom they met at Ainring on 9 May. Subsequently the two Fa 223s were transferred to British and American ownership for testing in the respective countries. A third aircraft, the V16, was meanwhile destroyed by Focke at Tempelhof, and about fifteen more in various stages of assembly were captured by the Russians when they marched into Berlin.

In total about eleven Fa 223s, including the prototypes, were actually completed and flown, and these logged some 400 hours flight time and about 9,654km (6,000 miles) of cross-country flying before the end came. Another thirty-seven Draches reached advanced stages of assembly, and component parts for a further twenty were manufactured at the three production sites between 1940 and 1945.

While Focke had been developing his lateral-rotor configuration, a second designer, Anton Flettner, was working with the German Navy to produce a helicopter able to operate from ships in the anti-submarine and reconnaissance roles. Flettner had originally built his first, unsuccessful, helicopter in 1932 before developing in 1936 his own cabin autogyro, the Fl 184 with cyclic-pitch control, for naval evaluation. This was written off within a few weeks of its maiden flight, but Flettner followed it with a second variant, the Fl 185, incorporating a powered rotor, before abandoning this avenue of development and concentrating on a new helicopter variant, the Fl 265. This retained the nose-mounted engine position and the familiar autogyro tail surfaces, but introduced a unique intermeshing rotor system, with two counter-rotating two-bladed rotors mounted close together side-by-side, synchronised to avoid collision.

Six single-seat Fl 265 prototypes were ordered for naval evaluation in 1938, and the first of these was completed in May 1939, although it crashed on its first flight when the synchronisation gear failed and the rotors struck each other. Nevertheless, the basic concept proved successful and the type was operated in 1939–40 aboard cruisers in the Baltic.

Flettner followed this with the much improved Fl 282 Kolibri (Humming Bird), with the powerplant relocated under the main rotors and greatly enhanced forward visibility. In 1940 forty-five prototype and thirty pre-production Fl 282s were ordered for trials and evaluation, and some priority was given to development as German military ambitions grew. The first prototypes were completed in 1941, with both open and enclosed cockpits, and a year later the cruiser *Köln* was used for

THE HELICOPTER'S FIRST WAR

The Fl 265 carried out trials aboard the German cruiser Köln *during the early days of the war, operating from a platform built over a gun turret.*

rudimentary sea trials in the Baltic, with a Kolibri operating from a 4 x 4m (13 x 13ft) platform built over a gun turret.

Production was initiated at the Flettner factory in the Berlin suburb of Johannisthal and a new facility at Bad Tolz, but was frustrated by the Allied bombing raids. By 1943 only about twenty Fl 282s had been completed, and probably not more than twenty-four in total were delivered by the end of hostilities. This was despite an order placed with BMW in 1944 for a further 1,000 aircraft, none of which were completed. Despite this, early Fl 282s entered service in 1943, cleared for evaluative shipborne operations to protect German convoys in the Baltic, Aegean and Mediterranean.

Meanwhile, Flettner began work on a larger variant, the Fl 339, for army co-operation and gun-spotting/reconnaissance. One Fl 282 was modified with an observer's cockpit behind the powerplant, but further development was largely overtaken by events. Nevertheless, three Fl 282s did enter service in 1944 with Luft-Transportstaffel 40 for artillery spotting. In February

Top: *First flown on 30 October 1941, this is the second prototype Flettner Fl 282, fitted with a fully glazed cockpit. This machine was later cannibalised to provide spares. The Fl 282 Kolibri (above and below), underwent sea trials as early as 1942, operating from a platform built on the Travemünde airfield safety ship based in Lubeck Bay. Its intermeshing rotor system was unique among wartime helicopter designs. The Kolibri's great potential as the first shipborne antisubmarine helicopter was frustrated only by Allied bombing attacks on the production plant in 1942-43.*

Despite the popular myth, Sikorsky was not the first to fly a practical helicopter. Indeed, his early efforts with the VS.300 were frustrated by control problems. Only after many modifications was he able, in December 1941, to begin serious flight testing.

1945 Fl 282s operating on the Russian Front spotted the Soviet advance in Far Pomerania, and subsequently at least three Fl 282s based at Berlin-Rangsdorf were used in support of artillery units in the final defence of Berlin. Most were shot down by Russian anti-aircraft units and fighters. Two other Fl 282s survived with Luft-Transportstaffel 40 at Aigen in early May 1945 but, with only one pilot available and the Russians just 30 km (18 miles) away, an attempt was made to destroy one airframe before taking the survivor to Ainring and the advancing US forces. A second airworthy Fl 282 was surrendered to the Americans at Munich on 13 May, and both were later shipped to the USA for trials. At least one other serviceable example was captured by the Russians, and a fourth, non-flying, example was taken to the UK.

In the USA the prewar development carried out by Cierva/Weir and Focke was closely studied by Kellett and Pitcairn, who recognised that, had it not been for the Nazi leadership in Germany, Focke and the British companies would have almost certainly gone ahead with their cross-licensing agreement to develop and build the Focke-Achgelis helicopter designs, using the Cierva cyclic/collective-pitch hub control system.

In 1938 Kellett chief engineer Lawrence LePage had visited Dr Focke to study the Fa 61 and, following his return to the USA he developed the similar but unsuccessful lateral-rotor Platt lePage XR-1, which first flew in June 1941. In the meantime Pitcairn, which as the Cierva

licensee in the United States held the patent rights to the cyclic/collective-pitch hub mechanism, mistakenly stayed with the Autogiro.

The patents held by Pitcairn made it very difficult for any other American designer to develop a controllable helicopter, and this was certainly the problem facing Igor Sikorsky when he returned to rotary-wing development in the immediate prewar period. Initially his VS-300 prototype went through a variety of major changes involving the number and layout of rotors, blade design, powerplants and fuselage structure before he finally admitted defeat and used a hub control system that infringed the Pitcairn-held patent. The VS-300 was first flown untethered in May 1940, but not until December 1941 was final success achieved.

In part Sikorsky was driven by the US Army Air Corps, which was beginning to show great interest in the helicopter but insisted that only a single-motor configuration was practical. The experimental VS-300 was therefore followed by the VS-316, which used the same main rotor/anti-torque tail rotor configuration and the patented hub control but introduced a two-seat cockpit and a fabric-covered fuselage. Development of this new model, designated the XR-4 by the USAAF, was approved on 17 December 1940. The first prototype was rolled out in December 1941, the month the USA declared war on Japan, and three days before Germany and Italy declared war on the USA.

First flown on 14 January 1942, the XR-4 soon

Deck landing trials with the Sikorsky XR-4 equipped with pontoon floats were carried out by the US Army early in the development programme, encouraged by the Royal Navy, which saw the R-4 as the answer to the U-boat threat in the Atlantic.

demonstrated real potential as a practical helicopter, and Vought-Sikorsky began to negotiate a licence agreement with Pitcairn for the production and sale of the hub control mechanism. In July 1943 Pitcairn agreed, and in a patriotic gesture asked for only a negligible royalty on all helicopters manufactured for the US government for the duration of the hostilities. (This patriotism was later rewarded by the government reneging on the agreement and purchasing postwar large numbers of Bell, Hiller, Piasecki and other helicopters which infringed the patent. Pitcairn sued, and in 1977 was awarded compensation amounting to more than $32 million.)

In April 1942 the XR-4 was demonstrated at the Vought-Sikorsky factory in Stratford, Connecticut, before a gathering of US and British military officials, and this was followed a month later by a 760-mile (1,223km) delivery flight from Stratford to Dayton, Ohio, where the helicopter was to undergo official USAAF evaluation. Over the next several months tests were carried out to establish the value of the XR-4 for bombing submarines, pilot training, and all-terrain operations with large rubberised floats. By January 1943 the trials had been completed and the Army had decided to order thirty pre-production YR-4 models for further Service evaluation. The first three of these, designated YR-4A, were basically similar to the XR-4 but had a more powerful, 180hp engine. The remaining twenty-seven were YR-4Bs with an enlarged cabin. Subsequently seven YR-4Bs were transferred to the RAF as the Hoverfly I, and three

to the US Coast Guard as the HNS-1, all for evaluation and training.

Initially the US Navy had showed no interest at all in the XR-4 or any other kind of helicopter, on the grounds that 'no rotary-wing aircraft had yet been able to carry 453kg (1,000lb) useful load, and was never likely to do so'. (They were obviously unaware of Focke's success.) The Coast Guard and the British Royal Navy were more optimistic, and now saw considerable value in helicopters for anti-submarine convoy protection. By early 1943 continuing German U-boat successes against Atlantic convoys reinforced British and American interest in the helicopter's potential for convoy protection, and in May 1943 the XR-4 was used for a two-day demonstration of its shipborne ability, flying on and off a rudimentary 50ft (15m) square slatted wooden platform aboard a tanker, the ss *Bunker Hill*, moored in Long Island Sound.

May 1943 also marked the delivery of the first US Army YR-4 (42-107234) which, accompanied by the XR-4, was flown from Stratford to Fort Monmouth, New Jersey, for tests with the Signal Corps, followed by the first public demonstration of the helicopter in front of the Capitol in Washington D.C.

In July 1943 a second series of deck-landing tests were carried out, this time on a wooden platform over the stern of a troopship, the ss *James Parker*. On this occasion take-offs and landings were carried out by both the XR-4 and YR-4 while the vessel was under way in

The R-4 became the first American helicopter to enter production when it was ordered in quantity by the US Army in early 1943. Operational service followed a year later.

open seas off Long Island. During the second day of trials the ship was rolling at up to 10°, and the wind over the deck was reaching 40mph (64km/h). Nonetheless both helicopters, one with a wheeled undercarriage and the other with pontoon floats, were operated on and off the deck with little trouble.

Despite the success of the trials, the US Navy still took little interest, although the Coast Guard received its first HNS-1 variant in October 1943. This was delivered to Floyd Bennett Field, where the USCG began experimenting with rescue techniques and equipment, and on 3 January 1944 a helicopter from this base was used to deliver blood plasma from lower Manhattan Island to Sandy Hook, New York, where survivors of an explosion aboard the destroyer USS *Turner* were being treated. Later that same month a helicopter pilot training operation was set up at Floyd Bennett Field, to be equipped with twenty HNS-1s transferred from an Army order for 100 full-production R-4Bs being manufactured during 1944.

In November 1943 a new YR-4B (42-107240) was handed over to the Army at Stratford and immediately dismantled at nearby Bridgeport for shipment by Curtiss C-46 transport to Alaska for cold-weather trials. These included tests with a litter (stretcher) capsule on the port side and practice 'casevac' rescue operations. Although the helicopter carried out no real rescue missions in Alaska, the experience was to prove useful five months later, when an urgent request was received to use the R-4 to carry out a casevac operation in the CBI theatre.

On 20 April 1944 a Vultee L-1B light aircraft of the 1st Air Commando Group, supporting Chindit operations against the Japanese in Burma, was flying three British soldiers, two wounded and one with malaria, to hospital when its engine failed and the pilot was forced to land in the jungle some 100 miles (160km) behind enemy lines. All four men survived the crash, but there was nowhere nearby where an aeroplane could land to effect a rescue. Following a request from the local Army commanders, five early Sikorsky YR-4B helicopters had just been airlifted to the Group base at Hailakandi in India, although three were almost immediately written off in accidents, leaving just two for operational use by mid-April. These were based at Lala Ghat in east Bengal, and a message was sent to the unit, which agreed to attempt a rescue.

On 21 April a single YR-4B (43-28223), piloted by 1st Lt Carter Harman, took off from Lala Ghat and staged north-west to Jorhat, crossing a 6,000ft (1,800m) mountain range *en route*. Refuelling stops were necessary approximately every 160km (100 miles). After an overnight stay, Harman continued the flight to Ledo, and then to Taro, where an extra fuel tank was roped to the roof of the cabin for the last leg over more mountains to a Chindit strongpoint codenamed 'Aberdeen'. The helicopter arrived on the afternoon of 23 April and was immediately refuelled and sent on the rescue mission. Initially Harman flew the YR-4B some 20 miles (32km) to a light-aeroplane strip on a sandbar, while the stranded group was told by a dropped note to descend from the ridge where they were hiding and head for a paddy

The Sikorsky XR-5 was built in 1943, with the Royal Navy very much in mind as the future customer. Lack of interest from the US Navy and other war priorities conspired to delay development, and the war was over before it could enter service.

field about five miles (8km) from the strip. Harman then made two flights to the paddy field, returning to the airstrip each time with one of the wounded, who were recovered to 'Aberdeen' by light aeroplane. After the second flight the underpowered YR-4B went unserviceable owing to the engine overheating in the high temperatures, but on the following morning Harman was able to rescue the remaining two men before returning to 'Aberdeen' later the same day.

This was the first rescue operation performed by a helicopter. Over the next ten days Harman carried out four more missions from 'Aberdeen', including one into a 3,000ft (900m)-high clearing close to Japanese forces, where two wounded soldiers (one clinging to the undercarriage struts) were successfully lifted out in one flight. Harman was subsequently awarded the DFC, having completed eighteen successful rescues before the surviving YR-4Bs succumbed to a lack of spare parts and the harsh operating conditions.

In the final stages of the war R-4s were used in the Philippines by the 38th Infantry Division to evacuate casualties from mountain positions.

Despite the successes achieved with the R-4, it had never really been intended as much more than an experimental and training helicopter. As early as February 1942, therefore, Sikorsky was planning a larger aircraft, the VS-327, capable of carrying a more realistic payload and with greater range and performance. Designated the XR-5, the new helicopter was originally intended for the short-range reconnaissance and liaison role but, although this was later broadened to include rescue and air ambulance roles, senior Army officials showed little interest. However, intense interest from the British Air Commission (BAC) in the XR-5 for the anti-submarine role finally won the day. Initially four prototypes were ordered, two for the USAAC and two for the British, despite continuing and considerable opposition from the US Navy. The first XR-5 flew in August 1943, and was followed by contracts for a total of 450 aircraft, 200 for the USAAF and the remainder for the BAC. The first twenty-six, designated YR-5A, were to include fourteen for Great Britain, a total of sixty-nine British deliveries being included in the first 104 off the line. In the event, manufacturing delays and war priorities saw the production schedule slip to a point where the war was over before the R-5A entered service. The British order was cancelled outright and substantial cutbacks were made in the USAAF contracts. Postwar, the basic design was successfully reworked as the S-51/H-5 series.

While Sikorsky was developing the entirely new R-5, the company was also refining the basic R-4 with the intention of increasing the payload and performance. To begin with the plan was simply to modify a YR-4, but in September 1942 the recommendation was made to build four new helicopters, designated R-6. Subsequently a contract was placed for five XR-6s, including three for Army trials and two for the US Navy. The first XR-6 flew in October 1943, but it was several months before various control and vibration problems were overcome and the prototype delivered to the Army for official

Intended as a much-improved development of the R-4, the Sikorsky R-6 arrived too late to see wartime service and, as a result, was produced in relatively small numbers.

evaluation. Meanwhile, the type had already been ordered into production for both the US and British military. The latter received no R-6s until after the war, but the US Army did take delivery of a few for evaluation.

British interest in the Sikorsky helicopter development programme had begun to crystallise in 1941, following a demonstration of the VS-300 before key members of the BAC, and was confirmed with the failure of the PA-39 Autogiro to come up to expectations. Thenceforth the BAC put its full weight behind trials of the Sikorsky R-4, to assess the suitability of the helicopter for convoy protection and the use of the R-4 itself as a training machine. At the same time the Commission put pressure on the US Defense Department to proceed with development of the R-5, placing an order for thirteen YR-4s and 250 R-5s in July 1942 to show encouragement. This was bitterly opposed at the time by the US Navy, which needed the Vought-Sikorsky plant for more urgent fixed-wing aircraft orders and, as recounted earlier, the British R-5 order was eventually cancelled before deliveries could begin.

Meanwhile, British deck-landing trials with the YR-4 had been planned for July 1943, but were set back when the first British YR-4A was badly damaged at Bridgeport in an accident on the 4th, when a tail-rotor blade came adrift during a 10ft (3m) hover and the helicopter crashed. It was replaced by an early YR-4B, which was officially delivered to the Royal Navy at Bridgeport on 22 September and was itself badly damaged five days later in a landing accident during pilot training. Despite these mishaps a small team of RAF, Royal Navy and US

Coast Guard pilots began to evaluate and train on the R-4 at Floyd Bennett Field and, belatedly joined by a now enthusiastic US Navy, carried out combined trials on a British cargo ship, MV *Daghestan*, in US waters during November 1943.

At the beginning of 1944 a joint service helicopter unit was established in the UK at Hanworth, Middlesex, coinciding with an ongoing ocean trial in which two YR-4Bs sailed aboard the MV *Daghestan* with a transatlantic convoy to the UK. Atrocious weather during the sixteen-day voyage limited flying to just three days and less than two hours total flight time, and even then the ship was rolling at up to 20° with a flight deck rise and fall of some 30ft (9m) and windspeeds of up to 46mph (74km/h). Although more flying could probably have taken place had the vessel been permitted to alter course to minimise some of the ship's motion, it was concluded that the YR-4B was not suitable for employment as an anti-submarine weapon, and that such operations would have to await the advent of a more capable design. The two YR-4Bs were flown off the ship on its arrival in Liverpool and dispatched to Feltham in Middlesex for overhaul, one flying direct and the second going by road, since only one set of the fabric-covered main rotor blades had survived the Atlantic crossing. A third YR-4B was crated and shipped to the UK in February 1944. Deliveries of further YR-4Bs and production of R-4Bs against British orders continued throughout 1944 and into 1945, the aircraft being divided between the Royal Navy and the RAF.

In August 1944 one R-4 was issued to No 529 Squadron for evaluation in the radar calibration role, marking the first use of the helicopter by an operational RAF unit, and in February 1945 No 43 Operational Training Unit was formed at RAF Andover as a Helicopter Training Flight, equipped with nine R-4s and charged with converting the No 529 Squadron Autogiro pilots and Army Auster AOP pilots. Plans to dispatch R-4Bs to mainland Europe for artillery spotting and liaison during the final stages of the war did not materialise.

In February 1945 the Royal Navy issued several R-4Bs to a Fleet Requirements Unit, 771 Squadron at Hatston in the Orkneys, for evaluation in the air-sea rescue, gunnery calibration and other roles. The flights included deck landings on warships, both at anchor and under way, but the war ended before the training and experience could be put to any real use.

Deliveries of the later R-6 to the UK began after the German surrender and just before the Japanese capitulation. Consequently none entered service until the postwar period, and even then only in small numbers.

Thus it was that the helicopter's first war came to an end. It was an unusual period which, had things turned out differently, might easily have seen Europe dominating development and postwar production. Instead, the

British use of the R-6 was restricted to postwar evaluation to determine future uses for the helicopter with all three Services.

British and French decisions virtually to freeze helicopter development at the beginning of the conflict, and the complete destruction of the German production capability towards the end of the war, effectively handed leadership over to the USA – an advantage that has been held ever since.

Bibliography

Brooks, P W, *Cierva Autogiros*, Smithsonian Institution Press (Washington DC, USA, 1988)

Luftwaffe Profile Series No 6, *Flettner 282*, Schiffer Publishing (Atglen, Pennsylvania, 1996)

Nowarra, H J, *German Helicopters 1928-45*, Schiffer Publishing (West Chester, Pennsylvania, 1990)

★British Air Commission papers, 1940-1945

★Focke-Achgelis Fa 223 papers

★Weir Helicopter Development, 1935-1941

★Sikorsky R-4 to R-6 historical files

Items marked ★ are held in the Helicopter International *archives*

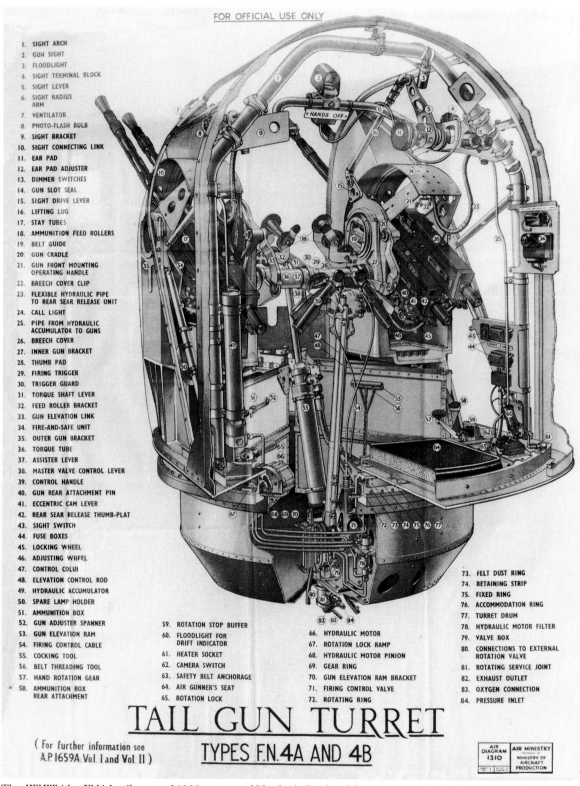

1. SIGHT ARCH
2. GUN SIGHT
3. FLOODLIGHT
4. SIGHT TERMINAL BLOCK
5. SIGHT LEVER
6. SIGHT RADIUS ARM
7. VENTILATOR
8. PHOTO-FLASH BULB
9. SIGHT BRACKET
10. SIGHT CONNECTING LINK
11. EAR PAD
12. EAR PAD ADJUSTER
13. DIMMER SWITCHES
14. GUN SLOT SEAL
15. SIGHT DRIVE LEVER
16. LIFTING LUG
17. STAY TUBES
18. AMMUNITION FEED ROLLERS
19. BELT GUIDE
20. GUN CRADLE
21. GUN FRONT MOUNTING OPERATING HANDLE
22. BREECH COVER CLIP
23. FLEXIBLE HYDRAULIC PIPE TO REAR SEAR RELEASE UNIT
24. CALL LIGHT
25. PIPE FROM HYDRAULIC ACCUMULATOR TO GUNS
26. BREECH COVER
27. INNER GUN BRACKET
28. THUMB PAD
29. FIRING TRIGGER
30. TRIGGER GUARD
31. TORQUE SHAFT LEVER
32. FEED ROLLER BRACKET
33. GUN ELEVATION LINK
34. FIRE-AND-SAFE UNIT
35. OUTER GUN BRACKET
36. TORQUE TUBE
37. ASSISTER LEVER
38. MASTER VALVE CONTROL LEVER
39. CONTROL HANDLE
40. GUN REAR ATTACHMENT PIN
41. ECCENTRIC CAM LEVER
42. REAR SEAR RELEASE THUMB-PLAT
43. SIGHT SWITCH
44. FUSE BOXES
45. LOCKING WHEEL
46. ADJUSTING WHEEL
47. CONTROL COLUI
48. ELEVATION CONTROL ROD
49. HYDRAULIC ACCUMULATOR
50. SPARE LAMP HOLDER
51. AMMUNITION BOX
52. GUN ADJUSTER SPANNER
53. GUN ELEVATION RAM
54. FIRING CONTROL CABLE
55. COCKING TOOL
56. BELT THREADING TOOL
57. HAND ROTATION GEAR
58. AMMUNITION BOX REAR ATTACHMENT

59. ROTATION STOP BUFFER
60. FLOODLIGHT FOR DRIFT INDICATOR
61. HEATER SOCKET
62. CAMERA SWITCH
63. SAFETY BELT ANCHORAGE
64. AIR GUNNER'S SEAT
65. ROTATION LOCK

66. HYDRAULIC MOTOR
67. ROTATION LOCK RAMP
68. HYDRAULIC MOTOR PINION
69. GEAR RING
70. GUN ELEVATION RAM BRACKET
71. FIRING CONTROL VALVE
72. ROTATING RING

73. FELT DUST RING
74. RETAINING STRIP
75. FIXED RING
76. ACCOMMODATION RING
77. TURRET DRUM
78. HYDRAULIC MOTOR FILTER
79. VALVE BOX
80. CONNECTIONS TO EXTERNAL ROTATION VALVE
81. ROTATING SERVICE JOINT
82. EXHAUST OUTLET
83. OXYGEN CONNECTION
84. PRESSURE INLET

(For further information see A.P. 1659A. Vol. I and Vol. II)

TAIL GUN TURRET
TYPES F.N. 4A AND 4B

AIR DIAGRAM 1310

AIR MINISTRY
MINISTRY OF AIRCRAFT PRODUCTION

The AW Whitley FN4A tail turret of 1938 was a world leader in bomber defence (see page 207). It posed a serious threat to any attacking fighter, delivering a lethal cone of fire from its four Browning guns.

8

Armament Diversifies

R Wallace Clarke

Aircraft Guns

After the carnage of the First World War it seemed unthinkable that another confrontation could occur in Europe. Yet fifteen years after the Armistice had been signed there were ominous signs that the German Chancellor was intent on retrieving German land annexed by the Treaty of Versailles. By 1935 General Feldmarshall Milch, under the guise of Director of Deutsche Lufthansa, had covertly built up the German air force to a state where international protests could be shrugged aside. Intelligence reports reaching France and Britain confirmed their worst fears; it was revealed that the prototype bombers being tested at the Luftwaffe research centre at Rechlin were all designed for tactical use in offensive warfare. Reports of a similar build-up of naval and army forces confirmed the fact that war with Germany was a distinct possibility.

Consequently, the issue of specifications for new equipment assumed a new urgency. The new aircraft designs would need armament systems far in advance of the vintage equipment fitted to the obsolescent biplanes then in service. The major powers realised that the air weapons dating back to the First World War had reached the limit of improvement. More reliable and faster-firing guns were needed which would keep them abreast of any future adversary. These were the weapons which would take the lives of so many eager young airmen.

Britain

After protracted trials in the 1920s the Air Staff had concluded that, although there was a need for a large-calibre gun to counter the expected use of armour protection, the new aircraft types should be armed with fast-firing, rifle-calibre weapons. The American Browning (Colt) model 40/2 recoil-operated gun was chosen following comparative trials with other weapons in 1934. After being modified by Maj Thompson of the RAF gun section to take 0.303in (7.7mm) cordite ammunition, it proved to be an excellent air weapon, arming most RAF aircraft by 1939. The belt-fed Browning was not, however, an ideal free-mounted observer's gun, and the new Vickers Class K gas-operated weapon was adopted to replace the then-obsolescent Lewis. The Air Staff saw the need for heavily armed 'bomber destroyers'. Several designs armed with the ponderous 37mm Coventry Ordnance Works (COW) gun had been mercifully rejected in the early 1930s, but a specification issued in 1935 called for a twin-engine fighter armed with four 20mm Oerlikon cannon. Westland Aircraft submitted its design (later named Whirlwind) and received an order to

The Browning MkII 0.303in-calibre machine-gun was the standard fixed fighter and turret gun at the outbreak of hostilities. It is seen here in a test rig.

The Hispano-Suiza H5404 20mm cannon, first used by the French Air force, was adopted by the RAF in 1940, and manufactured in the UK. The Hispano was later modified by G F Wallace and proved to be a reliable hard-hitting aircraft weapon. Here it is mounted in its intended position between the cylinder blocks of the Hispano HS 12Y Aero engine.

proceed with production. Another specification, P.9/35, was issued for a single-engine fighter armed with a four-gun powered turret. It was envisaged that it would intercept bomber formations and proceed to decimate them. Unfortunately the bombers did not come from Germany, but arrived from France with a fighter escort. The unfortunate crews of the Boulton Paul Defiants paid dearly for this mistaken theory. When the Swiss Oerlikon was rejected for aircraft use by the RAF gun section there was an urgent need for a 20mm shell-firing gun. After receiving reports from the Air Attaché in Paris of a new Hispano-Suiza 20mm aircraft cannon, members of the Air Staff and Maj Thompson visited the works in Paris to evaluate the weapon. They found that the gun, the Hispano-Suiza 404, would be an ideal shell-firing gun for service use, and an agreement was eventually signed for licensed production in the UK. After some early production problems the Hispano provided the RAF with a hard-hitting gun which gave excellent service throughout the conflict.

France

The Armée de l'Air introduced two new rifle-calibre guns for use in the mid-1930s, the fast-firing Darne gun and the MAC, both designed and produced in 7.5mm calibre. The Hispano type 404 20mm gun was the standard cannon fitted to French aircraft. It had originally been designed to be mounted between the cylinders of the Hispano HS12X aero engine, to fire through the hollow propeller shaft and consequently being known as the *Moteur cannon*. The first fighter so armed was the low-wing Dewoitine D.510, but it was later fitted to the D.520, which had a single 404 firing through the propeller hub, plus two MAC machine-guns in the wings.

Russia

The armed forces of the USSR and Germany were able to develop and produce their military equipment without the constant calls for financial cutbacks which plagued the defence departments of democracies. In the Soviet Union any promising design of military equipment was given Service trials. A number of gun designers were also given facilities to develop a series of aircraft guns which were probably the best in the world at that time. The first to be accepted for use was the ShKAS, designed by B G Shpital'nyi. This was a fast-firing 7.62mm calibre gas operated gun used in the 1930s and throughout the war. The same designer was responsible for the ShVAK 20mm cannon, a very advanced gun which also saw widespread use in the war. The standard Russian heavy-calibre machine-gun was the Beresin BS 12.7mm, which compared favourably in some respects with the 0.50 calibre Browning and was gas-assisted recoil operated. It was introduced in 1941. Another formidable gun was the 23mm Volkov-Yartsyev (VYa), which was also brought into service in 1941. It fired a 200g (7.07oz) shell at a phenomenal 920m (3,020ft) per second, and was used with great success against the German Panzer units. The Soviet Air Force also used some Vickers and other foreign designed aircraft guns, but the foregoing were the main weapons used by the airmen of the USSR in the initial stages of the war.

Germany

The strength and ingenuity of the German armament industry since the turn of the century has provided its armed forces with weapons which often seemed one jump ahead of the opposition. In the First World War the aircraft, guns, and synchronising gear supplied to German aviators often gave them an advantage over

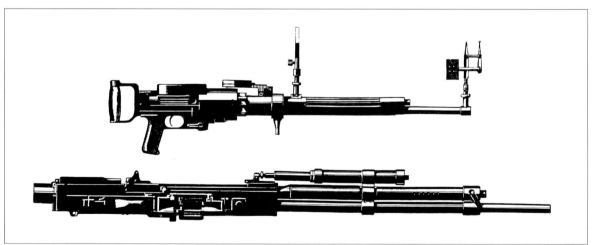

Russian air weapons in 1940. Top: *the ShKAS machine-gun: Designed by B G Shpitalnyi, this belt-fed 7.62mm-calibre gun was the fastest firing (1,800rpm) air weapon used in the Second World War.* Bottom: *the Beresin UB was the standard heavy-calibre machine-gun used by the USSR. It compared favorably with the US Browning 'Point Fifty'.*

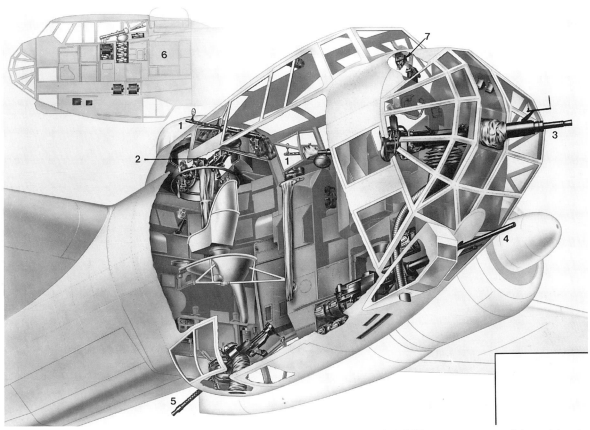

A typical Luftwaffe bomber armament layout on the Dornier Do 217E3.

Key:

1 MG15 7.62mm machine-gun fed by 75-round saddle-type magazine

2 MG131 13mm-calibre machine-gun mounted in an EDL turret, powered in rotation only

3 Free-mounted MGFF 20mm cannon, mainly used for air-to-ground attacks

4 MG151/20 20mm cannon, sighted and fired by the pilot

5 MG 131 in lower rear defence position, movable mounting

6 Layout of ammunition magazine stowage

7 Revi 12D (bottom), and Lofte (top) sights for fixed cannon and dive bombing respectively.

their Allied opponents. When the Armistice was signed in November 1918 there were several new types of aircraft guns about to come into service. One of these was the revolutionary Gast gun, firing 1,600 rounds a minute; another was the STB Szakats 20mm aircraft cannon. The Dreyse model 1918 was an advanced rifle-calibre gun which was covertly developed after the war; it was to have a great influence on the design of later aircraft and ground service guns, the most important being the MG 15 and the MG 17 of 1934. These weapons, produced by Rheinmetall-Borsig, were recoil-operated, rifle-calibre guns, the free-mounted MG 15 being fed by a 75-round saddle-type magazine. The fixed MG 17 was belt fed and was fired electrically by a solenoid. Designed in 1932, these guns were to be fitted to most Luftwaffe aircraft in 1939.

The general trend of aviation armament was towards larger-calibre guns with more striking power. As early as

1933 Rheinmetall commissioned a talented designer, Louis Strange, to design a 13mm automatic gun suitable for air use. This gun, the Rheinmetall-Borsig Model 131, was adopted by the Luftwaffe as the MG 131. It was in mass production by 1939, and was widely used on fighters and as a bomber defence weapon. Electrically fired, it was chambered for a special round fired at 750m/sec.

It was generally agreed that the ideal fighter gun would be a 20mm shell-firing weapon, and all the European powers adopted guns of this calibre for air-craft use. All such guns in use at the outbreak of war were descended from the German Becker cannon of 1916. The Swiss Oerlikon concern produced three auto-matic 20mm guns in 1935, all based on the Becker. One of these, the Type F, was adopted by the Luftwaffe in 1935 as the MG FF. It was manufactured under licence by Rheinmetall-Borsig, being used as a fixed fighter gun

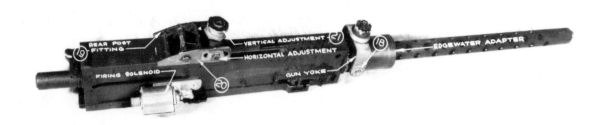

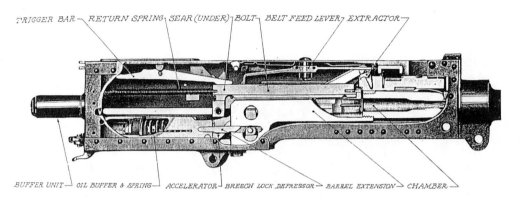

The 0.50in-calibre Browning, used in most US aircraft in the Second World War. The gun shown is fitted out for turret mounting (top). The cutaway drawing shows the main features of the recoil-operated action.

and as a movable weapon for bomber defence. It was operated by a blow-back action and fed by a 60-round drum.

USA

In 1918 Gen John Pershing convinced Washington that there was a need for a heavy-calibre machine-gun for ground and air use. Consequently an 0.50in (12.7mm)-calibre automatic gun designed by the great John Browning was adopted for service use, being manufactured by the Colt firearms company in seven versions. The air-cooled model was modified in 1932 by a Dr S G Green, and became the famous model M2 'Fifty Caliber' which, with minor modifications, armed most US aircraft throughout the Second World War. Although, as will be seen later, other weapons were used by the USAAF, the policy of standardising the M2 Browning resulted in long production runs of the gun and ammunition. The rounds, based on a German anti-tank bullet of 1917, were fired at a velocity of 2,750ft (836m) per second, giving an effective range of 1,100 yards (1,005m). The model 40/2 0.30in (7.62mm) Browning gun had been dropped as an air weapon by 1941, its only use being as a nose gun on some early versions of bombers.

Italy

In the mid-1930s SAFAT, the arms division of Fiat, developed a series of machine-guns for the Italian army. After trials the Ministry for Air ordered three versions for aviation use, to be made by the Breda concern. Designated the Breda-SAFAT 1935, they were produced in three bores, 7.7mm (0.303in), 7.92mm and 12.7 (0.50in). These were the standard guns in use by the Regia Aeronautica when war was declared on the Allies.

Hostilities commence

When UK Prime Minister Chamberlain declared war in September 1939 the theories and planning of the previous years were put to the test. In the first month of the war a force of Handley Page Hampden bombers attacking German destroyers off Heligoland were intercepted by Messerschmitt Bf 109s and lost half their number. The Hampden's defensive guns were all hand-aimed Vickers on rudimentary mountings, and proved to be totally inadequate. The Luftwaffe hailed the operation as a victory. On 18 December a force of twenty-four Wellingtons was sent on an armed reconnaissance to Wilhelmshaven. This sortie revealed armament shortcomings on both sides. Prewarned by radar, German fighters were waiting, and attacked the formation from the beams, where the Wellingtons' multi-gun turrets were least effective. Ten were shot down, and one Messerschmitt dived into the harbour. Although this was, from the German viewpoint, a successful operation, reports showed that the MG FF 20mm cannon in the Bf 109 was less effective than hoped. Ammunition was soon exhausted, and the shells detonated immediately on contact with the airframes of the Wellingtons.

The RAF Air Staff had hoped that the combined fire from powered gun turrets would fend off attacking fighters, but after the attrition of the Wilhelmshaven operation it was reluctantly decided that such losses could not be sustained, and the coming strategic bombing campaign against Germany would have to be carried out under the cover of darkness. This decision was to prove disastrous for the civilian population of Germany. Another painful lesson was also to be learned by the British. It had been presumed that German bombing attacks would come from distant airfields, and fighter tactics consisted of squadron attacks in tight formations against slow groups of bombers. After France was overrun the short distance from French airfields enabled Luftwaffe bombers to come with 'little friends' who proceeded to bounce the tightly grouped formations from above. The RAF soon adopted the loose line-abreast 'finger four' tactics of the German fighter groups, in spite of resistance from the 'textbook' fraternity.

The decision to arm RAF fighters with eight rifle-calibre guns was more successful than the 'cannon lobby' had forecast; it had been feared that the longer-range 20mm guns of German fighters would give them an advantage. It was soon realised, however, that very few pilots could hit anything at a range of more than 200–300 yards, and while the pilot of a Bf 109E could fire only thirty-five 20mm and seventy-three 7.92mm rounds in a two-second burst, British pilots got off 320 bullets from their Browning guns. This partly made up for the generally low standard of marksmanship.

The Air Staff had realised that their decision to rush the French 20mm Hispano into production was going to be vitally important in view of reports that new and faster firing heavy guns were soon to be installed in German fighter aircraft. Tactics and equipment developed by the Luftwaffe in the Spanish Civil War gave their pilots an initial advantage over the British, but the hectic air battles over southern England and France gave RAF Fighter Command valuable experience, and the scene was set for the fight for air superiority, which neither side was to achieve completely until the closing months of the war, when fuel and pilot shortage seriously affected Luftwaffe operations.

The introduction of the Hispano gave the RAF a much harder hitting fighter gun, but surprisingly tests proved that ball (solid steel) shells were more destructive than high-explosive (HE) projectiles, though the most effective rounds were semi-armour-piercing incendiary and composite explosive/incendiary types. From 1942 these were the standard 20mm shells used by the RAF. Two other shell-firing guns used by specialist squadrons were the Vickers Type 'S' 40mm, used mainly by ground-attack Hawker Hurricane IIDs, and the Molins 57mm gun used to great effect by the de Havilland Mosquito XVIIIs of Coastal Command. The American M2 Browning was the only large-calibre machine-gun used by the RAF and FAA, although Rolls-Royce submitted two alternative designs, but the availability of the American gun saved tooling-up for the British weapons. The M2 was of course fitted to US aircraft used by Britain, and tail turrets fitted to Bomber Command aircraft in the later war years also carried them. Four new factories were built to produce the Hispano, and production at Vickers and BSA was at full stretch throughout the war; consequently there was no thought of producing new types of aircraft gun. Speed of production, reliability and commonality of ammunition was thought to be more important than any possible increase in firepower.

Germany, on the other hand, had greater arms producing capacity, and constantly upgraded its air weapons, her industry producing an unbelievable number of new and often revolutionary aircraft guns. The first new wartime gun was the MG 81, developed by the Mauser company. Based on the MG 34 infantry weapon, it was adopted in 1940 as a fast firing fighter and bomber defence gun. Probably the most important new weapon was the Mauser MG 151/20 20mm cannon, developed from the earlier 15mm MG 151. Introduced in 1940, it featured electrical firing, and was used in large numbers on fighter and bomber aircraft. Mauser made 29,500 examples, and both Britain and America considered producing it for their own use.

The first 30mm gun used by the Luftwaffe was the MK 101, which was primarily used on the Eastern Front as a ground-attack weapon but was the first of a number of heavy-calibre guns to be used against Allied air attacks. The MK 101 was followed by the MK 103, another 30mm gun made at the same Solithurn plant of Rheinmetall. This was used against the early US 8th Air Force formations with some effect, the big 30mm shells causing major damage. Rheinmetall then produced a short-barrelled 30mm gun, the MK 108, which used a simple blowback, action and, being made mainly of steel pressings, was cheap to manufacture. It was designed specifically as an anti-bomber weapon, with a fairly low muzzle velocity and firing high-capacity HE shells. German nightfighters using the gun accounted for many RAF night bombers. It was also used against American day bombers, but its heavy weight affected fighter performance against US escort fighters. Rheinmetall also produced a novel anti-bomber weapon, the SG 117, consisting of seven short MK 108 barrels welded together and mounted vertically in the fuselage of Focke-Wulf Fw 190 fighters. It was intended to be ripple-fired when a photo-cell operated as the aircraft flew beneath a bomber.

By the time the SG 117 was brought into service in 1945, however, few fighters were penetrating the fighter screens. This weapon was one of many unique ideas to try to stem the Allied bomber offensive. Another was to use longer-range guns to enable fighters to stand off the formations and pump shells into the American bombers. One of these was the FLAK 18 37mm anti-aircraft (AA) gun, which was carried by a number of types. As will be seen later, rockets were also used, and an attempt was made to bomb the Americans from above.

The most significant aircraft gun to be produced during the Second World War was the MG 213C, built by the Mauser concern of Oberndorf. This was a gas-operated weapon in which the rounds were fed into a revolver-type housing in stages. This system enabled it to fire at a very high speed without overheating or excessive wear. The first model, tested at Oberndorf in 1943, was bored for 20mm rounds, but the final model was the 30mm MG 213. Although development was given high priority, none of the new guns saw service. However, after the war it was adopted (under many different names) by every major air force. Variants remain in service to this day, one of the latest being the 27mm gun arming the Panavia Tornado; made in the Oberndorf factory where the design originated. Because the Luftwaffe used many guns, as one type superseded another the armourers on the airfields had to cope with a bewildering array of manuals and ammunition types. This often led to confusion, but it has to be said that the German arms industry provided its airmen with the most innovative weapons of the war.

American developments

When the USAAF began operations in the Far East and Europe the main aircraft gun was the Browning 0.50in calibre machine-gun. It proved to be a hard hitting, trouble-free weapon, being used on both bomber and fighter aircraft, and as mentioned earlier, the use of one standard gun simplified production and maintenance. As the war progressed, however, other weapons were adopted for relatively minor roles. The first was an American-made version of the 20mm Hispano, designated the Gun Automatic, 20mm AN-M2 (Aircraft). Made by the International Harvester Co and Oldsmobile, it was used on the Lockheed P-38 Lightning, later US Navy Vought Corsairs, and in the tail position of the Boeing B-29. The Bell P-39 Airacobra had a Browning (Colt) 37mm M9 automatic gun firing through the airscrew boss. This weapon was also specified for a number of experimental fighters, but its slow rate of fire was not really suitable for aircraft use. A gun with an even slower rate of fire was the massive M4 75mm field gun, which fired huge 15lb (6.7kg) shells. This was installed in the North American B-25G and H Mitchell medium bomber for ground-attack operations, being mounted in a cradle under the pilot's seat and loaded by a 'cannoneer' from a 21-round box. Together with the B-25G, 1,000 H models were built, and used in North Africa and the Far East. The weapon was not a resounding success, and was generally discontinued in favour of a multiple battery of 'Point Fifty' Brownings.

Japan

If America and Britain fitted very few different types of guns and ammunition in the interest of production and commonality of aircraft weapons, the Japanese did the opposite. The Army used different weapons to the Navy,

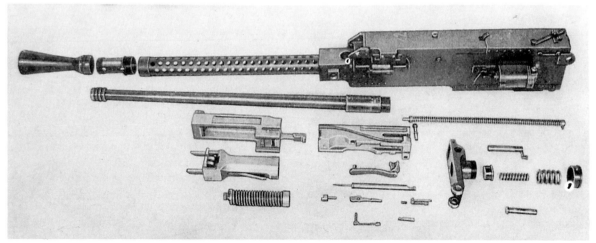

The Japanese Army Model HO-5. This was a scaled-up Browning 0.50in-calibre gun, the parts shown here being identical to the American weapon. Ironically, Colt Browning tried to do the same thing without success.

and both Services adopted weapons of different types and calibres. Most of the machine-guns were copies of Western designs, and the heavy-calibre guns were mostly based on the 0.50 M2 US Browning gun. This was because a large number of Brownings captured in the invasion of the Philippines were found to be superior to their own designs.

The army used the Type 98, which was a German MG 15 copy, the Type 89 Model 2, based on the Vickers Mk II 0.303in, and the Ho103, a copy of the M2 Browning. The Type 97 20mm gas operated cannon was used as both an observer's and fixed gun, the Type 1 Ho5 was a Browning scaled up to 20mm, and the Ho105 was a 30mm cannon. Also used was the Type 98, based on the 1916 model 37mm Hotchkiss. The Navy also used the Vickers, but called it the Type 97, the Type 1 was their version of the German MG 15. The Type 2 was an observer's gun copied from the MG 131. The Navy did standardise its 20mm weapon; this was the Type 99 Mks 1 and 2, based on the Oerlikon FF&FFL. The same gun was also scaled up to 30mm and was known as the Type 5. There were other weapons used, but the only Japanese design was the Ho301, a 40mm gun which fired shells with an in-built rocket propellent, discharged through 12 holes in the base. It had a very low velocity and was only a short-range weapon. In 1944 400 German MG 151/20s were taken to Japan by U-boat, some being fitted to Kawasaki Ki-61 fighters.

USSR

After the German advance into Russia the tide was gradually turned, and Soviet forces' equipment was updated and improved. After initial defeats, new types of aircraft and guns were introduced which enabled Russian airmen to fight on equal terms. In 1942 the Nudel'man-Suranov NS-37 anti-tank aircraft gun was issued to the Stormovik close-support units. This was a 37mm recoil operated gun firing projectiles which could penetrate 40mm armour from an angle of 40°. In 1944 it was redesigned to fire 45mm rounds which could pierce 58mm armour. Another anti-armour air weapon was the OKB-16, which fired 57mm AP shells at a velocity of 980m (2,789ft) per second. The Beresin UB 12.7mm heavy machine-gun was improved in 1944, and in the same year the B-20 20mm cannon was issued. The latter gradually replaced the trusty ShVAK weapon, being used in fighters and in the multi-gun turrets of the Tupolev Tu-4 heavy bomber. In the last year of the war the Nudel'man-Suranov team produced a 23mm version of their 37mm gun; this was the progenitor of a series of guns designed by A Rikhter which have remained in service until the present day.

Italy

The Regia Aeronautica fought with the same weapons as were in service in 1939 with the exception of the Mauser MG151/20, which was supplied by their German partners.

Main Aircraft Guns Used by the Major Powers in the Second World War

Weapon	Bore (mm)	Weight (kg)	Amm Feed	Action	M/V (Mts/S)	Rounds per min
Great Britain						
Lewis Mk III	7.7	8.3	97rd drum	Gas operated	744	600–1,000
Vickers Mk III	7.7	10.9	Dis/l belt	Short recoil	744	850–900
Vickers K (VGO)	7.7	9.3	97rd drum	Gas operated	744	950–1,000
Browning Mk II	7.7	9.9	Dis/l belt	Short recoil	744	1,150
Hispano Mks II & V	20	49/38	Drum/belt	Delayed blowback	878/820	650/850
Vickers Class S	40	134	15rd drum	Long recoil	615	125
Molins 6 Pdr	57	816	23rd mag	Recoil	791	60
Browning 0.50in	12.7	29	Dis/l belt	Short recoil	838	750–950
America						
Colt Browning M2	12	29	Dis/l belt	Short recoil	838	750–950
AN/M2 Hispano	20	49	Drum/belt	Delayed blowback	878	650
M4 Field gun	75	408	21rd mag	Recoil	580	Manually loaded
Colt Browning M4	37	112	30rd drum	Short recoil	580	150
Germany						
MG 15	7.92	7.1	75rd mag	Short recoil	800	1,100

MG 17	7.92	12.2	Dis/l belt	Short recoil	800	1,100
MG FF	20	28	60rd mag	Blowback	585	520
MG 81	7.92	6.3	Dis/l belt	Short recoil	800	1,300
MG 131	13	16.8	Dis/l belt	Short recoil	710–750	850–960
MG 151/20	20	180	Dis/l belt	Short recoil	710–800	700
MK 101	30	180	30rd mag	Gas operated	960	250
MK 103	30	141	Belt	Gas operated	790–960	420
MK 108	30	60	Dis/l belt	Blowback	505	600
BK 37	37	295	6rd mag	Recoil	820–914	160
BK 5	50	530	22rd belt	Recoil	835–930	50
MG 151	15	42	Dis/l belt	Short recoil	850–960	700
USSR						
ShKAS	7.62	10	Belt	Gas operated	825	1,800
Beresin UBS	12.7	21.5	Belt	Gas operated	855	1,000
VYa	23	68	Belt	Gas operated	920	600
ShVAK	20	40	Belt	Gas operated	790	800
NS-37	37	146	Belt	Recoil	900	250
B-20	20	25	Belt	Gas operated	800	800
France						
MAC	7.5	9.2	Belt	Recoil	810	1,000
Darne	7.5	9.2	Belt	Gas operated	820	1,700
Hispano-Suiza 404	20	49	Drum/belt	Delayed blowback	878	650
Japan						
Army Type 98	7.92	7.1	75rd mag	Short recoil	800	1,100
Type 89 mod 2	7.7	11	Belt	Short recoil	744	850–900
Type Ho-103	12.7	22	Belt	Short recoil	780	750–950
Type 97 (Ho-1/Ho-3)	20	32/43	15/50rd mag	Gas operated	840	400
Type 1 (Ho-5)	20	32.5	Belt	Short recoil	750	850/960
Type Ho-105	30	44	Belt	Short recoil	716	450
Type Ho-301	40	132	Mag.	Rocket propellent	232	450
Type 89 mod 1	7.7	9.0	69rd drum	Gas operated	744	750
MG 151/20	20	42	Belt	Short recoil	710–800	800
Ho-203	37	89	25rd mag	Recoil	576	120
Navy Type 92	7.7	8.4	47–94 drum	Gas operated	744	600
Type 97	7.7	10.9	Belt	Short recoil	723	850
Type 1	7.92	7.1	75rd mag	Short recoil	800	1,100
Type 2	13	17	Belt	Short recoil	720	900
Type 3	13.2	30	Belt	Gas operated	790	800
Type 99/1&2	20	23–37	Mag/belt	Blowback	600–760	490–750
Type 5	30	70	42rd mag	Delayed blowback	750	400
Italy						
Breda SAFAT	7.7	12.5	Belt	Short recoil	730	800
Breda SAFAT	12.7	28	Belt	Short recoil	723	800
MG 151/20 (German)	20	180	Belt	Short recoil	710–800	700

Aircraft Gunsighting

It is difficult enough to hit a running rabbit with a shotgun, but the airborne marksman faces a situation in which both he and his quarry are cavorting around the sky at high speeds. Air firing is by far the most difficult form of shooting. There are three main problems. The first is judging the angle of deflection; the guns must be aimed at a point in space where the bullets and target will meet. The second is range estimation; without any fixed reference it is difficult to assess distance, and many pilots wasted valuable ammunition by firing when out of range; gravity influences projectiles enough to affect accuracy when firing at targets at ranges of 200 yards (180m) or more. Thirdly, air gunners also had to allow for the impetus imparted to the bullets by the speed of their aircraft, and pilots had to ensure an accurate linear approach when firing. Tracer ammunition helped assessment of these allowances, but was notoriously misleading.

Top-scoring pilots and air gunners were usually natural marksmen with an instinct for the various allowances, but it was generally agreed by both sides that firing was usually very inaccurate. Indeed, an official Luftwaffe report stated that only three rounds of every 1,000 fired hit the target. Every air force established gunnery training schools to teach the finer points of marksmanship, but in the heart-thumping heat of battle the rules of correct allowances were often ignored.

By 1939 all the major air forces had adopted the reflector sight for fighter use. This gave the firer an illuminated aiming mark, or reticle, projected on to a glass screen in the pilot's line of sight. It usually consisted of a circle bisected with vertical and horizontal lines. The reflector sight was invented by Sir Howard Grubb in 1900, but was not used for aircraft gunnery until 1918, when some Albatros D.Va aircraft were fitted with a sight produced by Optische Antal Oigee of Berlin. Vickers submitted a design to the British War Office in 1915, but

it was not accepted for Service use. The circular reticle was designed to give a rough estimation of range and deflection angle. Gunnery schools stressed the importance of learning how to compare the target with the circle for various ranges, and a rough deflection allowance could be given by placing the target on the edge of the ring, flying towards the centre. Gunners in powered turrets also used reflector sights, but in general the free-mounted guns of bombers at this time used ring-and-bead sights. As will be seen, the major breakthrough in air-to-air gunnery came when the gyro sight was introduced. This presented the firer with an aiming mark (reticle) in which all the various allowances had been automatically computed. The development of gunsighting by the major powers throughout the 1939–45 conflict can now be followed.

Great Britain

The first reflector sight submitted for trials by the RAF was produced by Barr & Stroud of Glasgow in 1926. This company was renowned for its single-operator rangefinders and periscopes for military use, and in the early 1920s decided to develop reflector sights for the Services. They produced several designs in the following years, but it was not until the RAF expansion schemes of the late 1930s that the Air Staff issued contracts for series production of reflector sights for squadron aircraft. By 1939 two types were in use, the Barr & Stroud type GM2 (RAF Mk II pilot's sight) and a compact turret sight, the Barr & Stroud type GJ3 (RAF Mk III). The Mk II was fitted with a unique range finding device. The horizontal bar of the reticle was broken in the centre, the gap being adjustable by two knurled rings. A pointer on the top ring was set to range required in yards, the bottom ring's pointer being set to wingspan of the target aircraft. When the target was the same size as the gap, it was at the range indicated.

A crisis arose in 1938, when Barr & Stroud had to advise the Air Ministry that it could not produce the Mk II in sufficient quantity for the new Spitfires and Hurricanes, and to overcome the shortage a contract was signed with Goerz of Vienna for 700 sights made to Barr & Stroud drawings. In spite of the Anchluss pact with Germany, these sights were delivered, being produced in parallel with Revi sights for the Luftwaffe! Soon after the last delivery war was declared, and they were used in Fighter Command aircraft.

The Mk III turret sight was used in virtually every British turret until the advent of the gyro sight in 1944. It was a compact sight with a built-in rheostat for dimming, and a hood over the reflector glass to minimise searchlight dazzle. A dimming screen could be raised to reduce sun and cloud glare, and the circular orange reticle could be used for rangefinding and deflection for a

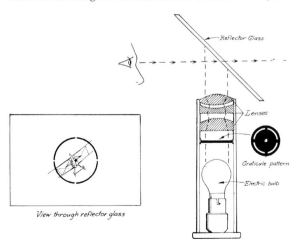

The principle of the reflector sight

Set required range on the upper dial

Set bottom dial to wingspan of target aircraft

The Barr & Stroud GM2 pilot's sight (RAF pilot's sight MkII). The original model had a circular reflector screen and sun screen. This model, the MkIIL, was fitted with a rectangular reflector which could be adjusted to suit the trajectory of rocket projectiles by means of the knob marked in degrees. The ranging procedure is shown in the diagram, with *(bottom)* the appearance of the target in the reticle.

*The Barr & Stroud GJ3 (RAF Mk III Series) turret sights. The Mk IIIA★ (left) was fitted to all RAF turrets until the advent of the gyro sight. The reflector screen was covered by an anti-dazzle hood; a smoked-glass screen could be raised at the rear, and the reticle brilliance was adjustable by the side knob. The MK III N (*right*) was used by Coastal Command and on daylight operations for quick alignment.*

target crossing at a relative speed of 50mph. The free-mounted Vickers gas operated guns used in side-hatch and cabin window positions were sighted mainly with 2in (50mm) ring-and-bead sights, larger rings being used by naval airmen. Under-defence turrets used optical periscopic sights, but gunners using these had great trouble acquiring an attacking fighter. As will be seen later, more-sophisticated sighting systems were developed later in the war.

Germany

After the First World War Germany was forbidden to produce military equipment but, as with air weapons, gunsights were developed in secret. The Carl Ziess company of Jena produced the Rexexvifier Revi series of reflector sights for the Luftwaffe, early models being used in aircraft of the Condor Legion in the Spanish Civil War. The main pilots' sights were the Revi 12D and 12F, the F with a suitably revised aiming reticle also being used for rocket sighting. After injuries to pilots in hard landings, the brightness control knob was moved from the front of the sight body to the right side, a thick rubber pad being fixed to the front. The Escania and Leitz companies were also engaged in sight production, and many specialised sights were made in addition to Revi models by these concerns. However, the main producer was Ziess.

This company also produced the Revi 16 series, which were similar to the British Mk III turret sights in size and operation. German reflector sights were fitted with standby blade sights in case of electrical failure.

In the first years of the war German bombers were defended mainly by free-mounted MG 15 and MG 18s on ball mountings fitted into cabin windows, and these were aimed by ring-and-bead sights. Rear defence positions were fitted with the 'VE' ring-and-bead system mounted on a sight bar which was compensated for deflection. Many cock-a-hoop fighter pilots closing in for the kill were lost to gunners using this sight. Designed primarily for tactical blitzkrieg operations, Luftwaffe bombers were fitted with forward-firing armament, these weapons being aimed by Revi 12D reflector sights. Some Dornier Do 217 bombers had four MG 81s in the extreme tail which were sighted and fired by the pilot using an RF2A periscopic sight mounted in the cabin roof.

Identifying a distant aircraft as friend or foe was often difficult, and Germany was alone in producing a reflector sight with a built-in telescope. There were two models, the Zielfernrohres ZFR3 and ZFR4A, with magnifications of 2.5X and 3.8X respectively. The upward-firing guns of nightfighters were aimed with Revi 16 sights aligned to 20° from vertical with the two MG FF cannon. Although other specialised sights were used, these were the main types used by the Luftwaffe.

America

When America entered the war, US aircraft were fitted with a wide variety of gunsights. The N3A reflector sight was used on the early turrets of B-24s and B-17s, but the main turret sight was the N6 and 6A. Sperry ball turrets used K4 computing sights which compensated for deflection and range. Another turret sight was the N8 series of retiflector sights in which the reticle was projected upwards to a mirror under the hood, which reflected it down on to the gunner's sight screen. US fighters also used a number of different reflector sights. Lockheed P-38s were fitted with the N3A (early) and L3 (late), and Republic P-47 Thunderbolts used the N3A, and an American-made version of the British Mk II without the ranging facility, designated the US Mk 8. The P-51 Mustang used the N3B sight initially, but later marks had the type N9 with a standby ring and bead. Many Mustang pilots also used the British Mk II pilot's sight. When the British gyro sight was adopted as standard it was fitted to most US fighters. The Sperry K9 computing sight gave the gunners in Martin turrets a point of impact allowing for deflection, using the rate-by-time system, measuring angular velocities of the target with respect to own aircraft motion. They were accurate if level flight was maintained, but any movement caused errors. The side-hatch guns of B-17s and B-24s were mostly sighted by B13 ring-and-bead sights, but these hand-operated guns were renowned for inaccurate shooting, and from November 1944 many Groups installed K13 computing sights which worked

The Revi C/12D was the standard Luftwaffe fixed gunsight. It was fitted with a built-in rheostat and standby ring-and-bead sight. There were various subtypes: one, the C/12F, had a radar input angled mirror behind the reflector screen. The RAF Mk II sight (opposite) is included in the background for scale.

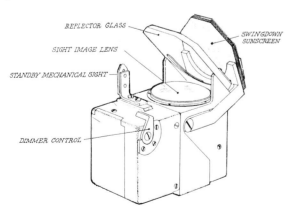

German turrets used the Revi 16B gunsight, very similar to the British Mk IIIA. The 16B was also used for some Luftwaffe fixed-weapon installations.

A Typical US compensating sight, the Sperry K13 was fitted to US 8th Air Force waist guns from November 1944. The gunner set airspeed and height and was presented with a point of aim allowing for bullet drop and the effect of his aircraft's forward movement on the trajectory of the bullets.

A Russian ASP gunsight fitted to a Polikarpov I-153 fighter in 1943. USSR aircraft sights were similar to the Revi series, and were usually equipped with ring-and-bead standby sights.

on the same principle as the K9. The British Mk III was also used by some groups in this position.

Russia

Fighter aircraft of the USSR used ASP series reflector sights, which were similar in some respects to the German Revi. They were fitted with blade standby sights, and the earliest known use was on Polikarpov I-15 fighters used in the Spanish Civil War. They were up-rated in 1940 and remained in use, with various modifications, throughout the war. Free-mounted bomber defence guns used large ring-and-bead sights. During 1944 late-version Petlyakov TB-7 bombers were armed with multigun turrets sighted by ASP reflector sights.

France

The French air arm was ill-equipped when war was declared. Political decisions had held back production of promising aircraft types, but the few that were available gave a good account of themselves. The only fighter available in any numbers was the Morane Saulnier MS.406, which was outclassed by German opponents. The reflector sight used by French interceptors was the Bailie Lamare, bomber aircraft being fitted with ring-and-bead sights.

Japan

The Imperial Japanese Air Force imported some German Revi fighter gunsights in 1938, and used some features from these in the Japanese Type 98 pilot's sight. This was adopted as standard, and incorporated a built-in dimming rheostat, sun screen and standby ring-and-bead unit. Bomber defence guns and some naval fighters used ring-and-bead sights of various dimensions.

All pilot's reflector sights were a hazard in a crash or heavy landing, being mounted in a position where the pilot's head was thrown forward. Most were fitted with rubber pads to lessen facial injury, but many pilots suffered from cuts and bruises known in some squadrons as 'sight face'.

The Gyro Sight

The invention of the gyro sight solved most of the problems of air gunnery; it was found to improve the average fighter pilot's accuracy by 50 per cent, and air gunners became magically accurate. Most of the major powers funded development contracts for a gunsight which would automatically compute the various deflection allowances needed for air-to-air gunnery. The first companies to produce such sights were Sperry and Fairchild in the USA. But although these gunsights certainly predicted deflection and were programmed for altitude, they were very bulky and were not always accurate when the aircraft was not flying straight and level. They were used quite effectively in US turrets, but were not suitable

The Mk II C gyro sight. Designed at Farnborough and produced by Ferranti from 1944, the gyro sight gave the pilot/gunner a point of aim allowing for range, bullet drop, and, most importantly, deflection. This sight transformed aerial gunnery to the point where, once the ring-of-diamonds reticle was on the target, the target would be hit. The principle was adopted by most of the world's air forces.

either in size or specification for fighter use. As will be seen later, Germany produced such a gunsight, but far too late for it to have any significant effect. It was the British who finally solved the problem with a relatively simple system based on the properties of the gyroscope. In 1938 an exercise was carried out by the RAF to assess the standard of gunnery of fighter squadrons equipped with Spitfires and Hurricanes, using camera guns. It was proved that deflection shooting was so bad that if the combats had been in earnest the enemy would have escaped almost unscathed. At a symposium at the Royal Aircraft Establishment (RAE) at Farnborough, attended by the Air Staff and leading scientists, it was decided to proceed with an urgent programme to produce a predictor gunsight based on a theory propounded by Wg Cdr L J Wackett and Capt (later Professor Sir) Melville Jones RFC in 1917. It was based on the fact that a gyroscope will resist any rotation of its axis. Such a sight would present the marksman with an aiming mark held back by the gyro. This principle is also used on rate-of-turn instruments, and the Ferranti company was asked to participate in the project, codenamed the Type 6 Mechanism. A team was formed at the RAE, and by October 1939 two types of experimental sights had been completed, one for fighters the other for use in turrets. Although both types predicted the correct lead angle, they were found to be unsuitable for squadron use. A

modified sight was then produced in which a revolving mirror was influenced by the gyro mechanism. This turned out to be an unqualified success, Ferranti setting up a factory in Edinburgh and beginning series production in November 1943.

Looking into his reflector screen, the marksman saw a ring of six diamonds. He adjusted the ring to fit the target, set the type of enemy aircraft on a dial, lined up the target, and opened fire. A delegation from the USAAF were so impressed with the new mechanism that it was ordered into production in America immediately. The British designations were the Mk IIC GGS (turret) and Mk IID (fighter), the US versions being Mk 18 (Navy), and Mk K14 (USAAF). Early scepticism vanished once pilots and gunners gained experience, and results bore witness to the system's effectiveness. The basic mechanism devised at Farnborough was to be used by most air forces for the following three decades.

In Germany the Eskania company produced the Eskania EZ42 Eagle gyro sight, in which two gyros controlled servo motors which moved a mirror to give the required lead angle. This project was considered to be top priority by the Luftwaffe, but it was not ready for squadron use until 1945, and very few saw service with fighter units.

Radar sighting

Once airborne radar had been developed for night-fighters, a team was set up in the UK under Dr P I Dee to develop a device with which gunners could locate and fire at an incoming fighter before seeing it. The design leader was Dr Alan Hodgkin and the project was codenamed 'Village Inn'. At this time (1943) German nightfighters were beginning to take a significant toll of RAF bombers, and tail defence turrets equipped with such a device would be much more effective. Given the official title of Airborne Gunlaying Turret (AGLT) the system consisted of a small rotating radar scanner mounted under the turret from which radio signals were transmitted and where the echoes were received from any aircraft approaching from the rear. Black boxes remote from the turret then processed the signals and transferred the resulting 'blip' to the gunner's gyro sight screen by way of a small cathode ray tube at the side of the sight, and a prism. To overcome the serious problem of friendly aircraft being detected and fired at, a system was devised in which infrared lamps would be installed in the nose of bomber aircraft which would project 'code of the day' signals. Infrared detectors mounted at the side of the gunner's sight would identify these transmissions. Testing was carried out at the Telecommunication Research establishment at Defford, and in 1944 No 101 Squadron became the first to have Lancaster turrets with AGLT installed. Three more units were equipped, and some success was reported, but trouble with the scanner linked with computers which calculated the deflection and angular differences of the barbettes and sight, was remarkably effective in preliminary trials. However, further development ceased when the war in Europe came to an end.

The General Electric Remote Control Turret system (RCT)

The Boeing B-29 was the ultimate bomber of the Second World War, and its defence system was also the most advanced to see service during this period. As mentioned in the turret section, this system consisted of low-drag turrets armed with 0.50 calibre Brownings which were remotely controlled by gunners from sighting stations, the tail turret being manually controlled. Each gunner had a fire controller incorporating a reflector-type sight. As he aligned the sight on to a target, a central fire control computer analysed the signals and sent electrical impulses to the turret concerned. These signals were amplified and fed into an Amplidyne generator, which energised the turret drive motors to the required aiming point directed by the gunner. If the target moved out of his line of sight, the gunner could pass the target on to another gunner. Looking into his screen, the gunner saw a circle of red dots, and adjusted these to fit the size of the target. He then tracked the target, keeping a centre dot on target. As in the gyro sight, he would already have set the target's wingspan on dial. Although this system was very effective, Japanese fighters accounted for quite a few B-29s during the attacks on the Japanese homeland, and as with all gunnery from bomber formations there was a high risk of hitting other aircraft in the group.

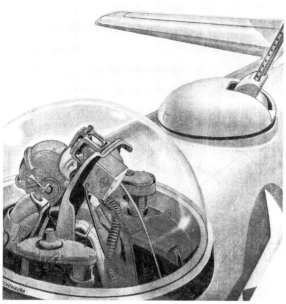

The top sighting station and upper turret of the Boeing B29 RCT defence system. Designed by the General Electric Company, this was the most advanced bomber defence system of the Second World War. Signals from the gunner's sights were processed in a computer which automatically aligned the turret guns on the target.

drive, and modification of the system, delayed further installations and the project lost its priority status. Meanwhile the war was drawing to a close, and further conversion of turrets ceased.

Remotely sighted turrets

In May the British Air Ministry placed an order for comprehensive remotely controlled turret systems for Bomber Command aircraft. The main contractors were Boulton Paul, British Thompson Houston and Vickers. Vickers-Armstrongs worked on a system in which cannon armed barbettes in the rear of engine nacelles were controlled by means of their Metadyne all-electric system. The gunner was to be seated in a tail sighting cabin, with an unimpeded field of view. Trials of the system revealed that distortions set up in the wing structures seriously affected gun alignment. An additional requirement for AGLT delayed the project further, and although it was showing great promise it was eventually cancelled with the end of hostilities. Boulton Paul and BTH were also nearing completion of the parallel project when the war ended. This comprised mid-upper and ventral turrets armed with twin Hispano cannon, sighted and controlled by a gunner in a remote tail position. Boulton Paul completed the two turrets, and the BTH control system, using an electric Amplidyne layout

The Development of Powered Gun Turrets

History

As higher-performance bombers came into service in the 1930s, it was soon realised that defensive gunners would have to be protected against the stronger slipstream forces and freezing temperatures encountered at higher altitudes. Some manufacturers provided elaborate windscreens, while others fitted transparent cupolas mounted on circular rings which could be manually rotated by the gunner, who elevated his gun by hand. Some of these enclosures, such as the Bristol 'parrot cage' turret on the Bristol Type 120 aircraft of 1932, were mounted on the revolving ring of a Scarff ring mounting. There were some ingenious variations, Armstrong Whitworth patenting a linkage which balanced the weight of the gunner with his gun, giving effortless elevation.

Although these manually operated turrets sheltered the gunner from the elements, slipstream forces on the barrel when firing to the beams made gun alignment difficult. The obvious solution was to provide some means of powered control, and although many countries set up design teams to investigate such systems, it was the British who did most of the pioneering work. The Bristol Aeroplane Company produced a hydraulically powered pillar mounting in 1934, and in the same year Barnes Wallis designed a slipstream-powered turret for the Vickers G.4/31 biplane and Westland designed a rear defence turret, operated by a 24V motor, for its tailless Pterodactyl V fighter. However, the most promising turrets were produced by two concerns who were to become world leaders in turret development, Boulton Paul and Frazer-Nash. When Boulton Paul announced that their new Overstrand bomber was fitted with a fully powered front turret, the world aviation press hailed it as a breakthrough in aircraft armament. In practice, however, the compressed air bottles of the pneumatic power system could not be maintained for a sufficient time to be practical.

In 1932 Archibald Frazer-Nash and his partner, Gratton Thompson, submitted a half-scale model of a hydraulically powered gun turret for evaluation at the Air Armament School at Eastchurch. It was seen to give accurate control, and the partners were given a contract for a turret to be fitted into the new Hawker Demon two-seat fighter. The development period of the Demon turret was rather protracted, but with the help of a team of talented engineers the system was improved, being used in the enclosed power turrets which armed Avro, Short and Vickers-Armstrongs bombers during the 1939–45

war. Frazer-Nash carried out developmental work at Tolworth in Surrey, and the Parnall Aircraft works at Yate, near Bristol, was purchased for turret production. Output from Yate during the Second World War amounted to over 60,000 turrets; 219 different designs are listed, of which 27 were fitted to RAF aircraft.

After the problems with the Overstrand turret, Boulton Paul, under the dynamic John North, signed an agreement with French designer J B A de Boyson to manufacture a turret control system for the company's new two-seat Defiant fighter. The concept of a two-seat fighter, dating back to the successful Bristol Fighter of the First World War, proved to be a costly failure, but the new four-gun turret was a success. The control system consisted of a self-contained hydraulic power unit inside the turret, the only requirement from the aircraft systems being electrical power and oxygen. After the success of the Defiant turret (the Type A), the company went on to produce other designs for Bomber Command aircraft using the same power unit. Handley Page used Boulton

One of the most effective mid-upper turrets was the Boulton Paul Type A. This company used an electro-hydraulic power unit contained in the turret, requiring no vulnerable oil piping in the fuselage. The type A was used on many RAF and Lend-Lease US aircraft.

Although it was the most advanced turret of its kind at the outbreak of war, the Armstrong Whitworth Whitley's FN4A tail turret of 1938 proved to be very cold and uncomfortable on long night operations over Germany. (See also page 192.)

207

Paul turrets in its Halifax, and many American bombers used by the RAF were fitted with Boulton Paul turrets on arrival in the UK. Many cannon-armed designs were submitted by Boulton Paul and Frazer-Nash for RAF use but not accepted, as were a series of designs for turrets armed with 0.50 calibre Browning guns. The reason these turrets were not accepted was an edict from the Ministry of Aircraft Production, which stated that the upheaval of production involved could not be justified in those critical early years of the war.

Another pioneer turret producer was the Bristol Aeroplane Company, which introduced a semi-retractable turret for its twin engined Blenheim bomber of 1937. The turret, designated the type B1, was fully powered by a hydraulic system based on the company's powered pillar gun mounting of 1934. The armament of a single Lewis gun was progressively increased after war was declared, but the Blenheim was by then obsolescent and very vulnerable to fighter attack. As will be seen later, Bristol produced the most effective British turret later in the war.

American turrets

After studying early reports of the war in Europe, the USAAF's planning staff soon realised that their existing and planned bomber aircraft were woefully under-armed. A rapid bomber rearmament programme was organised, and the major manufacturers were told to submit designs for power operated turrets armed with 0.50 calibre Browning guns. An urgent request was sent to the British Air Ministry to send current power turrets to Wright Field, where they could be used either as patterns for possible licensed production, or for assessment by US designers and engineers from prospective manufacturers. The British were only too pleased to oblige, as vital Lend-Lease material was greatly assisting the war effort. The general layout and controls of the British designs were used on some of the resulting American turrets, but in general, given the huge manufacturing and design capacity of the US industry, they were original and highly efficient, using the latest power and control technology. As the Browning M2 0.50 calibre gun was adopted as standard, all ammunition and associated equipment was common to the different turret types.

As in Britain, the power source varied. Bendix, Martin Emerson and Grumman used an electrical Amplidyne system which gave a very accurate response. This system was free from the oil leaks associated with hydraulics, and it was also simpler to fit with gunfire safety cut-off equipment. Sperry, Motor Products and Consolidated opted for hydraulic power units, in which an electrically driven pump provided pressurised oil independent of the aircraft hydraulic system. The guns were cocked by hydraulic rams on these turrets, while gunners in the electrically powered turrets were provid-

The Boulton Paul Type T turret with 0.50in-calibre guns was sent to America in 1941 to assist US designers formulate new designs. The similarity to Sperry and Bendix designs is notable.

ed with geared cable-operated chargers. Guns on all US turrets were fired by means of heavy-duty solenoids controlled from triggers in the turret control handles. The heavy ammunition belts were drawn into the guns by powered ammunition feed assisters, which fed the belts from replaceable ammunition cans.

American gunners were also protected by extensive armour plate and bulletproof glass panels, and provision was made for oxygen, intercom, and heated clothing outlets. All the new turret designs were extensively tested and modified where necessary. As in Britain, the manufacturers were expected to work closely with the aircraft makers to co-ordinate the various structural and power requirements.

Although they were late starters, the US manufacturers carried through the rearmament of their bomber aircraft in record time, and when the 8th Air Force

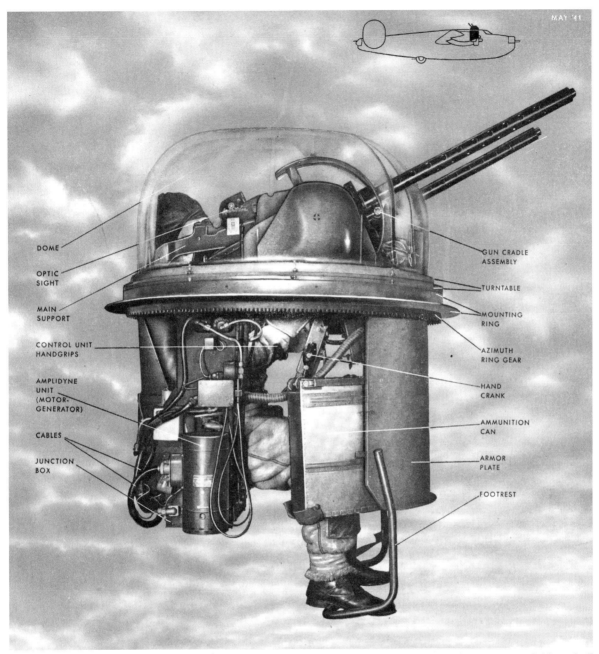

One of the first of a new generation of American turrets, the Martin 250 mid-upper turret. The armament of this and all American turrets was two 0.50in-calibre Browning guns. Bendix, Emerson and Martin turrets were powered by Amplidyne electrical systems; Consolidated and Bell used hydraulics. This illustration is taken from a 1941 manual.

launched its bomber offensive from East Anglia their aircraft were equipped with defensive armament second to none.

France
French bomber aircraft of the 1930s were mostly armed with rifle-calibre guns in manually operated turrets, or

had gunners in open cockpits. Although the SAMM and Hispano companies had developed powered turret designs, only one heavy bomber, the Farman F.223, was fitted with two SAMM type 109 turrets armed with single Hispano 404 20mm cannon at the outbreak of war. The Armée de l'Air had planned to use mostly twin-engined attack bombers, but political machinations had

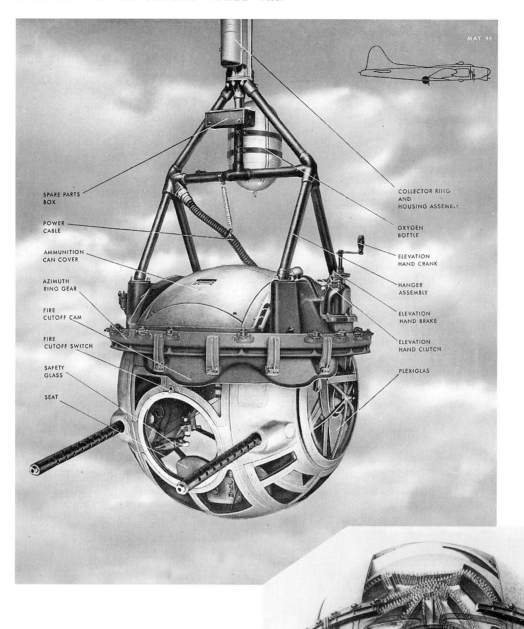

MAY '44

SPARE PARTS
BOX

POWER
CABLE

AMMUNITION
CAN COVER

AZIMUTH
RING GEAR

FIRE
CUTOFF CAM

FIRE
CUTOFF SWITCH

SAFETY
GLASS

SEAT

COLLECTOR RING
AND
HOUSING ASSEMBLY

OXYGEN
BOTTLE

ELEVATION
HAND CRANK

HANGER
ASSEMBLY

ELEVATION
HAND BRAKE

ELEVATION
HAND CLUTCH

PLEXIGLAS

The Sperry ball turret was the only really effective under-defence turret to see service in the Second World War. Top shows a page from a manual of May 1944. The guns were sighted by the K4 computing sight from the position shown in the lower *picture, which also shows the ammunition storage system.*

held back production, and American aircraft ordered to build up the strength of the bomber squadrons had not been delivered by 1939. The only modern bomber available in any numbers was the Lioré et Olivier 451, which was fitted with a retractable SAMM dorsal turret similar to that in the F.223. Unfortunately this did not prevent a very heavy loss rate against German fighters in 1940.

Italy

Italy's air force was at its peak in the mid-1930s, when it was the strongest in Europe, but by the time Italy declared war on the Allies most of its aircraft were obsolescent. However, the famous CRDA CANT Z.1007bis Alcione and Savoia-Marchetti SM.79 torpedo bombers were very effective. The Alcione was armed with a Breda SAFAT dorsal turret powered in rotation only and armed with a 12.7 gun by the same manufacturer. The defensive guns of the SM.79 were hand operated.

Germany

Germany entered the war with bombers designed primarily for tactical operations. Although plans were formulated in 1936 for a strategic bomber force, they were not carried through. The triumphant progress of the Condor Legion in Spain and the subsequent all-conquering blitzkrieg seemed to confirm the decision to concentrate on medium bombers, and the hand operated, rifle-calibre guns seemed quite adequate against the light opposition encountered. However, it soon became obvious that the defensive armament of these aircraft would have to be upgraded, and the failure to carry through the plan for heavy strategic bombers was a mistake. Heavy-calibre MG 131 machine-guns were installed in medium bombers, and powered turrets were designed, a priority programme being rushed through to reintroduce Project 1041 of 1937, the Heinkel He 177 heavy bomber. Like the Americans, the Luftwaffe had not seriously considered defensive turrets, but after its aircraft had been mauled by British fighters, development contracts were issued to Rheinmetall-Borsig, Mauser, and Focke-Wulf for powered turrets armed with 13mm MG 131 machine-guns and MG 151/20 20mm cannon. The first turret to see service was the hydraulically powered HDL. An upper turret armed with either an MG 151 15mm or MG 151/20 20mm cannon, it was very roomy and was used mainly on Blohm und Voss and Focke-Wulf Fw 200 aircraft. It was also used on other types including the Junkers Ju 188. The EDL was an electrically powered mid-upper turret armed with a single MG 131 13mm machine-gun and powered in rotation only, the gunner elevating his gun manually. It was first used on the Dornier Do 217, and later on the He 177 and Ju 188. The HL/131 V tail turret, armed with four MG 131 guns, was hydraulically powered from the main aircraft system, and the gunner was protected by

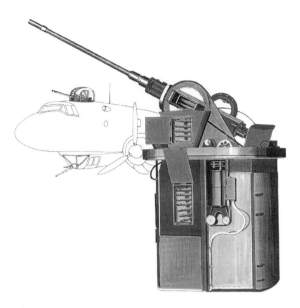

The German Hydraulische Drehringlafette HDL151 was hydraulically powered, and armed with single 15mm or 20mm cannon. It was very roomy, and made an ideal lookout position on the Fw 200 maritime strike aircraft.

thick armour plate. Although it was pressurised and provided with warm-air heating, it could only be operated by very small gunners, and weighed 453kg (997lb). This advanced turret was designed for the He 177 and large flying boats, but it is doubtful whether it was ever used operationally. These turrets were designed and produced by the Rheinmetall-Borsig company, one of the most prolific producers of air weapons in the Second World War.

The Focke-Wulf concern produced the 'Ferngerichtete Drehringlafette' (FDL) remotely controlled turret. This was electrically powered, and was operated by a gunner in an adjacent sighting station. It was used operationally on the He 177 and was specified for the Ju 290 series. This was a low-profile turret armed with two MG 131 guns, and its remote sighting and power system was reported to be quite successful. The gunner had two control handles; one was used for elevation, and the other rotated the sighting station and the turret. There were other German turret designs, such as the LB204 bow turret of the Blohm und Voss Bv 138, but they were mainly unsuccessful in service use.

USSR

The Soviet Air Force was known for its huge bomber aircraft in the 1930s, but when Germany invaded the USSR only one, the Petlyakov TB-7 series, could be compared with contemporary heavy bombers. The defensive armament of these four-engined bombers, which bombed Berlin in 1941, consisted of nose and tail turrets armed with single 20mm ShVAK cannon. In 1944 turrets fitted with four Beresin B20 guns of the same calibre were installed on the latest variant of this design. Another important Russian bomber was the Ilyushin Il-4, originally armed with 7.62mm ShKAS guns in manually operated turrets. In 1942 these enclosures were modified to take 12.7mm UBS guns.

Japan

One of the most rudimentary turrets to see service was fitted to the Japanese Mitsubishi Ki-21 Type 97 bomber, which had a large conical turret powered by bicycle pedals driving a chain-and-sprocket mechanism and mounting a heavy 12.7 machine-gun aligned in elevation by hand. However, this was not typical of Japanese equipment. Although the nation's guns and other equipment were often copies of western designs, Japanese aircraft armament was generally equal to the other major powers. The Mitsubishi G4M bomber was fitted with the first fully powered Japanese turret, which was hydraulically powered and armed with a Type 19 (Oerlikon) cannon. The Mitsubishi Ki-67 had an electrically powered dorsal turret armed with an Ho5 20mm cannon, two heavy-calibre machine-guns in the nose and tail, and similar guns mounted in side-hatch positions. This was the most efficient Japanese bomber, having a fighter-like performance. Apart from these aircraft, all other Japanese bombers were defended by manually aimed guns, protected by cupolas or mounted in open cockpits.

Later Turrets

In the later war years the RAF introduced rear defence turrets armed with 0.50 calibre Browning guns. (As mentioned earlier, heavy-calibre gun turrets were designed in 1939–40 but were not accepted for use.) These later designs gave the gunner more room and added armour protection; they were also fitted with gyro sights, and in some cases radar blind tracking. The main advantage, however, was the replacement of rifle-calibre guns with the hard-hitting Brownings. The smaller weapons were adequate until the advent of armoured fighters. The first of the second-generation turrets was the Boulton Paul type D, powered by an upgraded BP electro-hydraulic system. The type D was fitted to late-series Handley Page Halifaxes, the guns being mounted low and to either side of the gunner and fed by ammunition boxes back in the fuselage via ducts and feed assisters to the base of the turret. The Frazer-Nash FN82 was made to a similar specification with the exception of the power system, which was a beefed-up FN hydraulic unit powered from pumps fitted to one of the aircraft's engines. The third heavy-calibre turret was a private-venture design produced by Rose Bros of Gainsborough. Designed by K H Nickolls, the principle designer of the STAAG

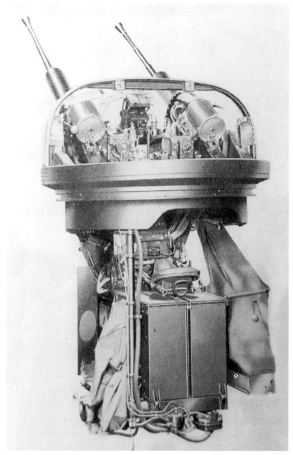

The Bristol B17, armed with twin Hispano MkV guns, was used on the Avro Lincoln. It was powered by the Bristol 'All Electric' System, giving very quick and accurate responses.

radar-controlled naval AA system, it was controlled by the gunner manipulating his gunsight, which was connected to hydraulic valves. As he aimed the sight at the target the guns automatically followed. It was armed with 0.50 calibre Brownings, and was so roomy that two gunners could be accommodated for training purposes. Mention must be made of the Vickers-Armstrongs heavy dorsal turret, in which a huge 40mm gun was mounted. The Wellington prototype was used for firing trials of this big mushroom-shaped turret, which was specified for a Wellington 'heavy fighter'. The concept of a heavy bomber destroyer was proved to be mistaken and the project was dropped. Much more successful was the Bristol type B17 dorsal turret, by far the most advanced turret produced in the UK. Powered by the Bristol 'all electric' system, it was similar to the US Martin and Emerson turrets, and was armed with two 20mm Hispano Mk V cannon, aimed with a gyro sight. It was not used operationally as its scheduled host, the Avro Lincoln, did not see wartime service. As mentioned in

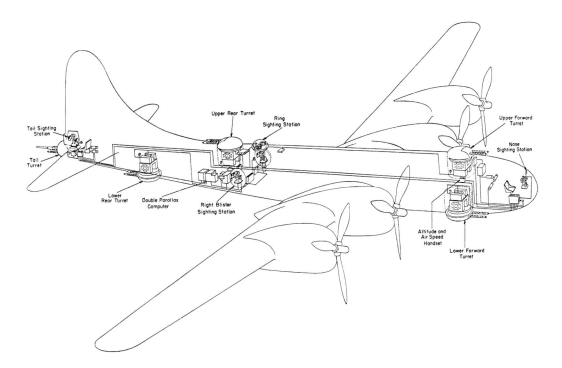

The General Electric Remote Control Turret system (RCT) was fitted to US B-29s. Each of the remotely controlled turrets were armed with twin 0.50in-calibre Browning guns.

the sighting section, Boulton Paul produced two remotely controlled turrets for the Lancaster remote control defence system, comprising dorsal and ventral turrets controlled from a tail sighting position. Fitted with twin Hispanos, these turrets were controlled by a computer linked with Amplidyne generators and a Ward Leonard system. The gunner could select either or both turrets, his gunsight being controlled by servo-motors linked to the computer. The scheme was initiated as early as 1942, but various problems prevented its introduction into squadron service.

The General Electric Remote Control Turret system

This system is described in the sighting section. It was remarkably similar to the British system described above, but with the advantage of American technical resources and production facilities it was completed in time for operations in the Far East. The turrets of the Boeing B-29s were compact units armed with twin 0.50s, each turret carrying 1,000 rounds of ammunition. The guns were re-cocked by a built-in pneumatic charger which operated automatically after firing ceased, the charger also released the firing pin of the gun when fire was opened. The tail turret was armed with twin Brownings and a 20mm Hispano in the first production B-29s, but the Hispano was not fitted in later versions of

the aircraft. This turret was not part of the RCT system, being operated and controlled by the gunner. The RCT turrets were all electrically powered, Selsyn generators in the turret housing powering the drive motors in response to signals from the sighting stations.

While B-29 gunners were seated in pressurised and heated sighting stations, RAF and 8th Air Force gunners had to endure hours in freezing conditions, flying through shell splinters and fighter attack. RAF gunners could not even see fighters climbing into position from below, hidden in the land mass. It has been suggested that the turrets should have been taken out to improve bomber performance, but many German fighters were lost to the fire of their rifle-calibre guns. The fact that they were there, especially in daylight operations, was a deterrent to attacking fighter pilots, who often broke away prematurely. It must be said, however, that the fighter always had the advantage of a relatively stable target, and could choose his approach. The gunner had to manipulate his turret in the few seconds of an attack and, before the advent of the gyro sight, make the necessary allowances to hit his fleeting attacker.

It could be argued that, had the production of Mosquito bombers been vastly increased, they could have replaced the Lancasters and Halifaxes and saved thousands of lives, but this would not have been possible in the time available.

Le Prieur rocket installation on a Sopwith Pup at Eastchurch in October 1916.

Aircraft Rocket Weapons

When a state of war exists, the combatants proceed to drop or project missiles and explosives at each other to cause death and destruction. The means of delivery have varied over the years, but have mainly been guns or aeroplanes. However, as the Chinese discovered in AD 1200, rockets can be used. The advantage of rockets is that they need no heavy launch or firing mechanism, a simple rail or tube being all that is required.

The first air-launched rockets were invented by a Frenchman, Lt Y P G LePrieur, who fitted electrically ignited firework-type rockets into tubes fixed to the interplane struts of biplanes in 1916. With experience, pilots were able to set fire to enemy observation balloons.

RS-82 rocket rails mounted under the wings of a Polikarpov I-153 on the Eastern Front in early 1942.

During the uneasy peace after the Armistice, Russia, Germany and Britain saw the possibilities of these missiles, and formed design teams to develop rocket types and launchers which could be used in any future hostilities.

USSR

In 1929 a team under B S Petrpavlovskii at the Leningrad Gas Dynamic Laboratory produced a spin-stabilised rocket missile with an explosive warhead which could be launched from rails for ground use, or from aeroplanes. Research facilities were increased and three types of rocket missiles were developed in the 1930s which were to play a major role in the war against Germany. These were designated RS-75, RS-82 and RS-132 (the numbers indicating the diameter of the warhead). These weapons were used mainly on ground-attack operations, but were also fired against enemy aircraft. Some Il-2 units specialised in close-support operations using RS-82 rockets. Launching tubes were produced for the three rocket types, and could could be quickly fitted to the underside of fighter and bomber aircraft. The advantage of the rockets was that, as opposed to large-calibre anti-tank guns, once the rounds were fired there was little loss of performance of the aircraft. The big RS-132 proved to be a potent anti-tank weapon. With a warhead of 23.1kg (50.9lb) it could immobilise Tiger tanks. The smaller RS-82 was also extensively used, production amounting to 2½ million. Soviet

A Messerschmitt Bf 110 of ZG26 with twin launchers for 210mm Wgr 21 air-to-air rockets. One hit usually proved fatal, but they were inaccurate and the launch tubes affected the aircraft's performance.

rockets used powder propellent and explosive, with impact fuses and small stabilising fins. They were sighted by specially graduated reflector sights.

Germany

German scientists carried out extensive work on big liquid fuelled rockets in the 1930s, and some development also took place with multiple projectors for tactical ground use. The famous Nebelwerfer proved to be remarkably accurate, the screaming 190mm projectiles doing nothing for the morale of enemy troops. When the Allied bomber fleets began their massive bombing

campaign against Germany, Nebelwerfer projectiles were upgraded to 210mm and adapted for air use, fitted with timed fuses. These were first introduced in 1941, being launched from tubes slung beneath the wings of fighters, which fired them from the rear of the formations, out of range of the defending gunners. The launch tubes adversely affected the performance of these aircraft, and the appearance of long-range US fighter escorts put an end to these operations.

Rheinmetall-Borsig produced the Föhn series of aircraft rocket missiles which were issued in three calibres: 65mm, 73mm and 100mm (FZ 65, FZ 73 and Fz 100).

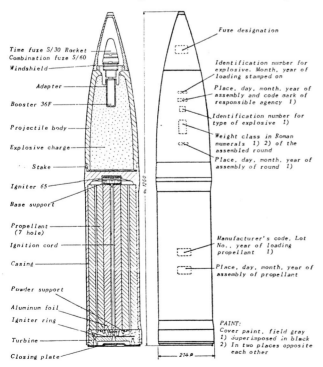

Section of the 210cm aircraft rocket, developed from the ground-service 190cm Nebelwerfer assault projectile.

A near-miss by an R4M air-launched rocket on a B-17 of 482nd BG. It appears that the photograph, taken from the side hatch of another B-17, captures the moment of bomb release.

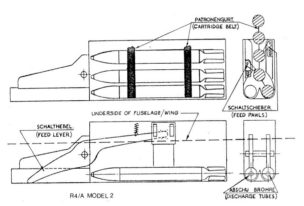

The Rheinmetall R4M rocket discharge unit Model 2. The missiles were stored in the aircraft's fuselage or wings and fed into the twin discharge tubes via a belt system and feed pawls. When fired, each round activated the feed pawl for the next, and capacity was limited only by available storage space.

They were similar in construction to the earlier 21cm missile, with the warhead and powder propellent in an elongated shell-shaped body. Multiple-tube launchers were designed from which the missiles were ripple fired. However, compared with heavy-calibre guns, the range and accuracy left much to be desired, and there are very few reports of operational use other than by some units on the Eastern Front.

Towards the end of hostilities a rocket similar to the British 3in missile, the Panzer Blitz, was used, but the most promising was the R4M rocket system. These 55mm (2.17in) air-to-air missiles were designed by Rheinmetall. The Mauser company produced two types of automatic low-drag firing systems, one a nine-round automatic launcher, and the other a pod with twin tubes fed by belted rounds from a magazine in the fuselage or wing. The missiles were 810mm (32in) long and had a launch velocity of 500m/sec (1,640ft/sec). After launch, stabilising fins extended outwards, giving a relatively stable trajectory. The Mauser launchers fired the rounds at a cyclic rate of 300 rounds per minute, but they were never used operationally, the only R4Ms fired in anger being launched from Messerschmitt Me 262A-1a jet fighters fitted with simple wooden racks under each wing, from which twelve rounds were ripple-fired. The Americans saw the advantages of the R4M system and used it as a basis for their postwar Mighty Mouse air-to-air missile system.

The weakness of the R4M rocket was its short range. A much less demanding missile for pilots attacking US bomber formations was the longer-range Rheinmetall R100BS, which had an effective range of 1.2 miles (1.8km), well outside the reach of US machine-guns. It delivered a hefty 40kg (88lb) warhead consisting of a high-capacity bursting charge and 460 small incendiary bullets into the centre of a bomber formation where it was detonated by a time fuse linked with a radar ranging device. This rocket was about to be issued when the war ended.

German Guided Missiles

It had long been realised that the ideal weapon to counter bombers and hit ground targets was a missile which could be guided to the target from a position beyond the reach of intercepting fighters. The first guided air-to-air missile was the Kramer X4. This consisted of a 20kg (44lb) warhead fitted to a small airframe with cruciform wings, which was propelled by a BMW liquid-fuel rocket motor. Tail mounted control surfaces were operated by 0.2mm wires trailing from the launch aircraft. It had a range of 1.8 miles (2.9km) and was about to become operational when hostilities ceased.

Probably the most significant guided air weapon system introduced during the Second World War was the Henschel Hs 293 series of guided air-to-ground missiles. The first model, produced in 1940, was a SC 500kg bomb fitted with wings and aerofoils controlled by radio signals during its glide to the target. The later Hs 293A had a purpose-made airframe with an underslung Walter liquid-fuelled rocket and a built-in 500kg warhead. The rocket motor propelled it forward to a position where the operator could observe its path, and he then controlled its glide by radio link on to the target. The Hs 293A was first used by II./KG 100 aircraft in the Middle East in the summer of 1943, when the sloop HMS *Egret* was sunk by a missile launched from a Dornier Do 217. This was the first of many successful attacks; another was to disable the battleship *Warspite*. The design leader of the project was Dr Herbert Wagner, who went on to design a TV-guided version. The success of these missiles and the V1 and V2 projects was acknowledged by the major powers, and the design teams were highly sought after by America and the USSR after the war.

Great Britain

In 1934 His Majesty's Master of Ordnance, Sir Hugh Elles, called a meeting at the War Office to 'Review our present knowledge of the rocket as an offensive weapon'. Two years later a working party had prepared a report recommending four possible uses. These were anti-aircraft defence, long-range offence, recoilless armament for aircraft and assisted take-off for aircraft. Considering later developments, this proved to be quite a prophetic summary of future use of the rocket. Dr (later Sir Alwyn) Crowe was appointed to lead the rocket weapon development team at the newly constructed Projectile Development Establishment (PDE) at Aberporth on the coast of Cardiganshire. It was decided that cordite would be used as a propellent, extruded into blocks, or 'grains' which were packed into a steel tube, the warhead being screwed on to the forward end, and small stabilising fins attached to the rear end of the tube. The rocket motors were ignited electronically. When the first test rounds were fired they proved to be reasonably accurate, having a burning time of 1.5sec and reaching a speed of 1,200mph.

After the Munich crises of 1938 Crowe was told to concentrate on an anti-aircraft missile to protect cities and production centres from the expected hostile bomber formations. Multiple projectors were designed, and a trials team was sent to Jamaica to test the timing mechanisms in the clear air. It was found that the accuracy of the spoiler operated timers did not compare with AA shells, but the project went ahead. Batteries of the projectors were set up round several cities. Known as Z projectors, they could ripple-fire a volley of 128 29lb (13kg) shells, each with a lethal radius of 70ft (21m). On

7 April 1941 a Heinkel was brought down in flames, but the spent rocket tubes posed a considerable threat to property on their return to earth. By December the Home Guard were manning ninety-one batteries.

In October 1941 an urgent call was sent to Crowe to drop all other work and adapt the AA rocket as an air launched anti-tank projectile. The war in North Africa had shown that Army tank and anti-tank guns were useless against German armour. Once the project started it moved swiftly. Four launching rails were mounted under each wing of Hurricane fighters, and armour piercing warheads were fitted. The first air launch took place on 25 October 1941, and during the following trials it was found that 4in (100mm) of armour could be pierced; the thickness of German Mk IV tank armour. In three months rocket-firing Hurricanes were in action against the Afrika Korps, but Tiger tanks had appeared which were immune to the new weapon.

In the meantime anti-ship rockets with HE warheads had been developed at Aberporth, but it was found that they entered the ship's plating and did little damage when they exploded inside. Production facilities had been built up for round-the-clock production, but the whole project was now in doubt. The solution came when a howitzer unit reported it had stopped Tiger tanks, hits and near misses having blown off their turrets and tracks. The howitzer shells relied on HE blast, and it was soon realised that the HE anti-ship rockets were almost identical in operation. Rockets with 60lb (27kg) HE warheads were quickly dispatched to Africa, and were found to be just as effective as the howitzer. By a coincidence it was found that if armour piercing projectiles struck the water short of the target when fired against ships and submarines, they curved upwards and entered the target below the waterline. Against submarines they entered the hull and flailed around inside, causing major damage.

The trials Hurricane, showing the first British airborne rocket installation. The first air launch took place over Chichester harbour on 25 October 1941.

217

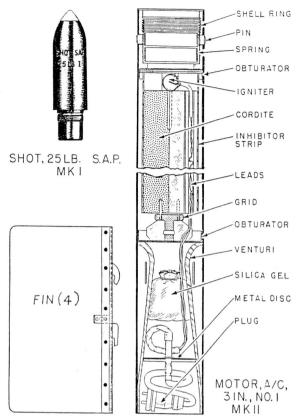

SHOT, 25 LB. S.A.P.
MK I

FIN (4)

SHELL RING
PIN
SPRING
OBTURATOR
IGNITER
CORDITE
INHIBITOR STRIP
LEADS
GRID
OBTURATOR
VENTURI
SILICA GEL
METAL DISC
PLUG

MOTOR, A/C,
3 IN., NO. 1
MK II

A section of the British 3in rocket, with the shell (SAP warhead shown here) screwed into the shell ring, and the fins slotted into the base.

As they were launched from short underwing projector rails, these weapons were naturally not as accurate as guns, but a salvo of eight 60lb warheads hitting a small area at supersonic speed had a devastating effect. When used against ships or submarines, two rounds were usually fired to keep AA gunners' heads down, followed by the remaining six fired from closer range, a hit from any one of which often proved decisive.

There followed a programme in which many types of Coastal Command aircraft were fitted with projector rails for maritime operations. The first successful submarine strike occurred on 14 May 1942 when a Fairey Swordfish from the escort carrier HMS *Archer* sank U-572 in the Atlantic. British rockets were longer and more unwieldy to store and fit than the equivalent German round, owing to the nature of the cordite propellent, but a salvo from an aircraft's eight projectiles had the destructive power of a naval cruiser's broadside. After many fatal accidents the electrical firing circuits were wired through a multiple socket at the rear of the projector, the plug connecting it to the aircraft firing system not being inserted until shortly before take-off. As the trajectory of the rockets was different to that of the guns of the aircraft, a Mk II reflector sight was designed in which the reflector glass could be tilted to the correct angle for rocket firing. This was done by means of a calibrated knurled knob, which could return the reflector to gun alignment after the rocket had been fired. The pilot could select pairs or full salvo from a firing panel, which also contained a master switch and firing button.

Probably the most important installation was on the

A Hawker Typhoon with double 60lb SAP rockets, the maximum number carried on tactical aircraft of the RAF.

The 'Stooge', produced by Fairey Aviation to counter Japanese suicide attacks on the fleet in the Far East. The four primary rockets were jettisoned after launch; four 5in then cut in for the final radio controlled phase.

Hawker Typhoons of the 2nd Tactical Air Force. This aircraft had developed from a less-than-ideal fighter into one of the most formidable close-support aircraft of the war. Operating from forward airstrips in Normandy, Typhoons fired millions of cannon shells and rockets in support of ground troops. They were particularly renowned for accurate rocket attacks, and when a strong force of Panzers was set to escape from an encircling movement at Falaise, Typhoons with bombs and rockets destroyed most of the Tiger tanks and vehicles in a classic attack, 175 tanks being immobilised by blast in a single day. The ultimate development of the 3in rocket was the double 60lb missile, giving the Typhoon an even greater punch. Once perfected, it was found that double RPs could be carried at speeds of up to 450mph (720km/h) provided no violent manoeuvres took place.

In 1943 research staff at Aberporth were directed to begin work on a large air-launched anti-ship missile with some means of automatic release. Codenamed 'Uncle Tom', the project was given priority status. A specification was issued for the radar ranging system, and a special sight was designed by Barr & Stroud which co-ordinated the approach line with the radar imput. A warhead of 350lb (158kg) of torpex was to be propelled by three 3in rocket motors stabilised by six rectangular fins. A double impact fuse was to be armed by the heat of the rocket motors, and a 3sec self-destruct device was designed to give a near miss a chance of damaging the target. The missile was ready for trials in mid-1944, but the release system was not ready until 1945 and the project was terminated after further trials.

After the end of the war in Europe, the British fleet was threatened by Japanese suicide bombers in the Pacific Theatre. The Fairey company produced a missile to counter these attacks. Called the Stooge, it was produced in record time, and was a radio controlled vehicle of conventional aircraft configuration with a 500lb (226kg) warhead. Four 3in rockets powered the launch phase; these were then jettisoned and four 5in rockets powered the final radio controlled phase to the target. The Stooge did not see action because, by the time the missile was ready for production, any kamikaze pilots still living had taken up safer occupations.

America

Although experiments were carried out by individual groups in the USA during the 1930s, no serious attempt was made to develop rocket weapons. After reports of the British work in this field, three visits were made to Aberporth and propellent manufacturers in England. As a result of these visits a complete pilot cordite extrusion plant was shipped to America for appraisal by nominated contractors. By late 1942 cordite rocket motors were being produced for army use, and in 1943 the USAAF adopted the army infantry rocket for aircraft use. This 4.5in (114mm) calibre weapon was 34in (86mm) long and weighed 384lb (17.4kg). It was ignited electrically, and was air-launched from twin or triple 10ft (3m)-long

A Douglas Skyraider with the US 'Tiny Tim' 11.75in (298mm) assault rocket, intended for use against Japanese bunkers. The smaller projectiles are 3.5in (89mm) anti-ship Folding Fin Aircraft Rockets.

underwing tubes, usually from fighters. A heavier development of this weapon, specially developed for air use, had a 50lb (22kg) warhead, but was not accepted.

The US Navy and Marine Corps soon saw the potential of the air-launched rocket as an anti-ship weapon, and adopted the 3.5in (89mm) Folding Fin Aircraft Rocket (FFAR) for use against Japanese vessels. Following British experience, the warhead was a solid armour-piercing type for maximum penetration. In 1944 the warhead was replaced by a 5in HE head containing 50lb (22.7kg) of torpex. US rocket development was now making up for lost time, and the Navy next adopted the 5in High Velocity Aircraft Rocket (HVAR). Known as the 'Holy Moses', it weighed 134lb (60kg). It was used by all US services for anti-ship and close-support operations.

As American forces started to recapture Japanese-held islands, pill boxes and bunkers were skilfully used by the defenders, and a request was made for a suitable rocket to pierce these emplacements. A massive rocket, 10ft 3in (3,124mm) long with an 11.75in (298mm)-diameter warhead was quickly produced and tested. Known as the 'Tiny Tim', it packed the punch of a 12in Navy shell. Primarily designed for the final assault on the Japanese mainland, it was put to use in the later stages of the island war by Marine PBJ Mitchells. They carried two Tiny Tims, and a few were used in action before the end. In March 1944 the McDonnell Aircraft Company fitted its Gargoyle glide bomb with an acid/analine rocket motor. Known as the KSD/1, this missile was tested, but the proposed guidance system was not perfected until after the end of hostilities.

Rocket-powered missiles, guided or otherwise, are now the main weapons used by the world's air forces, but compared with the spectacular advance of rocket technology during the war years, development has naturally been more leisurely.

Bibliography

Chinn, George M, *The Machine Gun* (US Bureau of Ordnance, 1951).

Clarke, R Wallace, *British Aircraft Armament Vol 1, RAF Gun Turrets from 1914 to the Present Day* (Patrick Stephens, Sparkford, 1993).

Clarke, R Wallace, *British Aircraft Armament Vol 2, RAF Guns and Gunsights from 1914 to the Present Day* (Patrick Stephens, Sparkford, 1994).

Gunston, Bill, *Encyclopaedia of Aircraft Armament* (Salamander Books, London, 1987).

Hoffschmidt, E J, *German Aircraft Guns and Cannons* (W E Inc., Greenwich, Conn.)

Wallace, G F, *The Guns of the Royal Air Force 1939–45* (William Kimber, London, 1972).

US Air Forces Information File Manual No 20 (United States Air Force).

9

The Well-equipped Warplane

L F E Coombs

Introduction

A well-equipped warplane in the 1940s, as with present aircraft, was one intended to complete all the specified operational requirements. Some aircraft were well equipped, others less so.

Failures on the part of designers and manufacturers to provide aircraft capable of matching the operational requirements laid down by the Air Staff were often the result of frequent changes of mind. In turn, apparently perverse rewriting of specifications arose because of sudden changes in air war tactics. It was extremely difficult for an air staff or any other organisation concerned with air defence or offence to foresee future tactical and strategic changes.

The initial European war of 1939 eventually spread to all parts of the globe. But in the 1930s air strategies and consequent design decisions were very much aimed at Northern Europe, the Mediterranean and the Middle East. British, French, German and Italian aircraft were equipped for those potential theatres of operation rather than for more remote parts. In America aircraft systems and equipment reflected long-range operations related to the Pacific.

The extent to which the aircraft that went to war in 1939 were well-equipped depended very much on the length of their gestation. It has been suggested that the Second World War started one or perhaps two years too soon. In 1930 the curve of technological achievement had only started to raise a little up from that of 1918. By 1935 it had risen much further but for a number of reasons manufacturers and air forces were not always able to take advantage of all the possible developments in systems and equipment. At this point it is important to differentiate clearly between experimental ideas and production equipment.

Few, if any, types of aircraft at the end of the 1930s could claim to be well-equipped. It might be thought that to be 'well-equipped' meant numerous guns of large calibre or the ability to carry a great weight of bombs. There were aircraft that met those criteria but there were far more that were not well-equipped because they were not, within our present meaning, 'weapons systems'. The modern weapons system concept was virtually unknown in the 1930s when the aircraft of the 1940s were on the drawing board. Systems and equipment were usually separate 'stand-alone' items. Aircraft manufacturers figuratively shopped around for equipment from outside companies; a com-

pass here, an undercarriage leg there, a generator there, and so on.

This reliance on outside suppliers was common to the majority of aircraft companies in the principal 'aviation' countries, i.e France, Italy, Germany, Britain, Japan and the USA. The state control of everything from a rivet to a complete aircraft in Russia was an entirely different approach. However, the similarities in the types and number of systems and accessories among the principal countries were more important than the differences. Therefore, for example there was, to some extent, a common inventory of equipment among American, German and British fighters.

A single-seat fighter of the late 1930s' generation such as a Bf 109 can be compared with a Hawk 75A or a Spitfire. Setting aside the obvious structural and configuration similarities, each might have had the following equipment in common:

- Cockpit instruments including reflector gun sight.
- Multiple gun installations, including arming circuits and ammunition magazines.
- Radio, both aircraft-to-aircraft and air-to-ground.
- Electrical generator and circuits for operating other equipment.
- Hydraulic system.
- Undercarriage operating system.

Comparable inventories for two bombers of the same generation, the Vickers Wellington and the He 111, included, in addition to a pilot's cockpit and equipment, the following:

- Space for a navigator and his specialised equipment.
- A radio-operator's position and equipment.
- Bomb-aiming equipment and associated arming and release circuits. Some of these were duplicated so that they could be operated either by the bomb-aimer or by the pilot.
- Protective armour plating for critical areas and crew positions. This was not provided for the earlier marks of Wellington. In the He 111 the racks of vertically stowed bombs provided some protection for the pilot and navigator.
- Movable guns for defence and in the Wellington power-operated, enclosed gun turrets.

The last item will be discussed further because it reflected an approach by the RAF air staff to defence that, at the time, differed significantly from that of other air forces. In turn it affected the systems and equipment of American and British aircraft.

A Luftwaffe Bf 109G, showing the ready access to the engine provided by the large hinged cowling panels. Note that some of the ground crew are pushing on the wing by placing their hands behind the automatic leading-edge slats.

Throughout the history of warplane development designers have had to chose between simplicity and complexity when attempting to comply with the specification issued by an air staff. In the mid-1930s an

Airmen hand-crank the Rolls-Royce Merlin engine of an RAF Hurricane Mk I in early 1940. The pilot does not appear to be equipped with flying clothing or parachute, or to be concentrating on the start-up procedure. This is more than likely one of the numerous 'photo opportunity' posed shots which characterised press activities of the time.

extreme example of the choice between simplicity and complexity was the undercarriage. The systems designer would favour a fixed undercarriage because it relieved him of much concern over arranging a suitable power system. On the other hand the aerodynamicist obviously wanted the wheels out of the way once the machine was airborne. The design problem was exacerbated in the mid-1930s because of the general lack of reliable power-operated systems, be they hydraulic, pneumatic or electric.

Furthermore, would a hand-operated hydraulic pump suffice for raising the undercarriage or should there be an engine-driven pump and a far more complex 'plumbing' system? The former would keep down weight, simplify maintenance in the field and reduce cost. The latter, however, would take up more room in the cockpit and burden the pilot with physical exertion and the dedication of one hand to the task when he needed both hands on the controls during take-off.

An important factor related to aircraft systems and equipment in general is the degree to which a particular aircraft type was intended to be serviced and maintained away from hangars, hard standings and second- and third-echelon support services. Both the Luftwaffe and the RAF exercised their aircraft support services away from established bases. A simple example of self-sufficiency or dependency in design is the method of

A Lockheed P-38 Lightning with turbosupercharged Allison V-12 engines. The turbosupercharger units can be seen on the upper surface of each tail boom. This method of maintaining power at high altitude was a feature of many American aircraft, but was not used to any extent by other nations.

starting the engines. Should an aircraft have sufficient internal battery power to start an engine, or would complete reliance be placed upon mobile accumulator trolleys, with hand cranking as the last resort?

During the Second World War 'new' systems came into operational use that had been experimented with during the previous ten years. Turbosuperchargers, airborne radar and UHF radio, to name a few, were around in the 1930s but they were not fully developed. Many ideas were delayed either because of production difficulties or because other systems had not been brought up to the same technical standard. An example is the airborne radar that was installed in Blenheim nightfighters of the RAF at the end of 1939. Its effectiveness as a contributor to the well-equipped nightfighter had to wait until a big powerful twin-engine aircraft, having a sufficient speed margin over its victim, became operational. Another example is that of oxygen systems for high-altitude flight. Had the B-17 been operational in 1935 it may not have been fully effective because of an inadequate oxygen system. It may also have suffered losses from fighter attacks because power-operated gun mountings were not available. Again, using the B-17 as an example, navigational equipment and techniques at the time were not developed sufficiently to ensure operational success.

Another factor that delayed the introduction of new technologies for systems was uncertain specification writing; particularly by an air staff. In the second half of the 1930s none of the world's air forces had experienced a full-scale, all-out, air war since 1918; albeit the Luftwaffe had gained some experience from the Spanish Civil War, the Japanese from its invasion of China and the RAF from 'tribal' wars and policing mandated territories in the Middle East. However, neither the French nor the air services of the USA, or for that matter the Italians, had other than limited experience of large-scale, intensive air warfare.

Only after many months of intensive air operations, with frequent changes of tactics to counter enemy initiatives and the need to keep aircraft airworthy when operating from other than well-equipped bases, could an aircraft's systems be proved and refined. Germany capitalised on involvement in Spain by building an air force dedicated to close support of the army. In doing so it made sure that its aircraft could be maintained in the field whatever the environmental conditions. In contrast the RAF suffered from a lack of certainty over the type of air war in which it might be involved. By 1938 the RAF had evolved essentially into three major commands: defensive fighter, offensive bomber, and maritime. Each of these commands operated aircraft types

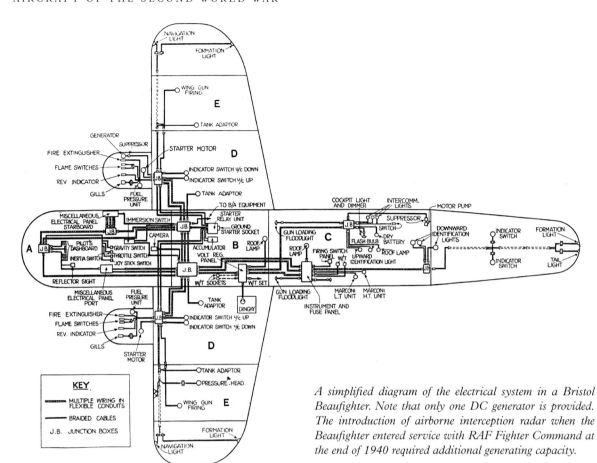

KEY

— MULTIPLE WIRING IN FLEXIBLE CONDUITS
— BRAIDED CABLES
J.B. JUNCTION BOXES

A simplified diagram of the electrical system in a Bristol Beaufighter. Note that only one DC generator is provided. The introduction of airborne interception radar when the Beaufighter entered service with RAF Fighter Command at the end of 1940 required additional generating capacity.

requiring specialised systems and equipment. After the first year of the Second World War fighters were converted to the bombing role and bombers undertook maritime patrols. These conversions required corresponding changes and additions to their systems and equipment. The Luftwaffe had to undergo a similar conversion. To some extent the changes were even greater than those of the RAF because it had to metamorphose from a mostly tactical force to being a strategic weapon and, in the second half of the war, a defence force against heavy and sustained day and night bombing.

The development of aircraft systems in general during the second half of the 1930s owed much to military and civil developments in the USA. High-altitude flight and turbosuperchargers, along with long-range bomber development, required considerable research and development of systems and equipment. American all-metal monocoque construction was well advanced by the time the other aviation nations started to go 'all-metal'. By 1939 and the start of the Second World War the majority of American, German and Japanese first-line aircraft were of all-metal construction. In contrast the RAF's order-of-battle in that year included the mainly fabric-covered Wellington and Hurricane.

Electrical power systems and actuators

In the 1930s those charged with developing technology and equipment in anticipation that war was fairly certain to engulf Europe at the end of the 1930s sometimes failed to foresee the demands of war. A notable example is the growth of electronic equipment. Radio systems for communication and navigation, and radar for detection and weapon systems and for navigation required a significant advance in electrical generating capacity. At the outbreak of war a typical RAF twin-engine aircraft had limited electrical power available. There were usually two 40 or 60 amp/hr 12V accumulators in series and an engine-driven generator for the 28V (nominally 24 V) system. Among the warring air forces, the aircraft of the Luftwaffe generally had electrical systems which were far better than those in the aircraft of other countries. However, in the second half of the war there were considerable improvements in the electrical systems fitted to American and British aircraft. This was one consequence of the increase in electronic systems, such as radar.

Generators in the 1930s were small in output compared with those at the end of the war. By the middle of the conflict electrical systems were coming into use with inverters for providing AC power that could be

224

In the absence of sufficient internal electric power, trolley-accumulators were a feature of many air forces in the late 1930s and 1940s. This is a 'short-nose' Blenheim Mk I of 1938. The trolley-accumulator is seen toward the tail of the aircraft.

transformed and rectified to supply the 1,000V or more needed by electronic systems such as radar.

In some respects the three major players in the European air war exhibited marked individualistic 'national' characteristics for electrical systems: they included alternators, direct current generators, twin-wire systems or earthed (grounded) systems using the airframe for DC current return. American aircraft usually had single-wire electrical circuits, with earth (ground) return through the aircraft's structure. Although this

A Messerschmitt Bf 110G. Once the radar scientists were allowed to specify external antennae for Luftwaffe aircraft, they lost no time in coming up with some drag-inducing arrays. These are the antennae for the Lichtenstein nightfighter radar.

simplified and reduced the weight of wiring it caused interference with electronic equipment, such as remotely located repeater compass systems. There were these and other differences among German, American and British aircraft. The larger types of American aircraft might have a petrol (gasoline)-driven engine auxiliary power unit to supply electric, hydraulic and compressed power. Small two-stoke petrol engines were used in some German aircraft for engine starting.

Throughout the Second World War the choice between electric or hydraulic operation of equipment was often a difficult one to make. Each had its advantages and disadvantages. However, when pressurised crew compartments became necessary, designers preferred electrical systems because it was less difficult to pass wiring through a pressure bulkhead than pipes. Electrical operation was also preferred to having to arrange satisfactory pressure resistant seals for moving mechanical components such as rods and shafts.

Radio and radio navigation

Radio communication sets usually covered VHF, HF and MF bands with direction finding (DF) loops, a common feature of all medium and large aircraft types irrespective of nationality. An example of a well-equipped aircraft, in the radio sense, was the Junkers Ju 88G nightfighter. In addition to its SN-2 Lichtenstein AI radar and standard Luftwaffe radio equipment there was the FuBl 2 blind approach receiver, the FuG 120a Bernadine which provided a visual record on a chart of bearings from radio beacons and the PeGe 6 radio compass. An important item of radio equipment found in Allied aircraft

The side-by-side cockpit of an RAF nightfighter. This is a Mosquito II equipped with 200MHz air interception (AI) radar. The cathode ray tube with viewing hood is on the right, with the controls below. Positioning the radar operator alongside the pilot and not, as in the Bristol Blenheim and Beaufighter, at a remote location in the fuselage, significantly improved the 'teamwork' vital for a successful interception.

operating from aircraft carriers were the radio homing beacons without which crews would have been lost, because while they were away their carrier might have moved far from its original position.

Radar

By the middle of the Second World War airborne radar equipment of one type or another was to be found in German, Japanese, American and British aircraft. The records do not indicate that production standard airborne radar was fitted to Russian aircraft.

The principle of reflected radio waves had been demonstrated by scientists in the nineteenth century. In the first decade of the twentieth century Marconi of Italy and Hülsmeyer of Germany designed some of the earliest systems for the detection of objects over useful distances and not just confined within a laboratory.

In the 1930s scientists in many countries developed a number of object-detecting techniques based on the

well-known phenomena that radio waves are reflected in ways analogous to the reflection of waves in water, air and light.

By force of circumstances, Britain and Germany in particular advanced radar from its experimental status to a practicable method of detecting aircraft and ships at distances greater than that of human vision and hearing. In Britain in the first half of the 1930s it was realised that, in the event of war, standing patrols of fighters for intercepting attacking bombers would require far too many fighters and would have little chance of success. This spurred the development of a radar 'barrier' around the shores of Britain. As the defensive Chain Home was developed and stations erected it was also realised that although the system could be used to direct fighters to within visual range of attacking formations in daylight, at night they would more than likely escape interception. Therefore airborne radar equipment had to be developed. Airborne radar was ready by September 1939, although the sets were still in the experimental stage and

The distinctive dipole radar antennae on the nose and wingtips of RAF Mosquito II nightfighter DD737, c.1942. The eventual development of centimetric radar replaced the external arrays with a streamlined radome in the nose of the Mosquito and produced an even more successful destroyer of night intruders.

it was not until the autumn of 1940 that the first successful night interception was made by an RAF nightfighter.

In 1939 and 1940 RAF Blenheim fighter crews had to use radar equipment that was bulky, unreliable and needed a specially trained operator to interpret the cathode ray tube (CRT) display. By the end of the Second World War radar interception sets were more compact and reliable, with displays that could be read directly by the pilot and were able to 'see' with far greater range and discrimination.

The importance of these early developments is their impact on the overall equipment of aircraft in general. As the war progressed airborne radar was rapidly improved in terms of compactness, lower weight, target discrimination and range.

In 1939 the most important development target was high transmitted power at centimetric as opposed to metric wavelengths. Sir Henry Tizard, the British scientist charged with the co-ordination and development of means to detect aircraft, stated that: 'The side that develops the radar with the greater transmitter power will win the war'. High power in a compact unit with operating frequencies higher than 500 MHz (60cm) was needed for nightfighter equipment. The race was won for Britain by scientists at Birmingham University (Randall and Boot) who successfully developed the resonant cavity magnetron capable of producing high power at centimetric wavelengths. This breakthrough led to the sharp or 'narrow' beam radar which had many advantages compared with the 1.5m 'floodlight' type radars being used by RAF Fighter Command in 1939 and 1940. One major advantage was the ability to discriminate between ground features, thereby enabling the display of an accurate representation of a target area.

In parallel with the development of a defence radar chain of stations around Britain, the German air force and navy encouraged the development of surveillance radar sets to guard the sea frontiers and of vessel-to-vessel search and gunnery radar. The Luftwaffe in particular demanded radar equipment that was accurate enough to lay searchlights directly onto a target. Further advances in radar technology in Germany provided the Luftwaffe with improved gunlaying sets. These projects tended to divert thinking away from airborne interception radars (AIs), but when it was realised that the RAF was increasing its night bombing sorties, airborne nightfighter sets were introduced.

Airborne radar for German aircraft evolved from pre-war radio altimeters. In 1940, nearly a year after the British, the Luftwaffe started to experiment seriously with radar for both interception and air-to-surface vessel (ASV). Development was delayed because the Luftwaffe insisted on buried antennae on its aircraft. Not until 1941 were externally mounted antennae permitted. By contrast, in Britain the drag of the Yagi type radar antennae was accepted as a necessary evil until centimetric radar, with its single antennae in a radome (dielectric radar dome), came into full production.

The first German nightfighter radar was the 'Lichtenstein', operationally tested in a Do 215. This used parts from the ground-based defence 'Freya'

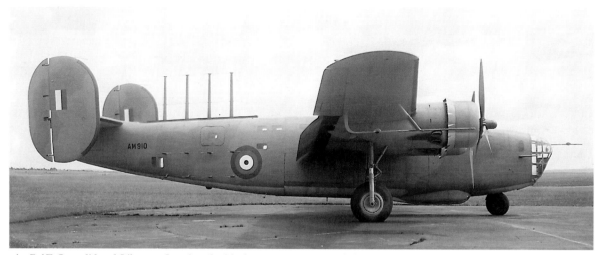

An RAF Consolidated Liberator I equipped with the antennae arrays of air-to-surface vessel (ASV) radar.

system. Like the early British equipment it was heavy and bulky. Research into air-to-surface vessel (ASV) radar went on in parallel with nightfighter radar development. By July 1941 an ASV radar ('Atlas') was installed in a Fw 200. To indicate the difference in priorities between the two opposing air forces the RAF had by then been supplied with over 6,000 ASV (200MHz) sets, which proved invaluable to Coastal Command despite a high percentage of failures and frequent damage to the projecting Yagi type antennae.

Although radar had been experimented with in the USA before 1941 and experimental sets had been evaluated in both ships and aircraft, it was not until British scientists visited the USA in October 1940 and disclosed the progress made with centimetric, cavity magnetron-

based systems that the technology took off at the Radiation Laboratory of the Massachusetts Institute of Technology. From 1941 onward the Allies were rarely short of ideas and production facilities for all types of radar. On the other side, although German scientists exhibited corresponding innovation and in the last two years of war were beginning to match system-by-system the radars arrayed against the Luftwaffe's aircraft and guns, they were handicapped by three non-scientific aspects of their work. Firstly, Hitler decided that all research, including radar, be restricted to projects which could be put into operation without delay. Secondly, the Luftwaffe high command failed to appreciate the potential of radar. Thirdly, German scientists, although aware of the need for centimetric equipment, did not realise the

An RAF Wellington VIII equipped with 200MHz ASV, with the characteristic antennae arrays along the top and sides of the fuselage and under the wing.

extent to which British and American cavity magnetron technology and production capacity had advanced.

A notable difference between German radar developed in the Second World War and that of American and British achievements was the H₂S radar developed by scientists at the Telecommunications Research Establishment (TRE) in the UK. It had been observed by those developing the early 1.5m AI equipment for the RAF that prominent, that is in the electronic sense, ground features could be distinguished on the CRT display.

However, the RAF had to wait until the centimetric technique had been perfected before H₂S with its plan-position indicator (PPI) display could be developed. So it was not until 30 January 1943 that H₂S was used operationally. This was fourteen months after the first 10cm radar tests in a Blenheim had proved the principle of a terrain-mapping radar. At the time American electronics experts were sceptical of H₂S and accused the British of wasting resources. It took much persuasion by the TRE to convince the USAAF of the advantages of

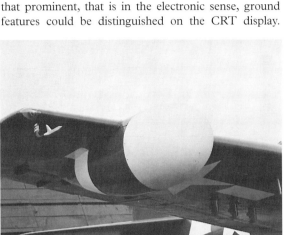

The US Navy's single-seat Grumman F6F-3N Hellcat was equipped with a pilot-operated 3cm interception radar Type APS-6. The set was installed in the fuselage behind the cockpit and connected to the antennae in a radome on the starboard wing, seen here, by a long waveguide.

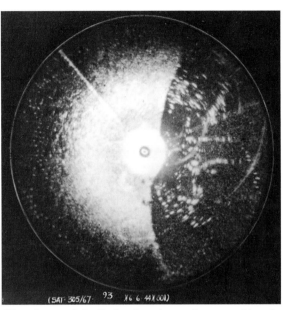

The picture of the D-day invasion craft approaching the beaches on the plan position indicator (PPI) of an H₂S radar. The line indicates the aircraft's heading.

The radome under this Austin-built Lancaster bomber housed the antennae for the H₂S system which provided the navigator with a 'radar' map of the terrain and targets.

the radar. Even the 10 cm H_2S was unable to provide enough discrimination for large inland targets, such as Berlin, and a rapid modification programme had to be started to change to a 3cm system (10GHz).

Not until an RAF Stirling bomber crashed in the Netherlands did German scientists appreciate the effectiveness of a resonant cavity magnetron in producing high powers at centimetric wavelengths. They were then able to develop a corresponding system. This was FuG 224 'Berlin'; one of a family of radars with PPI displays.

In parallel with ASV, AI and H_2S British scientists developed a number of radar-based navigation and blind-bombing systems. These were Gee and Oboe. In 1940 the Luftwaffe had made effective use of a radio beam to ensure the accurate location of important targets in Britain. This encouraged scientists of the Telecommunications Research Establishment, later the Royal Radar Establishment, to devise a radio beam guidance system for the RAF. At the time the standard of navigation, target finding and bomb-aiming was so low that most of the RAF's night bomber sorties were ineffectual. However, by 1942 RAF Bomber Command aircraft were equipped with the electronic navigation system Gee. Operating in the 22-85 MHz band, this was one of the first radio-lattice systems. There was also Oboe, in which radar stations tracked an aircraft and issued guidance instructions for steering it across a target and releasing marker flares. Oboe led to G-H, a system which enabled aircraft to interrogate the ground stations and obtain very accurate positional information.

One of the keys to radar success in the UK was the development of electronic displays, using CRTs, whose information was easy to interpret. For example Gee only required the operator in an aircraft to align two 'blips' (echoes) on two sets of time bases and refer the readings to a Gee chart from which an instantaneous and very accurate indication of position was obtained. By the end of 1942 the RAF's previously poor navigation, target-finding and bomb-aiming performance was being replaced by advanced electronic aids that provided hitherto undreamed-of accuracy and discrimination. Without Oboe and G-H for the target-making aircraft and Gee and H_2S for the main bomber force, it would have been impracticable and unsafe to dispatch hundreds of aircraft, but with these new electronic aids they streamed across a target in a short period, thereby saturating the defences. Independently of weather and visibility, targets were attacked with great certainty because the bombers of 1942 onward were truly 'well-equipped'.

As the war progressed first one side then the other gained the technical advantage. The electronic war was fought hard throughout the six years from 1939. The results can be seen in the wide range of electronic equipment fitted to all types of aircraft: radar for air

In the last year of the war, gunlaying radar for the rear turrets of RAF bombers was developed. This is one of the 'Village Inn' experimental radar installations on the rear turret of a Halifax bomber.

interception (AI), air-to-surface vessel (ASV), plan-position (PPI) and tail-defence. A significant radar development, in addition to more compact installations, was the growth of radar sets for direct use by the pilot. A notable example is the APS-6 pilot-operated interception radar installed in Grumman F6F Hellcats of the US Navy.

In addition to radar for navigation, target finding and attacking, each air force developed a range of electronic warfare devices intended to eliminate and confuse the enemy's radar. They also had to develop equipment which would modify the reflected radar signals from an aircraft so as to indicate that it was friendly, this being termed 'Identification Friend or Foe' (IFF).

Overall the approach to radar development was governed to a large extent by the strategic and tactical position of each air force in relation to its opponent. The British were forced to develop a defensive radar in a hurry in the mid-1930s with the result that airborne radar had to be given lower priority. One consequence therefore was the sparsity of aircraft electronic systems. In the beginning the Luftwaffe had no need for airborne radar. Its targets were within reach and easily identifiable in daylight. For night bombing there was a satisfactory radio beam system which was difficult to interfere with. Radar development was concentrated on long-range surveillance and flak control. Britain, and later the USA, eventually had to develop radar systems to cover a wide range of tasks. In doing so they literally swamped the efforts of German scientists as well as the Luftwaffe's ability both to attack and defend.

Fuel and oil systems

A typical arrangement of a fuel system consisted of a number of separate fuel tanks. The main tanks would be in the wings, arranged as inner and outer sets with electrically powered booster pumps to ensure that there was no interruption of the supply to the engines during critical stages of flight such as take-off. This applied usually to multi-engine aircraft. Single-engine aircraft such as fighters often carried the major part of their fuel in fuselage mounted tanks; either between the engine and the cockpit or under the cockpit: and in some aircraft, such as the Fw 190, both under and behind the pilot. In multi-engine aircraft the auxiliary or overload tanks might be in the fuselage, the bomb compartment or as jettisonable tanks under the wings.

Although the concept of the auxiliary tank carried under an aircraft had emerged before the Second World War the principal protagonists were slow to consider the use of such tanks. However, by the third year of war both the Germans and the British had adopted non-defensive fighter tactics. Aggressive fighter sweeps deep into enemy airspace required significant extensions to the operating range of fighters. Hence the adoption of the external jettisonable tanks. In the USA designers learnt from the experience of the war in Europe so that before war was joined with Japan, American aircraft had fuel systems designed from the start to permit both high-altitude and extreme-range operations.

The extended range and higher operating altitudes of both bombers and fighters required that the fuel tanks be pressurised to avoid fuel being lost through vaporisation at high altitudes. The use of auxiliary tanks often required the installation of immersed electrically driven pumps to ensure that the fuel was fed positively into the main fuel system collector tanks, from which the supply was taken to individual engines. Electrically operated booster pumps were used for take-off and landing phases of flight in order to ensure an uninterrupted supply of fuel to the engines, even though there were usually engine-driven pumps. They were also switched on at high altitudes. Incidentally, when fuel tanks had vents to atmosphere, to prevent a vacuum above the fuel, the vents had to be carefully designed and positioned, otherwise when the tanks were full the low aerodynamic pressure over the upper surface of the wing sometimes caused the fuel to siphon out through the vents. An important detail was the fuel strainers and drain cocks used to separate water from the fuel in the tanks. The water-drain cock for each tank system was a vital item. The denser water would separate out from the fuel and be at the lowest level so that it could be drained off before flight. Also of importance was the distinctive dye added to the fuel to indicate its octane rating; this generally prevented the wrong fuel being used for the type of engine fitted.

Although German, British, Japanese and American aircraft fuel systems were basically similar, there were some significant differences in detail. For example British engines were usually primed by means of a KiGas plunger-type hand pump. This was mounted in the cockpit of single-engine aircraft. In multi-engine aircraft the KiGas pumps were mounted on the underside of each engine nacelle. The technicalities of engine starting are often ignored by writers of fictional accounts of flying. They imply that wartime RAF pilots merely had to press the equivalent of a car's starter switch to get an instant start. American aircraft in contrast were usually equipped with electrically operated priming pumps that

Thirty-four-gallon jettisonable long-range fuel tanks under the wing of a Mosquito Mk 34. Like the Mosquito's fuselage, these tanks were made of moulded plywood.

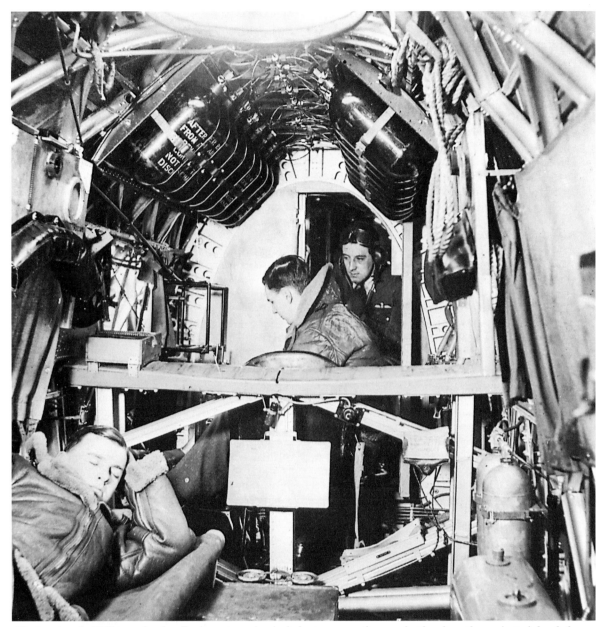

The interior of a Wellington bomber. Equipment on view includes: two rows of oxygen bottles above the navigator's head, the armoured bulkhead forward, the main wingspar with the fuel system management controls and system diagram, the crew rest bunk, and at the top the astrodome and the stowed padded supports for the navigator when using a sextant. Unusually the crew are not wearing lifejackets (Mae Wests), parachute harness or helmets.

could be selected by the pilot in the cockpit. German fuel priming methods were similar to American.

In general it can be recorded that as the war progressed fuel systems became more adaptable to operating requirements, and in consequence more complicated. The comparatively simple fuel systems of the 1930s were replaced by far more sophisticated equipment.

Fuel selector cocks could be manually or electrically operated. In the Consolidated B-24 of the USAAF the fuel system's principal selector cocks were located in the bomb compartment. The contents indicators were of the boiler gauge-glass direct reading type in which the fuel level was observed in vertical glass tubes. Of course there were shut-off cocks for isolating the gauge glasses when not in use. In British multi-engine aircraft the various fuel cocks were often positioned in a group located remotely from the cockpit. In the Vickers Wellington, with its early 1930s technology, fuel pipes and cocks were mounted on the aft face of the main spar where it passed through the fuselage. A mimic diagram of the fuel system was engraved on metal plates to remind the crew member sent aft which cock to open and which to close in order to effect a change in the fuel system. Another archaic feature of the Wellington's fuel system was the pull-wires which led from the fuselage out to the 60gal (276-litre) reserve fuel tank in each engine nacelle. It is a matter of debate whether the complexity of an electrical circuit and electrical actuator was better than the simplicity of the mechanical system in a multi-crew aircraft.

So far this survey of fuel systems has concentrated on petrol (gasoline)-powered engines. However, we must not forget that the German aircraft industry developed a number of diesel engines for aircraft use. Examples were the engines of the Blohm und Voss Bv 222 and the Bv 138. The latter had three Jumo 205-D diesel engines. There was a 760-litre (167gal) fuel tank for each engine along with reserve tanks. All the tank and cross-feed selector cocks were located in the flight engineer's station. There was also a hand pump for transferring fuel from the reserve to the individual engine tanks. Indicative of the avoidance of too much complexity, in the shape of remotely controlled valves and powered pumps, was the requirement when starting engines for both the pilot and the flight engineer to use hand pumps to raise sufficient pressure in the fuel lines.

There was no international standard of design and materials used to prevent damage to fuel tanks from flak fragments and the bullets of fighters and to provide a self-sealing action. A number of different techniques were applied: these included layers of vulcanised sponge rubber covering; another method was to apply layers of rubber and fabric so as to build up a thick self-sealing layer, similar to the composition of a car tyre. Some aircraft types, notably Russian, had a protection system which filled the void above the fuel in the tanks with an inert gas such as nitrogen. Others systems used the engine exhaust as a source of inert gas.

The subtle variations among the many different aircraft fuel systems mean that only a generalised description can be given.

Hydraulic systems

In the absence or impracticability of manual operation of equipment the aircraft designer could choose among electric, compressed air, pre-compressed spring, explosive, dynamic air pressure or hydraulic operation. The last, along with electric operation, was the most usual method of powering equipment, such as retractable undercarriages, lift and drag surfaces, such as flaps and dive brakes, as well as gun mountings.

A typical hydraulic system of the mid-war period emphasised the growth in the number of separate systems and in consequence the growth in aircraft complexity. Each engine drove a hydraulic pump. Hydraulic lines led from the pumps to selector valves in the cockpit where there was usually an emergency hand-pump. In some aircraft the selector valves were positioned close to the relevant system to be operated. These valves would be

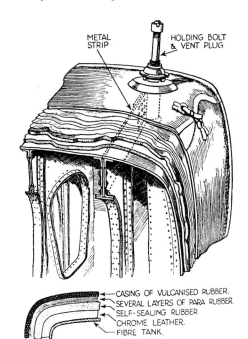

Construction details of the self-sealing fuel tanks used in the Junkers Ju 88. In the event of a bullet or flak fragment piercing the tank, leaking fuel caused the synthetic rubber to become plastic and seal the hole.

A Mustang II with experimental early-type long-range underwing fuel tanks, July 1943.

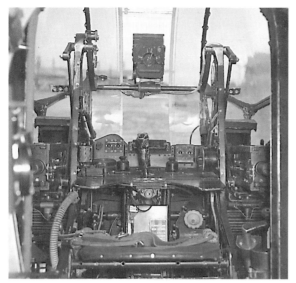

The interior of a Boulton Paul twin 12.7mm tail gun turret, equipped with Mk II gyro gunsight, in a Halifax bomber. The turret used an electrically powered hydraulic system for rotation and for gun elevation.

controlled remotely from the cockpit through electrical circuits and electric actuators. Hydraulic actuators would be used for a wide range of functions. This included: gun cocking (arming), undercarriage operation, bomb bay door opening and closing, wing flap and dive brakes, engine cowling flaps and, in naval aircraft, wing folding and arrester hook operation. Some British aircraft, notably the Whirlwind and the Stirling, had Exactor hydraulic engine controls which obviated the need for long and complex rod or cable controls between the cockpit and the engines.

The biggest load on a hydraulic system was often that of the flaps and undercarriage: in particular the large area of flap that had to be forced down into the airflow could impose a severe demand on the system. This was emphasised by the considerable number of hand-pump actions needed to lower the flaps or undercarriage in the event of pump failure.

The basic hydraulic system of pump or pumps, selector valves and actuating cylinders was comparatively simple. However, in practice there had to be many additional items to ensure satisfactory operation. These included check valves to prevent reverse flow, relief valves to protect against excessive pressure, flow equalisers, filters and pressure indicators. Also, in some aircraft there was a certain amount of redundancy designed into the system to enable it to withstand battle damage.

In some aircraft, hydraulic operation of equipment would be combined with electric power. An electric motor operated a hydraulic pump connected to a hydraulic jack. This arrangement was sometimes adopted

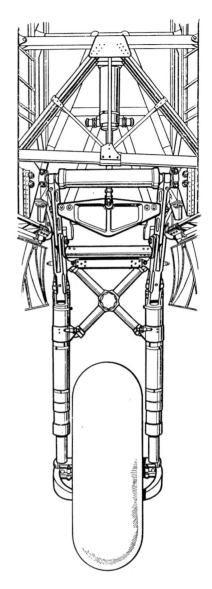

A typical undercarriage assembly, with hydraulic actuator jack (top centre) for retraction and extension. This is the starboard undercarriage leg of a Wellington, c.1940.

to eliminate the weight and vulnerability of long hydraulic pipe runs. It also avoided bringing hydraulic pipes and valves into the cockpit or the weight of mechanical linkages between the cockpit and a remotely located valve. An example was to be found in the Russian Pe-2 light bomber. An electrically powered hydraulic pump was provided in some aircraft for both emergency use and to enable hydraulic actuators of equipment to be operated prior to starting the engines. An example is the system in the Consolidated B-24. In the absence of an external starter accumulator or electrical power generator and with depleted aircraft batteries, the B-24 could be 'brought to life' by hand starting a small petrol (gasoline), lawnmower-size engine which provided electrical power. In turn the hydraulic system could then be used.

An unusual application of hydraulic power could be found in some Russian aircraft, in which a hydraulic engine-driven pump supplied remote power to a hydraulic vane-motor which in turn drove a fuel pump.

Vacuum systems

In American and British aircraft some instruments and camera equipment were operated by vacuum from engine-mounted pumps. Still visible on the exterior of British aircraft in the early years of the Second World War were the 1930s-vintage venturi tubes which provided vacuum power for the instruments. Three instruments in particular were operated by vacuum: artificial horizon, directional gyro and turn and bank (slip).

Pneumatic systems

A representative pneumatic system is that of the de Havilland Mosquito. Its components and functions were also applicable to other aircraft types. An engine-driven compressor charged air bottles from which supply pipes were fed to the radiator flap jacks, to the gun trigger units and to the wheel brake cylinders.

Undercarriages, alighting and other aircraft/terrain interfacing equipment

The use of tricycle undercarriages in the Second World War was confined largely to American aircraft. Although there were isolated examples of 'propeller' aircraft with tricycle gear outside the USA before 1940, it was not until the advent of jet propulsion that British and German designers considered the nosewheel arrangement to be essential. The choice of a nosewheel layout was often dictated by aerodynamic considerations. Incidentally, it is a misnomer to refer to a nosewheel undercarriage as 'tricycle' because the tailwheel, 'tail dragger', arrangement is also a tricycle. By the start of the Second World War the nosewheel type undercarriage was being referred to as a 'tricycle' to distinguish it from the then-conventional three-unit undercarriage, the tailwheel type.

In the USA the nosewheel undercarriage, often steerable, was being specified before 1939 and eventually it was considered essential for the future generation of medium and large bombers. Examples are the B-24, B-25, B-26, and B-29. It was also applied to the twin-engine P-38 and the P-61. The Consolidated B-24 reflects the change in 'undercarriage' thinking since the advent of the Boeing B-17 Flying Fortress in 1935. US Navy aircraft in general and single-engine fighters of the USAAF, with the exception of the P-39 Airacobra and P-63 Kingcobra, had a tailwheel.

To achieve a soft 'footprint', Arado provided its Ar 232 Tausendfüssler with a multiplicity of wheels. Altogether there were 25 wheels, including the conventional tricycle nosewheel retractable landing gear.

The German air force's range of aircraft types included only a few with a nosewheel undercarriage: notably the Me 262, Do 335, the Arado 232 and 234 and the He 162 and 219. The Arado 232 Tausendfüssler (Millipede) had altogether 25 wheels. Three were in the tricycle nosewheel retractable landing gear. The others, in eleven pairs along the underside of the fuselage, enabled the aircraft to be taxied over soft or uneven ground once the main wheels were partly retracted. The Arado 232's multi-wheeled undercarriage anticipated those of modern military transport aircraft such as the C-130.

A version of the Bf 109, the G-2/R1, was equipped with a 'tricycle' undercarriage in which an extra, jettisonable oleo leg was fitted, long enough to keep the fuselage level. This was devised so that a 1,120lb(500kg) bomb could be carried under the fuselage. However, none of the principal types of German propeller-driven bombers had a nosewheel undercarriage. The Do 335 fighter was twin-engined, with one propeller pushing and one pulling; it had to have a nosewheel

An experimental version of the Messerschmitt Bf 109 equipped with an auxiliary undercarriage wheel to provide ground clearance for exceptionally large items carried under the centre section, such as this 500kg bomb. After take-off the auxiliary wheel and leg were jettisoned and descended by parachute.

A Spitfire Vc with the 'tropical'-type air intake designed to keep dust and sand particles out of the engine. This was a less elegant solution than that adopted for the DB 600 series engine of the Bf 109 and the Italian Re 2000. The long-range, droppable, slipper-type tank holding 170gal and an extra 29gal tank in the rear of the fuselage increased the total fuel available for ferrying a Spitfire V to 284gal.

undercarriage in order to keep the fuselage level when on the ground because of the tail-mounted pusher propeller.

British designers were constrained by a combination of tradition and the pressures of war to stick to the tailwheel layout. Only when the RAF began to acquire American aircraft such as the Boston, Marauder, Liberator and B-25 Mitchell did the merits of the nosewheel undercarriage become so apparent that the Air Ministry encouraged its use. At the same time it has to be noted that many of the aircraft designs submitted by individual companies competing for Air Ministry contracts would have had nosewheel undercarriages. Some companies, however, such as Handley Page and Avro in the UK, tended to specify a conventional tailwheel arrangement.

As far as the mechanism and 'plumbing' were concerned the nosewheel undercarriage presented no serious design and construction problems. However, there were sometimes difficulties with avoiding nosewheel 'shimmy' (a rapid oscillation from side to side). An essential accessory was an anti-shimmy hydraulic damper. It also required a strengthened forward section of the fuselage and room in which to house the nosewheel and leg when retracted.

The nosewheel undercarriage introduced a different landing technique compared with tailwheel aircraft, which were often set down on all three 'points'. This technique could not always be used safely with a nosewheel, although by the mid point of the war 'tail draggers' were usually landed in what was termed a 'wheeler', with the tailwheel held off until the main wheels had made contact with the ground. Those pilots who used this method found the transition to landing a nosewheel aircraft fairly easy.

Extreme environments

With the exception of Russia, the principal air forces of the late 1930s and early 1940s paid only slight attention to the needs of operating aircraft in extreme conditions of temperature, humidity, dust and mud. However, even the Russian air force found itself in difficulty in heavy snow and extremely low temperatures during the Russo-Finnish war in the winter of 1939–40, and an RAF Blenheim squadron sent to help Finland was unable to cope with the winter conditions. The Luftwaffe was faced with the problem of excessive engine wear from dust ingestion when operating from unprepared runways in Spain prior to 1939. The RAF, which exercised military control over the north western parts of the Indian sub-continent and Mesopotamia, had long experience of clogged radiator cores and engine lives reduced by ingested sand. However, in general, it was not until air forces were forced by circumstances in the war to continue air operations in extreme environments and not wait for more favourable conditions, that extraordinary steps had to be taken to mitigate adverse effects.

Additional filters, designed to reduce sand and dust ingestion, were added to engine air intakes. The fine nose lines of Spitfires and Hurricanes were spoilt by the bulky filters fitted for use in North Africa and other 'dusty' areas. In contrast the DB 601 engine in the Bf 109 and the Italian Macchi C.202 had a comparatively compact filter alongside the engine on the left of the cowling.

A North American B-25 of the USAAF in Alaska. The engines are pre-heated by a small petrol engine unit which feeds hot air through trunking to the engine nacelles.

Starting engines in extremely low temperatures required the provision of mobile hot-air supply units. These fed hot air through flexible trunking connected to the covers placed over the engine. In the absence of heating systems the mechanics had to run the engines at

The leading edge of the wing of this Boeing B-17 is formed by inflatable rubber de-icing 'boots' that were cycled by compressed air to prevent a build-up of ice.

intervals to prevent them being damaged and to ensure that they could be started without delay. Another remedy for difficult starting in extreme cold was the dilution of an engine's lubrication system with fuel. Setting contained fires in the induction system was a regular practice on the Eastern Front.

Between the extremes of the Arctic and the desert environments were the tropical monsoon conditions that turned airfields into lakes. Aircraft and engines often had to be serviced in the open and with no special equipment to alleviate the problems of the mechanics. This applied particularly to the RAF and the Japanese air forces operating in South East Asia and to the USAAF, USN and USMC in the Pacific campaigns. De Havilland Mosquitoes used in that part of the world were lost because the adhesive used to join the composite wood structure failed under effects of high humidity and temperature. This is an example of where there was no specialised equipment available either to detect, other than by visual means, or remedy structural failure.

Ice prevention and removal

Operational demands meant that pilots had to take their aircraft through air conditions in which ice would form on wings and empennage; it might even form on the propeller blades. Various methods were in use to prevent (anti-ice) or disperse (de-ice) ice such as: fluid pumped

This Focke-Wulf Fw 190A-3 cockpit emphasises the comparatively high standard of finish and details applied to German cockpits, including the provision of a floor. To the left of the Revi reflector gunsight are the round counters for the armament; a detail not provided in British fighters.

out through holes along the leading edge or through a porous wick; rubber 'boots' fixed along leading edges that could be inflated and deflated by the cyclic application of compressed air, hot air ducted from the engine exhaust or from a combustion heater and electrically heated elements on critical surfaces. The last method placed a heavy load on an aircraft's electrical system.

Cockpits and their equipment

Introduction

Before describing the principal characteristics of the cockpits of Second World War aircraft it is important to consider the relationship of the cockpit and its equipment to the aircraft as a whole.

At the end of the 20th century we have become used to the concept of the man–machine interface and to integrated systems throughout an aircraft. We now expect that avionic systems will have built-in intelligence so that they can perform their functions without human intervention. In 1939 the idea of built-in test (BIT) and self-monitoring were virtually unknown within the present meaning of those terms. Two aspects of the Second World War cockpit illustrate these concepts: First, some instruments had to be interpreted by the pilot in order to obtain the required information. This interpretation included applying correcting factors in order to obtain a 'true' reading. Second, engine control and monitoring was often without the benefit of automatic systems. For example American engines were not, in general, equipped with automatic boost and mixture controls. This meant that the pilot had to watch carefully the engine instruments when making large throttle movements. In contrast British and German engines were given more comprehensive automatic controls. These relieved the pilot of the need constantly to monitor engine indications, particularly when concentrating on a target or evading the attentions of enemy fighters during an aerial battle.

German cockpits had equipment, including instruments which made them instantly distinguishable from American British, Italian and Japanese types. In general German cockpits were equipped, both in detail and overall, to a very high standard compared with those of British aircraft. Switches, selector levers, instruments and the minutiae, such as labels, were carefully designed. Wiring was confined to conduits. The cockpit equipment reflected the generally high quality of German design and manufacture. American cockpits, compared with British, were in general far more comfortable for the crew. There was extensive padded lining to isolate the crew from external noise. Ash trays were often provided.

French cockpits prior to 1940, as a man–machine interface, were a mixture of German and British ideas. With only six months in which to perfect better cockpits, based on air war experience, the French were unable to make any contribution to design in general.

Fenestration

In the 1930s and 1940s cockpit fenestration design for multi-engine aircraft could be divided into two basic profiles: the traditional stepped nose, as common in civil transports, and the unbroken nose line favoured for many German aircraft; and, later in the war, adopted by Boeing for the B-29. Although the semi-spherical array of small windows was intended to give wide fields of view forward, upward, below and on both bows it exposed the crew to intense sunlight. At night, particularly in rain, the multiple reflections of lights on the ground, such as when landing, gave the pilot a dangerously distorted view.

Perhaps one of the most significant changes in cockpit fenestration that occurred at the end of the 1930s concerned the design of canopies on single-seat aircraft. Pilots of 1930s biplane fighters disliked a completely enclosed cockpit because it added to the difficulties of visually searching for the enemy. This pilot's view upward, downward and to the sides was already hampered by the wings, the interplane struts and rigging wires. The increase in performance of the monoplane fighters predicated an enclosed cockpit. Each of the three principal fighters in the Battle of Britain in 1940 had a distinctive cockpit windscreen and canopy. The Bf 109 canopy and windscreen had an angular shape made up of individual flat panels. The canopy was hinged on the right to allow access to the cockpit. However this had the disadvantage that the aircraft could not be taxied with it open. The American Bell Airacobra had a car-type door, as did the early mark of the Hawker Typhoon: the door had to be closed once the engine was started. The Bf 109 cockpit closely confined the pilot: its dimensions seemed to have been related to the average shoulder width and seated

The cockpit of a Bf 109F, showing the hinged canopy which had to be closed before taxying. A section of the armour plating for the pilot's seat was fixed to the canopy.

Before the 'bubble'-type canopy became common, various methods of improving a pilot's all-round view were tried. One was the Malcolm hood, here seen fitted to North American Mustang III FX889.

height of pilots and therefore made no allowance for the large man. The Spitfire started life with a windscreen and canopy that proved unsuitable for air combat. The curved panels distorted the pilot's view and he could not turn his head sufficiently to see astern. The demands of air fighting prompted major changes to the shape of the cockpit canopy. The Hurricane's canopy was made up of many small flat panels and, unlike the Spitfire, the type never acquired a bubble canopy.

During the Second World War there were few departures from the excepted position for the pilot or pilots. This was close to the nose in multi-engine aircraft and behind the engine in single- and tandem-seat aircraft. Other crew positions could either be concentrated close to the pilot, as in many German aircraft, or dispersed in

remotely located gun, bomb-aiming and navigation positions. An example of a unique attempt to be different was the Bv 141B. This was an asymmetric single-engine monoplane with the crew in a nacelle to starboard of the engine. The latter was extended aft to carry the empennage, the tailplane of which extended to port. This arrangement of crew and engine provided excellent fields of vision in most directions except to the left.

Single- and tandem-seat cockpits world-wide were usually built to a standard arrangement. Whereas multi-engine crew postions exhibited significant differences among the 'airwar' nations. For example and as mentioned, German designers favoured concentration of the crew members in a forward location as in the Do 217 and Ju 88 and their subsequent variants. There was usually only one set of pilot's controls and this was to the left of the centre line. A basic set of flight controls might be provided for a seating position on the right.

American multi-engine aircraft cockpits often reflected the civil flight deck arrangement with two pilots sitting side by side and with the copilot on the right responsible for managing the engines and systems. This layout was also used in Japanese bombers. However the cockpit layout of the Douglas A-26/B-26 Invader was a departure from the usual American two-pilot side-by-side seating because there was only one pilot's position. The pilot sat to the left of the gangway. The engine controls pedestal was on the centre line. The Invader pilot also benefited from advances made in the forming of large one-piece cockpit windows: there was only one centre pillar to obstruct the forward view, whereas in earlier aircraft types there was a multiplicity of small windows. In contrast British medium and heavy

The crew positions in the Blohm und Voss Bv 141 were housed in a wing-mounted 'fuselage' to the right of the single engine, which was mounted in an extended nacelle that carried the empennage. This was an attempt to provide wide arcs of view forward and aft for the crew of a single-engine aircraft.

The navigator's, wireless operator's and flight engineer's stations in a Saunders-Roe Lerwick flying boat of 1939. This is a splendid example of a non-ergonomic layout of the instruments and controls. Apart from the haphazard juxtaposition of individual items, the confusion was added to by the fact that the controls for the starboard engine were to the flight engineer's left when he faced the controls. The large disc on which are mounted 17 selector levers is the control panel for the complicated fuel system. Although intended as a companion to the RAF's Short Sunderland, the Lerwick was not a success.

bombers usually only had one pilot's seat. This was on the left in order to leave room for a gangway on the right leading to the navigator/bomb-aimer's position in the nose. Examples were the Blenheim, Wellington, Whitley and Hudson. Although the last type was a Lockheed design the crew positions were arranged to meet the RAF's specification. British aircraft with 'two-pilot' cockpits included the Stirling and the Sunderland.

Although a number of stereotype arrangements have been described there were also many exceptions to any apparent rules about cockpit design and equipment. Perhaps one of the greatest variations of design in multi-engine aircraft were to be found among the throttles and other engine control levers. There were examples of throttles to the left and examples to the right of the pilot. In German aircraft the engine controls were more often to found to the left of the pilot. Some types of British aircraft had them to the left and others on a central controls

pedestal as in a civil airliner. American bombers also exhibited differences. The B-17 and the B-24 had the throttles on a central pedestal, whereas each of the two pilots in a B-29 had a set of engine control levers to his outboard side. (The throttle-like levers close to the centreline of a B-29 flight deck were the brake control levers.)

On the subject of throttle levers, it is interesting to note the French and Italian preference for the throttle movement of pull back for increased power. French and Italian pilots were accustomed to this arrangement. However it could have fatal consequences when pilots of other nations attempted to fly French and Italian aircraft. It so happened that in 1940 a number of American aircraft, such as DB-7s (Bostons) and Curtiss Hawk 75s, originally intended for the French air force, were acquired for the RAF. An important modification was the reversal of the throttle movement.

The cockpit of an RAF Whitley bomber. This emphasises the preference for having only one set of pilot's controls in the majority of British and German multi-engine aircraft. In contrast, the majority of American multi-engine types had two sets of controls.

Instruments

Instrument panels also exhibited national characteristics. A notable example was the RAF's Basic Six 'blind flying' panel. This was an orderly arrangement of the airspeed, artificial horizon, altimeter, vertical speed, directional gyro and the turn and bank (slip) instruments. In the United States generations of pilots had learnt to fly using an entirely different instrument scanning technique. The result was an apparently confused arrangement of the instruments on the panel in front of the pilot; sometimes with the engine instruments mixed in with the flight instruments. However, the arrangement suited American pilots having originated with the instrument layout in primary trainers. A seemingly haphazard arrangement of the instrument panel was used in German aircraft. Often this could not be avoided because the characteristic extensive fenestration forward, with views from the pilot's seat downward, upward and to the sides, militated against a neat athwartships panel. In the He 111, for example, many of the flight instruments were above the pilot's eye level.

The two principal American heavy bombers in service before the advent of the B-29, the B-17 and B-24, had their main instrument panels arranged so that the second pilot could monitor the engines and systems. This meant that the captain had few instruments on his part of the panel. The flight instruments were concentrated on the centre of the main panel. Being an earlier aircraft, the cockpit of the B-17 had fewer electrical systems switches and controls compared with the B-24. On the controls pedestal between the pilots there were throttle, propeller and mixture control levers for each engine along with a master control unit for all four exhaust-turbine superchargers. A Boeing 'trademark' was the arrangement of the four engine throttle levers. These had horizontal grips so that the pilot could, with one hand, move all four together or select either pairs of engines or individual engines.

In the first two years of the war there was one particular item of equipment which set British cockpits apart from those of other nations. This was the principal compass display. American and German aircraft had remotely located master compass units with repeater instruments in front of the pilot and navigator. The cockpit of an RAF aircraft of the Second World War could not be mistaken for any other because of the large-diameter aperiodic magnetic compass with rotatable grid ring which took up a lot of space. In single-engine aircraft it

A characteristic of American two-pilot bomber cockpits was the concentration of engine and system instruments in front of the second pilot. This is an early mark of the B-24 Liberator as operated by RAF Coastal Command, and is not equipped with the turbosuperchargers and their master electronic control box fitted to USAAF B-24s; hence the boost control levers to the left of the pedestal.

The P Type aperiodic magnetic compass, lower right, in the cockpit of a Wellington Ic. This was the principal heading instrument in RAF aircraft until superseded by the remote reading gyro-magnetic compass system as used in American and German aircraft.

was usually positioned between the pilot's feet. After about 1941 the RAF made increasing use of the gyro magnetic distant-reading compass system based on a magnetic flux gate detector unit mounted remotely from the pilot's and navigator's positions.

Instrument design differences

Engine instruments in American multi-engine aircraft were usually of the type in which one instrument case housed two mechanisms, thereby giving two pointer-on-dial presentations; one for each of two engines. This arrangement economised in space on the instrument panel. The British also had some twin read-out instruments, such as rpm indicators. The American twin-display instruments, for example, when set in a row covering four engines and two different sets of parameters, had to be scanned carefully to make sure that a particular reading applied to the correct engine.

Automatic flight system controls

The autopilots in use at this time were selected and programmed through a control and display unit in the cockpit. Typical of the wartime generation of automatic flight

The crew of an RAF Vickers Wellington bomber about embark for a sortie in 1941. They are wearing Irvin parachute harness and carrying their clip-on parachute packs. This photograph emphasises the RAF's policy, established in the mid-1930s, of fitting power-operated gun turrets.

control systems (AFCS) was the Honeywell system with its distinctive control and selector unit and two rows of small lamps to indicate when the pilot could engage the system. In the B-24s the unit was mounted on the left side of the central control pedestal. In contrast British multi-engine aircraft were equipped with the less sophisticated Smiths pneumatic autopilot that had been developed in the early 1930s.

An early example of the modern side-stick controller was to be found on some B-24s. A small control column or joystick was mounted alongside the left leg of the aircraft captain. This enabled him to control the aircraft directly through the autopilot when flying in formation. It was an extension of the system whereby the bombaimer exercised control of the aircraft in yaw when approaching a target.

Crew Safety

Parachutes
Fashions in parachutes varied among the air forces of the Second World War. There were harness fastenings favoured by the British whereby one turn and a bang with the hand released all four parts of the harness. American harness in contrast had four individual release

hooks. An innovation adopted for some RAF squadrons was the Irvin suit, which combined a flying coverall with integral harness to which a chest type parachute pack could be fastened. This type of personal safety equipment had the advantage that there were few projections and hooks for catching on equipment when moving about in the cramped conditions of RAF bombers. Luftwaffe aircrew sometimes wore a back type parachute as opposed to the seat type favoured by American and British pilots flying single-seat aircraft. Crews of B-17s and B-24s were further encumbered by having to

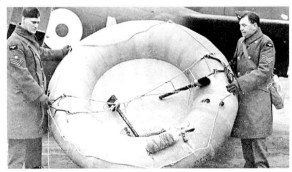

A typical Second World War inflatable dinghy carried by RAF multi-engine aircraft.

Bristol Beaufighter VIF nightfighter V8526 displays external equipment including the nose and wing antennae of its Mk IV AI radar, 'cheese-grater' flame-damping exhaust pipes, and the access hatches which formed windshields to facilitate emergency exit by parachute.

wear armoured jackets (flak jackets) and steel helmets when flying through intense German flak and fighter attacks.

Inflatable liferafts, along with inflatable lifejackets ('Mae Wests'), provided aircrew with extra assurance that even if the worst were to happen and the aircraft had to ditch, then they stood a second chance of survival. Because liferafts were usually installed in the wings or fuselage there was always the risk that they might inadvertently inflate in flight and damage or obstruct the tail controls.

Armour plating

In the first year of war few aircraft were equipped with armour protection for their crews. As the air war became more intense, pilots in particular were given armoured seats or bulkheads and armour added to protect other vital parts of the aircraft. For example the He 111 had an 8mm armoured bulkhead abaft the radio position; 8mm armour also formed the back of the pilot's seat in the Bf 109. The damage inflicted by Bf 109s on Wellington Is in December 1939 operations highlighted their vulnerability to both 7.7 and 20mm bullets. An armoured bulkhead was installed abaft the navigator's position in subsequent versions of the Wellington. The armoured

glass windscreen fitted to the nightfighter version of the Bf 110 was 60mm thick. On the Bf 109G the windscreen was 90mm thick.

Ejection seats

Athough the jet aircraft of the last year of war highlighted the difficulties of escaping by parachute, ejection seats were only fitted to some. The Meteor and Vampire were designed with a conventional pilot's seat. The Me 262, despite its performance, did not have an ejection seat for the pilot.

The test pilot in the He 280V1 who found that suddenly he had no control of the aircraft made history by

This is the Dornier Do 335 Pfeil of 1943, with one engine 'pulling' and the other 'pushing'. An early example of a piston-engine aircraft with an ejection seat.

245

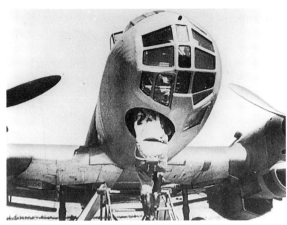

The Junkers Ju 86P with pressurised crew compartment. The appearance of these photo-reconnaissance aircraft over the UK in 1942 prompted the development of the Westland Welkin and of a high-altitude version of the de Havilland Mosquito; the Mk XV equipped with AI Mk VIII interception radar.

being the first to use an ejection seat 'in anger'. This was on 13 August 1942. The compressed air-operated seat was the first of a number developed for the Luftwaffe's final generation of aircraft: the He 162 and Do 335 Pfeil for example. The latter had an ejection seat even though it was a piston-engined/propeller type.

Pressurised crew compartments

Above about 10,000ft the crew of an aircraft experienced increasing discomfort with every additional 1,000ft. However, provided they were supplied with a regulated supply of oxygen, were in heated cockpits or wore electrically heated suits and did not have to move about too much or exert themselves, they could retain their effectiveness even when flying at 30,000ft. At that altitude the air pressure had dropped to 4.4psi and the outside air temperature was down to around minus 44°C.

As the air war developed each of the combatant air forces tried to gain the ascendancy by a number of technological advances in order to achieve, in addition to higher combat speeds, extreme cruising altitudes. This placed an aircraft out of reach of accurate flak. It also enabled it to get above the worst of the weather. Importantly it also made it difficult for interceptor fighters to get into an attacking position.

The Luftwaffe introduced a pressurised crew compartment for the Ju 86, a bomber conversion used for photo-reconnaissance. The presence of these aircraft over the UK prompted the development of high-altitude fighters for the RAF, such as the Westland Welkin. The Wellington V and VI were attempts to develop a high-altitude bomber for the RAF. The crew were sealed in a pressurised cylinder with limited external vision and a difficult exit in the event of trouble. Including prototypes, 67 high-altitude Wellingtons were built, but only a few went into squadron service, primarily for early trials with Oboe.

None of the British and German methods of providing an acceptable working environment for the crew was entirely satisfactory and in no way were they a precursor of the modern pressurised airliner. However, in the United States Boeing, which had introduced the civil pressurised Stratoliner, developed a successor to the

The high-altitude version of the ubiquitous Vickers Wellington bomber. This is a Mk VI with Merlin 60 engines. The crew were located inside a pressurised cylinder with a transparent dome for the pilot's head and shoulders.

Germany's Mistel (Mistletoe) composite used its piloted fighter upper component to guide an unmanned explosive-laden bomber on to its target. This is an S3A trainer using an Fw 190A-3 and a Ju 88A-6.

B-17. This was the B-29 in which the crew could operate in a virtual shirt-sleeve environment except when attacked or over the target. Two sections of the cylindrical hull were completely pressurised. These were connected by a tunnel equipped with a small trolley so that a crew member could propel himself from one section to the other. The technology applied to the structure of the B-29 showed the way to the pressurisation of civil aircraft after the war.

Emergency flight controls

Some aircraft in the Second World War with only a one-pilot cockpit were equipped with an emergency set of controls at another crew position. Examples are the Martin Maryland and the Douglas DB-7 Boston. A similar arrangement was provided in the Martin Baltimore. The emergency controls of the Maryland were located in the navigator's isolated position in the nose. In the DB-7 the emergency flight and engine controls were in the wireless-operator's position aft.

The final years in the cockpit

In the chapter covering armament reference is made to the introduction of the lead-computing gyro gun and rocket sights fitted to Allied aircraft from 1942 onward. In contrast German aircraft retained the simpler Revi type reflector sights until the end of the war. The significance of this difference in equipment standards is the effect the gyro sights had on the look of fighter cockpits. The gyro sights were very much larger than the non-gyro reflector sights and therefore filled much of the space behind the windscreen.

The introduction of the gas turbine and rocket propulsion systems did not have an immediate effect on the design and equipment of cockpits in general, apart from turbine temperature indicators reading up to 1,000°C and rpm indicators graduated from 0 to 10,000rpm. However, the need for ejection seats required some major structural changes to provide room for the mechanism.

Few of the aircraft design offices in the Second World

War had the resources or time to allow in-depth studies of what we now call human factors or ergonomics in the control interface such as the cockpit. Attempts were made by some designers to improve the control interface. There were many cockpit layouts proposed by pilots who, after all, were in the best position to comment based on the experience of sitting for many hours in discomfort, unable to obtain accurate instrument readings or employ safe instrument scanning techniques, unable to see ahead clearly in precipitation and so on. One designer in particular made a big effort in this respect. This was Martin-Baker, whose M.B. 5 was not only one of the most advanced of all piston-engined aircraft but had a cockpit in which ergonomic considerations had been applied.

STOL, VSTOL, JATO

The rotary-wing aircraft only just made it in time for the war. However, its impact on operational effectiveness was small. Design offices in Germany, Japan, Italy, Britain and the USA were aware of the potential of the rotary wing but realised that for high speed and for large aircraft there were both drawbacks and limitations. Even at this early stage of development the helicopter was limited in its use to specialised functions. The rotating wing was not ready to give fighter and bomber type aircraft the ability to take-off and land in a short distance or to hover. Neither was it going to help with over-the-normal-load take-offs.

Therefore recourse had to be made to in-flight refuelling, rocket assisted take-off (RATO) and to composites such as the Ju 88 carrying a fighter on its back. Other methods of enabling take-off weight to be above the normal or to extend the range included the use of additional lifting surfaces that could be jettisoned once the aircraft was airborne.

Bibliography

The Aeroplane journal, various, London, 1939–40.

AP 1565: Manual for the Spitfire.

AP 2019: Manual for the Mosquito.

Aircraft Engineering journal, various, London, 1939–45.

Bekker, C. *Die Radar Story* (Stalling, 1964). An important survey of the history of German radar development and operational use.

Bowen, E G, *Radar Days* (Hilger, Bristol, 1987). The 'father' of airborne radar for interception covers all the important British and American wartime developments.

Brown, E, *Wings of the Wierd and Wonderful* (Airlife,
Shrewsbury, 1983). Includes detailed descriptions of aircraft equipment.

Coombs, L F E, *Cockpits of the RAF* (Series in *Aeroplane Monthly*, London, 1983.

Coombs, L F E, *The Aircraft Cockpit* (Patrick Stephens, Wellingborough, 1990). The chapters on military cockpits provide a comprehensive survey of developments and problems.

Flight journal, various, London, 1939–1945.

Grover, J H H, *Radio Aids to Air Navigation* (Heywood, London, 1956). Out-of-print descriptons of wartime navigational systems.

Gunston, W T, *Avionics* (Patrick Stevens, Wellingborough, 1990). Very useful clearly set out descriptions of how wartime radar and other electronic systems operated.

Hartcup, G, *The Challenge of War* (David & Charles, Newton Abbot, 1970). Includes details of aircraft equipment such as gunsights, bomb sights and radar.

Her Majesty's Stationary Office, *Laboratory of the Air* (London, 1948). An out-of-print insight into the development of aircraft equipment by the RAE.

Jewell, J, *Engineering for Life* (Martin-Baker, Denham, 1979). Covers safety equipment, ejection seats and cable cutters.

Lovell, Sir Bernard, *Echoes of War* (Hilger, Bristol, 1991). As the 'father' of plan position radar, such as H$_2$S, Sir Bernard covers the complete development of systems which enabled the RAF to navigate and bomb with deadly accuracy.

Miller & Sawers, *The Technical Development of Modern Aviation* (Routledge & Keegan Paul, London, 1968). An essential source of dates and technologies. Covers both civil and military applications.

Price, A, *Aircraft Versus Submarine* (Kimber, London, 1973).

Price, A, *Instruments of Darkness* (Macdonald & Janes, London, 1977 edn). Price's two books provide clear descriptions of aircraft operational equipment.

Pritchard, D, *The Radar War* (Patrick Stevens, Wellingborough, 1989). A semi-technical review of German radar development. It covers all the principal airborne radar systems used by the Luftwaffe.

Reuter, F, *Funkmess* (Westdeutscher, Opladen, 1971). The history and development of German radar.

Robinson, D H, *The Dangerous Sky* (Foulis, Oxford, 1973). A valuable source of reference to aircrew life support and safety equipment in the aircraft of the world's principal air forces.

Saward, D, Group Captain, *'Bomber' Harris* (Buchan & Enright, London, 1984).

Saward, D, Group Captain, *The Bomber's Eye* (Cassell, London, 1959). As radar adviser to 'Bomber' Harris, Saward was close to the 'sharp end' of airborne radar development in the RAF.

Trenkle, F, *Bordfunkgerate der deutschen Luftwaffe 1935–45* (Dusseldorf, 1958). One of the top radar scientists. His book is a detailed study of the different radar systems used by the Luftwaffe.

Williams, T I, *A History of Technology Vol VII Part II* (OUP, Oxford, 1978). A useful source of references to technical developments in aviation.

Zeffert, H, *Aircraft Electrical Engineering* (Newnes, London, 1960). A standard work whose importance is its description of electronic technologies that owed much to wartime developments.

Curtiss P-40 production. The cylinder banks and cam-boxes of the Allison V-12 cylinder liquid-cooled engines are clearly visible.

10
Propulsion
Andrew Nahum

Introduction

The aero engine has always been one of the most demanding products of engineering science, and it is important, for an understanding of the air war, to understand that in 1939 the piston engine was as much a virtuoso example of engineering development and manufacture as a modern fan-jet engine is today.

Because of the nature of high-power engine manufacture, few countries could design and produce military engines of the first rank. This effectively meant, at the outbreak of war in 1939, the ability to produce a reliable engine capable of some 1,000hp and weighing approximately 600kg (1,300lb). This was an extremely demanding target, and implied that any industrial nation which sought to attempt it needed a whole suite of supporting technologies. There was the requirement to forge difficult shapes and components, such as crankshafts, to the highest strength factors then available, a need for metallurgical expertise in the development of continually improving alloys, and the application of aerodynamic analysis to supercharger performance.

These demands meant that in 1939 only Britain and Germany had engines in the very front rank, and it is both significant and surprising to note that the Battle of Britain, a year later, was in part a struggle between two of the oldest and most respected names in the automotive industry; Rolls-Royce and Daimler Benz. The initial pre-eminence of these two nations was partly a consequence of German rearmament and the British response to it. There is no doubt, for example, that the USA could have produced an engine in the same league at that time, but the requirements for its air force seemed less pressing than for European powers, and engines had been optimised more for the emerging airline network than for short-term combat power.

At the outbreak of the Second World War the powerplants available for aviation were all piston engines. Development starting in the First World War and continuing through the interwar years had produced two well-defined types. Firstly, for front-line combat use, there was the liquid-cooled in-line engine. The other major type was the air-cooled radial, which had found a niche as the favoured type for airlines.

Liquid-cooled engines

Since the First World War various numbers of cylinders and different configurations had been tried. Thus, in that conflict, German manufacturers had produced in-line six- and eight-cylinder engines, while the British Napier Lion had been one of the pioneers of the 'broad-arrow' engine, with twelve cylinders in three banks of four. This configuration was also promoted by Lorraine-Dietrich in France and Isotta-Fraschini in Italy during the interwar years. A Napier-powered Supermarine S.5 seaplane won the Schneider Trophy contest in 1927 with a Lion tuned to the limit of its endurance at 875hp, although the layout was by then becoming outmoded.

The problem for the aero engine designer was partly the eternal one of creating a motor at the limit of attainable power-to-weight ratio. However, there was the other important consideration, from the point of view of aircraft design, of 'power density' – providing the most power possible for the smallest cubic volume, and making an engine that was slim enough to allow a finely streamlined nose or engine nacelle. For all these reasons the V-12 engine with two banks of six cylinders at an angle of 60° emerged as the best compromise. It was reasonably short, without too much wasted airspace between the cylinder banks, and also had the virtue of excellent mechanical balance and freedom from vibration. That was the reason that this configuration had been adopted by a few top-quality makers such as Rolls-Royce, Packard and Cadillac for some of their most exclusive cars. However, the mechanical balance of a V-12 was not simply a luxury in the aviation application. Unbalanced forces and vibration are much more destructive in an engine built to minimum weight, compared with a substantial car engine, and the adoption of the V-12 configuration allowed the engines and mountings to be lighter and more reliable than they might otherwise have been.

The prime examples of this technology could be seen in the Rolls-Royce Merlin and the Daimler Benz DB 601 engines which respectively powered British and German fighters at the outbreak of war. However, there was a certain difference in the design philosophy behind them, for while the German engine had a capacity of 33.93 litres, the Merlin was a mere 26 litres. The reason that the Merlin was directly comparable in power lay in its much greater reliance on supercharging, a technology in which Rolls-Royce had become adept. This technological choice proved to have been a wise or a lucky one, for Rolls-Royce was able to continue to improve the power of the Merlin throughout the war, taking it from approximately 1,000bhp to 2,300bhp without changing the basic geometrical form of the engine itself. The

A Rolls-Royce Merlin 65 in North American P-51 Mustang I AL975G, October 1942. Although the Mustang was originally equipped with the Allison V-12, the switch to the Merlin produced the outstanding Allied fighter of the latter part of the war, combining the speed to meet enemy fighters with the range to escort bombers over Germany.

pattern of development throughout the war was that supercharger and gas flow research at Derby would reveal further potential for power, and this would then be tested mechanically. The uprated engines would be run for hours on the test beds to establish at which point mechanical components might start to fail at the new rating. The 'Derby hum' of engines on test lay over the city night and day throughout the war.

Other liquid-cooled V-12s did exist. From 1933, in France, Hispano-Suiza produced the 12Y series, rated between 800 and 900hp and used in fighters such as the Morane-Saulnier MS.406 and the Dewoitine D.510, but it had not benefited from the same degree of development as the Merlin and it is significant that, from the mid-1930s, there were continuing moves to establish a Merlin assembly plant in France. In Italy Fiat also produced a series of well-engineered V-12 engines, although these, too, were rather low on power output. The other V-12 worthy of mention was the Allison V-1750, produced in the USA. This was similar to the Merlin in general architecture but again had not had the benefit of such intensive development, and in a well-known episode was displaced by the Rolls-Royce Merlin in the North American Mustang fighter, to make it a far more capable aircraft. In a turbosupercharged form, the Allison did become extremely effective, particularly in its application for the twin-engined P-38 Lightning.

Air-cooled engines

The other important class of piston engine was the air-cooled radial, which also dated back to the First World War but had made amazing advances in the interwar years. Air-cooled in-line engines were also tried, but failed to succeed in the highest power classes owing to the difficulty of providing an even supply of cooling air to the cylinders. Thus the radial, with its star-like arrangement of cylinders around a compact and light drum-shaped central crankcase, became the only high-power air-cooled type. Its advocates claimed that it had the advantage over liquid-cooled engines both on the

The Messerschmitt Bf l09G began to reach squadrons in 1942. This pre-production example is fitted with a 33.9-litre liquid cooled V-12 Daimler Benz DB 601 engine rated at a take-off power of l,270hp. However, the production series received the enlarged 1,475hp DB 605A engine, which had been developed from the earlier type by increasing capacity to 35.7 litres. The side-mounted centrifugal supercharger can be seen at the rear of the engine.

One of the mysteries of French aero engine development is that the Gnome-Rhône company, which had pioneered the innovative rotary in the years before the First World War, failed to follow-up with new products of its own and took a licence for Bristol radial engines. However, it did do considerable development on the basic Bristol designs and marketed a successful range of engines. This 18.98 litre 14M, seen here in a Henschel Hs 129, was rated at 710hp for take-off.

A Boeing B-17 Flying Fortress in the Middle Fast, showing its air-cooled Wright Cyclone radials with cowlings removed for servicing. The nine-cylinder R-1820 (1,823in³, 29.88 litres) gave 1,000hp for take-off.

score of lower installed weight (no water jackets, coolant and radiator) and reliability. Certainly airline experience pointed to the undesirability of water joints in aircraft required to perform reliably over long distances and to timetables. Thus Imperial Airways made particular use of air-cooled Bristol radials developed by the single-minded engineer A H Roy Fedden. In the USA the emerging airline network used radials from the Wright and Pratt & Whitney companies.

Mention should also be made of the Japanese radials, made principally by Nakajima and Mitsubishi. Licences for Bristol and Pratt & Whitney engines had been taken out in Japan, and although these undoubtedly contributed to the learning curve, the Japanese engines showed originality. Particular features were the use of very fine cylinder fins, fan cooling and close-fitting cowls. These features were clearly intended to reduce the drag of the radial installation, but a penalty was the tendency of the fine-pitched fins to fill with oil and dust. Although Japanese radials were good at the beginning of the Pacific war, they were barely powerful enough, and the superiority enjoyed by the Mitsubishi Zero fighter for a period was obtained at the sacrifice of both protective armour for the pilot and the number and calibre of

guns. As the war progressed the Japanese engine industry was unable to spare the resources to develop and build the more powerful units which would have allowed the aircraft to meet the newer, heavily armed American aircraft on equal terms.

The major difference between American radials and those by Bristol, the pre-eminent British make, was that from 1927 onwards Roy Fedden at Bristol steered the company to development of the single-sleeve-valve engine. In these engines the task of arranging inlet and exhaust opening is done by a sliding inner cylinder liner, the sleeve, with specially shaped ports cut in a band near the top. As the sleeve rises and falls with a circular motion, the ports line up in turn with inlet and exhaust passages. This layout was actively promoted at high level in the Air Ministry by Harry Ricardo, the noted British internal combustion consultant, on the basis of his experimental work. The attraction was that it abolished the conventional poppet exhaust valve with its red-hot head, which was a potential source of both pre-ignition and 'knock'. With the current fuel of low octane rating this meant that the engine could be designed for a significantly higher compression ratio, giving a major improvement in power output and economy. For Fedden

Left: *The Bristol company was the pre-eminent British maker of air-cooled radial engines. In 1932 it introduced the sleeve-valve to overcome problems with the low octane rating of contemporary fuel and to replace the maintenance-intensive pushrod-operated four-valve cylinder heads in their previous range. The 24.9-litre Perseus, seen here in a de Havilland Flamingo, could give 890hp and proved extremely reliable, but it depended on high-grade hand assembly and fitting. The subsequent challenge for the Bristol company was to transfer this technology to quantity production for the expanding Royal Air Force after 1935.*

arrangement of camshafts, pushrods and rockers for four valves per cylinder became almost 'an impossibility to contemplate'.

Many regarded the pursuit of the sleeve-valve engine as a chimera, for it required advances in both materials and machining technique. The difficulty is that the fit of piston in the sleeve must be right, at all conditions from cold start to high temperature at maximum power. So, too, must be the fit of the outer diameter of the sleeve in the outer finned cylinder barrel. The problem cannot simply be solved by making these fits rather loose, because an intimate contact is essential between sleeve and barrel to allow heat to flow to the cooling fins. Even David Pye, Deputy Director of Scientific Research at the Air Ministry, was sceptical, remarking: 'The single-sleeve-valve engine has been a sickly child ever since it was brought to birth' and querying whether it might be a case of 'infant mortality'. It was a serious criticism that no-one had made a success of it, and he felt that there would be little interest in it if it were not the only way out of the 'impasse of the red-hot exhaust valve'. The programme, with hindsight, might have been a huge

there was also another attraction. Bristol engines had aimed at a higher output per litre than its competitors, and in consequence used four valves per cylinder rather than two. This had been possible to arrange in the single-row engines, but as power requirements rose and two-row engines became necessary, Fedden reflected that the

A Bristol Blenheim nacelle, showing the nine-cylinder Mercury engine. The 24.9-litre engine had the same internal dimensions as the Perseus but used the earlier four-valve cylinder head. The valves, with springs and rockers, can be seen in this view.

The twin-row Hercules was the mainstay of Bristol engine production during the Second World War. Seen here without its normal cooling shrouds to direct the air around the cylinders, the 14-cylinder 38.74-litre sleeve-valve Hercules developed up to 1,725hp and was used in the Lancaster, Halifax and Stirling bombers, as well as in Wellingtons and Beaufighters.

diversion of effort, and it is noteworthy that Bristol radials cost about twice as much per horsepower in the Second World War as the Rolls-Royce Merlin. It is significant that no other engine manufacturer brought an air-cooled sleeve-valve into production, although it was tried, as we shall see, in some liquid-cooled in-line motors which were scarcely less problematical. A combination of the improvement of gasoline to 100 octane and the liquid-sodium-cooled exhaust valve served to postpone detonation in high-power engines by the early war, and even Harry Ricardo, as 'godfather' of the single sleeve valve, came to wonder if the effort had been worthwhile, regretting that:

> so many years … elapsed between … the research … and its practical development … since the advantages of the sleeve valve were most apparent in the early days when we were using relatively low octane fuels.

Liquid or air cooling for fighters?

During the 1930s there was considerable discussion about the most suitable power unit for high-performance aircraft. On commonsense grounds it appeared that the radial was obviously going to cause more drag, but cowling experiments, such as those with the Townend ring in Britain and the NACA cowl in the USA, showed that the drag could be hugely reduced. Nevertheless, it was

The BMW 801 was normally supplied as a complete exchange unit or 'power egg' with all accessories and cowlings fitted, allowing rapid engine changes in service conditions. This is a captured example from an Fw 190 undergoing examination in the UK in 1943.

generally considered that the drag of a liquid-cooled engine, even with a radiator, was less than that of the blunt radial and its cowling. This advantage was not necessarily permanently in favour of the liquid-cooled engine, as was shown by the temporary superiority of the Focke-Wulf Fw 190 with its BMW 803 radial engine, which alarmed British pilots when it appeared in mid-1941. The impressive performance of the big American fighters powered by powerful two-row radial engines that appeared later in the war was also a powerful argument for the radial.

However, in the early part of the war the problem of the temperature control of cylinder and head in radials meant that the liquid-cooled engines had the edge in performance. At this time, and with the fuel available, the cooling of radials at full power was marginal, and the advantage given by liquid cooling allowed a greater output, as well as a leaner cruising mixture and more economy. As noted below, liquid cooling also allowed charge cooling to improve the efficiency of the supercharger. However, the argument about the advantage between the two types was never finally resolved, and was still a matter for debate as the new jet engines began to sweep away all high-power piston engines in the postwar era.

High-octane fuels

The high-power piston engine is uniquely dependent on the quality of its fuel. Before the First World War, engine researchers had begun to puzzle over the phenomenon of 'knock' – a ringing noise sometimes encountered when an engine was running at high power, as if the cylinder had been struck with a light hammer. If the engine was kept running at the same power this sound often heralded a feed-back cycle of knock and eventual self-destruction.

Detonation was a concern in all the combatant countries in the First World War, but in Britain Harry Ricardo, then a student at Cambridge, was among the first to set up a systematic study. He begun to appreciate that, although raising the compression ratio of a particular engine design would produce more power, it also made the occurrence of knock more likely. Ricardo researched the problem by using an experimental engine of his own design with a variable supercharger ratio. As the supercharge pressure was increased with a given fuel, knock would begin to occur, giving for the first time an objective method of comparing fuel quality. One of the first interesting results that Ricardo obtained was that gasolines originating from different sources of crude oil differed in their propensity to knock. At the time the usual test for gasoline was its volatility, but although this would indicate whether the fuel would allow good cold starting performance and reasonable mixture distribution between cylinders, it was not a reliable predictor of knock. In fact, Ricardo found that a fuel with

excellent anti-knock properties was being burnt to waste in Borneo because it did not meet the volatility specifications that were then in place for British forces.

It was generally supposed at the time that pre-ignition and knock were the same, since both could lead to destruction of the engine in the same way. In pre-ignition a specific point in the engine, which might be the tip of a sparking plug or part of a component, such as an exhaust valve, becomes incandescent during running and itself functions as the initiator of combustion, in advance of the timed spark. Since this combustion occurs early, more heat is released to the combustion chamber walls and the hot spot becomes hotter. The ignition point thus automatically advances, leading to 'runaway pre-ignition', further heat build-up and probable seizure. A cure for pre-ignition therefore lay in better design of the surface geometry within the combustion chamber, attention to cooling and the heat path, and sparking plug design.

However, Ricardo glimpsed that knock was a different phenomenon. Combustion caused by pre-ignition still consisted of a normal flame front passing through the compressed air/fuel gas, and studies showed the normal rate of pressure rise in the cylinder. A 'knocking' combustion, by contrast, started normally, but part of the way through the remaining unburnt gas detonated abruptly. If the knocking continued, rapid heat build-up occurred, since the shock wave scoured the insulating boundary layer gas off combustion chamber surfaces and failure, usually of the piston crown, soon followed.

Immediately after the First World War Ricardo began a programme with Henry Tizard and David Pye to survey all possible fuels for spark ignition engines. Their work showed that 'the best fuel was the one that showed the least tendency to knock'. In fact, knock was an aspect of chemical stability of the fuel under the specific conditions in a gasoline engine. A good fuel would withstand compression and high temperature, waiting, as it were, for the timed spark and the arrival of the flame front. A poor fuel, heated by radiation from the advancing flame front, would reach a point where it spontaneously detonated. Ring chain 'aromatic' hydrocarbons seemed often to be more stable than straight chains, and some improvement could be had by selecting the crude oil source for gasoline refining. But apart from that it seemed that little could be done and the gasoline engine would have to put up with this inherent fuel limit. In fact, as a result of their research, Pye, who became Director of Scientific Research at the Air Ministry, and Tizard, who became chairman of the Aeronautical Research Committee and an important figure in defence science, expected gasoline engines to reach a natural power limit imposed by the knock rating of fuel. Throughout the 1920s and early 1930s both men spent much effort in encouraging development of the aircraft diesel engine, which they

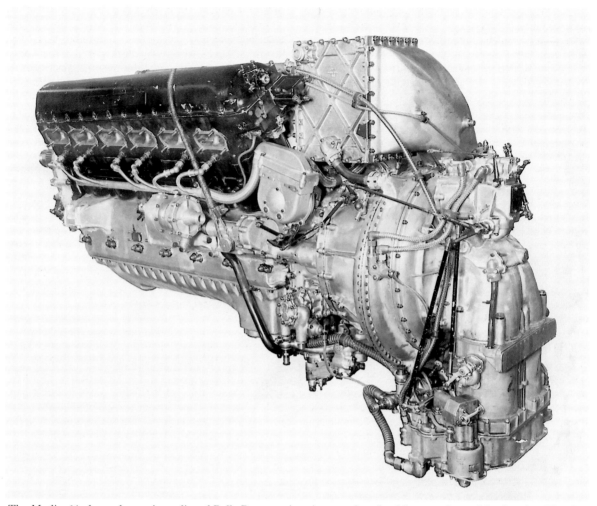

The Merlin 61 shows the poetic quality of Rolls-Royce engineering, utterly refined by necessity and by function. The classic and sound V-12 cylinder overhead camshaft engine is supplemented by a two-stage supercharger, drawing mixture from the updraught carburettor and passing it, via the charge cooler radiator (in the box-like structure) to the cylinders. The superchargers are also equipped with two-speed drive to enable supercharger output to keep pace with falling atmospheric pressure as the aircraft climbs. Using developments of this layout the Merlin was able, by the end of the Second World War in 1945, to develop 2,000hp at 15,000ft (4,580m), compared with 1,000hp from the Battle of Britain Mk III in 1940.

expected to overtake the gasoline engine owing to its immunity to knock and tolerance of fuel quality.

However, in the USA, a more pragmatic approach was adopted to the knock problem. Again it had been noted that gasolines from different sources varied in knock quality, and Thomas Midgley and C F Kettering, then studying fuels for the Liberty engine programme, realised that California gasolines were superior to many others and also developed a synthetic experimental blended fuel containing benzine and cyclohexane which allowed the engine to run at high compression on test. The fact that specially selected blends of organic chemicals could demonstrate knock resistance was theoretically interesting and useful, but it did not really help the

practical problem of providing good fuel in quantity. The discovery of anti-knock additives by Midgley, of which the most important was tetra ethyl lead, and their experimental use by the US Army from 1922, paved the way for the mass production of high-octane aviation spirit. By the Second World War, using both tetra ethyl lead as an additive, selecting crude oil stocks and refining technique, allowed the production of sufficient 100 octane fuel for Allied air forces.

Supercharging

Throughout the interwar period supercharging developed as a technology to improve the power of aero engines, and by the outbreak of war all the important engines had some form of forced induction. Part of the impetus for this derived from the car racing world, where the potential of a supercharger for forcing in a greater weight of mixture per stroke than a cylinder could aspire naturally pushed up the power output dramatically. Bugatti, Alfa Romeo and the German 'State' Grand Prix designs by Auto-Union and Mercedes all made extensive use of the technique. It was also used in aviation for the Schneider Trophy contests, the best-known example being the Rolls-Royce R engine used in 1929 and 1931 in the winning Supermarine S.6 and S.6B seaplanes. With a supercharger designed by J E Ellor, a former RAE Farnborough engine expert, the R engine produced 2,330hp on a special fuel containing gasoline, benzol, methanol and tetra ethyl lead. The development work for the 1931 engine gained Rolls-Royce, according to company lore, the equivalent of five years' experience at the normal pace of development.

However, the attraction of supercharging for military engines was not so much to increase the ground-level power of the engine, since that usually was already set at the maximum that the engine could stand continuously without beginning to suffer mechanically or through detonation. Rather, the supercharger was added to allow the engine to maintain its rated power at altitude, for otherwise the power of a piston engine decreases directly as the aircraft climbs and the air becomes thinner. Thus combat in the Battle of Britain could frequently take place at 15,000ft, and the aircraft of either side could not have fought at these altitudes without superchargers to maintain an artificially dense atmosphere in their inlet manifolds. As the war progressed the struggle in the air became, to a certain extent, a competition for altitude to escape the enemy, leading to increasingly powerful and better designed superchargers and culminating, as in the Merlin, in a two-stage, two-speed supercharging arrangement with intercooler.

The competition for power, which ruled combat engine development, was also a competition for height. The First World War had proved that the aircraft with higher altitude capability had the option of avoiding interception, or had the advantage if combat occurred. However, as piston-engined aircraft climb they enter thinner air and the engine receives less fuel/air mixture at each power stroke.

Aero-engine superchargers were almost invariably of the centrifugal type, spinning at very high speed (around 20,000rpm). This was driven by a step-up gear train from the engine, although the rotational inertia of the spinning rotor was so enormous that it had to be driven through a slipping clutch system to protect the gear drive train and shaft from destruction if the engine itself changed speed too quickly.

Supercharging, however, was not a simple way to gain altitude performance. The efficiency of the compressor was vital, since wasted energy appeared in the compressed charge as excess heat, reducing engine efficiency and also making detonation more likely. The downside can be seen by the illustration that if a supercharger is fitted to give an engine the same power at, say, 10,000ft that the normally aspirated version would have at ground level, there is a penalty in take-off power in the supercharged engine owing to the charge heating. One solution was to arrange a two-speed supercharger with two different gear ratios, controlled by clutches. The other strategy was to arrange for charge cooling; passing the compressed mixture through its own radiator before leading it into the inlet ports. This was another argument for the liquid-cooled engine, since a supply of coolant was available for the intercooler matrix.

In the USA the mechanically driven supercharger gradually gave way to the turbosupercharger, a centrifugal compressor driven by an exhaust turbine. The General Electric company had pioneered this development, and during the war exhaust turbochargers were to appear increasingly on American engines.

New engines and problematic engines

As might be expected in a complex and highly stressed device like an aero engine, novelty inevitably implies expense and trouble. Virtually all the new engines that were under development at the beginning of the Second World War posed development problems. Some never came through the process, while even those that did enter service sometimes came close to cancellation.

Firstly, developments of the standard piston engine should be considered. By the late 1930s defence planners were looking beyond the 1,000hp level of the engines coming into service to 2,000hp for new aircraft because the weapon load, whether guns and cannon on a fighter or bombs and defensive armament in a bomber, is directly related to the installed power. Long-range planning also looked forward to a new generation of piston engines of 3,000hp and more.

The major constraint on design was to achieve this increase without a large increase in frontal area and drag, which would partly defeat the purpose of the power gained. One interesting example of an ingenious attempt to overcome this was in the Napier Sabre. Colonel Frank Halford, who had designed the practical de Havilland Gipsy light aero engines, devised for the Napier company a twenty-four-cylinder 'H' engine. The Sabre was, in effect, two flat (i.e. horizontally opposed 'boxer') twelve-cylinder engines each with its own crankshaft, joined through coupling gears. This arrangement certainly ensured the tightest possible packaging of the engine cylinders, but the project had enormous problems. In addition to the unconventional layout, which brought problems of torsional vibration in the coupling gear train and crankshafts, the engine used single sleeve valves, as

The Napier Sabre was the single greatest problem encountered in British engine procurement in the Second World War. The complexity of the untried, geared 24-cylinder layout was compounded by the new technology of liquid-cooled single-sleeve valves. Since a new generation of high-power fighters, the Hawker Typhoon and Tempest, had been ordered, it was essential to crack the development problem, and the Sabre eventually entered service at a rated output of 2,200hp. However, it always consumed a far higher proportion of maintenance and service effort than other engines.

recently brought to a state of reliability by Bristol. However, the Sabre was to be liquid cooled, introducing another new element to complicate development. The programme was extraordinarily troubled, and a Ministry of Aircraft Production official called the Sabre in 1945 'a miserable failure', noting that in the development programme 'two incompatibles were brought together – an unusually poor producer and an unusually intricate article'.

Another interesting project, which has been little discussed until recently, was the development of a two-stroke fighter engine. The design emanated from Harry Ricardo in late 1935, and derived from his attempts to force up the power output of the diesel to suit it for aviation. The impending war, and the realisation that the possession of early warning from radar would change air defence strategy, directed the attention of British Air Ministry planners to the use of engines of very high power to give interceptors a rapid climb. This project also used a single sleeve valve, so that unlike the common piston-ported two-stroke, where some mixing of fresh

charge and exhaust is inevitable, the gas path was 'uniflow' with inlet ports at the head and exhaust ports in a belt at the bottom of the piston stroke. The engine, known as the Crecy, was developed by Rolls-Royce as a V-12 of similar proportions to the Merlin, but although its supporters believed it would give double or more the power of the four-stroke equivalent, it was never far enough ahead of the Merlin to justify a decisive commitment of resources.

Pratt & Whitney in the USA also experimented with the coupled double-crankshaft 'H' liquid-cooled engine in the interest of high power and maximum power density. Like the Napier Sabre and the Rolls-Royce Eagle (see page 262), which shared the same layout, these engines all used the single sleeve valve, partly to reduce the overall size of the engine by removing the need for rocker boxes or overhead camshafts. Another important attraction of the sleeve valve was the permanence of adjustment of the valve gear. With four valves per cylinder on high-performance engines, the adjustment of tappets on a twenty-four-cylinder engine at manufacture and

The Rolls-Royce Crecy petrol-injection, supercharged sleeve-valve two-stroke. It was hoped that this 26-litre V-l2-cylinder engine would be an ideal interceptor unit with twice the power of a four-stroke of equivalent size and weight, but its development never overhauled the Merlin. Thus in 1944 it was bench tested at 1,600bhp, but by this date the Merlin had been worked up to 2,340bhp. Postwar tests promised huge power outputs of up to 3,500hp from the Crecy, but the gas turbine made further development unattractive.

during maintenance must have seemed intimidating. The other much-vaunted feature of the sleeve valve, its relative immunity to 'knock', was certainly an attraction at the outset of these programmes, but by the late 1930s the availability of 100 octane had made this theoretical advantage less important. The Pratt & Whitney H-3130 reached 2,650hp but the company, in discussion with the USAAC, decided that development effort was best concentrated on the company's sturdy twin-row air-cooled radials, and it was cancelled.

Other high-power projects with unusual conformations included the Rolls-Royce 'X' engine, the Vulture, which had four banks of six cylinders in X formation, working on a single crankshaft and giving a capacity of 2,592in³. The Avro Manchester bomber was designed to take a pair, but the engine proved troublesome and was withdrawn. The redesigned Manchester, adapted for four Merlins, was rechristened the Lancaster and became extremely successful.

There were also double engines made by coupling two existing engines together. Allison's V-3420 was one

The experimental Fairey Prince represented one of the gallant attempts by aircraft manufacturer Sir Richard Fairey to break into the 'family' of aero engine companies supported by the Air Ministry through contracts. The Prince, like the Napier Sabre and Rolls-Royce Eagle, consisted of two opposed twelve-cylinder units sandwiched together. Unlike the other two, however, the cylinder banks were not geared together, but each drove one half of a contrarotating airscrew.

261

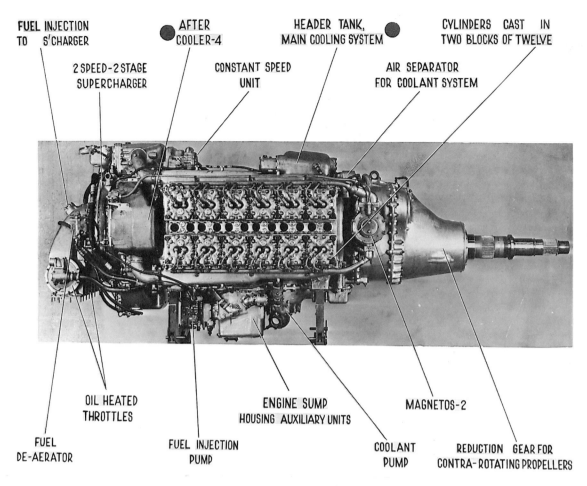

FUEL INJECTION TO S'CHARGER

2 SPEED-2 STAGE SUPERCHARGER

AFTER COOLER-4

CONSTANT SPEED UNIT

HEADER TANK, MAIN COOLING SYSTEM

AIR SEPARATOR FOR COOLANT SYSTEM

CYLINDERS CAST IN TWO BLOCKS OF TWELVE

OIL HEATED THROTTLES

FUEL DE-AERATOR

FUEL INJECTION PUMP

ENGINE SUMP HOUSING AUXILIARY UNITS

MAGNETOS-2

COOLANT PUMP

REDUCTION GEAR FOR CONTRA-ROTATING PROPELLERS

The 46-litre 3,500hp Rolls-Royce Eagle shows the double-layer 'H' configuration of two horizontally opposed banks of twelve cylinders with crankshafts geared together. Although the liquid-cooled sleeve-valve Eagle seems to have avoided the troubles which plagued the architecturally similar Napier Sabre, it arrived to late for military use in the Second World War, and high-power piston engines were rapidly displaced by the gas turbine in the postwar era.

such, comprising two V-1750s geared together. This was started in 1937, but the requirement for it was dropped. A similar stratagem was also adopted by Daimler Benz in the DB 606, which consisted of two DB 601s. On the subject of unusual piston engines the Lycoming XR-7755 should also be noted. This had nine banks of four cylinders each arranged radially around a central crank, and was intended to give 7,000hp.

In fact almost all of the new generation of unusual piston engines which departed from the classic liquid-cooled V-12 or air-cooled radial pattern proved exceptionally troublesome and played almost no significant part in the war, although it could be argued that the Napier Sabre was strategically important as the power unit for the Hawker Typhoon. This proved useful for ground and tank attack in co-operation with the Anglo-American armies after the Normandy landing, although

the Sabre always took a disproportionate share of repair and maintenance capacity.

The Rolls-Royce Eagle was also an exception, since it appears to have been the only engine in this category which proved mechanically sound. It was a flat-H sleeve-valve twin-crankshaft engine, and could produce 3,500hp, but it arrived too late to see action.

Jets

The other class of engine which was both new and problematical was of course the jet, although the development of the gas turbine is also usually considered as one of the technological landmarks of the Second World War.

The idea of a gas turbine is quite ancient, but by the 1920s there were numerous inventors and scientists, in several countries, who believed that the time was now right to develop it. In Britain, A A Griffith, a government

The Heinkel He 178, which made the first jet flight in August 1939. The engine is a centrifugal compressor turbojet of 450kg (1,000lb) thrust, designed by young physicist and inventor Hans-Joachim Pabst von Ohain and built by the Heinkel company. Although the project had a powerful propaganda effect in aviation circles, the Heinkel unit was not a direct progenitor of any of the German wartime jet engines which entered service.

scientist working at RAE Farnborough, proposed a turbine based on his new theory for producing a more efficient aerodynamic flow in compressors and turbines. Stanford Moss in the USA also believed a practical turbine was attainable, but his hopes were premature and he subsequently became the champion and developer of the turbosupercharger for the General Electric company. It is an interesting comment on the selectivity of history, too, that in 1937 a 100hp gas turbine test unit was run in Budapest by the Hungarian engineer Gyorgy Jendrassik, who created in the same year a practical and beautifully

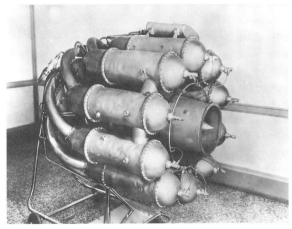

The Whittle W.1X engine that was shipped to the USA in October 1941, along with full drawings and technical information. The W.1 X was a bench-test engine made of second-line parts, but to the same design as the W.1 which made the first Allied jet flight on 15 May 1941. The W.1 gave 1,000lb (450kg) thrust at special rating and propelled the Gloster-Whittle E.28/39 at 370mph (595km/h).

designed turboprop of 1,000hp, but this achievement is almost unknown.

A major problem in the way of developing a gas turbine was that of materials technology; in particular, the challenge of developing alloys for the turbine blades that could retain strength to cope with the enormous centrifugal stress while approaching red heat. Other problems were obtaining even and rapid combustion in the high-velocity airstream in the combustion chamber, and making the compressor efficient enough for the overall efficiency of the engine to be worthwhile. There were, of course, more difficulties, including dynamic balance, harmonic and vibration effects from the interaction of airflow with compressor blades, and a new area of aerodynamic behaviour, to analyse.

The growing complexity of the piston engines reviewed earlier certainly suggests that the gas turbine would have come about in time. However, the effect of the war was to accelerate this process. What would have been accomplished eventually as the various enabling technologies caught up was done in half the time, at enormous expense and effort.

In Britain, Frank Whittle, as an RAF cadet in 1928, also argued that a gas turbine would be better than a piston engine for the coming generation of high-altitude, high-speed aircraft he envisaged. It was two years later that he realised that much complication could be avoided in the design if the engine did not drive a propeller, but was used to produce a high-speed jet directly. This meant that the energy in the exhaust did not need to be extracted by a series of turbine stages, as in a propeller turbine, coupled to a shaft which will drive the airscrew. Instead, a single turbine stage would be matched to the power requirement of the compressor, which maintained the cycle, while the excess energy in the exhaust was used to produce a high-speed jet stream in the engine nozzle. It was this simplifying variation which persuaded backers to support Whittle, for it made the engine more attainable with the technology of the time. His company, Power Jets, was founded in 1935 with private capital raised in the City of London, while the Air Ministry contributed Whittle himself.

In Germany the initial idea for a jet engine came from the young physics student Pabst von Ohain, who developed from 1934 an engine with a centrifugal compressor. Ohain's idea was taken up by aircraft manufacturer Ernst Heinkel, and the engine first ran in 1937. Thus in both countries the jet engine was initially promoted by young men who were not in the mainstream aero-engine business. From there the pattern diverged. In Britain, in spite of the frequent suggestion that Whittle was ignored and badly treated, his company became the main government focus for the development of the jet, and his prototype flight engine, the W.1, first flew in the Gloster-Whittle E.28/39 in May 1941.

In Germany almost the opposite happened. Although von Ohain continued to work throughout the war on gas turbine projects, the RLM encouraged the mainstream manufacturers Junkers and BMW to start work on the new engine, while the AVA aerodynamic institute at Göttingen, equivalent in some respects to RAE Farnborough, contributed its research on axial compressor design to the companies. The first flight of the Messerschmitt Me 262 with jet engines took place in July 1942. However, the development programme did not take account of the enormous potential of the aircraft, and too few were finally deployed to affect the final air war over Germany.

In Britain, the major concentration of effort was placed on Whittle's Power Jets team, and RAE personnel were also seconded to work there. To produce the engine in quantity the Rover automobile company was brought into the scheme as manufacturer, with Power Jets as the design authority, but the impressive behaviour of the first Whittle W.1 experimental flight engine did not translate into a similarly trouble-free production unit. Neither did the hoped-for collaboration between Power Jets and Rover occur. The question of whether the fault lay with Rover has always been contentious, and some have cited the car company's lack of experience and its 'unnecessary' design changes, perhaps intended to 'Roverise' the design and safeguard a commercial position for the new turbine after the war. On the other hand, it has been suggested that the Power Jets W.2B engine was being put into production prematurely when design was far from settled.

Certainly the fighter planned for the engine, the F.9/40 or Gloster Meteor, teetered on the verge of cancellation, and the RAF view was that by the mid-war period, with the thrust then promised from the Rover/Whittle units, it would scarcely be a useful fighter at all. One incident which must have sapped official confidence was the propensity for the W.2B's impeller to burst at full speed. For a while reliable development engines were built up with imported impellers from General Electric in the USA. This was a curious state of affairs, since General Electric had started in jets when furnished with drawings for the Whittle design by the UK in October 1941 and, in one year, had made airworthy engines which flew in the Bell P-59A eight months before the British W.2B was flown in a Meteor prototype. Fortunately the programme was rescued by being placed in the hands of Rolls-Royce for development and production, and Gloster Meteors entered service with the RAF in July 1944. Although the Meteor was useful against V1 flying bombs, it was never deployed against the Me 262 over Germany. Indeed, it is perhaps fortunate that the two fighters never met, as the Meteor had a speed disadvantage of some 100mph at 20,000ft to the German type.

Nevertheless, the interesting fact remains that, although the jet engine was too late and produced in insufficient quantities to be of strategic significance – in the widest sense – during the war, it has proved to be one of the most significant inventions to come out of the Second World War.

Bibliography

Banks, F R, *I Kept No Diary* (Airlife, Shrewsbury, 1978). Engaging personal account from an engineer who helped promote 100-octane fuel and tetra-ethyl lead in the interwar period. During the war he ran engine programmes at the Ministry of Aircraft Production.

Golley, J, *Whittle, the True Story* (Airlife, Shrewsbury, 1987). Essentially an expanded version of Whittle's own 1953 account, developed by the author in association with Whittle.

Gunston, B, *By Jupiter! The Life of Sir Roy Fedden* (Royal Aeronautical Society, London, 1978). A readable account of the life of the Bristol chief designer. An enlarged and reprinted version is in preparation by Rolls-Royce Heritage.

Gunston, B, *Rolls-Royce Aero Engines* (Patrick Stephens, Sparkford, 1989).

Gunston, B, *World Encyclopaedia of Aero Engines* (Patrick Stephens, Sparkford, 1986).

Harvey-Bailey, A, *The Merlin in Practice* (Rolls-Royce Heritage Trust, Derby, 1981). A personal memoir from one of the great team of Merlin engineers.

Hooker, Sir Stanley, *Not Much of an Engineer* (Airlife, Shrewsbury, 1984). Hooker was one of the great figures in the British aero-engine industry. Much of the book deals with his postwar work in Bristol, but he joined Rolls-Royce in 1938 and worked during the war mainly on the Merlin superchargers.

Lloyd, Ian, *The Merlin at War* (Macmillan, London, 1978). Lloyd had unique access to Rolls-Royce records in the postwar period.

Nahum, A, Foster-Pegg, R, and Birch, D, *The Rolls-Royce Crecy* (Rolls-Royce Heritage Trust, Derby, 1994). A very complete account of this aero engine.

Postan, M M, Hay, D, and Scott, J D, *Design and Development of Weapons* (HMSO, London, 1968). One of the series of official histories commissioned after the war. It contains a good history of British gas turbine development based on the 'government side' of the story.

Ricardo, Sir Harry, *The High-speed Internal Combustion Engine* (Blackie & Son, London, 1953). Ricardo was the pre-eminent independent internal combustion engine expert in Britain in the interwar period, with a powerful influence on national aero-engine policy.

Schlaifer, R, and Heron, S D, *The Development of Aircraft Engines and Fuels* (Harvard University, Boston, 1950). The best work of history on aero engines written to date.

Setright, L K J, *The Power to Fly* (George Allen & Unwin, London, 1971). An eclectic but stimulating look at aero engines.

Smith, H, *Aircraft Piston Engines* (McGraw-Hill, New York, 1981). Its best sections are those on American air-cooled radials.

Whittle, Sir Frank, *Jet* (Frederick Muller, London, 1953). Indispensible reading.

Comparative views of the Curtiss XSB2C-1 Helldiver prototype and a production SB2C-1 illustrate the drastic changes made to the design in an effort to rectify its faults and shortcomings.

11
Testing and Ferrying
Capt Eric Brown and Patrick Hassell

Flight Testing in Wartime

The threat of war will inevitably speed up the rate of progress in national aviation technology, but when war is actually declared such progress will accelerate to a top priority. The aggressor will always start with the advantage of intent, but those he attacks may well have superior assets such as industrial capacity, strategic mineral resources, and so forth, and will seek to develop these with all possible speed. Therefore to both combatants time is of the essence.

In aviation, the areas of technological development in the Second World War were largely dictated by the type of enemy threat, and concerned both attack and defence. Geography was a prime factor in determining the parameters for dealing with the threat. For example, Britain's proximity to Germany was totally different from that of the USA to Japan, while the Soviet Union had the unique situation of virtually bordering her major enemies.

Experimental flight testing plays a prime role in advancing aviation technology, and this was realised by all the major combatants, who had remarkably similar concepts of how to conduct such activity. Each had central government combined military/civilian bodies with overall control of all aviation technological resources and aircraft production. Flight testing, both experimental and production, was undertaken by aircraft manufacturing companies, but experimental research flight testing was mainly confined to specialist centres staffed by scientists and professional test pilots. In Great Britain these centres were located at the Royal Aircraft Establishment (RAE) at Farnborough, the Aeroplane and Armament Experimental Establishment (A&AEE) at Boscombe Down and the Marine Aircraft Experimental Establishment (MAEE) at Felixstowe; in Germany at Rechlin (Neubrandenburg), Peenemünde (Karlshagen) and Travemünde (Lübeck); in the USA at Wright Field, Ohio, the US Naval Air Test Center, Patuxent River, Maryland, and the USAAF Test Center at Muroc, California. In Japan, the Soviet Union and Italy, more reliance was placed on the manufacturing companies, with only limited test facilities outside their spheres.

The role of the aircraft manufacturers was obviously crucial in all of these national systems, but since such companies concentrated their resources on their own products, it was vital for the research establishments to keep them informed of technological advances by distribution of scientific reports. On the other hand, the manufacturers could turn to those establishments for help as troubleshooters if their products ran into difficulties, so liaison between the respective test pilots and scientific staffs was of the utmost importance.

Operational requirements

The design of any military aircraft is normally initiated as the result of an Operational Requirement (OR) issued by the Air, Naval or Army Staff as relevant. That OR then becomes the focal point for manufacturers' interested in competing for the design contract. It is therefore essential that the military staffs have close liaison with the research centres, so that they are aware of the latest state of the aviation art known to these founts of knowledge. Thus both the pilots working for manufacturers and those attached to research centres are made fully aware of the OR in all its aspects.

In the matter of design there were differing national criteria to be observed, particularly in structural stressing, where Britain, for example, set the most exacting standards. It was also important for all concerned to study any intelligence reports on enemy aircraft construction and performance, equipment and tactics, and also to keep abreast of reports that would throw light on political thinking that might affect strategic decisions. For example, the Japanese accent on attack at all costs meant sacrificing defensive measures such as armour plating protection, bullet-proof windscreens and self-sealing fuel tanks in fighters such as the ubiquitous Mitsubishi A6M Zero (see page 268).

One of the methods employed to keep test pilots *au fait* with what was going on 'at the sharp end', was to give them short operational attachments in front-line squadrons, or at least extended visits to such units.

Test pilot training

At the outbreak of the Second World War the selection of test pilots was a haphazard affair, being mainly by recommendation from superior officers in the military field, who recognised outstanding flying ability and an equable temperament. This military source of supply was virtually the only one that could provide the experience for such a career. In 1943 Britain sought to regularise the selection and training of test pilots by setting up a training school, open to military and civilian pilots sponsored by aircraft manufacturing companies. The courses encompassed both ground school and flying instruction, and the concept was copied by the other leading aviation

A captured Mitsubishi Zero wearing American markings undergoes evaluation. Japanese aircraft lacked the defensive armour and self-sealing tanks of their Allied counterparts, trading protection for speed. The Zero ruled the Pacific skies for the first three years of war.

nations, although most did not achieve this until after the war ended.

An immediate benefit from this system was that graduates of such a school knew each other well and kept contact after they dispersed, so that a much closer liaison developed between the test pilots at the various research centres and aircraft companies.

Manufacturer experimental flight testing

Aircraft and engine manufacturers were usually only involved in experimental test flying of their own products, although they were occasionally given contracts to test equipment that would be compatible with their products.

The testing of prototype aircraft included the initial flight and subsequent refinement of the handling characteristics by both aerodynamic and engineering changes to a standard that would make the aircraft suitable to undertake its acceptance trials by the military. This could be a relatively straightforward procedure, as in the case of the superb Supermarine Spitfire, or a long, exasperating process, as with the Curtiss Helldiver, which in

eighteen months of development suffered 899 major design changes. These in turn necessitated many thousands of minor changes, yet still the end result was an inefficient aeroplane.

Generally, the gestation time for an aeroplane is dictated by its size. The tiny Heinkel He 162 jet interceptor fighter made its first flight a mere ninety days after the issue of the OR, whereas the Heinkel He 177 four-engined bomber took almost two years to achieve a similar milestone.

The flight testing of new-design piston engines was only undertaken after considerable bench running, following which the engine was matched with an already proven airframe. The flight tests mainly concerned reliability, performance in terms of power output, fuel consumption and flexibility of response to throttle movements and to aerial manoeuvres likely to be met in operational conditions. These tests then had to be repeated in either actual or simulated extremes of climate and environment likely to be encountered.

The design time for a piston engine was, as for

Both Britain and Germany sought to investigate the aerodynamics of new large aircraft by building piloted, flying scale replicas. The Short S.31, a half-scale Stirling bomber powered by Pobjoy radial engines, was small enough to be tested in the RAE's 24ft windtunnel in 1940, as seen here, as well as being flown on manufacturer's trials.

aeroplanes, generally dictated by size, and was of the order of one-and-a-half to three years. However, such engines were more likely to be subjected to continuous development during their lifetime than the aeroplanes they powered, as the military strove to keep ahead or at least abreast of contemporary enemy aircraft.

The wartime ratio of aircraft manufacturers to engine manufacturers was generally in the region of 3.5:1, and most had a multiple number of factories but concentrated the experimental flight test facilities at one or two sites.

Experimental research flight testing

The core of a nation's technological effort in aviation lies in its pure research centre, which is usually civilian controlled, with a large scientific staff and a cadre of military test pilots, although some also have their own permanent civilian test pilots. In particular such centres were normally equipped with low-speed and high-speed wind tunnels. Examples of pure research centres in the Second World War were the RAE in Britain, the

National Advisory Committee for Aeronautics (NACA) Aeronautical Laboratory at Langley Field, Virginia, in the USA, and the Aerodynamische Versuchsanstalt (Aerodynamic Test Establishment) at Göttingen in Germany.

In wartime, the programmes of flight testing at those establishments were necessarily very flexible, to meet the varied and unpredictable demands that poured in from the military, but apart from the *ad hoc* element there was a steady flow of pure research going on, the guidelines for which emanated from government-appointed bodies of eminent scientists. In Britain that body was the Aeronautical Research Council (ARC), in the USA it was NACA, and in Germany the Technisches Amt (Technical Office) of the Reichsluftfahrtministerium (RLM or Air Ministry).

The general pattern of research being undertaken was remarkably similar in these three countries, while Japan, the Soviet Union and Italy were some rungs lower on the ladder of sophistication. This becomes apparent when the pattern is examined in detail.

Messerschmitt Bf 109E-3 'White 1' of JG 76 forced-landed at Woerth in the Bas-Rhin Department of France on 22 November 1939. Restored to airworthiness, it was tested by both the French and British, and is seen here under test in England as AE479 in 1940.

Performance comparisons of Axis and Allied aircraft yielded data that could be of great value to combat pilots. Here a Republic P-47D Thunderbolt leads captured Focke-Wulf Fw 190A-4 PM679 in a flypast during evaluation.

Assessment of enemy aircraft

Enemy aircraft fell into both Allied and Axis hands as a result of combat damage or malfunction causing a forced landing, navigational errors leading to an un-scheduled landing on enemy territory, or, in rare cases, defection by the crew. Such aircraft were given a full technical examination whilst being made flyable in readiness for handing over to the research test pilots, who would 'wring them out' as a matter of urgency to assess the strong and the weak points in handling. These were immediately communicated to the front-line squadrons

so that they could capitalise on them.

A classic example of this was the RAE's testing of the German Messerschmitt Bf 109 fighter, which revealed that if lured into a really tight turn whilst attacking a Hurricane or Spitfire, its wing slats would snatch open unevenly and ruin the pilot's gunnery aim. Also it showed that, if dived to 440mph, the Bf 109's elevators virtually froze solid, and at low level this would cause it to dive into the sea or the ground. It was apparent, too, that in a dive attack the German pilot would have

Another pair undergoing comparison: Messerschmitt Me 410A-3 TF209 and a de Havilland Mosquito NF XVII.

difficulty keeping his aim straight, as there was no rudder trimmer fitted to the aircraft, and there would consequently be a strong tendency to skid. On the plus side, the Bf 109 had an unusually steep angle of climb, which made it almost impossible for an attacker to follow.

At about this same period a similar routine was being conducted at Rechlin, where the German testing of a Spitfire IIA gave rise to two criticisms of note, namely the heaviness of the lateral control, which resulted in an inferior rate of roll, especially in comparison with the Focke-Wulf Fw 190 fighter, and secondly the proneness of the Merlin engine to cut when bunted into a steep dive. RAE pilots had already noted this shortcoming during mock dogfights with the Bf 109, whose Daimler Benz direct fuel injection engine continued to run smoothly under all conditions of manoeuvring flight.

As the war progressed, the scope of this type of work broadened considerably, as it was realised how effective it was not only in helping one's own combat pilots, but also as a valuable intelligence pointer to the enemy's technological state-of-the-art with regard to aerodynamic developments, engineering construction methods, the use of strategic metals and minerals, and armament and engine developments.

Up to the end of 1942 it seemed that Allied and Axis aviation technologies were running neck-and-neck, but this false surmise was soon to become apparent when photo-reconnaissance pictures of Peenemünde-West, taken in early 1943, showed long scorch marks on the grass, and then later the shape of a tiny sweptback tailless aircraft — the first clues to the existence of the sensational rocket-powered Messerschmitt Me 163 interceptor fighter. It might be asked whether British lack of knowledge of this development was evidence of a failure in Allied intelligence work, but subsequent events have shown that German security was generally incredibly tight under its repressive political regime.

Transonic flight testing

The phenomenon of compressibility of airflow over a wing at high speeds was well known to aerodynamicists in the 1930s, but the extent of its effects on the controllability of an aircraft was still largely unknown at the outbreak of the Second World War. However, the problem became urgent as aircraft performance increased and they flew faster and higher.

Compressibility effects occur when the airflow past an aircraft reaches the speed of sound, but it is not necessary for the aircraft to be travelling at that speed, because the space it occupies causes the air to accelerate slightly in order to get past. The speed of sound in air varies with temperature, and is about 760mph (1,222km/h) at sea level and only 680mph (1,094km/h) at 30,000ft (9,150m), so it is of help to pilots in

particular for compressibility to be expressed in terms of Mach number (a fraction indicating the speed of an aircraft divided by the speed of sound) rather than indicated airspeed.

The Machmeter is a standard fit in modern high-performance aircraft, but it was only fitted to experimental aircraft in the Second World War, and not in any operational aircraft. This did not present any difficulties while aerial combat remained predominantly at low and medium altitudes, but the advent of the Boeing B-17 Flying Fortress in European skies, operating at altitudes of about 30,000ft, brought a host of problems for the long-range escort fighters, especially those which had to fly above the bomber stream as top cover and then dive down on the enemy fighters climbing up to attack the Fortresses. In these dives, Lockheed P-38 Lightnings, Republic P-47 Thunderbolts and North American P-51 Mustangs occasionally got into serious control difficulties, and some suffered fatal consequences in uncontrollable 'graveyard dives'.

Already in 1943 an intensive programme of transonic testing had been initiated at the RAE, involving the Spitfire and the three American fighters. It revealed grave shortcomings in the P-38 and P-47, whose critical Mach numbers were only 0.70 and 0.74 respectively, while those of the Merlin-engined P-51 and Spitfire were 0.80 and 0.88. The shock stall, a breakaway of the airflow from the top of the wing causing loss of lift and increase of drag, usually evidenced itself by a nose-down change of trim requiring increasingly heavy stick forces to counteract it until these forces taxed the pilot to his physical limit, which thus determined the critical Mach number. For operational pilots the risk of getting into compressibility trouble was exacerbated by the absence of a Machmeter. Their only alternative was to do some quick mental computing of height against indicated airspeed — hardly possible in the heat of battle.

This type of research flight testing involved much probing of the unknown, and it was also done under pressure to get data on both critical and tactical Mach numbers (the latter being the maximum Mach number at which the aircraft could be safely manoeuvred), so that these could be passed on to front-line units. It was high-risk flying, and casualties were commensurately high, but so, too, were the stakes in this gamble.

The Germans had made a significant breakthrough in the region of transonic flight by using sweptback wings to delay the onset of the shock stall, with highly successful results. Why the Allies missed out on this advance is a mystery, because the German aerodynamicist Professor Busemann gave a lecture on the subject at a conference in Rome in 1935, attended by scientists from Britain and America. Postwar testing by the RAE of the Messerschmitt Me 262 fighter with only 28° of sweepback showed that it had a critical Mach number of 0.86

and a tactical Mach number of 0.83, compared with the Spitfire's 0.80 tactical limit.

Stability and control were of course the main work-load of pure research flight testing, and wartime endeav-ours were aimed at producing perfect harmony of control and three-axis stability particularly suited to the duty of the aircraft type. Above all, determined efforts were made to lighten the controls on aircraft capable of transonic flight. Hydraulically powered controls gave the optimum answer, but care had to be taken that pilot 'feel' was not lost and that stability was not compromised; also in the event of hydraulic failure it was essential that a manageable manual reversion system was available.

By the end of the war it was clear that the so-called 'sound barrier' was capable of being broken, but not by piston-engined aircraft because of the excessive drag effect of the propeller.

The advent of jet and rocket propulsion

The birth of practical jet propulsion can be dated with certainty to 1930, when Frank Whittle patented his specification for a gas turbine jet engine. When theory was translated into reality and the Gloster E.28/39 made its first flight, on 15 May 1941, it was believed in Britain that this was the world's first jet aircraft. However, German security had managed to hide from the world that they had knowledge of the Whittle patent and had forged ahead with their own development to get their first jet aeroplane, the Heinkel He 178, into the air on 27 August 1939. That success was followed on 2 April 1941 by the first flight of the Heinkel He 280, the world's first twin-engine jet aeroplane.

In Britain, the development of the Whittle jet engine was painfully slow owing to lack of official support, and the E.28/39 did not get to the RAE until early 1943. Up to that point all flight testing had been undertaken by the Gloster Aircraft Company, which used this experience to

Although the British believed that the Gloster E.28/39, seen here at RAE Farnborough, was the world's first jet aircraft, the Germans had beaten them into the air with their Heinkel He 178.

produce the Meteor twin-jet fighter, examples of which reached RAE in late 1943.

The Whittle engine was of the centrifugal compressor type, a choice largely dictated by the simplicity of the de-sign and the need for reliability at that stage in the state of the art. The first German jet engines were likewise of the centrifugal type, but they changed rapidly to the more complicated but more streamlined axial-flow type, Britain eventually did in the postwar years.

In the USA, whither a Whittle engine had been sent, development then started on a twin-engine fighter pow-ered by General Electric Company-built Whittle 1-A turbojets. The first flight of the Bell P-59 Airacomet was made at Muroc on 1 October 1942, and an example was received at the RAE on 5 November 1943. The RAE jet stable was completed in early 1944 by a de Havilland Spider Crab (later to be renamed Vampire), powered by a single de Havilland Goblin turbojet.

Fritz Schäfer makes the first powered take-off of the world's first twin-engine jet aircraft, the Heinkel He 280V1, at Marienehe on 2 April 1941. Note the uncowled HeS 8 turbojet engines.

The Arado Ar 234 V5 takes off from a trolley in 1943. This reconnaissance-bomber suffered from its short-life Junkers axial-flow jet engines.

Jet flight testing at the RAE mainly covered engine performance and aircraft behaviour in high-speed flight. At that stage of jet engine development, the main problems were connected with fuel flow and consumption, and engine acceleration response to throttle movements. Erratic fuel flow or rapid throttle movements could cause the engine to 'flame out', and so a considerable effort was directed to producing a reliable in-flight re-light system.

The jet engine had of course stepped up aircraft performance dramatically, so the emphasis was on transonic flight behaviour. The characteristics remained basically much the same as for piston-engine aircraft, except that they tended to happen more readily because of the greater acceleration of the streamlined airframe and the fact that the jet engine was at its most efficient at high altitude. Machmeters thus became a mandatory fit to all Allied jets. Furthermore it was discovered that one of the piloting problems on the E.28/39 was slowing down the

aircraft in flight, particularly for landing, owing to its lack of drag, so airbrakes became a necessity for future designs.

At Rechlin the Germans were concentrating their efforts on the Arado Ar 234 reconnaissance-bomber and the Messerschmitt Me 262 fighter. Both had twin axial-flow jet engines of Junkers design. These engines proved to have very short lives because of lack of suitable heat-resistant strategic metals in Germany, and they had a low safety factor in the event of a crash as they used 87 octane gasoline with a 5 per cent mix of lubricating oil as fuel.

In their haste to get their jets into operational service the Germans did not explore the transonic flight region as thoroughly as they might otherwise have done, and as a result their jets had neither Machmeters nor airbrakes fitted. However, at the end of the day they were startlingly innovatory aircraft, and in the Me 262 they had potentially the most formidable aircraft of the Second World War.

Experiments with rocket-powered aircraft were predominantly carried out by Germany from as early as 1928, using at first solid-fuel rockets and then progessing to the liquid-fuel type. As an outcome of this work, the first operational rocket fighter in the world was developed in Germany, the end result being the tailless Messerschmitt Me 163 with 23° of sweepback to its wings. The airframe owed much to the experiments undertaken in the late 1930s by the Deutsches Forschungsinstitut für Segelflug (DFS) (German Gliding Research Institute) at Darmstadt, but the rocket flight testing took place at Peenemünde-West by ex-DFS test pilots serving in the Luftwaffe.

The Me 163 represents a landmark in aviation technology, although it was more of a threat to its own pilots

The 'startlingly innovatory' Me 262 was probably the most formidable aircraft of the Second World War, even if it did lack a Machmeter and airbrakes. This Me 262A-1a was surrendered on its maiden flight by a defecting company test pilot on 31 March 1945.

than to the enemy, mainly due to the highly volatile rocket fuels and the difficulties inherent in having to make a fast deadstick landing on a skid after every sortie.

Troubleshooting

A considerable amount of wartime flight testing concerned sorting out problems that degraded an aircraft's operational performance, and these usually involved panic remedies. A typical case was the cutting of the Merlin engine in the early Spitfires when they were bunted into a dive, and this put the British fighter at a disadvantage against the Bf 109 with its direct-fuel-injection Daimler Benz DB 600 series engines. On receiving the field reports, RAE Farnborough immediately went to panic stations and a brilliant female scientist, Miss Beatrice Shilling, very rapidly came up with a simple solution in the form of a small metal disc with a hole in the middle. When this orifice plate was brazed into the Spitfire's fuel pipe it enabled fuel to flow in normal conditions, but if acceleration was applied to the fuel in an axial direction the disc prevented the fuel surging away from one end and thus starving the engine even momentarily of fuel. Some urgent flight testing was necessary to get the disc hole size right and prove the system. In the event the effect of 'Miss Shilling's Orifice' on RAF morale was electrifying.

Another such panic fix, by the Americans, was the fitting of underwing dive recovery flaps to their early wartime fighters, the Lightning and Thunderbolt, which both exhibited dangerous compressibility characteristics resulting in loss of control in even shallow dives at high altitude. These flaps were carefully positioned at a point on the wing undersurface so that, when activated, they imparted a nose-up pitch to the aircraft, aiding recovery from the dive. Again much flight testing was required to determine the optimum flap position and prove the concept.

A different kind of troubleshooting consisted of countering some unexpected enemy innovations that presented a dire threat. Such a device was the German V1 pulse-jet pilotless flying bomb launched against England in the summer of 1944 from coastal launch ramps on the European mainland.

The V1 normally flew at about 1,000–2,000ft (300–600m) above ground level at 400mph (640km/h). Since no contemporary Allied fighters could match this performance, some drastic action was required. The engine manufacturers proposed boosting their engines to a much higher power for short 3min bursts, using 150 octane aromatic fuel instead of the normal 100 octane. Four fighters, the Mustang III, Spitfire XIV, Tempest V and Mosquito IV, were then tested at RAE with highly satisfactory results, and the V1 was effectively countered, 1,771 being destroyed in the air.

In troubleshooting, the aviation doctors played a significant role, particularly in the matter of developing pressure cabins for high-altitude flying, anti-'g' suits for combat flying, and ejection seats. The flight testing of such equipment was mainly done by experimental research test pilots, often with the doctors acting as test observers, and in some cases even as the test pilots themselves.

Marine flight testing

All of the Second World War combatants operated marine aircraft, but the percentage number of these was very small in comparison to the large forces of landplanes. Seaplanes and flying boats naturally have to be

Supermarine Seafire IIC MB141, with a tropical filter, makes a rocket-assisted take-off at RAE Farnborough in 1943. It transpired that there was little need for assistance, as the Seafire needed an into-wind deck speed of only 5mph to become airborne.

A Seafire is launched from Farnborough's rocket catapult. The two-colour quartered circles on the nose and rear fuselage were for calibration and film analysis purposes. A Bristol Buckingham dominates the foreground.

flight tested from appropriate marine establishments with sheltered mooring areas and long stretches of open water for taxiing, take-off and landing trials.

The critical factors in marine testing are ascertaining the take-off and landing characteristics. These tests determine the limitations of sea states and wind conditions for both take-off and landing, during which the main bugbear is the risk of porpoising, a dangerous motion which can lead to loss of the aircraft.

Specialist flight testing

Some areas of flight testing require the pilots to have in-depth experience of the special aspects involved, particularly aircraft carrier operations, which played key roles in the Pacific war and significant ones in the European theatre. Landing an aeroplane on the flight deck of an aircraft carrier is probably the most demanding task a pilot is called on to undertake as a matter of routine, so assessment of a naval aircraft's flying qualities require an experienced deck landing pilot. In consequence the American, British and Japanese navies had their own cadres of test pilots.

Naval aircraft require their own very special features: excellent view ahead in the landing attitude, a robust and energy absorbing undercarriage, effective controls at very low speeds, innocuous stall characteristics, high drag in the landing configuration, high lift in the take-off configuration and good ditching qualities.

Experimental research flight testing of naval aircraft included their initial deck landings and take-offs, catapult and rocket-assisted take-offs, low windspeed landings (for escort carrier operations) and crash barrier engagement. So important were these tests that the Royal Navy in 1943 assigned HMS *Pretoria Castle* as a dedicated carrier for trials of aircraft and equipment, with training as a secondary function. This vessel continued to operate in these roles until late 1945.

During the Second World War the landing speeds and weights of naval aircraft conducted at NATC Patuxent River in the USA and RAE Farnborough in the UK was closely co-ordinated, since cross-operation of American and British aircraft carriers was essential in war. Innovatory naval aviation developments included the British scheme for merchant shipborne catapult fighters for convoy protection, and the American system of single-point catapulting from carrier decks, which eliminated the weighty cradle and fuselage spools of the old system.

Japan was very active in naval aviation and produced a particularly successful shipborne naval fighter in the Zero. The Japanese Navy's flight testing infrastructure closely resembled that of Great Britain, maybe because both are island nations.

Germany and Italy both showed an initial interest in naval aviation and each built an aircraft carrier that never went into service. Neither power attempted to design a specialist carrier aircraft, but intended to adapt air force aeroplanes for carrier work. Naval aviation flight testing was therefore virtually non-existent in these countries.

The Soviet Union, with a huge coastline spanning half the world, had decided it could defend its territory with land-based aircraft, and showed no active interest in carrier aviation until the postwar era.

Production flight testing

Hundreds of thousands of aircraft of hundreds of different types were built in the Second World War, and though it might be imagined that factories producing a particular type would make them all perfect copies of the original, this was far from the case. Discrepancies between handmade components, and rigging differences in both engine and airframe manufacture, made it a necessity to check each aircraft to a set of standards which ultimately had to be verified by flight testing before acceptance. The immensity of the task of such wartime testing can be gauged from the following maximum production runs of the main combatant nations:

Country	Aircraft type	Numbers built
Soviet Union	Ilyushin Il-2	36,163
Germany	Messerschmitt Bf 109	33,000+
Great Britain	Spitfire/Seafire	22,759
USA	B-24 Liberator	19,203
Japan	Mitsubishi Zero	10,938

Obviously a large number of production test pilots was needed to meet this task, but because of the type of flying required, recruitment from the ranks of civilian pilots was possible. The permanent core of production test pilots could be expanded by the secondment of service pilots, and indeed this was a widely used option, since aircraft production rates fluctuated with the fortunes of war.

The pressures on production test pilots were high in wartime because of the constant demand for aircraft necessary to make good operational losses and to build up new squadrons. Such testing also had its own kind of dangers, as can be seen from the record of the chief production test pilot at Vickers-Supermarine's factory at Castle Bromwich (Birmingham), who had 127 forced landings in six years of production flight testing of Spitfires.

Aircraft Ferrying in the Second World War

From the earliest days of military aviation there has been a need for 'ferrying', the unglamorous task of delivering aircraft from their manufacturers or returning them to depots for overhaul. But the vast numbers of aircraft used in the Second World War and the thousands of miles which frequently separated the Allies' factories from the theatres of operations made ferrying an unprecedented logistical task. This led to the creation of specialist ferrying organisations, all of which relied heavily on civilian experience. By 1945 they had made a remarkable contribution to the war effort, with over 600,000 delivery flights, and in the process they inadvertently transformed the air transport scene.

The first of these new organisations was born as Hitler's troops prepared to invade Poland. Gerard d'Erlanger, a director of British Airways, had been promoting a scheme to use older private pilots like himself for communications flying in wartime, and at the end of August 1939 the Air Ministry agreed that d'Erlanger should invite suitable pilots to become 'Air Transport

Auxiliaries' employed by British Airways. Within ten days the first respondents had been flight tested, and after a brief conversion course twenty pilots were sent to reinforce the RAF's two small 'ferry pools'. All were men, but under pressure from experienced women pilots keen to 'do their bit' the Air Ministry allowed Pauline Gower to form a small, female ferry pool at Hatfield with the mundane job of flying de Havilland Tiger Moths to storage units. This unit attracted publicity and chauvinist criticism, but by months of reliable work the women overcame most prejudices and were allowed to fly more advanced types.

In February 1940 Air Transport Auxiliary (ATA) pilots were withdrawn from the RAF units to form a new ferry pool, administered by BOAC[1]. As the ATA's Commandant, d'Erlanger then had forty-three men and nine women pilots working for him. In the short days of that first winter they delivered about 100 aircraft a week. By 1944 there were fourteen pools, together averaging 1,500 deliveries weekly. But that figure masks the great peaks of demand, as in the month before D-day or after long spells of impossible winter weather. Then there could be over 500 deliveries a day, some pilots flying five or six aircraft, with a taxi flight in an Avro Anson between each collection. In the ATA's six-year life its aircrew made over 308,000 deliveries of machines ranging from ancient Hawker Hart biplanes to Handley Page Halifax bombers and Gloster Meteor jets.

The 'Ancient Tattered Airmen' and 'Always Terrified Airwomen' came from many backgrounds and included stockbrokers, grocers, farmers, journalists and even a conjuror. Most were from Britain and the Commonwealth, but there were many Americans, and representatives of two dozen other nations. Pauline Gower finally achieved complete equality for the women pilots, who,

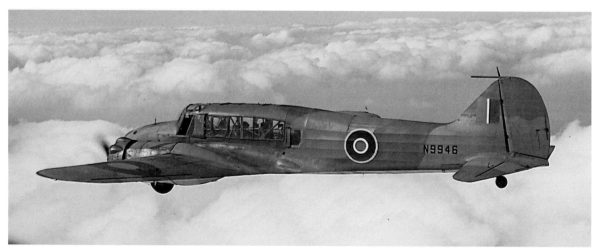

Although the Avro Anson I was operationally obsolete at the outbreak of war, it proved invaluable in many secondary roles. Ansons like N9946, seen here in 1944, were the mainstay of the ATA's air-taxi fleet, distributing ferry pilots to airfields across Britain and collecting up to eight of them for the trip back to base at the end of a long day.

Lockheed Hudson patrol bombers comprised almost 70 per cent of the 593 aircraft safely delivered in the first year of the Atlantic ferry service. Here an early batch of Mk.I Hudsons is prepared for the Big Trip; the crudely-blanked rear-fuselage cutouts are for the Boulton Paul turrets, which were installed upon the aeroplanes' arrival in Britain.

like the men, were expected to handle any aircraft of the Classes for which they had qualified. Thus pilots used to Hurricanes and Tomahawks might be sent to collect Typhoons without ever having seen one, with only the ATA's Pilot's Notes to warn them of handling problems and guide them round the controls' eccentricities[2]. They flew without radio or navigation aids in all but the worst weather, and sometimes in aircraft classed 'NEA' (Not Essentially Airworthy). Yet the pilot-error accident rate, including the minor mishaps, was only 0.25 per cent. Inevitably there were some fatal accidents. The ATA lost 153 aircrew over its six-year existence, about 10 per cent of those who served. Many accidents were caused by the weather closing in, as happened to Amy Johnson, who drowned in the Thames, the first of fourteen ATA women to die flying.

Lord Beaverbrook, who took over responsibility for aircraft production in May 1940, ensured that the ATA expanded rapidly to release RAF pilots for operational flying. In that crucial summer Beaverbrook adopted another idea for ferrying which had far greater long-term consequences. Many American-built aircraft shipped across the Atlantic were being lost to the U-boats, in-

cluding Lockheed Hudsons, which theoretically had sufficient range to reach Britain from Newfoundland. But the North Atlantic weather was still a great unknown, particularly in winter. In two decades it had been flown less than 100 times, and although Pan American had carried the first passengers across in 1939, a reliable year-round service was thought to be ten years away. But Beaverbrook wanted aircraft, not reliability, and flying them over might reduce the delivery time by three months. Some air marshals said that half the aircraft would be lost in winter, but George Woods-Humphery, ex-managing director of Imperial Airways, and his pilots with Atlantic experience, such as Wilcockson and Bennett[3], believed it was possible. Beaverbrook backed them, and under the wing of Canadian Pacific Railways they set up the small Atlantic Ferry Organisation (ATFERO) in Montreal. They recruited pilots and radio operators, mostly civilians from Canada and the USA, and when the first seven long-range Hudson IIIs reached Canada (towed across the border by horses to circumvent the letter of the US Neutrality Act) the crews were ready for the 'Big Trip'. Led by Bennett, they left Gander, Newfoundland, on the cold clear evening of 10

The promising D.H.95 Flamingo was just entering production at the outbreak of war, and de Havilland was allowed to complete only sixteen of its first all-metal airliners. Eight were operated by BOAC from its Egyptian base at Almaza, but by 1944, with American transports more readily available, shortage of spares led to their retirement. Here, G-AFYF King Alfred *of BOAC is seen in the Middle East. Delivered to Cairo in August 1940, it was shipped back to Britain in 1945.*

November 1940, flying by night in loose formation. Despite a towering Atlantic weather front and some other problems, all seven reached Northern Ireland safely. Beaverbrook was delighted. When the second and third groups also arrived safely, ATFERO's future expansion was assured.

Before those first transatlantic deliveries, another equally urgent ferry operation had begun, in a very different climate. After the fall of France, aircraft for the Middle East had to be shipped around the Cape. By offloading the aircraft at Takoradi in the Gold Coast (now Ghana), assembling them, and flying them across Africa

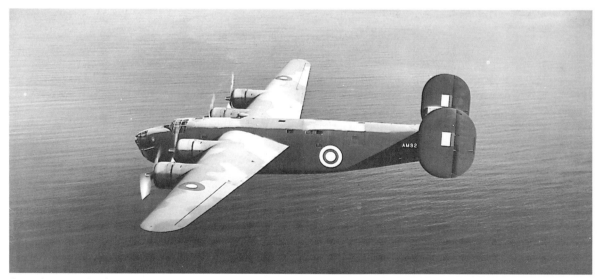

In early 1941 the Consolidated B-24 Liberator bomber was the only landplane able to fly the Atlantic regularly in both directions. The early production aircraft were used to start the Return Ferry Service taking ATFERO crews back to Canada in considerable discomfort. Their many VIP passengers fared no better on the freezing seventeen-hour trips, but were safe from the U-boats below. This Mk.I was brought across by an Anglo-Canadian-American crew, making landfall in just over eight hours.

In spring 1941 BOAC received nine new Lockheed Model 18 Lodestars to supplement its smaller Model 14s on the vital Takoradi–Egypt ferry route. As the crucial role of air transport at last became appreciated, more of these fast aircraft were obtained from US owners. Stripped out and fitted with bench seats for eighteen passengers, they formed the backbone of BOAC's African operations throughout the war. This example, G-AGCM Lake Mariut, previously NC33617 on the US civil register, is seen over Cairo.

in stages, demand on shipping was dramatically reduced. This route had been opened by Imperial Airways in 1936, but conditions were still extremely primitive, and for the Hurricane pilots, led in small formations by one or two Blenheims with navigators, the great stretches of empty desert must have seemed as daunting as the Atlantic. Nonetheless, by June 1941 over 150 aircraft a month were being sent 'up the line' to Egypt, and by the time Axis forces were expelled from Africa in May 1943 the RAF had ferried more than 5,300 aircraft across the continent.

A major obstacle to expansion had been returning ferry crews to Takoradi. Transport aircraft had been largely neglected in the RAF's prewar expansion, and though BOAC's D.H.95 Flamingos and Lockheed 14s shuttled across the continent taking vital spares and VIPs

to Cairo and returning with ferry crew, they had too few machines. So in mid-1941 Pan American Airways was contracted to operate a trans-African airline service, and later to deliver lend-lease transports and bombers direct from the USA to Egypt using the chain of airfields they were building (with US government finance) through the Caribbean and Brazil.

There was a similar problem in returning ATFERO crews to Canada until the arrival of the first six Consolidated LB-30A Liberators in the spring of 1941. These aircraft had unprecedented range, often flying direct from Scotland to Montreal. They transformed aircrew turnaround times, but for men huddled in sleeping bags for seventeen hours in the freezing draughts of the plywood-floored bomb bay, the flights were no picnic. Contract pilots claimed that they were not paid to deliver

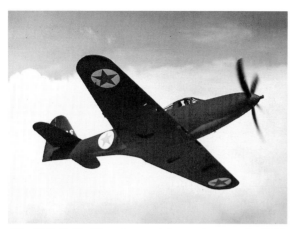

The Bell P-63 Kingcobra and its predecessor, the P-39 Airacobra, were unusual in having the Allison V-1710 engine behind the cockpit, allowing the installation of a 37mm cannon firing through the propeller hub. Nearly three-quarters of the 3,303 Kingcobras built were supplied to the Soviet Union, most being ferried via Alaska. This machine bears the USA's interpretation of the Soviet national markings it would soon carry.

aircraft but to take the trip back. BOAC took responsibility for this Return Ferry Service (RFS) in September 1941 and operated it until the end of the war, making over 2,000 crossings. This was the first year-round airline service across the North Atlantic, but those enduring the discomforts of the bomb bay (including many VIPs) might have disputed the term 'service'.

The Lend-Lease Bill of March 1941 presaged a rapid increase in the flow of bombers for the RAF, and

President Roosevelt realised that the USA would have to support their delivery. The formation of the USAAF Ferrying Command on 29 May 1941 was the first step, relieving ATFERO crews by flying aircraft from the factories to their US 'points of departure', where Roosevelt wanted them to be handed over directly to the RAF. Consequently ATFERO became RAF Ferry Command in July 1941 under Air Chief Marshal Bowhill, who the year before had been a pessimistic opponent of Atlantic ferrying. Bowhill fully recognised ATFERO's remarkable achievements, however, and made few changes; Ferry Command[4] remained a primarily civilian organisation under RAF leadership. By the time it disbanded on 16 February 1946 it had delivered some 10,000 aircraft across the oceans. The final loss rate was only 2 per cent, but even this meant that over 500 aircrew had died.

In spring 1941 the Americans proposed building more airfields in Canada, Greenland and Iceland. Besides handling the projected expansion, they would allow medium-range aircraft to be ferried without extra fuel tanks. Survey flights by Capt Elliot Roosevelt, the President's son, and by ATFERO, resulted in the selection of sites at Goose Bay in Labrador and the Greenland fjord locations later famous as Bluie West One and Bluie West Eight. The pace was remarkable. The Canadians' first ship reached remote Goose Bay in September 1941; the first aircraft landed on 9 December.

That autumn Roosevelt bent the US neutrality laws further, authorising Ferrying Command deliveries to the Middle East along the Pan American route, where more new airfields were being constructed. Thus before Pearl Harbor a start had been made on the new global infra-

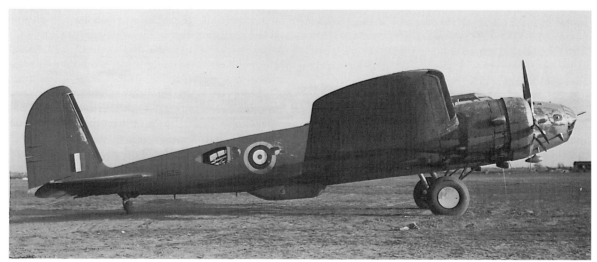

Twenty Boeing B-17 Flying Fortress Is, of which AN529 was typical, were delivered to the RAF by ATFERO in spring 1941, but these early models proved ineffective on operations. It was not until 1 July 1942 that a USAAF B-17 flew into Prestwick, the first of thousands for the 8th Air Force. Most were flown by crews who had never crossed water wider than the Great Lakes.

With its efficient, long-span 'Davis wing' and great range, the B-24 Liberator proved invaluable as a transport aircraft, whether flying Winston Churchill to Russia or anti-tank shells to Egypt. Two freighter variants of the famous bomber were built, the C-87 seen here and the C-109, a specialised tanker mainly used to carry fuel 'over the Hump' into China.

structure. However, real war exposed the logistic difficulties facing the USAAF even in its small initial deployments. There were no overseas fuel dumps, maintenance crews or spares stocks, no weather service and few experienced aircrew. Bombers to reinforce the Philippines had to be sent 'the wrong way', via the trans-African route and India, and after two months only forty-one of the sixty-five dispatched had reached the Southwest Pacific. But the USAAF learned quickly, and the first deployment of B-24 bomber squadrons to the Middle East in June 1942 went like clockwork. By then the route across Africa had also been used by Curtiss P-40E fighters on their way to China and by Lend-Lease B-25 Mitchells going on to Tehran, where their Pan American crews handed them over to the Russians. Later Russian deliveries would be mostly via Alaska, leaving the recipients with the long trans-Siberian trip to the front line.

June 1942 saw three other significant events: the first Eighth Air Force B-17s flew to England from Presque Isle, Maine, beginning the biggest ferry task of the war; USAAF Ferrying Command became Air Transport Command (ATC), responsible for both ferrying and strategic air transport, and the aircraft which would allow ATC properly to fulfil the latter role, the Douglas C-54, entered service only four months after its first flight. The USAAF found that demand for air transport to the operational theatres was insatiable. Vital spares, ammunition, blood plasma, specialist technicians and generals were all needed yesterday, and there was never enough capacity.

In December 1941 the entire USAAF long-range transport fleet comprised just eleven B-24s. Like the British, they turned to the civilians. The airlines' four-engined flying boats (only eleven aircraft) and some ninety DC-3s were purchased and their previous owners contracted to operate them. Thus in June 1942 General Harold George had 130 aircraft to support ATC's worldwide operations, but only fifteen of them had air force crews. The ATC also relied on the airlines to supply trained personnel at all levels; George's deputy was Cyrus R Smith, boss of American Airlines. Unlike RAF Ferry Command, ATC policy was that directly-employed civilian pilots were commissioned. This may have impeded greater use of women pilots, for though several women's auxiliary ferrying squadrons were formed, and received great publicity for their work, the air force would not recruit them and they were disbanded in December 1944 when sufficient male pilots were available.

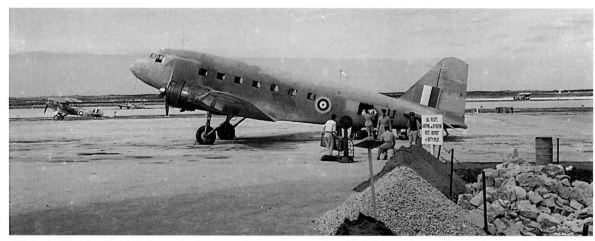

While the Douglas C-47 Dakota was the pre-eminent transport aircraft of the war, its smaller predecessor, the DC-2, also served. Britain purchased twenty-five of them from US airlines in 1941 for use in India and the Middle East, and after Pearl Harbor twenty-four more were impressed by the USAAF as the C-32A, though they were still mostly flown by their old airline crews. One of the DC-2s operated by No 31 Squadron, RAF, is seen here in the Holy Land in the early war period. (The aircraft in the left distance is a Hawker Audax.

The growth of the ferrying task paralleled the American 'production miracle'. In 1944 US manufacturers built 96,318 aircraft. In total weight, they increased production by a factor of twelve in just three years. In March 1944 alone they built more aircraft than Germany had in the whole of 1939. All of these aircraft had to be ferried from the factories, and the bombers and many of the fighters were then flown overseas. Fortunately for the ATC the majority of these flights were made by the aircraft's own combat crews. In 1941 ATFERO had shown that aircrew who had learned to fly

When Pearl Harbor was attacked, Douglas was starting to assemble the first DC-4 airliner. Put into production as the C-54 Skymaster, it entered service in the summer of 1942. By the end of the war 1,000-plus Air Force, Navy and airline Skymasters had transformed long-range logistic support, carrying passengers and freight around the globe on an unprecedented scale and paving the way for postwar air transport. Skymaster 41-37284 is seen here during evaluation in the UK..

in Canada could, with a little extra training, become successful 'one-trippers', the Atlantic crossing being their first long-distance flight. The USAAF followed this example. They were prepared for a 10 per cent loss rate, but of 920 aircraft despatched across the Atlantic in 1942, 882 arrived safely. With new and larger airfields, improved navigation beacons, better weather forecasting and the introduction of ground controlled approach radar, the loss rate fell as the numbers grew, and by 1944 even ferrying single-engined fighters across an ocean which for so long had been the preserve of heroic adventurers seemed almost routine.

The ATC still had to ferry the many replacement aircraft overseas, but this and its RFS operations were now overshadowed by its strategic transport role. It was this which drove the expansion from 130 aircraft in June 1942 to over 3,000 when Japan surrendered, including 839 C-54 Skymasters. The ATC was effectively running the biggest airline the world had seen, or would see for many years to come, able to fly 275,000 passengers a month, 50,000 of them transatlantic, plus over 100,000 tons of freight, most of it going 'over the Hump' into China. Under the ATC umbrella its contract airlines, Pan American, TWA, Northwest and others, were also expanding, gaining invaluable experience of flying across new oceans and continents while operating the latest airliner, for the C-54 was only a DC-4 in uniform.

In 1944 US airlines were still undertaking a third of ATC's operations and were well set to dominate postwar air transport. Air ferrying, which in 1939 had seemed a humdrum domestic task which might be delegated to amateurs, had grown through this mass-production war into a vast global operation. American investment in new

Typical of the civil aircraft impressed into RAF service for communications work was the Percival Q.6, designed in 1937 as a relatively fast four-passenger business aircraft. Two of the eleven impressed, including this rare retractable-undercarriage version, HK838/G-AFMV, were used in the Middle East, where the Air C-in-C, Air Marshal Tedder, was lucky to be rescued after his Q.6 forced landed with a failed engine.

hard-runway airfields with beacons and radar provided a worldwide network of facilities barely conceivable five years before, and if they spelled the end for the much-loved flying boats, they promised far greater regularity and safety. There were now thousands of aircrew with transoceanic experience and surplus aircraft to equip new operators. Wartime ferrying had changed air transport decisively, from an adventure for a tiny élite into a real travel industry.

Notes

1   British Airways and Imperial Airways were integrated into the new, nationalised British Overseas Airways Corporation (BOAC) through the winter of 1939–40, although the merger was not officially completed until 1 April 1940.

2   Ergonomics seems then to have been unknown to many designers. A typical example is that the air-brake control in Merlin-engined Beaufighters operated in the reverse sense from that in the Hercules-engined variants.

3   Australian Don Bennett was already well known for his record-breaking flights in the Short/Mayo seaplane *Mercury*, but after leaving ATFERO in June 1941 would become still more famous as the creator and leader of the RAF's Pathfinder Force.

4   Ferry Command became 45 Group, RAF Transport Command, when the latter was formed in March 1943, but the earlier name seems to have remained in colloquial use.

Bibliography

Barnato Walker, Diana, *Spreading My Wings* (Patrick Stephens, Yeovil, 1994). An entertaining personal memoir of flying with the ATA by an inexperienced pilot who survived more than her share of awkward moments. A daughter of 'Bentley Boy' Woolf Barnato, she also gives interesting sidelights on several aviation and establishment figures and a brief account of her family's astonishing rise to wealth and fame.

Bennett, Air Vice-Marshal D C T, *Pathfinder – A War Autobiography* (Frederick Muller, London, 1958, and Sphere Books, 1972) also covers his remarkable pre-war flying career and is more interesting than later biographies. He describes the early days of ATFERO and his pioneering trips in some detail and from a very personal (and typically opinionated) viewpoint.

Bergel, Hugh C, Flying Wartime Aircraft (David & Charles, Newton Abbot, 1972), reprints the ATA Pilots' Notes for seven types, including the

Hurricane, Wellington and Liberator, with comments by the author, who commanded No 9 Ferry Pool. This brings home the extraordinary variety in aircraft handling and systems, some quite eccentric, which ATA pilots faced daily. Hugh Bergel has also written a personal memoir, Fly and Deliver — A Ferry Pilot's Diary (Airlife Publishing, Shrewsbury, 1982).

Chandler, Robert, *Off The Beam* (Robert Chandler, 1969). An interesting perspective on Ferry Command by a radio operator, this memoir also covers the author's fascinating prewar career at Croydon and postwar with BSAA and with de Havilland on Comet proving flights.

Christie, Carl A, *Ocean Bridge — The History of RAF Ferry Command* (University of Toronto Press, Toronto, 1995, and Midland Publishing Ltd, Leicester, 1995). This 'academic' history is splendidly researched and scrupulously annotated yet remains very readable and fully aware of the human realities. Particularly interesting is the proper Canadian perspective it gives to the origins and continuing operations of ATFERO and Ferry/Transport Commands. It is unlikely to be bettered.

Craven, W F, and Cate, J L (Eds), *The Army Air Forces in World War II* (University of Chicago Press, 1948–58, reprinted 1983). The seven-volume Official History is not only comprehensive but remarkably readable and candid. There are two main sections relevant to the topic, and many useful details elsewhere. Volume I ('Plans and Early Operations') Chapter 9, 'The Early Development of Air Transport and Ferrying' by John D Carter, covers the origins of Ferrying Command, the involvement of the airlines, and operations up to mid-1942. Volume VII ('Services around the World'), Chapter 1 'Air Transport' by Carter and F H Heck briefly recapitulates the earlier work and continues the story of Air Transport Command through its great period of expansion. Essential reading for anyone interested wartime air transport or the origins of the modern age.

Curtis, Lettice, *The Forgotten Pilots* (Eastern Press Ltd, London, 1971, 1982). Easily the best account of the ATA, combining a carefully researched history with a well-written personal memoir which evokes the pleasure, anxiety, excitement and tedium of wartime ferry flying. Lettice Curtis joined the ATA in July 1941 and was one of only eleven women to convert on to heavy bombers. There are tables, maps and twenty-two appendices.

Gann, Ernest K, *Fate is the Hunter* (Hodder and Stoughton, London, 1961). This autobiographical work by the well known writer-pilot covers his pre- and postwar airline experience but includes wartime stories of flying DC-3s, C-54s and C-87s over the Atlantic, the Pacific and 'the Hump' into China on contract work for USAAF Air Transport Command. It confirms how much the ATC owed to airline staff and how the airlines sought to benefit from their opportunity. Gann's style now seems rather too self-conscious, but the content is still fascinating.

Luff, David, *Mollison – The Flying Scotsman* (Lidun Publishing, Lytham St Annes, 1983). This sympathetic and thorough biography of the pioneer long-distance flyer has interesting chapters on his, and Amy Johnson's, time with ATA.

McVicar, Don, *Ferry Command* (Airlife Publishing, Shrewsbury, 1981). The first of this Canadian pilot's trilogy of wartime memoirs, covering the rigours of ferrying on both North and South Atlantic, with a remarkable account of his arctic survey flights in February/March 1942. Brash and opinionated, with interesting details on flying types like the Norseman and Martin B-26, and the state of Brazilian brothels. The sequels are *North Atlantic Cat* and *Change of Wings*.

Powell, Air Commodore Griffith, *Ferryman* (Airlife Publishing, Shrewsbury, 1982). 'Taffy' Powell replaced Don Bennett when ATFERO became RAF Ferry Command, and ran its operations until July 1945. His aviation autobiography gives a readable and considered account of the organisation, its achievements and some of its personalities. It also covers his postwar career with Silver City Airways and BOAC.

Pudney, John (writing anonymously), *Atlantic Bridge* (HMSO, London 1945). Written during the war with help from Air Commodore Powell, this official account of ATFERO/Ferry Command activities, a slim ninepenny paperback, is still worth reading. It contains several first-hand accounts of early crossings, including the experimental trip by Waco CG-4a glider, towed from Montreal to Prestwick by a Dakota.

12
Training: a Vital Command
John Golley

During the Second World War aircrew training and aircraft production were the key factors in operating an efficient air force. They were also prime ingredients required to achieve command of the air. As the war unfolded the 'numbers game' in men and machines began to make its impact. Training systems had to accommodate advanced technology and supply increasing demands for aircrew, not simply to match losses but to service the rapid growth in aircraft production to meet operational requirements. The emergence of the four-engined bomber, for example, coupled with the growing European bombing offensive, began to suck in aircrew like a vacuum cleaner. Hence aircrew had to be trained on a 'mass production' basis, and output had to be geared to meet the growing needs of the air forces concerned.

Luftwaffe training
In September 1939 the Luftwaffe was in many respects the most powerful and efficient air force in the world, possessing some 4,300 aircraft manned by highly trained crews, some with battle experience (in Spain) and high morale. This was no mean achievement, as the air clauses of the 1919 Treaty of Versailles had stipulated that Germany was no longer to maintain or develop military or naval forces.

In the mid-1930s one of Hermann Goering's first priorities had been to overhaul the existing system of flying training provided by the commercial and sporting flying organisations. In 1936 these had been put on a war footing and a special training inspectorate created to centralise control and ensure the highest possible standards in all flying training schools. Before hostilities began the Luftwaffe had about fifty basic training schools across Saxony, the Rhineland, Bavaria, Silesia, East Prussia,

A typical Luftwaffe primary trainer, the Arado Ar 66C.

and Pomerania, plus facilities in Russia. As the war progressed, basic training schools were set up in Poland and Czechoslovakia, and advanced flying schools in France, Belgium, Greece, Norway, Denmark, and Italy, making a total of 75 to 100 schools. At the outbreak of war the Luftwaffe training scheme was turning out between 10,000 and 15,00 pilots a year. In 1940 it had a surplus of pilots, and operational and reserve training units were created to re-absorb them.

Initial Luftwaffe training – broadly corresponding to the RAF Initial Training Wing (ITW) stage – was quite different to that in Britain. German recruits, including officer candidates, spent from six to twelve months primarily on an infantry regimental course. There they were given a strong dose of Prussian discipline, taught to goose-step and use small-arms, and generally toughened up on the parade ground. This was somewhat akin to the American system for training air force officers (break them down first and build them up as you want them). Lectures on the basic principles of radio telephony and map reading comprised the only aviation aspect. Later, under the pressure of war, this course was reduced in duration to two or three months.

On passing out from the recruit depot, aircrew spent two months at a pool known as the 'Fluganwaerterkompanie', learning general-aviation subjects before being posted for *ab initio* training. Luftwaffe pupils arriving for this training were therefore highly disciplined in true Teutonic tradition and politically motivated. The Germans called it an AB school, which was a combination of the RAF's Elementary Flying Training School (EFTS) and Service Flying Training School (SFTS). The first 'A' course consisted of about thirty hours of dual and solo flying, comprising circuits and bumps, take-offs, simple banking turns and three-point landings. Aircraft which the student might fly included the Focke-Wulf Fw 44, Heinkel He 72, Gotha Go 145 and Arado Ar 66 or possibly the Bucker Bu 131. These light biplanes had a top speed of between 110 and 130mph (177 and 209km/h) and a landing speed of between 45 and 55mph (72 and 88km/h). The course was considerably shorter than that of an EFTS, and so was the 'B' course, during which the German pilot would do about seventy hours. He flew slightly more powerful aircraft, such as the Arado Ar 96 or Focke-Wulf Fw 56 monoplanes, both fitted with Argus engines of about 240hp.

The Luftwaffe trainee was given his wings after some 100 to 150 hours' flying, whereas an RAF cadet would

Another machine used by the Luftwaffe for 'A' course training was the Bücker Bü 131 Jungmann. This is the Japanese version, the Kokusai Ki-86a, codenamed 'Cypress' by the Allies.

log between 200 and 300 hours, depending where he trained, before he gained his wings.

One Englishman managed to arrange some flying hours at a large Luftwaffe flying school and wrote about his experience in the magazine *Flight* under the pseudonym 'Kismet' in January 1940. The writer had been flying for some time, so he received rather more advanced instruction than an absolute beginner. Naturally he was interested in comparing the basic flying training curricula of both countries. He said that German manufacturers often ran their own flying schools, under the control of the German air ministry. In England there were only two such instances he could recall. The advantages were obvious. Ease of maintenance by the factory itself, spare parts on the shelf, and opportunities for technical experts to see daily how their machines performed. In addition, pupils could visit the factory to

see how aircraft were constructed and study the design features which determined flying characteristics.

The writer was taken up in a Bücker Bü 131 Jungmann, and his first big surprise was to find that there was no telephonic communication between instructor and pupil; instead, the instructor used hand signals or sharply pulled the controls to take command. The German onlookers had laughed at 'der Englander's' helmet, with its novel ear fittings, and even more so when 'Kismet' did a smart ground loop when taxiing out – the Jungmann was fitted with a tailwheel rather than the accustomed skid. However, after that slight setback, he wrote:

I headed into wind and took oV as carefully as possible, it being the Wrst time that I had Xown an aircraft with duplicate ailerons. In spite of my care, the take-oV was bad, and the controls were pulled sharply from my hands. After a few seconds the instructor waved both his hands above his head in token of having quit the controls, and I again took over. Climbing with plenty of speed in hand failed to please him, and a series of violent upward jerks with his extended right arm made me steepen the angle until the earth had disappeared altogether, and I was convinced we were going to stall; but we did not.

A downward stroke of the right arm, and I eased the stick forward for straight and level Xying. The left arm extended with Wngers pointing left; I turned left, but not steeply enough, as extra pressure is put on the stick and we are turning vertically, or rather the machine is turning itself vertically, as there are the instructor's hands above his head again, and mine are gripping the seat!

All use of controls, their functions and objectives

The Argus engined Arado Ar 96 was one of the Luftwaffe's 'B' course aeroplanes.

The Fairey Battle Trainer, a variant of the early war period bomber. Under the Commonwealth Air Training Plan, 800 were shipped to Canada and 400 to Australia.

were explained on the ground first and then performed in the air by the instructor. Having acquitted himself satisfactorily in the Jungmann, 'Kismet' was allowed to fly the Bü 133 Jungmeister – a more powerful single-seat biplane trainer which all fighter pilots learnt to handle. Aerobatic training consisted of loops, half-loops followed by a roll, looping while gliding, inverted flying, slow rolls right and left, continuous rolls in right- or left-hand rotation, spinning, inverted spins, knife-edge flight and vertical slip-over wing – in that order. All of these aerobatics were first performed dual in the Jungmann.

The 'A' and 'B' training courses were fundamental, and on completion the instructors decided whether the candidate was most suitable to be a fighter or bomber pilot, an observer, or a reconnaissance pilot. Bomber or reconnaissance pilots were drafted to 'C' schools and trained on twin-engined aircraft on a course lasting from three to six months. This involved some sixty hours' flying, including night and cross-country blind flying. The RAF had incorporated most of this as part of SFTS training. Prospective German fighter pilots would fly some fifty hours at a specialist school on aircraft including the Arado Ar 68 and the Heinkel He 51, which were old operational biplane fighters. Later they flew early versions of the Messerschmitt Bf 109. Finally they would fly a further twenty hours at an operational training unit, where they handled the latest variants of the Bf 109 and the Focke-Wulf Fw 190.

The Royal Air Force, 1939–41

At the outbreak of war flying training in the RAF had no command structure or representation on the Air Council. In September 1939 there were only fourteen Service Training Schools, including one at Abu Sueir in Egypt. These establishments were being fed by the civilian schools, but the total output was very small when measured against squadron needs. The creation of the RAF Volunteer Reserve in 1936 had enabled 'weekend flyers' to be trained at existing airfields near towns in various parts of the country. However, by 1940 5,300 pilots were being trained annually (less than half of the Luftwaffe's output) against an average of 300 in 1935.

At this stage most Service training schools were operating with aircraft long since obsolete. Hawker Harts, Hinds and Furies, together with other Hart variants, were standard, as was the Armstrong Whitworth Atlas. All were open-cockpit biplanes equipped with very limited navigational instruments. Radio was unheard of on such aircraft, and the consequent lack of communication was a severe handicap. The introduction of the converted Fairey Battle proved successful on a short-term basis, as it provided the characteristics of the low-wing monoplane, together with Sperry gyro instruments, radio, flaps and the variable-pitch airscrew.

Gradually the Miles Master and North American Harvard trainer became more readily available, both being excellent low-wing monoplanes for the training of fighter pilots, while the old workhorse Avro Anson, together with the Airspeed Oxford, proved invaluable for the tuition of twin- and multi-engined aircrew.

Such was the shortage of pilots during the Battle of Britain that an extremely risky, and in the event unprofitable experiment took place. Described as 'X' courses,

Avro Ansons from 10 FTS, Tern Hill, Shropshire. The Anson was used to train all types of aircrew in the UK and throughout the Commonwealth.

selected pupils were taken direct from Elementary Flying Schools and sent to Operational Training Units (OTUs). At this stage they had done barely fifty hours' flying, of which only a little less than half had been solo, and all on elementary trainers. Some were sent to RAF Abingdon to fly Whitley bombers and others to RAF Bicester for conversion to Bristol Blenheims. The course lasted twelve weeks and involved over 120 hours' flying, a third of which was at night. However the loss rate, both during training and subsequently on squadrons, made it impracticable and the scheme was abolished.

Climate

The variable British climate disrupted flying training, especially as the majority of Training Command aerodromes were grass and prolonged periods of rain frequently made them unserviceable. Every hour available had to be used and dawn-to-dusk day flying was a matter of routine, followed by night instruction. Under blackout conditions on the darkest of nights, often in low cloud and with no discernible horizon, circuits were completed on instruments alone. Sperry gyro compasses would be set at zero and the take-off climb would be

to 500ft (150m), followed by a climbing turn on to 270° to 1,000ft (300m). The pilot would turn to 180°, when the flarepath could be vaguely visible on his left-hand side. He would then turn across wind on to 90° and begin his turn towards the flarepath and his final descent.

During the winter of 1940/41 enemy air attacks on aerodromes were frequent, especially at night. Night flying was therefore carried out at satellite airfields where flarepaths were hooded, making them invisible from 3,000ft (900m). The introduction of a primitive glide path indicator and, later, the generator-operated Chance light (which provided a floodbeam only at the moment of landing and was then switched off), gave some further relief, but night instructing continued to be a very dangerous business. Originally night flying ceased on the receipt of an air raid warning, but in October 1940 Flying Training Command was ordered to continue flying, irrespective of any form of attack. It is difficult to imagine, and for those who took part, to recapture, the dangerous and difficult circumstances facing instructors and pupils alike at this time. The result was that courses had to be shortened, and consequently standards deteriorated.

A Miles Magister, Miles Master II and Airspeed Oxford of the Central Flying School, photographed in September 1942. The Magister was a light monoplane used for primary training, the Master II was an advanced trainer for those converting on to operational fighters, and the Oxford played a major role in the training of multi-engine pilots.

Canada – the big deal

Meanwhile, the Empire Flying Training Scheme had become a reality, providing an opportunity for the RAF to decentralise flying training. Hard pressed by Canada and other Dominions, Britain had been forced to increase her commitment. She proposed the transfer of entire flying schools, but Canada went further and insisted on a supply of aircraft as a condition of acceptance. Some 3,500 training aircraft were required to launch the project in Canada. However, there was a problem with the type of aircraft. The vast projected expansion of Bomber Command swung the balance heavily in favour of multi-engine pilots (about five or six being needed to each single-engine pilot), and sufficient Oxfords and Ansons could not be provided. Consequently, many potential bomber pilots had to be trained on single-engined Harvards.

By the end of 1940 four SFTSs had been transferred to Canada and were in operation, as were thirty-six Empire Schools; 520 aircrew were trained, of which 240 were pilots. In early 1941 all RAF pupils going to Canada had completed EFTS training in the UK. As the elimination factor was high during primary training, this ensured that cadets making the long journey to Canada had proved their aptitude in the air. It was also more cost-effective, although the value of 'all-through' training in a stable background at adjacent airfields far outweighed the disadvantages. Consequently, grading schools were established in the UK to deal with the aptitude problem, and in the summer of 1941 the RAF began opening EFTSs in Canada. These foundations provided a basis for rapid development during the following year, when the output rose to 16,653 aircrew, including 9,637 pilots.

1941 – global expansion

In May 1940, with the need for aircrew becoming even more urgent, the British government held tentative talks with the US government regarding pilot training in the USA. They were told that all military flying schools there were fully occupied with America's own needs. It was then suggested that primary training could take place in American civilian schools, but the authorities in Washington expressed the view that pupils would be better trained in Canada, using American aircraft and instructors. Understandably, the US government did not

289

wish to compromise its neutrality, and although the Canadian offer was accepted, only very few US aircraft and instructors were provided.

The project was reopened in August 1940, when the British government was desperately anxious to explore any possibility of additional training. This time it was proposed to set up civilian schools in the USA to train British pilots under direct, paid contract. The problem of neutrality was again a stumbling block because of the Taft Act, but was circumnavigated by proposing to sell non-military training on a commercial basis. The solution did not, however, dispel all the difficulties, the main two being the enormous dollar cost to the UK and a lack of suitable training aircraft in the USA for civilian school use.

Nevertheless, the scheme was put into operation in July 1941, shortly after Germany had invaded the Soviet Union. The aircraft shortage was greatly alleviated by the introduction of the Lend-Lease Act earlier in the year, enabling the USA not only to provide the aircraft so urgently needed, but also to build six British Flying Training Schools (BFTSs) and bear a large proportion of the costs themselves. It was typical of US efficiency that the six schools were operating within a matter of weeks.

A novel feature of the BFTS scheme was that it provided a complete training course from primary to graduation at the same station; a continuous production line process. Furthermore, the RAF had taken a firm hand to ensure that the syllabus covered all aspects of EFTS and SFTS training. All of the instructors were civilians, most of whom had a great deal of flying and instructing experience. The schools took 200 cadets for a 20-week course, of which about 20 per cent were American cadets. They flew Stearman PT-17s or Fairchild PT-19s at primary level and North American AT-6 Texans (Harvards) or Vultee BT-13A Valiants at basic and advanced level. Thus the BFTSs could only provide graduates who had been trained on single-engined aircraft.

Phillip Murton (later Sqn Ldr), who trained at No 6 School at Ponca City, Oklahoma, comments:

> The quality of instruction is a diYcult one to assess. Generally the Xying instruction was good, in that the instructors sure could Xy. But they were, for the most part, unable to explain in the air or on the ground why an aircraft did certain things, or what one had to do to Xy correctly. From the student's point of view it was largely a question of copying.

This was described by Bill Williams, who also trained at Ponca, as a 'sitting by Nellie' technique!

Apart from the BFTS operation, there were two other schemes: the Arnold Scheme, operated within the South-east Army Air Corps Training Center, with its

Rear Admiral John Henry Towers USN, originator of the Towers Scheme, which played a major role in training British naval cadets in the USA.

headquarters at Maxwell Field, Alabama, and the Towers Scheme, named after Admiral Towers, US Navy, and operated within the US Navy organisation. The Arnold Scheme was named after Gen Henry 'Hap' Arnold, Chief of Staff of the US Army Air Corps, as it was in 1941.

During the initial stages of the Arnold scheme the USA was a neutral country, and to circumvent the Taft Act British cadets were issued visas in Canada and entered the country in grey flannel suits and wore KD uniforms on the stations. This was almost history repeating itself, because Germany had circumvented the Versailles Treaty in building the Luftwaffe. German pilots had posed as South Tyrolean tourists and secretly crossed the border into Italy to train with the Regia Aeronautica, and had worn Italian Air Force uniforms. The Germans had been accepted as students in Italy; the British cadets were officially civilians off-station, but came under Air Corps disciplinary rules and regulations at all times.

In their early stages of training RAF cadets found the discipline imposed on them by the Army Air Corps frustrating and somewhat crude. It took the form of a system known as 'hazing', which derives from the word 'haze',

The Consolidated PBY Catalina, employed as an advanced trainer under the Towers Scheme in the USA, was the only fully operational machine flown during training.

meaning 'to punish with unnecessary work'. This training was designed to break a man down and rebuild him the way the USAAC wanted him.

The Stearman used for primary training was a considerably larger and more powerful machine than the de Havilland Tiger Moth. It required firmer and more positive handling than the Moth, and its additional power

The Boeing Stearman PT-17 Kaydet was a widely used American elementary or primary pilot trainer.

was conducive to aerobatics. The American system of pilot training included three phases: primary, basic and advanced. Basic training constituted an intermediate stage between primary and advanced training. The BT-13A Valiant was used by the BFTS and Arnold and Towers schemes for this intermediate stage.

The aircraft for advanced training were the Curtiss AT-9 and the Cessna AT-17 Bobcat, two totally different twin-engined machines. While the Curtiss had a gliding angle like a brick, the Cessna AT-17 was more of a gentleman's aircraft, made of steel tube, wood and fabric, with the air and gentility of a more advanced Anson. The different flying characteristics of the two machines certainly made a pilot more adaptable, which was a considerable asset. Asymmetric flying, general handling, instrument, formation and night flying plus ten days at another school for ground and aerial gunnery, made up the course.

The Towers Scheme was operated by the US Navy for training naval flying personnel, its primary object being to train aircrew for service with RAF Coastal Command and the Fleet Air Arm. Naval cadets, however, received more flexible, and in most cases longer, training than their counterparts. At primary level the basic trainer was the Naval Aircraft Factory N3N, nicknamed 'Canary', an uncluttered, dual-controlled biplane

Popularly known as the 'Vibrator', the Vultee BT-13 Valiant was extensively used as a basic trainer in the USA.

Bombing and gunnery training in the USAAF was carried out in the Beechcraft AT-11 Kansas, a variant of the company's ubiquitous Model 18.

One multi-engined pilot trainer used on the Advanced course in the USA was the Curtiss AT-9, known as the 'Jeep'.

built by the US Navy. Pupils then went on to fly more advanced machines, the Vought O3U Corsair and Vought OS2U Kingfisher, a monoplane alternatively fitted with floats. In addition courses were run by Pan American Airways to train British navigators.

The Ottawa Conference, convened by the Canadians on 6 June 1942, re-evaluated all systems of flying training in an attempt to standardise and co-ordinate them throughout the North American continent. This agreement embodied major changes, not least a change of name, from the Empire Air Training Plan to the Commonwealth Air Training Plan. Under the control of the Royal Canadian Air Force (RCAF), all schools and supplementary units, together with resources, were

administered from one base in Ottawa. All SFTSs were to be expanded, and RAF EFTSs brought under civilian operation. This agreement made for greater efficiency, and laid the foundations for greater expansion. It also provided an invaluable forum for representatives of host countries who were providing overseas training at a crucial time during the expansion of their own air forces.

When the conference was taking place there were sixty-eight EAT schools and twenty-seven RAF transferred schools. By the end of 1942 these had increased to ninety-two BCATP schools supported by sixty-two ancillary units. The basic methods and systems of RAF flying training evolved over the years were, broadly speaking, adopted throughout. The Canadian experience of Bob Stanford, an RAF cadet, is typical of thousands of his contemporaries. He completed grading school in the UK at 15 EFTS Carlisle, flying Miles Magisters. The 'Maggie' was a low-wing monoplane powered by a 130hp de Havilland Gipsy Major 1 engine. It had a leisurely landing speed of only 45mph (72km/h), was fully aerobatic and introduced fledgeling pilots to the novelty of trailing-edge split flaps at an early stage. At 15 EFTS cadets had to solo before transferring to Canada, where Stanford was posted to 34 EFTS at Assiniboia in Saskatchewan. The EFTS occupied a grass airfield, with newly constructed hut accommodation. The aircraft type was the de Havilland D.H.82C, a standard Tiger Moth equipped with a sliding Perspex canopy. The station was, in fact, a standard RAF EFTS plonked down in the middle of the Canadian prairies,

De Havilland's D.H.82A Tiger Moth was one of the most famous and widely used primary trainers of the Second World War. This is a Canadian example, designated D.H.82C, with its Perspex canopy removed, leaving only the front windshield.

The North American Harvard advanced trainer was universally employed throughout the overseas air training projects. Here, three RCAF Harvards pose in vic formation in 1941.

Airspeed Oxfords from 24 Air School SAAF, Nigel, Transvaal. The original Oxford Mk.Is were used for all aspects of aircrew training, and the Mk.IIs extensively for pilot training overseas.

with RAF flying instructors and Service back-up. Flying conditions were ideal, and cadets were able to have four or five lessons in a full day's flying.

Learning to fly was far easier than in the UK. Navigation was simple because road and rail lines ran directly east and west, south and north in symmetrical fashion. Grain elevators displayed their location and the air was clear, with visibility of fifty miles or more. There was little turbulence and none of the complexities of a congested landscape. All of these factors helped to engender confidence, enabling the pupil to master his machine in the wide open spaces.

The Tiger Moth Stanford flew was the Mk II version of the D.H.60T with staggered and sweptback wings (the latter to allow ease of exit by parachute from the front cockpit). Powered by a 130hp Gipsy Major engine, this light, fully aerobatic, sensitive machine was a delight to fly. It demanded perfect co-ordination and a gentle touch, but could cope with the ham-fisted while allowing the uninitiated a great deal of licence. It is fair to say that most people should have been able to fly a Tiger Moth, but few could fly it accurately.

Stanford logged 78 hr 50min at 34 EFTS on a course lasting three months. Then he was posted to 32 SFTS at Moose Jaw flying the Harvard IIA, similar to the US AT-6C. Its qualities as an advanced training machine were such that over 20,000 Harvards were built in various countries. Stepping out of a Tiger Moth into the cockpit of a Harvard could come as quite a shock. Sitting up high in the 'office', facing a mass of instruments and the big Pratt & Whitney radial engine and feeling the stick and the toe brakes, could made one wary of touching any lever in case the undercarriage folded!

The SFTS course lasted for three and a half months, during which Stanford logged 122hr 55min, including twenty hours' night flying, despite the approach of the Canadian winter, when temperatures fell to minus 60°. His grand total of flying hours when he was awarded his wings amounted to 203hr 5min. He had started his flying training on 29 June, shortly after the Ottawa Agreement had been signed and the Commonwealth Air Training had become fully operational.

Meanwhile, global flying training had gathered momentum. Southern Rhodesia, now Zimbabwe, had opened 25 EFTSs at Belvedere, near Salisbury, in May 1940, as part of the Rhodesian Air Training Group. South Africa followed under the Joint Air Training Plan. New Zealand and Australia were already totally committed, and apart from local training, were feeding training schools in Canada.

The Luftwaffe

The losses sustained by the Luftwaffe during the battles of France and Britain were substantially increased when Germany invaded the Soviet Union in June 1941. By 1942, in spite of the territorial expansion of the Luftwaffe training organisation throughout Europe, it began to fragment. The major training schemes of 1940, 1941 and 1942 were being clipped or cancelled. Courses had to be shortened in order to replace combat losses, and there was a shortage of flying instructors and of twin-engined aircraft, such as the Focke-Wulf Fw 58 Weihe. The Luftwaffe training organisation was short not only of pupils, but also of ground staff, who were being diverted to infantry regiments to fight, mainly on the Russian front.

By 1942 the Luftwaffe was fighting on three fronts; the Soviet Union, the Mediterranean and the Atlantic. The manpower difficulty and shortened courses had to affect the quality of aircrews. In contrast, by courtesy of the global training scheme and accelerating aircraft production, the RAF was undergoing the biggest expansion of its history. During this period the USA had entered the war, and the USAAF was using the UK virtually as an unsinkable aircraft carrier. Thus, the 'numbers game' in men and machines began to make its impact on the air war.

The planning and timing of the Commonwealth Scheme was perfect, because it began to peak at the particular time that Luftwaffe training began to fragment. In 1942 the scheme produced 44,338 trained aircrew, and in 1943 this increased to 58,601. Germany, by comparison, was totally unable to compete with this vast training organisation which, at its peak, had three times the number of training establishments serving the Empire Air Forces. With a population of some 88 million, Germany had about double the number of potential UK pupils (healthy, educated youths born in the years 1922–4), but the global scheme was able to draw upon members of these age groups throughout the Commonwealth, and the USA with a population of 188 million. The US Army Air Forces alone graduated 193,440 pilots during the Second World War.

German ace Adolf Galland (left) talking to General Mölders.

Generalleutnant Adolf Galland's concise comments postwar reflect the Luftwaffe's situation from 1942 onwards:

Pilot training has never been sufficient. We had not enough training schools, not enough instructors, not enough aircraft, not enough time and finally not enough fuel. I have been twice to Winnipeg for the Commonwealth Aircrew Training reunions. I have admired your training organisation which was owned by a rich Air Force.

The UK

By the end of 1941 it became obvious that the global training scheme would be producing far more aircrew than OTUs and squadrons could absorb. Furthermore, pilots and navigators trained overseas were totally without experience of British weather conditions, the blackout and map reading. During 1942 Advanced Flying Units (AFUs) were established to solve these problems. These courses were not merely designed to keep pilots in flying practice as a stopgap, but as a definite stage in training policy.

Single-engine pilots completed forty hours' flying including day, night, and advanced flying in Miles Masters. Twin-engine pilots completed eighty hours including day, night, beam approach training, and advanced day flying with simulated night flying in Oxfords. Alongside this intensive training was a comprehensive ground programme involving navigation, signals and bombing. The AFUs continued to operate until the end of the European war, and were gradually phased out in 1946.

It is quite remarkable that over 88,000 aircrew were trained and graduated in the UK, despite the climate and other detractions. This is roughly half the total output from Canada, the mainspring of the global scheme. Furthermore, the UK provided the specialist courses enabling the graduate to go to war well able to master the technological developments in aircraft and systems as these became more complex.

Summary

Any flying training system which enables a graduate to progress on to more advanced machines and take part in aerial warfare justifies itself. The training schemes described above reflect, to a certain extent, the characteristics of the country concerned. Both Germany and America employed rigid military discipline combined with a 'copy the instructor' technique. There was no such discipline in RAF training, and instructors explained the behaviour of the aircraft in varying conditions of flight.

In early 1946 the author was an instructor at 17 SFTS at Spitalgate, outside Grantham, Lincolnshire, flying Harvards. There was an intake of Turkish and Dutch pupils and this brought considerable language

difficulties, especially with the Turks. Instructors were forced to adopt the 'copying' technique, and it worked well because the countries concerned paid large sums to the Treasury as part of the deal!

The global schemes outlined above had many other attributes apart from flying training. British cadets posted across the world, for example, found themselves acting as unofficial ambassadors for the 'Mother Country'. People wanted to know about the Battle of Britain and how the 'Old Country' was coping with the bombing. Blood ties linking Britain to her Dominions and Commonwealth were strengthened by the advent of war. This large-scale invasion, comprising the prime of British youth, did much to forge stronger links which were invaluable.

The schemes also provided the basis for the development of Commonwealth and Dominion air forces, and in so doing gave the impetus for the regeneration and development of the aviation industries within the countries concerned. The American schemes generated a close liaison between the RAF and the Fleet Air Arm and the US Army Air Force and the US Navy which proved invaluable during the course of the war.

The end product of the enterprise was the mass output of trained aircrew, and flying was the powerful magnet which attracted youth from all over the world. Flying provided the 'icing on the cake' during months of intensive training, and the ultimate challenge for all those involved. The Luftwaffe, whose flying training organisation was spread across the countries Germany had conquered, was unable to tap the reservoir of youth from within.

A cadet's ambition was to win his wings and then fly the aircraft of his dreams, but the war is riddled with unforeseen circumstances. Many of those who gained their wings in the summer of 1944 were hoping that the war would last long enough for them 'to have a go' in Europe, the only alternative being the Far East. Waiting for a posting was frustrating, with the Allies advancing swiftly through Belgium and into Holland. Events were moving fast and many felt that the end of the war was in sight.

Then, on 17 September, some 10,000 paratroopers, including glider pilots, 'hit the deck' at Arnhem, and only about 3,000 came out. Consequently the army became desperately short of glider pilots – so much so that Brig George Chatterton (a prewar RAF pilot) talked to his contacts in high places at the Air Ministry and succeeded in 'borrowing' 1,500 RAF pilots for conversion on to gliders. This was an incredibly large number of highly trained men, by any standard, to have available 'at the drop of a hat'. It demonstrated that the reservoir of talent created by overseas flying training proved invaluable in an entirely unforeseen context. The newly trained RAF glider pilots were then split into

Output of pilots and other aircrew – Dominion sources

Type and year of output	Canada	Australia	New Zealand	South Africa	Southern Rhodesia	Total
1940						
Pilots	240	60	318	–	110	728
Navigators	112	39	–	–	–	151
WOP/AGs and AGs	168	54	–	–	–	222
Total	520	153	318	–	110	1,101
1941						
Pilots	9,637	1,367	1,292	341	1,284	13,921
Navigators	2,884	681	–	629	23	4,217
WOP/AGs and AGs	4,132	1,296	–	–	110	5,538
Total	16,653	3,344	1,292	970	1,417	23,676
1942						
Pilots	14,135	3,033	943	1,529	1,666	21,306
Navigators	7,404	1,375	–	2,541	237	11,557
Air bombers	1,742	–	–	170	–	1,912
WOP/AGs and AGs	6,896	2,280	–	–	387	9,563
Total	30,177	6,688	943	4,240	2,290	44,338
1943						
Pilots	15,894	3,869	836	2,309	2,083	24,991
Navigators	8,144	1,662	–	3,250	239	13,295
Air bombers	6,445	–	–	918	–	7,363
WOP/AGs and AGs	8,695	3,838	–	–	419	12,952
Total	39,178	9,369	836	6,477	2,741	58,601
1944 (to 30 September)						
Pilots	8,807	1,684	502	2,025	1,188	14,206
Navigators	7,953	696	–	2,403	180	11,232
Air bombers	5,131	–	–	742	–	5,873
WOP/AGs and AGs	7,998	1,328	–	–	309	9,635
Total	29,889	3,708	502	5,170	1,677	40,946
Grand total	**116,417**	**23,262**	**3,891**	**16,857**	**8,235**	**168,662**

Summary

Pilots	75,152
Navigators	40,452
Air bombers	15,148
WOP/AGs	37,910
GRAND TOTAL	168,662 to September 1944

Remarks

1 The country is that in which the training was carried out and does not indicate the trainees' nationality.
2 The figures are those for outputs from the SFTS or its equivalent, i.e. an Australian trainee who did his EFTS training in Australia and his SFTS in Canada would be shown under Canada.
3 The figures include trainees retained to meet the Dominions' own local requirements.

two groups; about half of them were posted to UK airfields for the Rhine crossing, and the remainder were earmarked for India to take part in airborne operations in South East Asia. It was the luck of the draw for many cadets who had trained at a specific time during the course of the war. Sometimes courses had to be shortened, while later in the war they were extended. There were so many variables for training organisations to cope with, not least the ever-increasing targets for manpower to fly and operate the machines. Hence, 'Flying Training' was a Vital Command, and a key piece on the operational chessboard.

Bibliography

Golley, John, *Aircrew Unlimited* (Patrick Stephens, Yeovil, 1993).

Lee, Asher, *The German Air Force* (Duckworth, London, 1946).

Lee, Asher, *Goering Air Leader* (Duckworth, London 1972).

Tantum IV, W H, and Hoffschmidt, E J, *The Rise and Fall of the German Air Force* (W E Inc, Old Greenwich, Connecticut, USA, 1969).

Index